Just Capital

Adair Turner has combined a career in business, public policy and academia. He is currently Vice-Chairman of Merrill Lynch Europe and director of a number of media and Internet companies. He is also visiting professor at the London School of Economics. From 1995 to 1999 he was Director-General of the Confederation of British Industry and before that a director of McKinsey & Company, the international firm of management consultants.

Adair Turner

JUST CAPITAL

The Liberal Economy

PAN BOOKS

First published 2001 by Macmillan

This edition published 2002 by Pan Books
an imprint of Pan Macmillan Ltd
Pan Macmillan, 20 New Wharf Road, London N1 9RR
Basingstoke and Oxford
Associated companies throughout the world
www.panmacmillan.com

ISBN 0 330 48023 5

1 3 5 7 9 8 6 4 2

A CIP catalogue record for this book is available from
the British Library.

Typeset by SetSystems Ltd, Saffron Walden, Essex
Printed and bound in Great Britain by
Mackays of Chatham plc, Chatham, Kent

To my wife Orna

and for my daughters

Eleanor and Julia

Contents

Part Three
Implications for Policy

Acknowledgements

Many people have helped stimulate the ideas which this book tries to express: many too over the years have responded to my endless requests for information. But there are some to whom I owe particular thanks. Ralf Dahrendorf and Richard Layard have both provided invaluable encouragement and guidance. Ralf has been an inspiration for my political philosophy; Richard has critiqued my economics with meticulous energy – remaining errors of theory or fact lie almost certainly in the areas where I went against his advice. It was Richard too who invited me to join the Centre for Economic Performance (CEP) at the LSE and I am indebted to the CEP for the support it has given me, both intellectually and in the production of the book, on which Mary Yacoob and Linda Cleavely have worked many long hours.

Through the CEP too I found my research assistant Joana Quina, who has been relentless in her pursuit of factual accuracy and an excellent advisor. Many former colleagues at the Confederation of British Industry (CBI) must also be thanked, not only for their support when I was Director-General, but also for the good humour and alacrity with which they have responded to a former boss's request for the details of half-remembered analyses.

Those who have read sections of the book and provided criticism and encouragement include Sam Brittan, Paul Ekins, Will Hutton, David Metcalf and Jonathan Porritt – to each of them many thanks. Georgina Capel, my agent, has spurred me on, as has George Morley at Macmillan, and my especial thanks must go to Tanya Stobbs who worked with me to make a book of economics, I hope, accessible to the general reader.

My deepest thanks are, however, to my wife Orna Ní Chionna, to whom I promised that the year 2000 would be my sabbatical from business, a time for family, and who has supported and encouraged me amid our growing realization that writing a book is a project more all-consuming than any business activity. This book is dedicated to her.

Adair Turner
December 2000

Foreword
by Ralf Dahrendorf

Adair Turner's book is so thoroughly un-Marxian that one hesitates to describe it as a 'critique of political economy', yet it is just that. It takes on conventional wisdom, notably about globalization which it finds 'deeply flawed in terms of analysis and an impediment to intelligent policy debate'. In disentangling the 'mixture of the true, the half true but exaggerated, and the plain wrong' Turner steers an unwavering course between the Scylla of the hard economics of neoliberalism and the Charybdis of the soft politics of the third way. He has much to say on both, and he says it with clarity as well as irony. The result is a highly original political economy of liberty at a time of global pushes and local pulls.

Most readers will share the pleasure which Turner takes in exploding fashionable myths, like the 'competitiveness of nations'. ' "Competitiveness" is a meaningful concept at the level of an individual company, it is totally meaningless at the level of the world, and it loses its meaning as we progress along that spectrum.' Making countries more 'competitive' is therefore a misleading use of language, which is not to say that some of the measures taken to that end are not sensible for other reasons. What is wrong is to invoke 'globalization' for the purpose. Turner adds that there is nothing fundamentally new about global markets. Their effect is – and is intended to be – to make traded products cheaper and thus reduce if not the volume then the value of world trade rather than enhance it. As a result many of the remaining needs, and jobs, are local rather than global and, what is more, 'a subtle mixture of the high-tech and the high-touch, the "thin air" and the concretely physical, the knowledge based and the deeply mundane'.

One of the results of this dual trend is that we are faced with truly hard choices. They arise from five developments: 'rising inequality; an increased need for flexibility; increasing demand for key public services; increased demands for regulation; and the conflicts between physical development and the environment'. Turner significantly calls these developments 'essentially domestic', which means that the necessary choices – or trade-offs – are a matter for national governments and politics. Whatever global pushes and local pulls there are, the nation-state remains the central agent of reform.

For those whose primary interest is economic (and it should be emphasized that this is a book of political *economy*), Adair Turner offers much that is original as well as controversial; it is not hard to anticipate the arguments about productivity growth, trade, the e-conomy and the effects of redistribution. If one's interest is more on the political side of the debate, Turner has important things to say to elucidate the central issue of politics at the beginning of the twenty-first century: where and how should the line be drawn between the public and the private sphere, between public goods and private interests, between the visible hands of regulators and governments and the invisible hand of the market?

A number of contributions to this debate follow from Adair Turner's analysis. The first is that there are in fact choices to be made. It is simply wrong to see the forces of globalization as a kind of reincarnation of Hegel's 'world spirit' which sweeps everything else away and forces the hands of leaders and led. The statement that competitiveness in global markets compels us to curtail the welfare state or to take measures to increase labour flexibility is simply not true. There may be other reasons – of demography, for example – to do these things but it 'degrades the quality of public debate' to use a 'rhetoric of external threat, of "no-alternative"'. There are alternatives, and they can be spelt out clearly.

Second, there is much to be said for the claim that in recent years we – or some of us, some countries – have gone too far in reducing the public sphere in order to stimulate (or so it was argued) private initiative. Discounting state purchases and provision is plainly 'biased'. Turner himself, for example, 'would like us to spend more money on subsidized public transport in London to make it a more pleasant, less polluted city', and he also wants to 'make our villages and towns safer and quieter'. 'I would rather pay more tax to get those benefits than have the extra personal income available to buy more market goods, and I can only buy these consumer benefits through the tax and government route since they are inherently collective.' If enough others agree then a political choice can be made.

It is high time that this point be made clearly and calmly. For some time now taxation has been the great taboo of democratic debate. There was a case for taxes to go down in many countries, not only to encourage private choice but also to combat bureaucratization and waste. More recently a curiously unsatisfactory reversal has set in. Some political groups demand an increase in taxation without specifying the purposes beyond such blanket terms as 'education' or 'health'. Indeed governments begin to use windfall income in the same way. What is really needed is a policy debate about specific objectives – 'consumer benefits', if you wish – followed by an indication of how the necessary funding is to be found.

The third contribution of Turner's book to the public-private debate is possibly the most important. There is, he argues, no one blueprint, no 'Washington consensus' on where the line between the public and the private sphere should be drawn. Different countries have different approaches, and beyond a certain minimum of market conditions they are equally viable. 'There are bad policies which can destroy economic-growth prospects, but there is a relatively wide range of different policies, structures and cultures which produce rather similar results.'

This is a thesis of critical importance; the evidence for it which Turner offers deserves, therefore, the closest scrutiny. It is in fact a profound argument against the 'Washington consensus' on economic policy which stems largely from what might be called the Chicago School of (neoliberal) economics. This school is not as evil as, say, John Gray makes it out to be, nor is it to be rejected with the thoughtlessness – and violence – of the Seattle demonstrators. But it is overemphasizing one set of factors at the expense of many others. Turner is right to point to Russia as the supreme illustration of a 'rampant market fundamentalism' which may have done more harm than good.

The most interesting case in point is Europe, both in relation to the United States and with respect to its internal differences. It is often not realized how great these are. One striking case is the comparison between Britain and Italy. Two countries of equal population and equal wealth – thus of almost identical GDP per capita – nevertheless differ fundamentally in their economic and social culture. Italy's small and medium-sized, often family-owned companies seem capable of producing the same net effect as Britain's often large, shareholder-dominated firms. When it comes to unemployment, or even social security, families in Italy still bear much of the burden which has to be borne by the welfare state in Britain.

Not all these differences are sustainable, for a variety of often domestic reasons. Adair Turner makes sure that he does not have to repudiate everything which he (sometimes willy-nilly) stood for as

Director-General of the Confederation of British Industry. But he offers a pleasingly calm and pragmatic set of arguments to dispel all dogmatic assertions about the top rate of income tax, or minimum wage levels, or arrangements of co-determination. The point is not that these and other measures, since they work in one country, might as well be introduced in others. The point is that many countries in Europe have found a balance of social and economic policies which is viable, despite the fact that it differs from the models propounded by politico-economic missionaries.

For Europe, say, in relation to the United States, this means that 'there is no one "European social model" but many national models common only at the level of objectives and broad approaches'. For Britain, however, this analysis means that the line between the public and the private sphere has to be moved a few degrees in the public direction. Public transport in London, and safer and quieter towns and villages have already been mentioned. Education is another example. 'Investment both in excellent general education, focusing especially on ensuring high levels of basic skills, and in excellence at the elite end of education (excellent science and technical skills), therefore making undoubted economic sense (as well as being socially and culturally desirable in a civilized society) even if we have no precise understanding of how more specific educational and training initiatives affect economic performance.'

Once again, the quotation illustrates a style. Turner makes strong statements but does not overstate. His measured yet firm tone leaves no doubt where he feels sure of his ground and where he sees room for further questioning. This tone also characterizes his treatment of that most vexing of current issues of political economy, the European Union. It will be clear from this introduction that Turner does not see Europe as the salvation. It has its place in the scheme of things, notably through the single market. Monetary union – the euro – has certain advantages at the micro-level, not least for tourists and travellers, perhaps also for consumers. At the macro-level it may well contribute to desirable stability and to upholding the single market. On balance, therefore, he comes down in favour, but only on balance.

Adair Turner never leaves the slightest doubt about his belief that the invisible hand of the market is the best guide to economic growth and wealth creation. But GDP figures are not all there is to wealth, not even GDP per capita figures which tell us rather more. The fundamental questions of economics remain those of what we are trying to maximize.

Human welfare requires more than a high per capita GDP. The market has to be embedded in a supportive and sustainable state. The state is fortunately no longer regarded as an active manager of the economy. Its social role, however, remains vital and is becoming if anything more important because 'unless well-managed [it] can fracture the social compact on which modern capitalism must be based'. Limits on government's ability to tax and spend do not require 'radical downsizing of European welfare states' nor do they reduce 'the freedom of individual European countries to make significantly different choices about tax and spend levels'.

Where does all this place Adair Turner's analysis politically? Above all it takes the public debate about means and ends of contemporary politics forward. Arguments for and against the neoliberal project have become barren and ideological. This book is by contrast a breath of fresh air. Its author is naturally unideological. At the same time, the political language of the third way seems exhausted after but a short period. It is somehow based on the notion that the economy is a given; it has to be nurtured, even pampered ('it's the economy, stupid') but it offers no choices. Choices have more to do with lifestyle and generally with appearances. Turner takes us back to the real world in which hard choices are more than words. He tells us what they are and who has to take them. They have to do with the public-private boundary and have to be made by elected national governments.

Turner steers clear of political labels. He likes Sir Samuel Brittan's notion of 'redistributive liberalism', though it may be misleading to call a properly financed public sector a form of redistribution. Redistribution evokes the notion of taking from the rich in order to give to the poor whereas what matters is to involve all in the provision of goods available to all. Turner also likes Brittan's 'capitalism with a human face'. In my view he provides us with the political economy of liberty. His prime concern is not equality and his patent medicine is not fraternity, or communitarianism in more fashionable language. In fact he offers no patent medicine. His concern is to find ways to offer more life chances to as many as possible, and to do so in an open society, a liberal order.

Introduction: The Triumph of the Global Free Market

In November 2000 Bill Clinton visited Vietnam, the country which twenty-five years earlier had expelled America's military might, and which had set out to build a communist society. He brought a message of reconciliation but also a message of confidence in the capitalist model, urging the Vietnamese to embrace the 'force of nature' which globalization and the market economy appear to represent. He was well received and not surprisingly. For Vietnam is already integrating into the global market economy, its exports competing in developed-country markets on the basis of low labour cost, its factories producing goods for multinational firms, its domestic economy increasingly organized on market principles. In that conversion to the market economy it is following in the footsteps of its one-time communist models – Russia and China. The triumph of the global free market appears complete.

To many people that triumph is welcome, global free trade and capital flows the unique route to rising world prosperity. To others it is deeply troubling. Green groups see global capitalism as a threat to the world environment: protesters on the streets of Seattle and Prague attacked capitalism as a casino and a threat to the world's poor; protectionists in the US fear low-wage competition as a threat to 'real' jobs; European social democrats worry that low-wage and low-tax competition threatens the European social model. Both opponents and supporters of global capitalism, however, share the common assumption – the common conventional wisdom – that globalization is *the* key force for change in economic and social life, in both developed and developing countries. They often share too the belief that competition between nations limits economic and social choice, that the pursuit of desired social, environmental or ethical aims is constrained by the demands of national 'competitiveness'.

Much of what is assumed and feared, however, is based on confused economic theory and misinterpretation of facts. Globalization has huge consequences for some individual companies, and some implications for degrees of freedom in national policy, but at least in the developed world it is not the most important driver of economic and social change. Many of the most important challenges facing the developed world indeed are driven not by globalization but by internal developments, developments which would be occurring in the US, Europe and Japan even if the rest of the world did not exist. These societies at least are largely masters of their own economic and social destiny, and their ability to pursue desirable objectives – high quality healthcare, adequate social welfare, environmental improvement, a moral foreign policy – is undiminished provided they exploit the power of market economics but recognize its limitations. For developing countries the constraints are sometimes more severe. But integration into the global economy opens up more choices than it closes. The challenge for developing countries and for the global institutions is to achieve the clear benefits of global free markets while seeking to offset their inherent imperfections. Global capitalism is not the driver of environmental destruction and inequality between nations its opponents claim, but nor is it a faultless route to economic nirvana.

Throughout the twentieth century, belief in the desirability of a 'good society' was too often combined with suspicion of market economics. The market economy, however, if utilized rather than worshipped, is the best mechanism available for pursuing both economic dynamism and desirable social goals. The purpose of this book is to explore how we can use market economics to achieve those ends, and how we need to manage and moderate capitalism to make it humane and environmentally responsible. For if capitalism has undoubtedly triumphed we must still decide which specific form of capitalism we want, which variant of capitalism works best in both economic and social terms, where free markets work well and where they do not. The bulk of the book (Chapters 1–8) explores that choice within the already developed economies; Chapters 9–11 consider the more global issues.

Public debate on economic policy – the discourse of politicians, journalists and business people rather than academic economists – is marked by an intriguing mixture of changing fashions but constant underlying themes. It is the changing fashions which first strike us if we review the debates of the last ten years. For since 1990 we have passed through four quite different phases of belief, ending up with a complete reversal of 1990's dominant wisdom.

In the early 1990s many people in Britain and the US were

convinced of the superiority of the 'stakeholder' rather than 'shareholder' economies. Japanese and German manufacturing prowess seemed triumphant, and the reasons for this were attributed to their long-term investment approaches, their patient committed shareholders, and their freedom from short-term stock-market pressures. While for a few years in the mid-1980s the Anglo-Saxon model had seemed to enjoy a revival, by 1990 it was all turning sour, and it was obvious to many commentators that it was fundamentally flawed. US productivity growth in the 1970s and the 1980s had been painfully slow and as a result the average American worker had received hardly any real wage increase for fifteen years, but Germany and Japan and France had maintained relentless productivity improvement. With the Soviet Union's collapse capitalism had clearly beaten socialism but to many people it seemed obvious that the best form of capitalism was not the American variety, but what was labelled a 'Rhineland' variety. Michel Albert's *Capitalism Against Capitalism* (1991) could confidently tell the story of 'the economic superiority of the Rhine model' of capitalism, and noted as a fact that 'American industry is in retreat'. Books like Edward Luttwak's *The Endangered American Dream* or Clyde Prestowitz's *Trading Places* warned Americans of their failure in the competitive war versus Japan. And even as late as 1995, Will Hutton's *The State We're In* argued, to many convincingly, that Germany and Japan were the models for Britain to emulate. The World Economic Forum, held in Davos each year, hosts the world's biggest concentration of politicians, economists, journalists and businessmen, and its agenda is a pretty good reflection of the conventional wisdom of the day. In 1990 one of the sessions to get into was entitled 'Coping with Japan's Economic Might'.

By the mid-1990s, however, the predominant story had changed. The Japanese economy was stagnating, the European model looked tarnished, and America now felt threatened, not by high-tech, high-skill, high-investment competition from Japan and Germany, but by relentless waves of competition from low-cost East Asian countries. The causes of this East Asian success were debated, allowing both left and right to claim support for their views. To some on the left the success of Korea or Taiwan supported a new version of the stakeholder theory. A combination of distinctively 'trust-based' private-sector relationships and intelligent state intervention was seen as delivering long-term investment approaches impossible in stock market-driven Anglo-Saxon economies. To some on the right the reason was equally clear but quite different: minimal states, low taxes and free markets were delivering an overwhelming competitive advantage. But the threat, the challenge, was equal in either analysis. The East Asian tigers posed a competitive challenge to which the West must rise. South Korea's economy would overtake the UK by 2010. So the West must cut costs, tighten belts, and compete to win in the fierce world of global competition. America was threatened, but even more so was Europe. Europe's high unemployment, wrote the European Commission in 1994, was being driven by the fact that 'the countries of the south are stirring and competing with us at cost levels we simply cannot match'.[1] And, therefore, according to political taste, Europe needed either to invest in more roads, research and development and skills, or cut its welfare states and its wages. Otherwise it would be left behind in this race for the world. At Davos in 1995 you could have gone from a session on 'Challenges to European Competitiveness' to one discussing 'The Globalization of Asian Values'.

But then in 1997 Asia crashed. Starting in Thailand in July, a wave of devaluations, stock-market crashes and bankruptcies engulfed the miracle economies, driving them into recession. Suddenly it was obvious to many commentators, who had hitherto failed to share with us their insights, that the Asian tigers, far from being paragons of either the free-market minimal state or of private-sector trust-based relationships, were in fact disaster zones of crony capitalism, corruption, 'intransparent' accounting and poor corporate governance. The East Asian countries, even more than Europe, needed to change. They needed, so the conventional wisdom went, to become more transparent, more free market, more like America. For by now, the American economy was clearly on a path to renaissance which gainsaid the earlier pessimism, and the 'Washington consensus' of free-market certainty was increasingly in the ascendant. At the Davos meeting in January 1998 you could have attended any one of eight sessions whose title included the word 'crash', 'meltdown' or 'crisis', but each time governed by the word 'Asian'. And you could then have moved on to discuss 'How Will the US Use Its Unrivalled Position?'

By autumn 1998, however, the outlook for global capitalism seemed a lot less rosy. Global financial volatility and fear were rampant. Russia collapsed and defaulted on its debts. Brazil teetered on the brink

---

1. EU, *Growth, Competitiveness and Employment*, White Paper 1994. Why countries like Korea and Taiwan are deemed to be in 'the south' is a mystery.

of unwanted devaluation, falling over in January 1999. The US equity market lost almost 20 per cent of its value between mid-July and the end of August, the dollar:yen rate moved 15 per cent in just three days; and the collapse of the hedge fund LTCM threatened a credit crunch which some feared would push the whole of the global economy into severe recession. The consensus economic forecast for 1999 was for slow or negative growth in almost all regions of the world, and to many people it was clear that the whole edifice of global free-market capitalism was shaky at the foundations. Henry Kissinger regretted 'the indiscriminate globalism of the 1990s'. George Soros, having made a fortune from short-term financial speculation, warned us in *The Crisis of Global Capitalism* that short-term financial speculation would destroy the whole system of global capitalism. Paul Krugman, one of the world's most respected economists, warned of 'the return of depression economics', and John Gray was happy to be able to report that the 'false dawn' of global capitalism was over, its 'delusions' revealed.[2] Presidents and prime ministers of the G7 countries made thoughtful speeches on the need for new financial architecture, a rather technical subject previously left to technicians at the IMF and World Bank. And at Davos in January 1999 any session with those technicians was packed out, since only they appeared to know what was going on.

By spring 2000, however, all had changed again, and changed so completely that the events of 1997 to 1998 seemed like a bad dream. For suddenly we were not on the brink of impending disaster, but marching confidently, above all in America, into the 'new economic paradigm', the paradigm of the Net, of the dotcom, of the knowledge-based economy, with productivity rising and inflation dangers dispelled, where the only relevant question was 'Don't you get it?' Nobody at Davos in January 2000 wanted to hear those IMF technicians droning on about new financial architectures. No prime minister or president considered financial-market structures worthy of mention. But wherever two or three of the great prophets of the Net had gathered together – the leaders of Yahoo and AOL, Microsoft or Dell – there was the crush hoping to pick up a few crumbs of their wisdom. Most of those prophets, of course, are American. And so today's conventional wisdom, at the time of writing, has reversed entirely that of 1990. The American free-market system has proved not a failure but a startling

---

2. See John Gray, *False Dawn – The Delusions of Global Capitalism* (1999).

success, and a success above all in the 'new economy'. Europe's and Japan's challenge now is not to get left behind, to learn how to compete in the 'new economy', to meet the latest challenge of global competition.

Ten years with at least five dominant wisdoms. A story which should at least make us wary of the twists and turns of intellectual fashion. But while there have been changing fashions, changing because of apparent shifts in economic success, one theme has been constant throughout and one other growing steadily in importance. The common theme is globalization; the growing theme, the superiority of free markets.

'It is a truth universally acknowledged,' wrote Paul Krugman in *The Accidental Theorist*, 'that the growing international mobility of goods, capital and technology has completely changed the economic game.'[3] It is indeed a dominant conventional wisdom of business life and economic discourse and has been for at least the last ten years. It rests on the following observations. First, that we live in a world of seemingly relentless growth in global trade, with trade volume growth outstripping world output growth year after year. Second, that we have seen, in the 1990s, an explosion in global capital and financial flows: $26.5 billion of equity capital flowed from the developed world to the emerging world in the whole of the 1980s; $49.5 billion flowed there in just 1996 alone. About $1.5 trillion of turnover courses through the world foreign-exchange markets every day, a flow overwhelmingly larger than world trade and three times higher than in the mid-1980s. Superlatives and figures can be piled up in any number of ways. But the reality of a more interconnected world of global money, debt and equity markets is clear for all to see. Third – and this observation comes not from macro statistics but from the anecdotes of specific sectors and companies – that we live in a world of increasingly global competition. Products that used to be made only or predominantly in the developed world can now be delivered from across the world, from countries with much lower income levels, creating entirely new competition for existing companies, competition sometimes so cost-advantaged that no resistance is possible. And competition not just for goods but for services too – not just car parts from Brazil and China, or textiles from Egypt, but software support and reservation systems operations

---

3. Paul Krugman, *The Accidental Theorist and Other Dispatches from the Dismal Science* (1998).

outsourced to Bangalore. Anecdotes of such new competition are the staple of innumerable business-strategy books and conferences, and the reality of competition for many individual companies.

These are the facts which seem to justify the beliefs of globalization theory. The belief that the world is a fiercely competitive place in which companies must struggle to win or even to survive. The belief that countries too are locked in what Lester Thurow called 'head to head' competition, in which some will win and some will lose.[4] The supposed winners in this race for the world may have changed over the course of the 1990s, from Germany and Japan at the start of the decade, to Korea and Thailand in the middle, to America today, but the basic concept of a global competitive world in which countries must compete to prosper has been a permanent motif of the debate.

If global competition has been the common motif across the decade, the steadily rising theme has been the superiority and inevitability of the free market. Each shift in the relative economic performance of different countries seems to have proved the proposition that freer markets are better than less free markets. And each further intensification of international capital flows and trade, each year of increasing awareness of global competition and of the volatility of global financial markets, has fostered the belief that you cannot buck the market, even if you wanted to.

The dominant wisdom of today's economic debate is therefore that of the global free market, triumphant, it seems, as never before. From that dominant wisdom flows a range of assertions and assumptions about the degrees of freedom available to individual countries to pursue distinctive economic and social goals. Countries are no longer free to follow their own macroeconomic policies: they are disciplined by the global capital markets to pursue fiscal and monetary policies attractive to global institutional investors. Limits on financial market liberalization (such as capital controls) are either harmful or simply impossible. Stakeholder models of corporate governance are not sustainable because the capital markets will not allow them. Tax bases are under threat as a result of competition for mobile skilled labour and mobile capital, and as a result the levels of government expenditure seen in European countries are unsustainable and will have to be reduced.

---

4. Lester Thurow, *Head to Head – The Coming Economic Battle Among Japan, Europe and America* (1992).

Welfare states are thus becoming unaffordable. And across the whole range of government policies – from welfare to education, transport to the environment, research and development and labour-market regulation, competitiveness must be the key criterion, overriding other nice but unaffordable social objectives.

The striking feature of this analysis, this set of assumptions, is that it unites commentators of right, left and middle; the first in triumph, the second in despair, the third because it's a useful alibi. For 'right-wing ultra-liberals' (the terminology is rather arbitrary but reasonably well understood)[5] the realities of global competition and the realities of global financial volatility are powerful rhetorical sticks with which to beat the left. Redistribution via welfare states can be attacked not as undesirable but as unaffordable. Labour-market regulation can be condemned not for its specific, domestic labour-market consequences, but because it will affect external competitiveness. And if the financial crashes of 1997–8 led some to question the imperative of free markets in all things, to the true believer they simply proved that the Asian economies were not free enough.

For the left wing, the implications are doleful but the facts and challenges of globalization are equally accepted as given. Global free markets threaten to condemn countries to a relentless 'race to the bottom' in social and environmental standards. The Anglo-Saxon hegemony is a threat to the European social model. Global competition threatens jobs in developed countries. Global financial markets severely punish any emerging country which seeks to diverge from the free-market consensus. And the interconnected nature of the world economy means that the prosperity of the developed world can easily be upset by

---

5. To describe different schools of thought and models a terminology is needed. Somewhat arbitrarily I will use the following. The 'stakeholder' model, 'Rhineland' model, or 'continental' model will be used close to synonymously to denote a model of capitalism distinct from Anglo-Saxon capitalism in ways defined at the beginning of Chapter 6 (which also, however, warns against the belief that there is one European model). The term 'stakeholderist' (ugly but without obvious alternative) will be used for proponents of Rhineland or continental approaches. 'Anglo-Saxon' will be used to describe a free-market approach to product, capital and labour markets; the 'American model' will imply also a minimal state. 'Ultra-liberal' will imply a strong free-market approach to all economic issues; 'right wing' ultra-liberal to denote in addition support for minimal states and opposition to redistribution.

turmoil elsewhere. The policy prescriptions are different from those inferred by right-wingers. The European model must be reinforced to prevent 'social dumping', not dismantled to compete. But the diagnosis of the threat is the same.

And the same diagnosis is a staple of speeches by pragmatic politicians of the centre. For the language of globalization and global competition has a powerful appeal even to the least ideological of politicians, providing both a useful alibi and a unifying theme. Governments are always faced with competing claims which cannot simultaneously be satisfied, and much of the business of government entails trade-offs between different groups within society. Incompatible expectations are most easily managed down with reference to a harsh external world. Trade-offs are rhetorically denied by the language of 'no alternative'. The rhetoric of global competition would be appealing because it is useful even if it was not also so convincing.

The problem with these widely accepted assumptions, however, is that they are a mixture of the true, the half true but exaggerated, and the plain wrong. By focusing on globalization as the key driver of economic change, moreover, this conventional wisdom diverts attention from other forces powerfully at work in the developed world, forces which would be at work even if the developed world were the only world, having no capital or trade flows with anywhere else. And by legitimizing a rhetoric of external threat, of 'no alternative', of policy driven by the dictates of 'competitiveness', it degrades the quality of public debate on the trade-offs and choices which should be the essence of political decision-making. The conventional wisdom is both deeply flawed in terms of analysis and an impediment to intelligent policy debate.

It is, for instance, true that part of our economy is increasingly open to global trade and competition, but it is also true that a growing set of economic activity – in service provision and servicing – is inherently untradeable (try exporting a haircut), and that this untradeable sector is increasing as a proportion of the whole economy. In some ways, indeed, the world economy is becoming *less* rather than more global, more local indeed, and this, as we shall see in Chapters 1 and 2, has subtle implications that need to be understood.

It is also true that the growth of global capital and financial markets is a key development limiting some countries' degrees of freedom in macroeconomic policy: and in general global capital markets are a good thing. But it is not clear that liberalization of liquid, short-term financial markets is in all cases beneficial, and some of the policy prescriptions proposed after the Asian crisis were based on a faith in market liberalization as a cure-all medicine which is religious rather than scientific in nature.

It is meanwhile plain wrong to believe that the competition of newly emerging industrial economies threatens or can threaten the sustainable standard of living of the developed world, or that it threatens the sustainability of their levels of welfare-state provision, or that it is the cause of high levels of European unemployment. Each of these propositions is false and importantly false, since wrong description of the causes of problems (e.g. of European unemployment) could lead us to ignore the real causes, and to fail to prescribe required and available solutions. As we shall see in Chapters 5 and 6, there are good reasons for believing that Europe should liberalize its labour markets, but those reasons have nothing to do with the challenge of competing in global markets and the specific changes needed will not be optimally designed if increased competitiveness is the declared objective.

Finally, the idea that global tax competition limits the sustainability of government expenditure on welfare states is somewhat true but greatly exaggerated by those who in any case desire a small state and minimal redistribution as ends per se. And the resulting constraint on the size of the state still leaves us able to pursue a range of desirable social objectives, provided we focus the state on those objectives and remove it from functions where it adds no value.

The challenge, therefore, which this book attempts, is to strip away the nonsense and the hype of what Professor Paul Krugman has called 'globaloney', to distinguish clearly between globalization's real and imagined consequences, and to identify what other, unrelated forces are at work. Once we do that we are able to address coherently the optimal design of economic and social policy. We will then discover that states still retain a high degree of freedom to choose between alternative social, environmental and indeed foreign-policy options, and that the existence of the global economy, while it has changed some of the context in which countries operate, has not changed fundamentally the scope of social and political choice.

But if our degrees of freedom in social and political choice are not as radically constrained as conventional wisdom suggests, what has changed, partly because of globalization but even more because of changes in technology and customer preference, is the instruments through which desirable social and economic objectives need to be pursued. It is this change in appropriate instruments, rather than objectives, which poses a challenge to the traditional European social model.

The European social and economic model should therefore change. It should embrace, even more than it has already, the benefits of market competition in all sectors of economic activity, including the utilities previously seen as the preserve of the state. It should liberalize its labour markets to encourage the creation of jobs, especially in service sectors of the economy, and should accept that labour-market interventions (via high minimum wages or collective bargaining) are inappropriate routes by which to pursue desired levels of income redistribution. It should accept as highly likely the evolution of its corporate governance structures towards the Anglo-Saxon model of overt shareholder wealth maximization and towards more explicit measurement of corporate performance. And it should limit the size of the state by withdrawing the state from activities which serve no inherent social purpose, whether that be the ownership and management of commercial assets, or the transfer of income from middle class to middle class, for instance through state pension schemes. But there is no need to reject as unaffordable reasonably high levels of collective good provision (high environmental standards, good public health and education), and no case for rejecting a state role as, to a degree, the redistributor of income. (Indeed, as we shall see in Chapter 3, an increased need for such redistribution arises from a strong tendency towards pre-tax inequality unleashed by technological trends.) It is for such a reformed, refocused but not rejected European social model that this book argues.

The political philosophy of such an approach is clearly not socialist, nor even social democratic. But nor is it the philosophy of free-market conservatism – predicated on the assumption that market outcomes are either by definition desirable or, if undesirable, unchangeable because of external constraint. Instead it is a philosophy which recognizes the immense benefits of markets, but which also recognizes the need and the possibility of governmental action to achieve desirable objectives which the market itself will not automatically deliver, including some limited but still important element of redistribution of economic outcomes. And it is a philosophy which recognizes also that while markets in general are massively superior mechanisms of economic organization, they are not perfect in all circumstances, and they are capable (for instance in the financial markets) of moving in quite irrational ways.

Optimal policy needs to recognize and reflect this fact, not assert that market liberalization is by definition correct in all circumstances.

'Redistributive and managed market liberalism' would be a reasonable description of what is proposed. Unfortunately that's a bit of a mouthful. 'Capitalism with a human face' is catchier but Sir Samuel Brittan has already taken that as the title of a book, otherwise that might have been my favoured title. The key theme of this book indeed is that the potential for a 'capitalism with a human face' remains largely undimmed by the emergence of the global economy, and that we should be confident of our ability to combine the dynamism of the market economy with the needs of an inclusive society and of a preserved and improved physical environment.

Structure of the argument

Some readers like the discovery method: they can proceed directly to Chapter 1. Others prefer a map of the territory to be covered: for them the following outline will be useful.

Part 1 analyses the forces which are changing the context for economic and social policy. Chapter 1 begins with standard accounts of globalization and suggests that in some key ways economies are becoming more local not more global. It argues that the concept of 'national competitiveness', in which nations as well as companies compete, is a serious impediment to clear thinking about economic performance, and about social and political choice. And it identifies other forces apart from globalization – changes in technology and customer preference – which have a more fundamental impact on developed economies. Chapter 2 analyses those forces in detail, distinguishing substance from hype in the 'new economy' and identifying the implications of an increasingly service-intensive economy.

Given this context, Chapter 3 argues that internal challenges – such as rising inequality and increased competition for limited-supply 'positional' goods – have more important implications for optimal economic and social policy in developed countries than the challenge of competing in the global economy.

Part 2 assesses the economic performance of different economies and forms of capitalism and their relative ability to deal with the changing world described in Part 1. Chapter 4 explores how we measure economic success and warns against the belief that standard economic indicators are good measures of social or even individual welfare. Chapter 5 stresses that the performance of mature economies is much more similar than different, and rejects the idea that Europe is in any fundamental sense failing relative to the US. But the changes outlined in Chapter 2 have shifted the balance of advantage in favour of more free-market approaches and changes are therefore required in European policies. These changes are described in Chapter 6: they amount to a reform but not a rejection of a distinctive European model. Chapter 7 analyses British economic performance and its implications for policy choices. Britain has ceased relative economic decline but its performance still compares poorly with many continental economies. To achieve further improvement the priority is more investment in capital and skills, not more deregulation.

Part 3 considers policy implications and global issues. Chapter 8 defines the appropriate and sustainable role of the state in a world of free capital and trade flows. It supports the withdrawal of the state from direct involvement in the management of the economy, but argues that government's social role remains vital. It rejects the argument that European taxation and public expenditure levels must be dramatically reduced in pursuit of 'competitiveness'.

Chapter 9 turns to environmental issues. It argues that bad market economics is often used to oppose desirable environmental objectives, but that market instruments can be powerful tools to pursue those ends. It argues also for radical reductions in CO_2 emissions and rejects the idea that responsible action on climate change is a threat to the 'competitiveness' or prosperity of developed countries. Fiscal instruments such as high-energy taxes and road-congestion charges are needed to pursue vital environmental aims.

Chapter 10 deals with global financial markets and market liberalization in developing countries. It argues that global capitalism – combining domestic liberalization, freer trade and freer movement of long-term capital – has produced strongly positive overall results. But it identifies liquid financial markets as a special case where market imperfection is inherent, and where complete and immediate liberalization may not always make sense. And it analyses Russia's transition to capitalism as an example of market economics too simplistically and too optimistically applied. A pragmatic rather then religious approach to market liberalization is essential.

Chapter 11 covers trade issues. It argues the case for freer trade as in the interests of the developing rather than the developed world.

It supports integration of environmental issues into trade-policy discussions. And it explains why our economic prosperity does not require us to sell arms to odious regimes, nor to ignore human rights issues.

Chapter 12 summarizes key conclusions and sets out the political and economic philosophy implied.

PART ONE

Trends, Concepts
and Delusions

1. The Competitiveness of Nations: Myths and Delusions

The concept of national competition and of national 'competitiveness' is central to many popular accounts of how the global economy works. Not only has globalization created a world of intense competition between companies, but countries too are locked in head-to-head competition, making a high level of competitiveness essential if prosperity and high employment are to be achieved. The belief is pervasive and the language of competitiveness plays a crucial role in political debate. Governments issue Competitiveness White Papers and invite businessmen and women to join Competitiveness Councils. Global institutions issue tables ranking countries by competitiveness. Right-wing politicians tell us that competitiveness demands smaller welfare states and lower taxes. Lobby groups reach for 'the threat to competitiveness' as the easiest weapon with which to beat off unwanted government actions. Europe faces a crisis of competitiveness, and needs to compete more effectively with America in the new economy. The message is reiterated in countless books, and strikes a chord with practical business people facing competitive challenges to their own individual businesses. It feels right that if companies are locked in ever more global competition, so too must countries be.

But that assumption is almost entirely wrong: and the fact that it is wrong has profound consequences for our ability to think clearly about relative economic performance and about policy choices in economic and social life. This chapter, therefore, sets out what is wrong with the concept of national competition in the global economy, and suggests an alternative framework for thinking about economic objectives and economic policy issues. It outlines the real rather than imagined impact that globalization is having on developed-economy prospects and on the degree of interdependence between economies. And it identifies other factors, apart from globalization, which are central to what is happening to the economies of the developed world.

Some readers may think it odd that most of an entire chapter is thus devoted to explaining what is *not* going on rather than what is. The assumptions of 'national competitiveness', however, are so pervasive in public debate, so seemingly rational to practical people, but so confused that unless and until you dispel them you cannot think clearly about economic and social issues. If I cannot persuade you of the arguments of this chapter, you will either not fully understand or else disagree with much of what follows. The arguments in this chapter are therefore necessary.

Even though most of them, I readily admit, are not original. Indeed, as long ago as 1993 Paul Krugman devoted a series of articles (subsequently published as the book *Pop Internationalism*) to a devastatingly effective attack on the confusions of national competitiveness theory, and the key theoretical and empirical arguments against those confusions were set out in that book. Despite the power of his attack, however, the confusions of competitiveness theory have not gone away, and continue to pervade popular thinking. Despite what many economists believed was Krugman's stake through the heart of competitiveness thinking, this muddled concept seems to have the power to rise from the grave. A restatement of Krugman's case remains, therefore, essential.[1]

The assumptions of national competitiveness theory

The idea that the global economy is characterized by competition between nations is pervasive to popular thinking in most developed countries. Several of the American books which did much to set competitiveness theory into full flight have already been mentioned in the Introduction. Ira Magaziner and Robert Reich's *Minding America's Business* (1982) was an early example of the genre. Clyde Prestowitz's *Trading Places: How We Allowed Japan to Take the Lead* (1988) was a standard of the late 80s fear-of-Japan phase of thinking. Lester Thurow's *Head to Head – The Coming Economic Battle Among Japan,*

---

1. I recognize that some people familiar with the work of the Confederation of British Industry (CBI) will wonder, in reading this chapter, whether I am not attacking some of the very language which was used by the CBI when I was its Director-General. To which my reply is largely *mea culpa*. My defence for doing so, and for not more aggressively seeking to change that language, is presented later in the chapter. But it is a plea in mitigation, not one of total innocence.

Europe and America (1992) was perhaps, in its very title, the classic statement of the proposition.

'Competitiveness-speak' came slightly later to Britain and continental Europe, but from the mid-1990s on has become pervasive in public debate. The Conservative government created a Competitiveness Unit in 1993, and produced Britain's first Competitiveness White Paper in 1994. The threat that a Labour victory would pose to Britain's competitiveness was a crucial feature of the Conservatives' 1997 election campaign. New Labour, however, readily continued the theme with a Competitiveness Council on which I, among others, was asked to sit. The European Union, meanwhile, having slipped into competitiveness-speak first in 1994 with its White Paper on *Growth, Competitiveness and Employment*, was by 1997 also equipped with a Competitiveness Advisory Council to advise its Commission President. The CBI's 1996 policy programme was entitled 'Competing in the Global Economy', and by 1998 UNICE (the European-wide employers' federation) had launched 'Competitiveness in Europe', an analysis of Europe's dangerously uncompetitive position.

The assumptions which lie behind this use of the word 'competitiveness' include the following general and more specific European points. First, that the global economy is an increasingly competitive place because trade is increasingly important and increasingly global. Second, that the world economy is increasingly interconnected – that what happens in one economy inevitably and directly affects others, both in a competitive sense and through mutual reliance on each other's demand. Third, that nations as well as companies compete and that it is therefore essential for countries to improve their competitiveness. And finally, that Europe in particular suffers from a 'failure of competitiveness' in two respects. It is uncompetitive in basic manufactures versus emerging countries because its labour costs are too high and its taxes too onerous. It is uncompetitive versus the US in the new economy because it lacks entrepreneurship, perhaps as a result of burdensome taxation and regulation. This dual failure of competitiveness is then seen as a key cause of Europe's high unemployment.

Three European quotations across the 1990s illustrate these beliefs. First from the European Commission's *White Paper on Growth, Competitiveness and Employment* (1994), in which Europe's high unemployment is seen as deriving from the fact that newly emerging economies are 'competing with us at cost levels we simply cannot match'. Second from Professor Minford, a popular British economist, in 1995: 'the present travails of the OECD countries – slowdown, deflation, wage inequality and unemployment – are the direct result of the intensifying competition from emerging market economies whether in Asia, Latin America or Eastern Europe' (*Daily Telegraph*, 25 September 1995). Third, from the British Cabinet Office's Performance and Innovation Unit report on business and consumer Internet use in September 1999: 'if the UK fails to capitalise on the opportunities that e-commerce presents, then jobs and prosperity will be eroded by e-commerce competition from overseas'.

But these assumptions are confused in theory, wrong in empirical description of the world economy, and wrong in their description of the causes of European unemployment.

Theoretical confusions and the special case

The idea that the success of other economies can reduce the prosperity or the rate of growth of prosperity, or the employment level of a country, and that as a result success *relative* to other countries has a peculiarly important role in overall economic performance, is almost totally wrong. One cannot say totally wrong without the 'almost' because there are a few special case conditions which create the theoretical possibility of negative effects from the increased success of others. But if these special case conditions did pertain, the total impact on US and overall European performance would still be minimal, and they are the opposite of the conditions which have concerned most devotees of 'the failure of competitiveness' school of thought.

There are two obvious confusions found to different degrees in accounts of national competitiveness theory. The first is the implicit assumption of a limited pot of prosperity for which nations compete; the second is the use of the term 'competitiveness' without specification of the exchange rate. Both have to be rejected to think straight: rejecting them (particularly the second) requires just a bit of economic theory.

The simplest versions of competitiveness theory implicitly assume that the world economy is a zero or limited sum pot of prosperity and/or of employment opportunities for which countries compete. That was a fairly explicit assumption of Sir James Goldsmith's book *The Trap*, but it is also the implicit logic of Lester Thurow's title *Head to Head* and of his description of a world of 'win-lose' competition. But it is wholly wrong and so obviously wrong that most people who use concepts of competitiveness are quick to distance themselves from such a simplistic assumption. Just as within an economy, all citizens can simultaneously become richer, so at the world level all countries can simultaneously achieve economic growth. Economic prosperity is not in most respects contested – in general one nation's prosperity does not hurt another's. There are only two exceptions to that assertion. One applies if there are economic factors in fixed or limited supply – such as raw materials or, a more likely example, the capacity of the atmosphere to absorb CO_2 emissions. That exception raises important global issues which Chapter 9 addresses. The other relates to a special case of competitiveness theory, concerning changes in the terms of trade. This is discussed below. But both are exceptions which place only very small limits on our ability simultaneously to grow GDP per capita in all countries, and both are quite different problems from those which concern most devotees of competitiveness theory. As near as makes no difference, one country's prosperity has no inherent influence on another's prosperity; and one country's rate of growth has no direct influence on another's growth.

The more common error is the use of the word 'competitiveness' outside a specification of the exchange rate. Country A, we are told, has too high labour costs and as a result is uncompetitive in world markets. However, even for the externally traded sectors of the economy, this is a quite meaningless statement if the exchange rate is not specified. And if the external sector of an economic bloc (be it a nation or the Euro zone) was uncompetitive at some given exchange rate, a fall in that exchange rate would tend over time to bring about a new competitive equilibrium. For large economic blocs like the US or Europe the total economic impact of such exchange-rate movements is limited for empirical reasons to be discussed below, but the potential for such movements makes a nonsense of statements that economic area A or B is inherently, rather than temporarily, uncompetitive.

The potential movement in exchange rates is, however, relevant to the special case, the only set of mechanisms by which one country's prosperity or rate of growth can at least theoretically be threatened by another's increasing competitive success. This special case arises through adverse movements in the terms of trade. Trade between two countries will always increase the potential income in both countries, essentially because each country concentrates on the production of goods and services where it has a relative or comparative advantage, a concentration which increases overall productivity in both countries (if we don't believe this we shouldn't be in favour of free trade).[2] But although both countries gain, the balance of advantage depends on the terms of trade, that is on the relative price of the products that Country A exports to B versus those that Country B exports to A. The balance of advantage between Germany and Malaysia, for instance, might reflect the price of German machine tools relative to the price of Malaysian manufactured televisions. If for some reason the price of the machine tools falls relative to television prices, the result is to make Germany (slightly) worse off. Germans will either have to consume fewer television sets (or other imported goods), or more Germans will need to produce more machine tools (or other exported goods) and as a result will not be available to produce other goods and services which German people consume: either way Germans will be slightly poorer. Germany will still gain from free trade: it is still better off exporting machine tools and importing televisions versus making machine tools only for its own use and making its own televisions as well, but it gains less than it did before.

The mechanisms by which these adjustments occur differ according to whether Germany has a fixed or floating exchange rate versus Malaysia. If a fixed rate, then German nominal wages would have to rise less than inflation, with real wages falling to match the lower price achieved for the machine tools; if, as in the real world, a floating rate, the Deutschmark (or rather the euro) would tend to fall versus the Malaysian ringit and German real wages would fall slightly as a result. But the fundamental impact is the same in both instances. German incomes fall to the extent that it gets fewer television sets per machine tool: and there is no negative impact on employment.[3]

---

2. Paul Krugman, *Pop Internationalism*, Chapter 6 provides a simple account of this basic trade theory.

3. In the example given indeed the employment effect could be positive. In other cases, however, 'competitiveness' effects can produce transitional employment effects which need to be managed even if the long-term effect is nil. Two cases in particular are considered later. (1) The difficulties that can arise between countries in a fixed exchange-rate regime if nominal wages are inflexible: this has implications as a special case of the 'tax and competitiveness' effects discussed in Chapter 8. (2) The impact of sectorally specific taxes, which can create transitional employment effects, as well as real income effects; this issue is discussed in relation to energy taxes in Chapter 9.

Such an adverse movement in terms of trade is *the only way* in which changes in the economic performance of emerging countries can affect the prosperity or growth rate of the developed world. It introduces the possibility that technological progress by others could theoretically impact a technological leader's standard of living. Thus in the example, the relative price of German machine tools could be falling because other countries were developing a technological capability over which Germany previously enjoyed a monopoly. In this case Germany still gains from free trade but gains less than when it enjoyed that monopoly.

It is because of this special case that one has to say that national competitiveness theory is 'almost' totally wrong rather than totally wrong. It is a special case which has spawned a rich literature of 'strategic trade theory'. It is a special case which may make it sensible for developed nations to make high skill levels, a good science base, and a high level of research and development key government objectives (though the argument for these can be equally made without any reference to the special case or to national competitiveness concerns). But while it exists in theory, in practice it is not terribly important to the prosperity (and not at all to the employment prospects) of rich developed nations, certainly if we are thinking at the level of the US or Europe rather than specific regions or small nations.

That is for two reasons. The first is that in actual fact the terms of trade have not been moving against developed nations as emerging countries grow; if anything over the last twenty years the trend has been in the opposite direction. It is indeed the *collapsing* relative price of imports such as textiles and consumer electronics which is more often used to justify scare stories about a loss of competitiveness: but those collapsing prices *increase* rather than decrease the importer's prosperity. The second is that at the level of the overall US or European economy surprisingly little of total economic activity is traded with the rest of the world: only about 12–13 per cent in both cases.[4] Even massive terms of trade effects would therefore make only minimal differences to European or US prosperity: a 20 per cent shift affecting

---

4. There are two different ways to define trade intensity. One takes exports plus imports divided by GDP. The other takes exports plus imports divided by 2, and then divides this by GDP. This book uses the latter convention. Time trends and inter-country comparisons are of course unaffected by which convention is used.

half of all trade would, for instance, cut GDP by only 1.2 per cent, equivalent to about six months of growth. As a result Europe and the US have only limited potential to make themselves richer by careful selection of specific high-value traded sectors or by a determination to stay ahead of others in a competitive race. For smaller economic units, of course, the effects could be larger, simply because trade is bigger as a percentage of GDP. For Ireland or Bavaria, for instance, the composition of their traded sectors (whether focused on high- or low-value activities) can make an appreciable difference to overall prosperity. In general the principle is simple: 'competitiveness' is a meaningful concept at the level of an individual company, it is totally meaningless at the level of the world, and it loses its meaning as we progress along that spectrum. At the level of statements about the competitiveness of Europe or the US, it is almost totally devoid of meaning.[5]

---

5. Some readers will find it counter-intuitive that a specific European region, say Ireland, can become (somewhat) richer because its traded sectors are skewed towards specific 'high value' sectors but that all European regions together (i.e. Europe) cannot except to a trivial extent. The factor which makes this possible is that Ireland's 'high value' skew can be relative to and thus at the expense of other European regions. The point becomes clear if we think about the extremes: an individual person can choose for their career to focus 100 per cent on an activity (e.g. being a software engineer) whose output trades at a high price relative to the other goods and services which the individual wants to consume, but a closed economy (i.e. the world) cannot choose to skew its production even minutely towards 'high value' activities, it has to produce the products and services consumers in total want and in the proportion they want. If consumer demand requires 2 per cent of all people to be software engineers the world cannot choose to be more software focused than that. The only determinant of its prosperity is the average productivity with which it produces all goods and services. A town or district can be significantly skewed to 'high value' activities, i.e. towards high-value people (e.g. the City of London); a region can be somewhat skewed; Europe in total cannot except to a very small extent – the mix of its activities and employment is determined at least 90 per cent by the pattern of European consumption.

   It should be noted, however, that even at the level of a 'region' the ability to plan a positive skew by deliberate choice is limited. 'High value' for terms of trade purposes does not mean hi-tech (there are plenty of low-paid people assembling computers), and what is 'high value' today can cease to be in future. Even at the level of smaller regions the practical implications of the special case therefore tend to be simply focused on generic issues such as the skills and infrastructure likely to attract whatever are the 'high value' activities of the future, rather than on picking winners.

Some readers may protest, however, that since trade intensity is increasing, competitiveness must at the very least be becoming more meaningful over time. In fact that is not true. For contrary to the conventional wisdom of globalization, trade intensity is not on a relentless upward path, and in absolute terms the role of global trade in the economies of the developed world is greatly overstated. The reasons why are central to our understanding of the changing shape of our economies.

A more global economy, or more local?

The conventional wisdom is that the trade of developed countries (whether imports or exports) is rising relentlessly as a share of GDP, and that global competition is therefore an increasingly important factor, affecting far more of the economy than in the past. But this is wrong. Developed economies as a whole, as against sectors, are not becoming ever more open to the blast of global competition.

That is true if we take a long-term historical perspective. Britain's trade intensity was about 26 per cent in 1910, only slightly below today's figure of 29 per cent. US trade intensity has risen from 8 to 13 per cent between 1890 and today, but when one considers that in 1890 the US had an overtly protectionist industrial policy, and today has close to free trade, that increase hardly suggests a revolution in the fundamental nature of the world economy. In terms of capital flows too, the world economy of the late nineteenth century was by some measures as 'global' as today's.

Indeed, in many ways the post Second World War period has seen simply a return to the degree of globalization already attained before the First World War. If we look at trade intensities for the European Union countries since 1960 (see Table 1.1, overleaf) three features are striking. The first is that there was a period of rapidly rising trade intensity – between 1960 and the mid-1980s – well before globalization became the conventional wisdom of economic discourse. This was largely due to the creation of the Common Market. The second is that since the mid-1980s, there has been no significant increase in total trade intensity: it rises and falls with economic cycles, but there is no strong trend. The third is that the vast majority of this trade is either internal to the EU – i.e. between different European countries – or with other rich developed countries (the US, Japan, Australia).

Table 1.1 European trade intensity: trade as % of GDP*

	1960	1974	1985	1997
Total trade	18.9	26.1	29.2	30.5
of which internal, i.e. with other EU15 countries, or with Switzerland and Norway		14.0	17.1	20.0
with Japan, US, Canada, Australia and New Zealand		6.3	6.7	5.9
with other countries (mainly low-income and emerging economies)		5.8	5.4	4.7

* Sum of imports and exports divided by two.

Source: OECD *Monthly Foreign Trade Statistics*, OECD *Historical Statistics*.

Only 11 per cent of European Union GDP is traded outside the borders of the EU, and only 5 per cent is traded with emerging low-income countries. And that proportion has fallen not risen over the last twenty years.

The pictures are similar for the world's other two major and rich economies. Japan trades just 10 per cent of GDP and that figure is lower now than in the 1980s: it peaked in the 1970s at about 14 per cent. The US has seen an upward trend in trade intensity from its initially very low base, and now trades 13 per cent of GDP versus 10 per cent in 1980. But only 4.4 per cent of GDP is traded with countries outside the rich developed world, and 30 per cent of that is with geographically contiguous Mexico. Despite all the talk of globalization, the vast majority of economic activity in rich countries is either not traded at all, or is traded with other countries of roughly equivalent income level and especially with the countries which are geographically contiguous. The impact of trade with low-income countries at the other end of the world on the macro economies of rich countries is massively overstated in populist accounts of globalization. Imports of manufactured goods from low-wage economies into developed economies account for only about 1–3 per cent of GDP and it is simply impossible for these imports to pose the threat to jobs and living standards which the conventional wisdom asserts.

Many people find the facts of static trade intensity counter-intuitive. It goes against all the talk of car parts from Brazil, textiles from Egypt, software from Bangalore. It goes against the daily experience of many business people who are painfully aware that in their specific sector competition has become more global. And it seems mathematically impossible to square with the figures we hear quoted each year of trade volumes growing faster than GDP. A numerator growing faster than the denominator but with the ratio constant is not arithmetically possible.

The factor which such anecdotes and figures ignore, however, is that of changing relative prices. Trade *volumes* grow faster than GDP, but the value of trade does not because the relative price of the goods and services we trade keeps falling relative to those we don't trade. Figure 1.1 illustrates the process for Europe from 1984 to 1997. The volume of goods and services traded (imports and exports combined) rose 94 per cent, while GDP (i.e. all goods and services) rose 34 per cent in real terms. But while overall prices rose by 67 per cent, the prices of imports and exports rose by just 21 per cent: in real terms

Figure 1.1 The relative price effect on EU15 trade intensity*

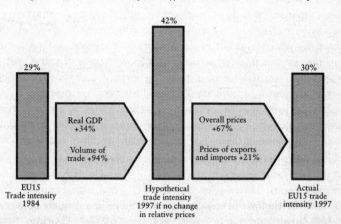

* (Imports and exports) ÷ 2 as % GDP.

Source: OECD *Historical Statistics*.

they fell 28 per cent. If the prices of traded goods and services had risen in line with general prices, trade intensity would indeed have risen from 29 to 42 per cent. Because traded prices fell in relative terms, trade intensity stayed roughly constant. In simple terms the price of television sets, which are traded, keeps falling relative to the price of haircuts which are not; that factor limits, and may eventually reduce, the proportion of our economy which is traded.

The key driver of these falling relative prices is different productivity growth rates in different sectors of the economy.[6] For inherent technological reasons productivity growth rates vary hugely sector by sector. Over time we get ever more productive in manufacturing and in those services which depend on information and communications technology; but productivity increases much more slowly in face-to-face services like healthcare, education, personal domestic services and restaurants. Relative prices tend to fall wherever productivity growth is fastest. It is because we get rapidly more productive in manufacturing television sets but not in providing haircuts that television sets keep falling in price relative to haircuts. If as a result people bought limitlessly more televisions the price effect could be offset, but at some point as people get richer they actually prefer to spend an increasing percentage of their income on more services rather than on more physical goods.

The implications of these factors for the overall shape of the economy will be explored in detail in Chapter 2. Essentially they mean that there is a relentless underlying tendency for economic value added and employment to shift to those activities, such as face-to-face services, which we are least able to automate, or which require direct customer contact, or which entail a non-automatable personal skill. As a result our economy becomes in some senses more local not more global: a powerful localization effect is at work. For the sectors where there is rapid productivity growth tend to be those that are most traded, and the activities with low productivity growth are least likely to be traded, and for reasons which are inherent not coincidental. We really can do airline reservations processing from Bangalore, but the very factors

6. The impact of differential productivity rates on the shape of the economy has been long familiar to theoretical economists but receives insufficient attention in popular accounts. See W.J. Baumol, 'Macroeconomics of Unbalanced Growth', *American Economic Review*, June 1967.

which make that possible – the information and communications intensity of the service, the non-emotive nature of the customer value to be delivered – also make the activity inherently susceptible to rapid productivity improvement, which in turn produces a collapse in relative price. The cost of providing airline reservations services will keep falling relative to the price of, say, a restaurant meal. The traded sectors of the economy are thus self-limiting as a proportion of GDP, because of their high productivity growth.

In short, there are strong forces at work in our economy tending to reduce trade intensity. If they were the only forces at work we would see trade intensities not only static but declining.

And at the level of individual cities or small geographic regions that is precisely what we do see. A far larger proportion of what is produced in a city or region is now consumed in that city or region than was the case fifty or a hundred years ago: a bigger share of economic activity occurs in the retail outlets, schools, hospitals, restaurants, sports centres and the like whose output is consumed in that location; a smaller share occurs in the factories which produce goods which are then shipped to other cities, regions or countries.[7]

But at the level of countries or continents this localization trend has been offset by two factors which go the other way. One is vastly improved transport and communications, which make it possible for those products which are inherently tradeable to be traded increasingly not from region to region, but across the globe – possible, for instance, for London's fruit and vegetable imports to come not just from Kent but from Kenya or Guatemala. The other factor is trade liberalization (elimination of tariffs and quotas) which removes artificial impediments to the influence of improved transport and communications. Together these two factors mean that trade as a percentage of sectoral activity does indeed keep growing in those sectors of the economy where products and services are inherently tradeable. What the conventional wisdom has missed, however, is the offsetting localization trend shifting more economic activity into inherently untradeable (or at least less tradeable) sectors.

---

7. Paul Krugman guestimates that Los Angeles today is a 75 per cent 'local' and only 25 per cent 'traded' economy, whereas late nineteenth-century Chicago was more than 50 per cent traded and less than 50 per cent local. *Pop Internationalism*, Chapter 13.

Actual observed trends in trade intensity therefore result from the balance of two offsetting sets of forces: inherent localization on one side, improved transport and communications and trade liberalization on the other. The balance between these two sets of forces has shifted over the years.

From 1914 to 1945 trade intensities declined because war and protectionism limited globalization even in the inherently tradeable sectors. From 1950 to 1980 Europe saw increasing trade intensity because the creation of the Common Market, combined with improved transport and communications, more than offset the localization effects of increasing service and servicing intensity. From 1980 onwards, however, the factors have been in balance. The US, conversely, has seen an increase in trade intensity in the 1990s driven by the creation of NAFTA (the North American Free Trade Area) – 50 per cent of the increase in US trade intensity is explained by Mexican and Canadian trade.

Looking to the future, we do not know which way the balance will tip. But it is possible that it will tip towards declining trade intensities. With world trade liberalization reaching the point of diminishing returns, and with transport and communications improvements already massively advanced, it may well be that the localization effects will in future dominate. At the very least we should not work on the assumption that our economies will become, in terms of trade intensities, relentlessly more global.

The myth of uncompetitive Europe

The conventional wisdom overestimates the importance of global trade to mature economies. It is even more wrong in its diagnosis of Europe's economic performance.

The standard story is that Europe is failing in the globally competitive market. Before the Asian crashes of 1997 the key concern was the competition from low-cost emerging economies. More recently the threat is seen as coming from a US pulling ahead in the new economy. But the basic assumption is the same. Europe is failing in global competition and that is a key cause of its high unemployment. Its costs are too high, its taxes too onerous, and its regulation too restrictive: it needs to change all that to become more competitive. A 1998 report from the European employers' federation UNICE quoted with approval a *Financial Times* article asserting that: 'Europe has a grim future ahead if politicians and business leaders fail to build support for measures to boost competitiveness.'[8]

But this description of Europe as uncompetitive just does not fit the facts. Chapter 5 will assess in detail Europe's economic performance compared with the US and with emerging nations, but for now two key points can be made to contradict the conventional wisdom. First, Europe's external sector is not uncompetitive nor unproductive nor in any sense failing. French, German, Swedish and Dutch companies are not failing in world markets, indeed they are performing rather well. French and German labour costs are high, but French and German companies achieve far higher productivity per hour worked than, for instance, the UK. As a result they can still be competitive in world markets. The Eurozone in total has tended to run a large balance of payments surplus, while the US runs a very large deficit.[9] Current account surpluses are by no means a sign of optimal economic policy but should at the very least give pause for thought to those who talk of Europe's uncompetitive position.

Second, while several European countries face a problem of high structural unemployment, this has almost nothing to do with a failure in global competition. As Figure 1.2 shows, the difference between Europe's employment rates and that of the US is accounted for by greater US job creation in the service sector, and primarily in specific service sectors which are almost entirely non-traded. The US has a higher employment rate because it has more people working in health-care, education, retailing, hotels, cafes and amusement centres. There are reasons why Europe has failed to create these jobs, reasons explored in Chapters 3 and 5, and reasons which require a change in European approaches, the reform of the European social model outlined in Chapter 6. But they are not reasons meaningfully explained through the language of national competitiveness.

---

8. UNICE, *Benchmarking Europe's Competitiveness* (1998).

9. Over the four years 1996–9 the Eurozone surplus was about $240 billion, the US deficit $830 billion. In 2000 the Eurozone was roughly in balance (a deficit of about –0.2 per cent of GDP) while the US ran a deficit of about 4 per cent of GDP.

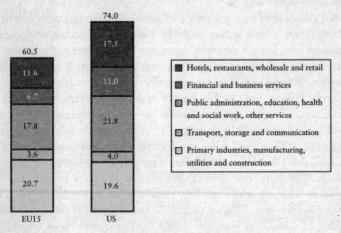

Figure 1.2 Employment rate in US and EU15, 1997
(% of working-age population)

Source: European Commission, *Employment in Europe 1999*.

If we want to understand why France has higher youth unemployment than Britain or the US we should not therefore wander around France looking for French exporting companies failing in world markets – we would find them doing very well and better on average than their British counterparts. We should ask instead why there are fewer staff employed in a French supermarket than there are in a Tesco or Sainsbury's. The use of the word 'competitiveness' is simply a distraction from our ability to answer that question.

Overall, therefore, national competitiveness scores low marks both as a theory and for its fit with the empirical facts. Ideally we should use a different framework for assessing economic success. But the language of competitiveness remains pervasive to public discourse and difficult to dislodge. Before suggesting an alternative framework, we should therefore ask two linked questions: (i) why is this confused theory so tenacious? and (ii) does it matter that it is confused; could we not despite its confusions use competitiveness-speak to achieve desirable ends even if that upsets logical purists?

Why so tenacious?

As was readily admitted earlier, much of the argument in this chapter is not original. Paul Krugman's *Pop Internationalism* articles attacked competitiveness-speak with vigour as early as 1994, and he has been echoed by writers such as Sir Samuel Brittan, in his *Capitalism with a Human Face* and in numerous *Financial Times* articles. Those attacks have scored a success of sorts, with a subtle shift by some people in their use of the term 'competitiveness' (described under 'Does it matter?' below). But despite the power of Krugman's attack, public debate on economic policy continues to be pervaded by the language and assumptions of national competitiveness theory. There seem to be four reasons for this.

The first is that the theory of national competitiveness feels right. Practical people prefer not to follow the latest twists and complexities of economic theory, and they like analogies with their direct experience – analogies between national budgets and household budgets, between national competition and the competitive challenges facing their own companies. In 1929 it felt right to practical people that if the national economy was in tough circumstances it should cut its expenditure to balance the books because that's what you would do as an individual, but it was a disastrously wrong assumption for the reasons which Keynes explained. Today it feels right to many practical business people that if they face intense competition from the other end of the world, and need to cut costs to compete, so too does the nation. But it is as wrong as the 1929 assumption (though fortunately with somewhat less disastrous consequences).

Second, the language of external competition serves a useful polemic purpose. It unifies people and helps justify and legitimize beneficial change. Change is unsettling: it typically creates winners and losers even if the net effect is positive. So it is often easier to justify change by reference to an external threat which makes change inevitable than on the basis of the true reasons. Industrial change – restructuring, downsizing, and rapid productivity improvement – is a good case in point. There are good arguments, explored in Chapter 6, for making it easier for European companies to fire workers in pursuit of higher productivity. Ease of restructuring generates productivity growth which delivers prosperity, and provided we run other elements of policy sensibly, the fired workers should find new jobs rapidly in other firms and activities, increasing national income. Paradoxically, indeed, if you make it too difficult to fire workers, you can reduce employment creation by reducing management incentives to hire labour in the first place. But it's pretty difficult to make that a compelling case to the ordinary workers concerned. It's much more appealing for company management to talk not about productivity and profit as an end per se, but about the inevitability of change in the face of global competition – and at the level of the company that is sometimes true. And it's much easier for politicians to argue for flexible hire-and-fire rules by suggesting that 'there is no alternative', that the jobs would be lost in any case if productivity improvement was not achieved, even though in many cases, in non-traded sectors of the economy, this is simply not true. The language of competitiveness is thus politically useful to justify policies which are sensible for other reasons.

Third, the language of national competition is of a particular use to right-wing advocates of minimal states and low taxes. Chapter 8 will explore the arguments in favour of constraints on the size of state (the share of GDP raised in taxes and spent on collective services and transfers through the social security system), but it will argue that there are trade-offs and choices to be made within a significant range of equally feasible solutions. Competitiveness theory can be used to deny that choice. Since it is 'obvious' that another country with a lower cost base, just like another company with lower costs, is a severe competitive threat, it follows that the need for low taxes, for a minimal state, can be argued as a blanket principle, not as a matter of trade-offs and choices within a range.

Fourth, and paradoxically, however, national competition and indeed the wider assumptions of globalization seem also to play a useful polemic purpose for many on the New Left. Talk of globalization provides a convenient cover for the retreat from socialism – it's easier to say that global conditions have changed than the more direct 'we were wrong'. The language of external competitiveness, moreover, provides a rosy glow of shared endeavour and shared enemies which can unite captains of industry and representatives of the shop floor in the same big tent. It is easier to cite the absolute necessity of competitiveness in the face of global competition when turning down the demands of traditional constituencies, such as trade unions, than to cite more robust but less appealing arguments in favour of the profit principle, managerial freedom, or flexible labour markets.

On all sides therefore there are strong reasons why the language of competitiveness appeals. But that doesn't stop it being deeply confused and misleading.

Does it matter?

It can be and often is argued, however, that it doesn't matter that national competitiveness is a confused concept as long as the results produced by its use are good ones. Indeed, many users of competitive-ness-speak seem to have moved, under the impact, perhaps, of Krug-man's attack, to a philosophy of pragmatic cynicism. Producers of 'competitiveness indices', for instance, have tended over the last five years to redefine competitiveness to mean simply 'relative success' with no implication of win-lose competition, and with the word 'competi-tiveness' simply surviving as a useful and recognized brand name from a previous era in which they did truly believe that global competition involved winners and losers.

Officials at the heart of the UK's competitiveness machine, the Department of Trade and Industry, tend, meanwhile, to the attitude that we should not worry too much about logical precision – the key thing is that policy is well designed, and if the language of com-petitiveness galvanizes management or trade unions, or British or European politicians to sensible market-friendly actions, that is all that matters. Thus, for instance, we (in the sense of a rather elite 'we') may all recognize that the real reason for encouraging rapid take-up of e-commerce is to drive accelerated productivity growth, shaking people out of existing jobs and freeing them up to do other jobs, but if the way to galvanize people is via the myth that, as per the Cabinet Office report, 'if the UK fails to capitalise on the opportunities. . . . jobs and prosperity will migrate elsewhere',[10] well so be it.

That pragmatic cynicism or pragmatic muddle-through was the attitude which I felt bound to take when running the CBI. By 1995 the CBI had carved out a name for itself as an advocate of competitiveness: in becoming its Director-General, in a sense I became the high priest of a cult whose beliefs I thought rather confused, but which I could not reject outright without causing more confusion, ineffectiveness and, indeed, offence. Invited to join a Competitiveness Council, it is churlish

---

10. Cabinet Office, Performance and Innovation Unit report (1999).

to say you will do so only if the name is changed, and one can seek to achieve sensible policy through such forums even if competitiveness is not a meaningful definition of the objective.[11] While I therefore made occasional speeches stating the arguments of this chapter and tried to reduce the 'competitiveness' count in CBI documents in favour of 'performance', 'productivity' or 'flexibility', I did not seek to ban the concept totally from our work. As long as I didn't do that, competitiveness would tend to creep into almost everything we did. Every issue – energy tax, parental leave, planning guidance on house building, corporation-tax levels, trade-union law, workplace parking charges, or the rights of part-time workers – could be given a competitiveness spin whether or not the real arguments were meaningfully connected to international competition. And if we omitted a competitiveness spin, journalists would encourage us to provide one or add one of their own, so used have they become to the language.

So does it matter? Does it matter that we are not being logical and precise in our use of language? Or is pragmatic cynicism acceptable given that competitiveness is so established in the language of economic debate? Increasingly I believe it does matter. It matters because while the aficionados of competitiveness indexes and government policy may reassure themselves that they can use this language without being misled by it, it is in fact close to impossible to apply the term 'competitiveness' to nations without most people assuming that it means competition in the normal sporting sense of the word, a competition where there are losers as well as winners. The idea that we can garner the rhetorical benefits of competitiveness-speak with none of the downside in intellectual confusion is a delusion.

Because that is so, the use of the word 'competitiveness' pollutes and confuses real, important debates about real, important issues of public policy.

It confuses the debate about the appropriate size and functions of the state, about the economic implications of different levels of tax and public spending. There are legitimate reasons for constraining the size of the state as a percentage of GDP, perhaps below some current

---

11. The recent DTI summary of *UK Competitiveness Indicators 2000*, reviewed by the Secretary of State's 'Competitiveness Council', is, for instance, a well-structured and insightful analysis of the drivers of UK economic performance. Only the title is confused.

European levels. There are some specific taxes on mobile factors of production, such as skilled labour and capital, where some concept of tax competition may make sense. There is certainly a need to consider how tax rates affect incentives, and how relative tax rates, for instance between unskilled labour (via payroll taxes) and capital (via corporation taxes), affect investment returns, labour substitution decisions and levels of employment. But there is no generalized competitive imperative to lower taxes across the board to compete with low-tax Asia or low-tax America. Those are, however, the terms in which the debate will be couched if the framework and language of national competitiveness continues to be accepted.

Equally competitiveness degrades debates about labour-market regulation, and labour-market regulation is a vitally important policy area for Europe to debate well. For while it is simply wrong to ascribe Europe's high unemployment to a failure of competitiveness in world markets, Europe does have high structural unemployment and that has a lot to do with inflexible labour markets. Labour-market interventions can create unemployment for reasons totally unrelated to external competition. Detailed debate on detailed policy reforms is therefore essential. But that debate will not be well conducted if its language of reference is that of external competition. For reasons discussed in Chapter 6, for instance, it is massively more likely that setting a minimum wage too high will increase unemployment of unskilled workers than that the introduction of parental-leave rights will have any appreciable employment effect. But it is impossible to make that distinction if we are trapped in the intellectual assumption that 'burdens on business' hit employment by hitting competitiveness.

Other examples abound. Energy taxes, considered in Chapter 9 may, under certain circumstances and if not carefully designed, slightly reduce national income, but if matched by payroll tax reductions they will not have any adverse long-term employment consequences. But the debate will be conducted in terms of a supposed threat to jobs if simplistic notions of competitiveness are allowed to dominate. Similarly with the arms-trade issues discussed in Chapter 11, the idea that we have to trade with murderous regimes in order to protect jobs in a harsh competitive world is almost entirely a delusion.

Finally, notions of competitiveness degrade the debate on many aspects of environmental regulation, such as planning rules. Part of the difference between US and UK productivity rates, to be explored in Chapters 5 and 7, seems to be due to differences in the ease of greenfield-site development. It is simply easier to run a highly productive retail store, or hotel or factory, on a greenfield site with expansive use of land, than in a more crowded brownfield development. America's greater ease of greenfield development reflects more relaxed planning rules which in turn reflect low population density. Those facts pose an important subject for public policy debate – whether we choose to take the inherent economic costs of population density through a small productivity penalty or through environmental degradation. It is a debate where economists can help by giving an idea of orders of magnitude, and a debate which might stimulate creative thinking about how far we can get the best of both worlds. But it is a debate whose clarity is simply destroyed by the introduction of a notion of competitiveness. For the moment we say competitiveness people assume, and are deliberately encouraged to assume, that the income costs are not one-off and limited but accumulating and large. And they assume too that an uncompetitive position will destroy jobs. But this is nonsense. Environmental regulations can reduce income, but they do not reduce attainable employment levels. That insight, however, becomes nearly impossible to grasp if we approach the world on the assumption that we compete for jobs by beating other countries in global competition.

Competitiveness-speak thus degrades public policy debate across a wide range of policy issues. It does so above all by directing public discourse away from the intelligent debate of trade-offs and choices, replacing it instead with the notion of externally determined necessity, of 'no alternative'. In reality across numerous areas of policy – in tax, the environment, transport, the labour market – we face trade-offs between desirable economic and non-economic objectives. We also face trade-offs between different groups in society, distributional issues which need to be faced squarely, particularly in the light of the trends in income inequality which Chapter 3 will describe. Competitiveness-speak is an impediment to sensible discussion of those trade-offs.

For these reasons language does matter, and the halfway house of pragmatic cynicism, accepting competitiveness as a sort of harmless proxy for overall performance, will not do. As Paul Krugman wrote in *Pop Internationalism*, it's time to 'start telling the truth: competitiveness is a meaningless concept when applied to national economies. And the obsession with competitiveness is both wrong and dangerous'.

We have to escape that obsession and develop instead a better framework for thinking about economic success, a clearer understanding both of what globalization does and does not do to our economies, and of the other forces at work, unrelated to globalization, which are changing the shape of our economies and the nature of the policy choices we face.

Economic objectives: what are we trying to achieve?

In principle the appropriate framework for thinking about economic success is clear. There are just two sensible economic objectives: a high-level of productivity and productivity growth (i.e. high and rising output per hour worked) delivering a high income per hour worked; and a low level of involuntary unemployment, jobs available for those who want them, and hours of work available in line with people's preferences.

These objectives often need to be balanced against other desirable aims, environmental, social, or distributional. And the second objective is sometimes difficult to measure, since involuntary unemployment is not always visible in the official statistics of those eligible to receive unemployment benefit. As a result there are several conceptual and measurement complexities to be clarified before we can compare the relative economic success of nations or types of capitalism. Measured GDP, for reasons to be discussed in Chapter 4, is by no means the perfect measure of true prosperity. But in principle the objectives are clear: we want maximum prosperity in return for effort expended, and we want people who want jobs to have them.

Three key implications follow from defining economic success in these terms, rather than with the language of competitiveness.

The first is that there is no particular distinction between productivity as an objective in traded and untraded sectors of the economy. Higher productivity delivers higher prosperity wherever in the economy it is achieved. Healthcare productivity is as important as manufacturing productivity.

The second is that it is quite possible for countries to be good at one of these objectives and poor at the other. Competitiveness theory suggests that jobs are created by achieving high productivity thus enabling a country to compete effectively for available jobs. But it just isn't so. There are two separate challenges of economic success, high productivity and high employment creation. In the long run they are not inversely correlated because there is no limited number of jobs to be shared out, but they are not positively correlated either. Germany, as we shall see in Chapter 5, has been very good at the productivity side of the balance, by some measures better than the US, but rather poor at creating jobs. An ideal economy, indeed, would have the productivity per hour worked of West Germany and the employment creation record of the Americans.

The third implication follows directly from this. If productivity and employment creation are two different and independent objectives, it is not surprising that different aspects of policy impact differently upon them. As already mentioned, environmental policy may involve some trade-offs between income levels and environmental stewardship, but has in general no long-term implications for the attainability of full employment. Conversely several aspects of labour-market policy can entail trade-offs between employment levels and desirable social objectives, but only rarely, if ever, have an adverse impact on productivity. Indeed as Chapter 7 suggests, high productivity may in some circumstances be stimulated by labour-market regulation.

What globalization really means

Misinterpretations of globalization and the confused notion of national competition in a global economy have confused economic-policy debate. But that doesn't mean that globalization is not a real phenomenon. It is real and it has important real implications which need to be understood.

Globalization is a daily reality for many companies in specific sectors of the economy. Within many sectors, the terms of competition have indeed shifted from being primarily local or regional to global. There really are those car parts from Brazil and software services from Bangalore, and for the individual companies facing this competition that is a more important reality than the macroeconomic implications with which this book is primarily concerned. If this were a book of business strategy, rather than of political economy, it would give a far more conventional and familiar account of the globalization challenge.

That globalization challenge for companies, moreover, is not limited to traded sectors of the economy. Globalization of trade may be more limited than most people think, but the globalization of capital flows and of the flow of ideas represents a powerful force for economic change with implications for retailing as much as for manufacturing.

We live in a world where ideas for new technology or for business system redesign can be transmitted across the world in seconds, where legions of professional consultants make their living from the transfer of ideas, and where capital is largely free to move to pursue investment opportunities, which will tend to exist wherever existing practice is behind the world best. We also live in a world where, for technological reasons explained in Chapter 2, it is becoming simultaneously easier to disintegrate companies vertically (concentrating on one slice of business activity only) and to integrate them across the world (combining the slices across many countries into one global company). That world is therefore one of huge opportunities and challenges for companies in almost all sectors. The fact that global competition is irrelevant to the aggregate level of employment in a country's retail sector, does not mean that globalization is irrelevant to the commercial fortunes of that country's retailing companies.

That accelerated flow of capital and ideas, moreover, probably has an important macro consequence for the global economy – increasing the attainable rate at which poorer countries can catch up with rich ones. Throughout economic history very rapid per capita growth rates have always been associated with technological catch-up. The country which at any time is the richest and most productive has never grown faster than 3 per cent per capita per annum or slower than 1 per cent for any significant number of years. But, as Table 1.2 illustrates, what seems to have accelerated is the feasible pace of catch-up. When Sweden was catching up with the US and UK in the period 1913–50, what that meant was a per capita growth rate of 2.3 per cent for the follower versus 1.6 per cent for the leader. When Germany and France had their catch-up spurt in the 1950s and 60s, growth rates of 4 or 5 per cent were attained. The Asian tigers in the 1980s were able to achieve rates of growth up to 6–9 per cent. What seems to have happened is that our improved mechanisms for transferring technology and know-how and capital across the world have made possible more rapid rates of catch-up.

This accelerated process of catch-up, assisted by globalization, does then have global consequences. It does not mean that rich countries get poorer or grow more slowly. Nor does it mean that Asian countries will soar past us in prosperity driven by some mysterious elixir of permanently rapid growth. In all likelihood when they approach rich country standards of living they will slow down to rich country growth

Table 1.2 Real national income per capita* (annual growth %)

	1860–1913	1913–50	1950–70	1970–90	1990–97
UK	1.1	0.7	2.3	1.9	1.6
US	1.7	1.6	2.0	1.5	1.4
Sweden	1.6	2.3	3.0	1.7	0.3
Germany**	1.5	0.7	5.1	2.4	1.4
France	1.1	1.2	4.5	2.3	0.9
Japan	1.1	0.7	8.7	3.4	1.6
Korea	–	–	–	6.9	5.9
China	–	–	–	6.3	9.1

* Figures prior to 1970 are GNP per capita, after 1970 they are GDP per capita.

** Figures for 1950–90 for Germany are for West Germany.

Source: David Landes, *The Wealth and Poverty of Nations*; OECD *Historical Statistics*; World Bank *World Development Indicators*; IMF *International Financial Statistics*.

rates. Germany and Japan did just that as they approached the US standard of living in the 1970s, and Hong Kong and Singapore seemed to be doing the same in the 1990s. But accelerated catch-up does have some pretty big geopolitical consequences, especially if it works in the case of China. If China catches up to half of US GDP per capita in the next fifty years it will by then be an economy three times larger than America's simply because its population will be six times bigger. Catch-up also has huge global environmental implications as developing nations claim their share of what is probably one of the world's few finite resources – the CO_2 absorption capacity of the atmosphere.

Globalization will thus create interdependency through environmental pressures. It also creates a more short-term interdependency, though not via the transmission mechanism often assumed. In 1998 almost every economic forecaster in Europe and the US predicted at best a sharp slowdown and at worst recession in 1999. The standard argument for those forecasts was based on trade effects arising from Asia's economic collapse. By March 1998, sales of British goods to Thailand were down 60 per cent on a year earlier, to South Korea by

51 per cent, to Malaysia by 44 per cent. It seemed obvious to many forecasters and to almost all business people involved in those markets, that this could not fail to have a strongly recessionary effect. But there was no rich country recession either in 1998 or 1999. That was because US consumer expenditure remained strong, and European consumption adequate, and for all the chatter about globalization rich economies are primarily dependent not on demand from elsewhere in the world but on their own domestic consumption. The Russian economy came close to imploding in autumn 1998. But even if it had disappeared completely, literally ceased to exist, that would have had less direct impact on US demand levels than a 4 per cent increase in the US personal-savings rate. The world is less linked together by trade dependencies than the conventional wisdom often suggests.

But we *are* linked together through short-term liquid financial markets, and it is their movements that created the real risk of global recession in 1998 and 1999. A global recession in 1999 was not a certainty deriving from trade interdependency but a possibility deriving from financial-market contagion, and the fact that the dice eventually fell on a favourable side should not lead us to assume that the possibility was not a significant and dangerous one. The implications of that financial-market interdependency are discussed in Chapter 10.

Finally, globalization may well have increased levels of inequality in the developed rich world. Trade theory tells us that logically it should have done so. Trade between nations tends to change the demand for different categories of labour and thus relative wage rates. In particular, it tends to reduce the relative wage rate of unskilled labour in rich countries. It doesn't make richer countries poorer but it can make them less equal. Or rather, it may create for rich countries a dilemma: accept increased inequality but keep unskilled workers in employment, the American way; or seek to offset rising inequality via labour-market interventions but at the expense of higher unemployment, the French way. Certainly as we shall see in Chapter 3, inequality is increasing in developed countries and this policy dilemma seems to result. What is less clear is whether the key driver of increased inequality is globalization or developments in technology which would be occurring in developed economies even if the rest of the world did not exist.

It is therefore to factors other than globalization that we should now turn, and to two factors in particular – the impact of technology and especially information and communications technology; and the relentless rise of the service and servicing economy. These factors are almost certainly more fundamental than globalization to what is going on in developed economies, and they have major implications for productivity and growth, for the shape of our economy and employment patterns, and for appropriate public policy.

2. The New Economy:
High-tech and High-touch

Excited, indeed at times almost breathless, accounts of the 'new economy' became the staple fare of popular economics during 1999 and 2000, relegating 'globalization' and 'competitiveness' to a supporting role. Globalization remained a theme because communications make the world economy more global; and competitiveness an important sub-plot because Europe must respond to the challenge of American leadership in information technology. But at least for a period the leading thought of the conventional wisdom was that information and communications technology had created a 'new paradigm' of economic performance, an information revolution as profound as the original Industrial Revolution. The Internet economy, the dotcom, the knowledge-based economy, was the focal point.[1] Or as British Prime Minister Tony Blair put it in a speech in November 1999, 'it's the e-conomy, stupid'.

To the true believers in this paradigm shift, the scale of the revolution is clear and the following propositions almost self-evident. First, that information and communications technology represents not just one of a series of waves of technological change, but something peculiarly rapid and peculiarly profound. Second, that this technology is having a profound effect on macroeconomic performance, accelerating the attainable rate of productivity growth and dramatically reducing inflationary pressures. Third, that information technology in general and the Internet specifically are profoundly changing the balance of strategic advantage in every sector of the economy, and profoundly changing rules of equity valuation. Fourth, that these changes have

---

1. There is a danger in writing about intellectual fashions that the fashion has changed again by the time the book is published. As I make final changes for the paperback edition, belief in the Internet economy is beating a rapid retreat with Internet shares now down 95 per cent or more from the April 2000 peak, and many Internet companies bankrupt. Despite this retreat, however, many of the basic assumptions that drive the euphoria of the tech boom – e.g. the belief that high-tech necessarily means high-growth, are still current today.

huge consequences for the jobs that people do, for the skills they need. Thus to Andy Grove, one of the founders of Intel, it is clear that 'all companies will be Internet companies' or by implication dead. To Charles Leadbeater, author of *Living on Thin Air*, meanwhile, it is clear that 'we are all in the thin air business', and that our children 'will make their living through their creativity, ingenuity and imagination'.

From these propositions follow policy priorities and actions. Britain must be made the most attractive business environment in Europe for e-commerce, equipped with its very own 'e-Tsar', for otherwise 'jobs and prosperity will be eroded by e-commerce competition from overseas'.[2] High-tech companies must be helped to attract top talent with special stock-option tax breaks. Europe, the Lisbon summit of April 2000 asserted, must focus on closing its competitive gap in ICT (information and communications technology) with the US. Skills in ICT must be given high priority, since 'we will all be knowledge workers in the knowledge-intensive economy of tomorrow'.

Some of this is at least partially true, and the focus on technology as the fundamental driver of economic change is a refreshing shift from the delusions of competitiveness theory. The new economy is at least a truer tale than the previous Asian threat horror story. But it is only true up to a point. For the implications of technological change, though profound, include some paradoxes too often missed in the excited accounts of the new economy. And many of the changes which ICT is now producing are essentially just accelerations of trends observable for many years. The economy which is emerging from these accelerated trends will not be a uniformly high-tech one, nor even a uniformly creative or imaginative one, but a subtle mixture of the high-tech and the high-touch, the 'thin air' and the concretely physical, the knowledge based and the deeply mundane. The most important challenges for policy emerging from this changing economic shape, meanwhile, have little to do with how Britain or Europe should compete with America, but are, paradoxically, non-technological and non-competitive issues, such as social inequality, collective-goods provision, the environment and transport.

This chapter therefore seeks to describe the changing shape of developed economies, while Chapter 3 explores the implications of that changing shape for public policy priorities. The story needs to begin with understanding what seemed to be happening in our economies up

---

2. Cabinet Office report.

to the mid-1990s, before we all began to chatter so excitedly about the new economy.

The rise of the service economy

The biggest structural change occurring in the rich economies for the past several decades has been not globalization but the relentless rise of the service economy. The increasing share of services in rich economies has indeed been evident for a century (see Figure 2.1). Initially the pattern of development was a decline in agricultural employment being replaced by jobs in both manufacturing and services, but in all rich economies manufacturing employment is now also in decline. Its decline has been greatest in the richest economy of all, the US, where the proportion of 'services' in the economy has grown from 62 per cent of GDP in 1960 to 76 per cent in 1997.[3]

Despite the longevity of the trend it is only in the last thirty or so years that the rise of services and fall of manufacturing has become an issue of controversy. It's controversial because to many people it is clear that this decline in manufacturing employment must be due to 'hollowing out' as a result of global competition, and clear too that it is regrettable and dangerous: regrettable because 'real jobs' have been lost and replaced by ephemeral service-sector jobs ('McJobs', hairdressing and the like); dangerous because an economy which doesn't 'make things' cannot remain sustainably rich.

In fact, however, the changing structural balance of the developed rich economies has almost nothing to do with global competition and everything to do with trends in consumer preference and technology internal to, and common to, all developed societies. Three factors, the first two closely linked and fundamental, the third separate and in some ways less profound, have driven these shifts in economic structure.

The first factor is customer preference. As societies and people individually get richer, they spend an increasing percentage of their income on services and a declining percentage on physical goods. British

3. The term 'services' as used in national account definitions is a catch-all for everything that is not manufacturing or primary industries (mining, agriculture). It covers several fundamentally different categories of activity, many likely to grow in future but some likely to decline.

Figure 2.1 Sectoral balance of employment, 1900–2000
(% of total employment)

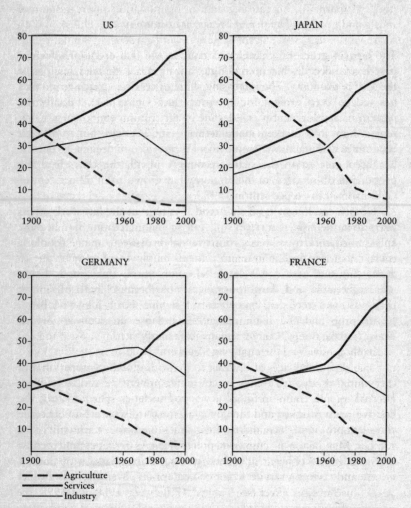

Source: OECD *Historical Statistics* for 1960–97, McKinsey Global Institute 1994 'Employment Performance' for figures for dates around 1900.

consumers in 1970 devoted 70 per cent of their total consumption to physical goods and energy products; by 1998 that had fallen to 52 per cent. In their place, expenditure had grown on transportation (air travel and rail journeys), on catering and accommodation (more restaurant meals and hotel stays), on leisure activities (more sports clubs), and on personal services (more cleaners, nannies and gardeners). Similar trends are seen in every rich developed country. In those countries where healthcare spend is determined directly by private demand, such as in the US, it too has risen relentlessly. Medical services expenditure as a percentage of personal consumption in the US rose from 5 per cent in 1960 to 10 per cent in 1980 to 15 per cent in 1998. (In the UK expenditure has also grown on housing, not a service, but a physical product where increased spend takes the form of competition for the limited supply of a locationally specific good. The importance of this growing demand is explored in Chapter 3.)

In some senses this shifting pattern of customer preference reflects simply a hierarchy of needs: as more basic needs are satisfied, others become more important. As people get rich enough to go beyond basic subsistence, they spend proportionally less of their income on food and more on cars and washing machines and televisions. Beyond a certain point, however, there is relative satiation in physical goods but a seemingly limitless demand for services. Few families have a passionate desire to own more than one washing machine, but demand for better health probably has no limit, and demand for more leisure services (more hotel stays and restaurant meals) is highly income elastic and can probably grow greatly from present levels.

The shift to services also, however, reflects a second factor, that of differential productivity rates in different sectors of the economy. If we become rapidly more productive at producing a specific good, the relative price of that good falls, and its sector falls as a proportion of the economy even if demand for the good is in volume terms still rising rapidly. Manufacturing employment has declined in part simply because we have got so efficient at manufacturing. A comparison of durable goods and catering-service volumes and prices over the last twenty years illustrates the effect (see Table 2.1). Between 1980 and 1998, the volume of both catering services and durable manufactured goods grew faster than GDP, and indeed durable goods were the faster growing, up 140 per cent in volume terms while catering services grew 77 per cent and the overall economy 53 per cent. Over that period at least, people did still want more cars, washing machines and television sets quite as

Table 2.1 Volume and relative price effects: UK, 1980–98

	Sector as % personal consumption 1980	Volume growth 1980–98 %	Price increase 1980–98 %	Sector as % personal consumption 1998
Whole economy		+53	+139	
Durable goods	10	+140	+62	10
Catering	6	+77	+215	9

Source: ONS *Economic Trends.*

much as more restaurant meals. But over that period durable goods' prices went up just 62 per cent, the average price level 139 per cent, and catering prices 215 per cent, simply because we got relentlessly more productive in the factories manufacturing durable goods but could not achieve the same productivity increase in restaurants. As a result durable goods stayed stable as a share of GDP but catering grew. The faster the productivity growth rate of an economic activity, the less it will rise or the more it will fall as a proportion of the total economy.

Customer preference shifts and differential productivity rates are thus two sides of the same coin, two forces together producing a relentless shift of economic activity to the service sectors of the economy, and in particular to any services where face-to-face contact is key, or where service quality depends on subjective human skills rather than on automatable activities. These forces explain why residential healthcare nurses, restaurant cooks, sports-centre professionals and domestic help are among the most rapidly growing categories of employment. They explain too why even when a physical good is purchased, an increasing percentage of the value added lies now in the distribution and servicing, less in the manufacture per se. Physical beer production and delivery costs, reflected in the wholesale price, now account for only 10 per cent of the price of a pint in a pub and only 15 per cent of the price excluding all taxes; forty years ago they accounted for about half. The proportion has shifted because consumers increasingly demand an attractive, stylish, fashionable retail ambience but also because you can automate a brewery but you cannot automate friendly bar staff. As a result there are now 509,000 people working in British pubs, bars and licensed clubs, but only 21,000 in British breweries. In the car market meanwhile, Ford Motor Company has said it now defines itself as a retailing and customer-service company as much as a manufacturing one, because it's in retailing and servicing that much of the value added lies.

It is this shift to a more service- and servicing-intensive economy which explains the increasingly *local* nature of the rich economies discussed in Chapter 1 and explains in turn why overall trade intensities are not relentlessly growing despite the globalization of competition in traded sectors of the economy. Over time, for all the talk of globalization, an increasing proportion of our economy is comprised of activities which are not only not traded across international borders, but which are literally local – produced and consumed in the same city or region, and inherently so because a restaurant meal or residential healthcare is delivered face-to-face.

The third and final factor behind the shift to the service economy is less fundamental, and in some ways indeed a statistical mirage. For alongside the shift of consumer demand and thus of employment towards services and servicing, the last two decades have seen a parallel but unrelated process of 'vertical disintegration' with companies and government bodies outsourcing non-core functions to concentrate on core activities and competencies. Catering, security and building-maintenance functions have been outsourced. Computer processing and software development have been handed over to specialist firms, often employing the same people previously employed by the company now doing the outsourcing. Corporate strategic-planning and market-research departments have been downsized and external consultants used instead. The causes and effects of this disintegration trend are in themselves an interesting subject for study but outside the scope of this book.[4] The overall impact is, however, clear from patterns of job creation in the US since the mid-1980s (see Table 2.2). Manufacturing and mining have continued to decline as a proportion of the total. Hotels, restaurants and retailing, after a huge expansion in the previous

---

4. One possible effect is that the growing role of outsourced management functions increases the pace of transfer of best practice and thus the potential rate of productivity growth. Consultants make their living by transferring best practice: the same people employed by companies guard best-practice secrets.

Table 2.2 Sectoral trends in US employment, 1988–98
(% of total employment)

	1988	1998	
Mining and manufacturing	19.0	15.4	Underlying
Construction, transportation, communications, wholesale and utilities	15.7	15.5	increases understated and decreases
Retailing, hotels, restaurants, catering	19.5	19.2	overstated due
Financial services	6.3	5.9	to outsourcing into 'business
Other personally purchased services	16.6	19.0	services'
Business services*	6.5	9.4	←——┘
Government	16.4	15.7	

* Includes 'Personnel Supply'.

Source: Bureau of Labour Statistics, *Employment Outlook 1998–2008: Industry Output and Employment Projections to 2008.*

decade, have held a roughly constant share; medical services, education, and many other personal services have increased. But so too have business services (accountants, consultants, lawyers, etc.), and the most rapidly growing individual line of all in the US government classification is a catch-all category entitled 'Personnel supply', not a new set of economic activities but a new category of employment contract, the same security guards, for example, but employed by different firms. In fundamental activity terms (i.e. the jobs that people actually do), the decline of manufacturing is overstated due to the growth of out-sourcing, but equally the growth in consumer services is understated, since retail and leisure and hospital companies have also outsourced activities.

The fundamental picture, however, would have seemed clear to anyone surveying the data just a few years ago. A combination of technological progress and changing customer preference was shifting employment and consumer expenditure from manufacturing to services of a face-to-face and human skill intensive nature, and as a result was producing an economy which, despite all the talk of globalization, was in some senses becoming more local. The trends were steady rather than exciting, the pace of technological improvement relentless but not accelerating. The cumulative effect was large, but the speed of change sufficiently slow that the story of an increasingly service-intensive, increasingly local economy captured few headlines, unable to compete with the more dramatic tale of globalization. And then along came the new economy, the new paradigm which is believed to be changing everything. Whether it really does change everything is the question to which we now turn.

The exceptional power of information technology

There are certainly some good reasons for claiming that ICT is distinctive from previous waves of technological change, and distinctive in ways likely to have profound economic consequences. Four distinguishing features in particular can be identified.

The first is the fact that ICT is pervasive throughout the economy. Many technologies are relevant to one or a few specific sectors of the economy but not to all sectors. The pharmaceutical industry is a sector currently achieving extraordinary technological progress, but that progress makes little difference to hotel companies, car manufacturers or airlines. Information and communications technology, however, gets everywhere, potentially increasing productivity in almost all sectors of the economy. That doesn't make it unique in technological history – electricity was a similarly pervasive new technology – but it results in something unique when combined with the second factor, a pace of technological progress which is an order of magnitude – literally ten times – faster than that seen in most other waves of technological advance. According to a rule of thumb (first enunciated in a more technical form by Gordon Moore, one of Intel's founders),[5] semiconductor and microprocessor performance per price doubles roughly every eighteen months (or alternatively the same performance costs half as much), and if anything the pace seems to have accelerated in the last

---

5. Moore's original rule, set out in a speech in 1965, actually relates to a more specifically technical issue – the capacity (in millions of transistors) of each new generation of memory chips, which, Moore observed, seemed to double each eighteen months. This technical progress then has the economic consequence of an equivalent doubling of performance relative to price.

several years. A similar pace of technological progress drives increases in potential communications capacity whether land line or mobile. The cost of computing per kilobit of processing power will likely fall by over 95 per cent in the next ten years. Between 1985–95, available transmission speeds increased four times, by 2005 they will increase another forty-five times.[6] This is quite different from most previous major technological developments. Even during the decade of most rapid productivity growth in electricity generation (1910–20), for instance, productivity was doubling only every eight years and in the initial decades of development every fifteen years.[7] As somebody once worked out (the original source is now unclear), if the automotive industry had achieved the same pace of price-performance advance over the last thirty years as the computer industry, the average family car would now cost £5 and do 200,000 miles to the gallon.

ICT's third distinctive characteristic is close to zero marginal cost in many functions. Incremental telecoms usage effectively costs zero up to the limits of capacities installed, and the cost of additional capacity is itself collapsing. Software-replication costs are just about zero once the software is developed. Some other technologies and industries have low marginal costs but none has anything quite so close to zero. Pharmaceutical manufacturing and distribution costs are low compared with initial research and development, but they are still a significant element in total industry economics. ICT's almost zero marginal cost is therefore truly exceptional, with important economic consequences, creating huge potential for natural monopolies if intellectual property rights can be defined or if dominant market positions can be attained.

Finally, ICT is likely to have distinctive economic effects, precisely because it affects information processing and information exchange, for information plays a vital role in determining industry structure. The relative efficiency of information flows between and within firms affects the optimal degree of vertical integration and the optimal size of firms. If we dramatically reduce the cost of information exchange, we should expect to see major changes in patterns of both horizontal and vertical integration, i.e. global mergers of companies focused on specific activi-

---

6. See 'A Revolution in Interaction', *McKinsey Quarterly* (1997).

7. See Paul David, 'General Purpose Engines, Investment and Productivity Growth: From the Dynamo Revolution to the Computer Revolution'.

ties, and those same companies outsourcing non-core activities. Equally, degrees of market efficiency or perfection are largely functions of information adequacy. If we reduce the cost of information, we expect to see changes in price-searching and price-fixing processes, and in the relative economic power of different players and markets.

So ICT has four quite distinctive features. It can be applied, moreover, to automate a huge slice of existing economic activity. For an enormous amount of work is not in any fundamental sense essential to deliver the product or service which consumers actually value, but instead is involved with all sorts of 'interactive' and information-exchange activities – with communicating or researching product availability, with placing orders and invoicing and accounting, with checking the location of products in transit, with producing reports and correcting errors. All of these are activities to whose disappearance the consumers of the final product or service would be completely indifferent; and all are inherently susceptible to ICT-based productivity improvement. The precise scale of these interactive or information-processing activities is difficult to estimate. McKinsey and Company, with that heroic absence of intellectual doubt which characterizes my former partners, has estimated that they account for 51 per cent of GDP and believe that, with available information and communication technologies, productivity in these functions could double, i.e. that the same work could be done with half as many people.[8] Few people would be willing to swear that the percentage is in fact 51 per cent rather than 53 per cent, or even roughly 50 per cent rather than roughly 60 per cent or 40 per cent. But the essential point stands: there is a huge swathe of economic activity, of employment, essentially concerned with information manipulation and communication, and inherently susceptible to efficiency improvement from the application of ICT. Combine that with a technology progressing at a superfast rate, and with specific features likely to have a profound effect on industry structures, and one seems to have a justifiable reason to expect the sort of paradigm shift which the devotees of the new economy predict.

While ICT does indeed have profound economic effects, however, the most fundamental are not those typically described in the more breathless accounts of the 'ever more knowledge-intensive economy'.

---

8. 'A Revolution in Interaction', *McKinsey Quarterly*.

The real impact of information technology

The shape of an economy can be gauged by looking at different employment patterns. The work which people do reflects both the products and services consumed and the technologies used to produce and deliver them. Technological progress changes employment patterns by changing both the array of goods and services available to the consumers, and the efficiency with which we produce and deliver them. Different technologies have very different effects on employment because they have a very different impact both on consumer demand and on the efficiency, i.e. the productivity, of processes.

The direct employment impact of technological change depends therefore (as Figure 2.2 shows), on the balance of two factors: the rapidity of the technological change and the extent to which the new technology generates new demand. A technology more towards the bottom right of the matrix directly generates increased employment. A technology towards the top left reduces employment as a first order effect, freeing up labour resources to do other quite unrelated things.

Agricultural technology throughout the last century was clearly on the left-hand side, its moderately rapid pace of technological advance

Figure 2.2 Direct employment impact of technology change

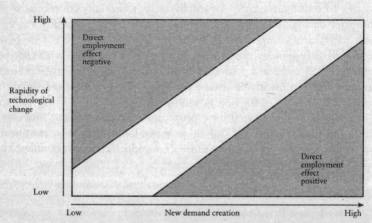

combining with minimal new demand creation to make its direct employment effect clearly negative, and its economic benefit deriving almost entirely from the fact that people were released from agricultural employment to find new jobs in other unrelated sectors of the economy. The automotive industry, at least until the last decade or so, was in a different category, on the right hand side of Figure 2.2. The technology created an entirely new category of consumer demand and for many decades new demand creation outstripped the pace of productivity improvement, with increasing numbers of people employed in the world automotive industry.

ICT is and will continue to be a set of technologies far closer in employment effect to the agricultural example than the automotive. It does create new products and services, new categories of consumer demand: it is to the right of agriculture on the matrix. But it does not create enough new demand to offset its extraordinary potential for productivity improvements, achieved both in the new products and services which ICT creates and, even more importantly, in a huge range of existing interactive activities. In its total economic effect, ICT is far more a technology which automates away existing jobs than one which creates new customer demand. Its role in delivering process improvement is in economic terms massively more significant than its role in product innovation.

That pattern of impact will surprise some readers. But it is clear from a few key figures (see Table 2.3). In the US economy, where the application of ICT is most advanced, all the ICT-producing industries combined accounted in 1999 for 8.2 per cent GDP, up from 5.8 per cent in 1990, and thus justifying the statements one hears that while ICT is still less than 10 per cent of GDP it accounts for a quarter of the total growth. But this ICT is primarily an investment, an input to other production processes, not a new category of consumer demand. ICT (hardware and software combined) now accounts for 44 per cent of all US plant and equipment investment, making it the central driver of productivity improvement in business processes in almost every industry. But only 2.4 per cent of total personal consumption is spent on the consumer goods and services of the ICT industry, all the mobile-phone hardware and services, all the consumer PCs and software, all the Internet connections and usage. ICT is a huge development in business investment but in the total scheme of things, a relatively small event in terms of personal consumption. That balance has major implications

Table 2.3 ICT within the US economy

ICT-producing industries as % of GDP, 1990–99

	1990	1995	1997–est	1998–est	1999–est
Hardware	1.8	2.1	2.4	2.5	2.6
Software/services	1.0	1.4	1.8	2.0	2.2
Prepackaged software	0.2	0.3	–	–	–
Other	0.9	1.1	–	–	–
Communications hardware	0.4	0.4	0.4	0.4	0.4
Communications services	2.6	2.7	2.6	2.9	2.9
Total	5.8	6.6	7.3	7.8	8.2

Personal consumption of ICT as % of total personal consumption

	1987	1990	1995	1998
Computer hardware and software	0.2	0.2	0.4	0.5
Telecoms services	1.7	1.6	1.8	1.9
Total	1.9	1.8	2.2	2.4

Investment in ICT as % of total business investment in plant and equipment

	1970	1980	1990	1995	1998
Hardware and peripherals	21	27	29	29	29
Software*	n.a.	n.a.	12	13	15
Total	n.a.	n.a.	41	42	44

* Offical investment figures for years prior to 1990 do not include software, and a comparable total cannot therefore be calculated; but if software was the same % of total ICT in 1980 as in 1990, the 1980 total would be about 38%.

Source: US Census Bureau, Statistical Abstract of the US; Bureau of Economic Analysis, Survey of Current Business.

for the changing shape of the economy, the changing pattern of employment.[9]

On the investment side the issue is whether all this investment is delivering the productivity improvements which the inherent nature of this technology would lead us to expect. For many years it seemed it did not. ICT investment reached about 38 per cent of total US investment as early as 1980, but productivity growth in the US in the 1980s, far from accelerating, seemed to slow.[10] Until a few years ago the common adage, originally stated by Professor Robert Solow, was that 'information technology is everywhere except in the productivity statistics'. But that does seem to have changed in the last few years and changed significantly enough and for long enough to make it likely that the US economy's underlying productivity growth rate has increased. US productivity per hour worked, having languished at 1.2 per cent per annum from 1980 to 1995, has increased to 2.7 per cent from 1995 to 1999, and seems if anything to be accelerating further.[11] The reasons for this delayed acceleration, and its macroeconomic consequences, will

---

9. ICT may also deliver significant increases in true customer prosperity but in ways which are not captured in GDP statistics, and which carry no implications for the shape of the economy, for the pattern of employment, or for private profit opportunity. If, for instance, the Internet reduces the time spent in customer-information search activities, or in shopping trips, this is a benefit to customers but it may well create no new profit opportunities (all suppliers may have to provide good information services as a condition of competitive parity) and only the most minimal new employment; the customer benefit will also not appear in GDP. The inherent economic characteristics of ICT, with minimal marginal costs and collapsing total costs, make it particularly likely to produce customer benefits which have no implications for economic activity – effectively the technology makes capabilities so cheap that customers gain some benefits from them at minimal or nil cost. The economic welfare benefit of the ICT revolution may thus be large even while ICT remains a small proportion of the total economy.

10. Prior to 1990 US statistics did not count software expenditure as an investment – a precise comparison of ICT's share in investment in 1980 with the 44 per cent reached in 1998 is not therefore possible. But software has exceeded 25 per cent of total ICT spend throughout the 1990s. Applying a 25 per cent assumption to 1980 produces a total ICT spend equal to 38 per cent of total investment in that year.

11. These figures are from the February 2000 *Economic Report of the President*. Cross-country estimates quoted later (in Table 2.4) suggest a still lower figure for the US for 1980–95.

be considered later in this chapter. For now the important conclusion is simply that ICT does at last seem able to achieve the efficiency improvements in interactive activities which have been long predicted.

That does not, however, mean that ICT grows in importance as a form of consumption, nor that everybody becomes an information-technology worker. By 1998 50 per cent of Americans already had a personal computer and 30 per cent were regular Internet users but total consumption of ICT-based products and services, including voice telephony, was still only 2.4 per cent of consumer expenditure versus 1.9 per cent in 1987, a fairly small increase. Nor is that figure likely to rise much in future, for the simple reason that ICT products and services are very cheap and keep getting cheaper: volume increases are continually offset by price collapse. Computers get relentlessly cheaper and better. Telecom services enjoy close to zero marginal costs and that means prices keep falling. Available bandwidth keeps increasing and that means that eventually all consumers will be able to enjoy high-quality video telephony, but when that time comes they will only pay what they used to pay for plain old voice telephony.

The fundamental driver of these falling prices is the relative productivity and relative price effect – the tendency of prices to fall wherever productivity growth is most rapid. That effect has been mentioned twice already in this book – helping to explain both the sectoral shift from manufacturing to services and the self-limiting nature of trade intensity. But it is an effect which works even more dramatically when we look specifically at ICT goods and services, precisely because ICT is characterized by such super-rapid technological advance. Given the eighteen months' price performance rule, it is quite possible that in twenty years' time consumers will be using, through their purchases of computers and telecoms services, 10,000 times as much computing and communicating power as they consume today, but it is also quite possible that the economic value of all that computing and communications power will have fallen, not risen, relative to the economic value of the world restaurant business.

The collapsing relative price of ICT reflects its extraordinary productivity growth; that productivity growth, meanwhile, has implications for employment. America's ICT-producing industries now contribute 8.2 per cent of GDP but they only provided (in 1998) 3.7 per cent of employment. Running a huge software company doesn't require many people because the marginal cost of software replication is zero. In autumn 2000 Microsoft had a market value eight times that of General Motors, but it employs 31,000 people while General Motors still employs 390,000; Walmart, the world's largest retailer, employs 1.1 million. Microsoft has a huge market value because, at least until now, it is making a huge margin over economic resources employed. That might suggest vulnerability in ICT valuations as prices eventually compete down to marginal cost. It certainly means that huge volume increases in ICT provision will only be accompanied by minimal employment creation.

The possible magnitude of that employment-creation effect can be gauged from the forecasts produced by the US Bureau of Labor Statistics. They foresee ICT industry employment growing from 3.7 per cent of the US total in 1998 to 4.9 per cent in 2008, with the increase concentrated almost entirely in computer processing and software services, rather than in hardware or packaged software production. The percentage will thus still be under 5 per cent of the total and there is no reason to believe that it will increase relentlessly thereafter, indeed it may fall. Meanwhile, in all those interactive activities mentioned earlier, the (roughly) half of the economy made up of administering, invoicing, processing and accounting, huge numbers of employees are likely to lose their existing jobs – the inevitable consequence of accelerated productivity growth.

We should therefore be clear about the likely effect of ICT on employment. ICT is almost certain, in its direct employment effects, to be a net job destroyer, to be closer in economic impact to improvements in agricultural technology than to the technologies of the car. But that doesn't mean that unemployment will rise, nor does it deny the huge economic benefits of ICT. A new technology does not need to create jobs directly in order to be economically beneficial. Improvements in agricultural technology destroyed jobs but the people freed up eventually found jobs in other completely unrelated areas of the economy.[12] That is what should and likely will happen with the ICT revolution.

---

12. In the case of agriculture and of other staple industries like coal mining and steel the transitional effects were of course huge, with significant regional unemployment and consequences for political stability. In the case of ICT, its pervasive character may well make transitional effects less severe, since the jobs displaced are not regionally or sectorally concentrated, but spread throughout the economy.

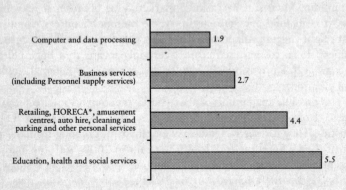

Figure 2.3 Forecast changes in US employment,
1998–2008 (millions)

* Hotels, restaurants, cafes, etc.

Source: Bureau of Labour Statistics, *Employment Outlook 1998–2008: Industry Output and Employment Projections to 2008.*

ICT will automate away huge numbers of jobs but, provided labour markets are reasonably flexible, provided nominal demand growth is kept steady and adequate and major unnecessary demand shocks are avoided, new jobs will be created.

The most likely source of those new jobs will be from a continuation of the trend to service and servicing intensity. That is certainly what the US Bureau of Labour Statistics' forecasts suggest (see Figure 2.3): 1.9 million new jobs will, they predict, be created in computer and data processing; 2.7 million will emerge in other categories of business service (with over 1 million in that catch-all category 'Personnel supply', a continuation of the outsourcing trend but not actually a change in what people do). The key new job-creation areas, however, fall into two categories: retail shops, restaurants, amusement centres, auto-hire cleaning and parking and other personal services are predicted to employ 4.4 million more people. And 5.5 million more jobs are expected in education, health and social services – more nurses, more teachers, more charitable workers. Of course these are just forecasts, but they fit the existing trends, they fit what we know about the fundamental economics, and they are likely to be broadly correct.

Leaving us with an apparent paradox which should not, however,

surprise us: which is that in this ICT-intensive world, many of
rapidly growing jobs will be in some senses high-touch rath
high-tech.

The high-tech, high-touch economy

The new economy is therefore a more complex one than some of the
more breathless accounts of the 'E-conomy' or 'wired society' suggest.
To understand it well, and understand the policy challenges which arise
from it, we need to recognize several simultaneous trends.

It is an economy of growing ICT intensity, and in some wider sense
also more high-tech. More people will make their living from the
provision and application of ICT, and more too in other high-tech areas
like biotechnology. More people with high quality technical skills will
be needed even if, in terms of share of total employment, the numbers
will not be huge. And most people in almost all jobs will need a basic
level of information-technology literacy in order to function successfully in their employment and in society. Information technology is
ubiquitous and most people will use it.

It is also an economy in which many people make their living
from the interpretation of information or knowledge processing, and
in which, at least for the foreseeable future, information analysis
and knowledge-processing capabilities are likely to be highly valued.
More employment in the media, in Internet companies, in business
services, in advertising, in information publishing, is certainly a part of
the story of the new economy. There will indeed be many people who,
in Charles Leadbeater's words, are in the 'thin air' business.

But it is also an economy which values highly many skills which are
essentially subjective, physical and intuitive, and values them highly
partly because the cost of ICT is collapsing. David Beckham earns
massively more than Stanley Matthews ever did; Posh Spice far more
than Lulu, and that is in part because the collapsing price of ICT
enables their images to reach a wider audience faster. It is in part a
consequence of ICT, but not well captured in the phrase 'the knowledge-based economy'. And more generally, the ability to create fashion,
or brand, or ambience or style – essentially intuitive, subjective skills –
are becoming more important and more valuable as richer people seek
to spend more of their money on perceived quality rather than quantity
of goods.

In sheer numbers of people employed, however, the new economy is above all an economy of increasing face-to-face services: more residential healthcare nurses, more sports-centre professionals, more waiters and waitresses, more restaurant cooks, more bag-packers in retail stores, or, if Internet retailing really takes off, more drivers of delivery scooters and vans. Some of these face-to-face service jobs are reasonably highly skilled, some more mundane. Some involve the use of information technology, but in most of them other skills are the key to distinctive quality of service. We can call this 'the knowledge-based economy' if we want because almost all jobs can be done better with higher skill, but there is nothing new about that.

The new economy, moreover, is one where many traditional jobs will still exist and in some cases grow. Manufacturing may have declined but for over 20 per cent of the UK population their experience of work is still either in factories or in other physical occupations such as construction, auto repair or driving buses, trains and lorries, and that number far exceeds all the information-technology workers and media workers and information processors combined. The productivity of what they do in those factories remains extremely important. Meanwhile, construction small trades – plumbers and painters and electricians – are not falling as a percentage of employment: richer people if anything want to consume more home improvement, and home improvement, unlike telecoms services, is not subject to rapid productivity improvement and price collapse.

Finally, the new economy paradoxically is an economy where some old-fashioned physical constraints matter rather a lot. As we get richer, we want better housing in the desired location to a greater extent than more television sets. But if desirable locations are fixed or limited in supply that means we compete with each other for that 'positional good' by pushing up the price. We also want to travel more – by road, by rail and by air – but we worry about the environmental impact, and we curse the congestion caused by others with the same aspirations as ourselves. The more we are able through technology-based productivity improvement to raise our income level, the more we compete for a limited supply of physical space. In the new economy we don't just live on thin air.

So the new economy is not just high-tech or knowledge based. It is a mixture of the high-tech and high-touch, the thin air and the physical, the knowledge-based and the plain old mundane jobs that need to be done. Nor in any fundamental way is the new economy really 'new'. It is the product of trends in place for many years, rather than the outcome of sudden revolution. That evolving picture poses complex challenges for public policy which are explored in Chapter 3. The urgency of the challenges will intensify under the impact of the accelerated rate of productivity improvement probably now unleashed. But they are not challenges best understood if we start from the proposition that we face a fundamentally new paradigm, a fundamentally changed economy suddenly quite different from that in which we have lived before.

A new paradigm of competition?

Some true believers in the new economy would accept much of the above, but still disagree with the conclusion that there is no new paradigm. They would accept that many more jobs will be created in face-to-face services than in information technology itself, but still claim for the e-conomy a special status for two reasons. First, because successful use of the Internet and ICT has become *the* key to company competitive advantage. Second, because the successful development of the knowledge-based economy is vital to 'national competitiveness' and thus prosperity, even if jobs will be created primarily in other sectors. Companies should grasp the challenge of the Internet, and Europe should close the Internet gap with the US, even if employment will come from the proliferation of jobs in restaurants, cafes and nursing homes. Is either of these claims well founded?

For a time in early 2000 the stock market seemed to reflect Andy Grove's assumption that 'all companies will be Internet companies', or by implication be uncompetitive. Dotcoms without a penny of profit to their name achieved billion-dollar valuations. American ICT companies accounted for only 10 per cent of private-sector GDP but 37 per cent of total stock-market valuation.[13] 'Old economy' companies which announced Internet plans achieved immediate leaps in their share price. Thirty-year-olds in Silicon Valley confidently predicted that much of the dinosaur old economy was dead meat, and its hierarchical

---

13. At the end of 1999. See David Hale, *Why the Equity Market is an Experiment in Corporate Resource Reallocation* (Zurich Financial Services, January 2000).

management structures and attitudes history. Consultants confidently asserted that the rules of the competitive game had changed radically.

The reality is and always was more mundane and more sector specific. The specific technology of the Internet has produced a major one-off shift in competitive advantage in some sectors. In addition the Internet is a communications tool relevant to businesses in all sectors. Finally, ICT more generally is a tool able to deliver productivity improvement in almost all businesses. But in many businesses, in many sectors accounting for the bulk of the economy, the idea that the Internet is the unique key to competitive advantage is simply nonsense.

The Internet has created a whole new category of business concerned with Internet access – the ISPs and portals, Yahoo, AOL and Freeserve. That world of ISPs and portals creates both big business opportunities and a potential threat to existing media and telecoms companies. The lines between access provision and information provision, distribution and production, educational services and entertainment are confused and unclear. The end result of the different possible relationships of the old and new media and telecoms companies is unpredictable, but the message that all media and telecoms companies have to think of themselves in a competitive space which includes the Internet is clearly a sound one.

The Internet has also had a dramatic impact on very specific areas of retail activity. Where there is a truly intangible product, like retail financial services, or a highly defined and easily delivered one, like books or CDs, or where we are delivering a right to a service, such as an airline ticket sold by a travel agent, we have seen dramatic shifts in market share with new entrants taking whole swathes of business. We have seen Amazon.com with a market capitalization at one time ten times that of Barnes and Noble, the traditional book-market leader.

Finally, the Internet has also made possible the emergence of new transaction marketplaces which create more efficient means of exchange. Consumer auction sites like E-bay have created an entirely new set of economic activities, encouraging individuals to trade possessions which they previously held on to out of simple inertia. Business-to-business transactions services have helped strip cost out of the interactive activities involved in goods and service exchange, allowing significant new businesses to emerge in markets where buyers and sellers are too fragmented to organize those services themselves.

In these three specific sectors, therefore, the Internet market has been revolutionary, with huge new fortunes made and dramatic shifts in relative market position. In other sectors, however, sectors which in total account for a far bigger share of the economy, the Internet's impact is as a new tool of business not as a new business per se. In retailing outside the special categories of intangible and easily delivered goods, what happened in 2000 was the onset of reality, the realization that in most retail sectors there is no such thing as a pure play e-retailer, and that even if orders are captured over the Internet some rather old-fashioned things – like warehouse management and stock control, range-buying decisions and delivery times, return levels and product quality – are vitally important. Boo.com, the Internet fashion retailer which went bust in July 2000, the many other e-retailers which have followed suit, and the over 80 per cent of all publicly quoted e-retailers now trading well below issue price have learnt that lesson the hard way. Almost all retailers now use the Internet, and some new retailers have emerged as a result, but the determinants of who wins between old and new players will not be the one new innovation nobody else thought of nor the fancy website design, but cost efficiency, customer service, and good buying.

As for the companies which provide face-to-face, physical move-ment, or basic services – hotels and restaurants, amusement parks, airlines and coach companies, rail companies, sports and leisure centres, hospitals and medical services, office-cleaning services and security services – the idea that there is a new competitive model going to sweep away the old is and always was nonsensical. Most of these companies, of course, use the Internet. All well-run hotel groups have or will have efficient Internet-based information provision and booking services. But the Internet booking services will not be what distinguishes the successful hotel, they will not be the source of distinctive competitive advantage, which will still derive instead from familiar sources – location, product design and pricing, and quality of service.

While in specific sectors therefore the Internet is already a key to competitive advantage, in many others it will be very soon a 'hygiene factor', a necessary attribute for competitive parity with other com-panies, but not a source of distinctive competitive advantage. Rather as is true today with the telephone. Almost any company today and for the last several decades would suffer severe competitive disadvantage if it didn't have an efficient working telephone system, but few would cite the telephone system as a source of distinctive competitive advantage. Few companies, other than telecoms providers, would say that they are 'telephone companies'. For many companies within just a few years that is how the Internet will be seen, necessary but banal.

Most companies in most sectors will, however, continue to make big investments in ICT as the key to improving productivity, stripping out huge swathes of costs in all the interactive functions which make up such a large element of present economic activity. As a result they will be big customers of the technology-providing companies. It is this huge purchase of ICT as an investment good by business which is the truly distinctive feature of the current phase of economic development. Stock-market values reflect that fact. In early 2000, at the height of the dotcom boom, all Internet companies in the US accounted for just 4 per cent of US stock-market valuation. But the software and hardware providers accounted for 23 per cent of the total. Whether those valuations were in absolute terms sensible depended on whether the huge margins information-technology providers currently enjoy can be sustained. But the relative valuation for technology producers and Internet companies reflected then, and reflects even more today, the reality of ICT's role in the new economy. ICT's impact as a consumer product is self-limiting because of collapsing prices. The Internet's role as a source of distinctive competitive advantage is limited to specific sectors. But ICT is a tremendously powerful driver of potential efficiency improvements in almost all business processes, and its core economic impact is above all to free people up from interactive activities to do other quite unrelated things.

American leadership: a 'competitiveness' challenge?

The US clearly leads in the new economy in three respects. First the US is ahead of Europe in the development of Internet applications. US Internet-penetration levels lead Europe by about two years and the US has created the first big Internet companies – Yahoo, AOL, Amazon.com and Ebay – companies which have established first mover advantage and which as a result play major roles in Europe as well as in the US. Second, US companies dominate the provision of the core technologies, the basic hardware and software that make all the applications work. Companies throughout the world use Dell, IBM, Hewlett-Packard and Sun computers with Intel chips, they use Cisco routers and license Oracle and Microsoft software. All those companies are American. Third, the US has achieved ahead of Europe a productivity spurt, very probably as a result of the intense use of ICT. Europe may be on the verge of one now, but even if it is, it is running three to four years behind the US.

These three dimensions of US leadership provoke fears that Europe is 'uncompetitive' in the new economy and generate calls for action to close the gap. Only one of them, however – the US's productivity advantage – carries major implications for public policy and none of them justifies the belief that we are facing a 'competitiveness' threat to prosperity and jobs. Indeed, while Europe should draw lessons from US leadership, there are some dangers in defining policy priorities in terms of a specific new economy challenge.

By far the most important of the three dimensions of US leadership is faster productivity growth. US superiority in this dimension is, however, very recent (see Table 2.4). Until the mid-1990s US productivity growth was much slower than the European average and slower than the US had itself achieved in the 1950s and 60s, and there was much perplexity as to why information technology investment, running at almost 40 per cent of total business investment from the late 1970s, was failing to deliver a productivity improvement. From the mid-1990s, however, the US has enjoyed superior productivity growth and the most likely (though not absolutely certain)[14] explanation is the impact of ICT. Three factors may explain the delayed impact.

---

14. For the alternative point of view on the US productivity spurt, see Robert Gordon, 'Has the "New Economy" Rendered the Productivity Slowdown Obsolete?', Northwestern University, 14 June 1999. Gordon argues that the productivity spurt is partly due to measurement changes and cyclical developments with the only underlying factor being productivity growth in IT *hardware* manufacture, i.e. with no proof so far of a pervasive IT effect on productivity throughout the economy. The 'counter-counter' argument has been set out by Christopher Gust and Jamie Marquez in *Federal Reserve Bulletin*, October 2000. They argue that the take-off in US productivity growth is driven by the pervasive use of ICT in the capital stock of many industries – with ICT as a percentage of US capital stock 7.4 per cent versus only 2–3 per cent in big European economies. This pervasive-use hypothesis is supported also in the public pronouncements of Federal Reserve Chairman Alan Greenspan.

This ongoing debate about the facts and causes of the US productivity spurt is another good reason for caution in defining public policy priorities in specific new economy terms.

Note also that a different statistical treatment of price deflators can produce significant differences in estimates of productivity. The US now applies a far larger

Table 2.4 *Labour productivity: output per hour worked*
(% growth per annum)

	1950s	1960s	1970s	1980s	1990–95	1995–9*
US	2.6	2.2	1.0	1.0	0.6	2.7
France	4.3	5.2	4.1	3.0	1.6	1.8
Germany	5.5	5.3	3.7	2.3	2.3	1.9

* French and German figures for 1995–9 are per person employed, rather
than per hour worked.
Source: O'Mahony (NIESR, 1999) for all pre-1995 figures; Council of US
Economic Advisors, *Economic Indicators* and *European Economy*, European
Commission, Supplement A, 'Economic Trends' for figures for 1995 on.

First, all new technologies seem to take several decades before
producing full results, essentially because it takes a long time for people
to work out how to use them to best effect. That was true of electricity
and the diesel locomotive and seems to be true also of information
technology.[15] Second, while the dollar value of ICT investment as a
percentage of the total increased more in the 1960s and 1970s than in
the 1990s, the sheer volume of ICT capability now being purchased is
massively increased. For each dollar spent, US industry is now getting
massively more capability – more capability in hardware due to the
relentless progress of the eighteen months' rule, and more capability in
software, with huge strides in software-development methodologies
dramatically cutting the cost and lead times for new productivity
enhancing investment. The third factor is that ICT now includes, far
more than ten years ago, a large element of 'C' (communications) with
huge improvements in connectivity, including but not limited to the

---

price deflator to IT equipment (i.e. its volume measures capture quality improvements). A similar approach applied to the euro area would increase recent estimates
of European output and productivity growth by about 0.5 per cent per annum. See
The Economist, 16 September 2000.

15. Jeremy Greenwood, *The Third Industrial Revolution* (American Enterprise
Institute, 1997); David, 'General Purpose Engines'.

Internet itself, creating major opportunities for process redesign spanning different sites or companies.

Whatever the causes the delay now seems over and US productivity growth has shifted upwards by a sufficient amount and for a sufficiently long period that most economists now accept that it is not a purely cyclical phenomenon. The improvement is not massive and will not be permanent: economists' estimates tend to cluster around the assumption that the US may enjoy a 0.5 to 1 per cent increase in its sustainable growth rate for perhaps ten years. Nor is such a shift at all unique in economic history. Productivity growth at the limit of present technology (i.e. the productivity growth rate of the country which at any time is the most productive) doesn't vary a great deal. Decade by decade it has never been below 1 per cent nor above 3 per cent since the start of market capitalism. But it does vary within that band. The 1960s saw US productivity growth of about 2–3 per cent compared with 1 per cent in the 1980s.[16]

This non-permanent non-unique shift is still, however, a major economic event. High productivity growth does not change the rules of macroeconomics, it doesn't kill inflation for ever, but it does for a period of time make the attainment of low-inflation growth easier. Even slightly higher total growth, powered by higher productivity growth, also makes an enormous difference to public finance. The US moved from a budget deficit of $164 billion in 1995 to a surplus of $124 billion in 1999, almost entirely because of accelerated growth. With all developed economies having to plan for the public finance strain of ageing populations, even temporarily improved public finances provide an enormously important window of opportunity to address long-term problems.

Europe has not yet achieved an equivalent acceleration in productivity growth and as a result is not yet enjoying the potential benefits of higher economic growth and improved public finance. The essential

---

16. Specific estimates for the US in the 1960s vary from 2.2 per cent for the whole economy (Mary O'Mahony, *Britain's Productivity Performance 1950–96: An International Perspective*, NIESR, 1999) to 3.2 per cent for the business sector only in US national statistics. The 1950s and 1960s were in retrospect, however, exceptional decades. Over most of capitalism's history productivity growth of the leader has stayed within a still narrower 1–2 per cent per annum band.

implication of the US's new economy leadership is therefore simple. Europe should ensure that it has in place the conditions likely to allow it to achieve accelerated productivity growth whether from the application of ICT or from other sources. The changes in European policy required to ensure this are discussed in Chapters 5 and 6. Only a few of those changes, however, focus specifically on success in the new economy or on closing some specific technological gap. Instead they are concerned with general conditions of product, capital and labour markets likely to generate productivity growth and employment creation. That should not surprise us – it follows from the nature of America's leadership and from the nature of ICT's impact. The most important economic impact of ICT lies not in the scale of the ICT-producing sector but in its potential to improve productivity throughout the economy, i.e. the intensity with which it is used. And increasing ICT intensity is not the only big trend in the economy; increasing service intensity is equally important. Europe's challenge is to create conditions conducive to the intensive use of ICT and to job creation in a service-intensive economy. That is an important challenge but it has nothing to do with the threat of American 'competition' in specific new economy sectors.

The other two dimensions of American leadership, though more eye-catching, are actually far less important. US leadership in core-technology provision is certainly dramatic and has roots which go back twenty to thirty years. The technological spin-off of military and space programmes helped create in the 1950s to 1970s a critical mass of scientists and businesses working in information technology: the intensity of links between universities, businesses and venture capital helped launch fifteen to twenty-five years ago the companies which are now household names throughout the world. And some of those companies have achieved dominance because ICT's close to zero replication costs and the need for 'standards' create conditions for natural monopoly – we all buy Microsoft software because everybody else does. Once leadership in such industries is established it is extremely difficult to dislodge.

That story has some lessons for Europe: it suggests the need for policy initiatives which could make it more likely that European companies participate in future waves of technological change (though even today European companies lead in some ICT sectors – such as mobile telephony). But it does not imply that Europe faces a 'competitiveness challenge' from the US, nor that Europe's prosperity is constrained by our lack of leadership in the sector. The key challenge is not to produce ICT but to use it, and the fact that many of the big companies are American does not give the American economy privileged access to the technology – anybody can buy software and hardware and at continually collapsing prices. The only way American leadership in ICT provision could make a difference to Europe's standard of living (though not to its employment) would be if we faced here an example of the special case of competitiveness theory discussed in Chapter 1. If the US had achieved a 'skew' in its traded sector towards high output per worker products (i.e. if the US was selling Europe 'high value' products in return for 'low value' ones) then a terms of trade effect could be at work. But in fact there is no evidence that this is the case. US exports of high-value software are matched by German exports of high-precision engineering goods, French exports of luxury goods and Italian fashion goods: there is no clear winner in terms of overall skew, and it is the ICT products which are collapsing in price relative to, for instance, fashion and luxury branded goods not vice versa. The conclusion of Chapter 1's discussion of the special case therefore stands. The possibility of terms of trade effects provides a general justification for societies to foster high levels of scientific and technical skill (or design and creative skill) but should not make us focus on a specific country's dominance in a specific sector and declare that a 'competitiveness' problem.

That argument applies with yet more force when we turn to America's highly visible lead in Internet penetration and in the creation of Internet companies. The stunning success of Yahoo and AOL, and the more tentative success of Amazon.com make great newspaper stories but the implications for public policy are few. The fact that European consumer Internet penetration lags the US by about two years is a fact but not a terribly important one. The striking thing about the lag indeed is not how long it is but how short: when cars and televisions were first introduced the lag between US and European take-up was much longer. The Internet lag is shorter because Europe and the US are now closer in terms of prosperity, because the product is much cheaper to the consumer and because the mechanisms for rapidly transferring ideas across the world have become ever more effective. In five years' time almost all consumers in both the US and Europe will have Internet connections, and when the economic history of this period is written, the fact that the European penetration curve lagged the US by two years will hardly feature.[17]

Business Internet penetration is more important simply because the use of e-commerce applications is one of the means by which accelerated productivity growth is likely to be achieved. For this reason, measures to ensure a workable legal framework for e-commerce and to ensure competition in high-speed local telecoms access are important (and already in hand). Some government role in encouraging best practice take-up by small businesses can also be justified. Beyond that, however, governments can rely on the private sector to keep any gap in product provision and take-up shorter in Internet applications than in most other categories of business investment. That is for three reasons. The first is that American Internet companies can offer their services in Europe more easily than is the case with many other new business tools: and what matters to productivity is that businesses use these services not who produces them. The second is that there is an army of venture capitalists and entrepreneurs dedicated to scouring the US for any Internet ideas not yet applied in Europe. The third is that many Internet applications do not require technological leadership, or large and sustained investments in either physical plant or intellectual capital, with competitive success instead dependent on executing more rapidly and effectively than competitors ideas which are in concept obvious and for which the basic technology already exists.[18]

The Internet's specific characteristics therefore make it highly likely that private-sector activities alone will drive its application in Europe only a few years later than in the US. These characteristics (in particular the third) also explain why the opportunities for rapid private wealth creation are in some instances large. But they also mean that this is not

---

17. Nor will it matter if many European consumers use, say, Yahoo as an Internet-service provider rather than, say, Freeserve. Part of Yahoo's value added may be created by people working in Europe rather than imported. And the fact that a country imports a specific product is in itself economically irrelevant: all that matters is the *overall* balance of payments and the overall mix of trading sectors between higher-value and lower-value products.

18. What they do often entail is high marketing investments both to persuade consumers and businesses to conduct business in new ways, and to establish first-mover advantage and maintain share of voice in crowded markets.

a challenge requiring specific government focus and support. Indeed for a time in 2000 there was a danger that too much government focus on the Internet, added to over-hyped valuations of Internet shares, could lead to too much capital and too many skilled people being directed into Internet start-ups rather than to other more long-term and difficult categories of business development.[19]

Governments need to focus on difficult things, on the things where we cannot rely on the motivation of private profit to achieve desirable ends. The changing shape of our economy is in fact creating major challenges for government. These are described in Chapter 3. But they are not the challenges of competing with the US in specific high-tech sectors. In terms of public policy priorities it's not 'competitiveness' and it's 'not the e-conomy, stupid'.

---

19. See Robert Schiller, *Irrational Exuberance*, for an account of how stock-market irrationality can drive misallocation of capital. Also W.J. Baumol, *Enterpreneurship, Management and the Structure of Payoffs* (MIT Press, 1993).

3. It's *Not* the E-conomy, Stupid

The conventional wisdom believes that globalization is the most important factor shaping our economies, and that achieving national 'competitiveness' is the most important public policy challenge – a challenge requiring changes to traditional economic and social models. But as Chapter 2 has argued, the key forces changing the shape of developed economies – trends in customer preference and in technology – are essentially internal. As a result many of the key challenges facing rich countries are internal too.[1] Rather than the threat of external competition, it is five essentially domestic developments which create a need for reform of some traditional economic and social models: rising inequality; an increased need for flexibility; increasing demand for key public services; increased demands for regulation; and the conflicts between physical development and the environment. These are far more difficult issues than those posed by external competition, or indeed by the need to compete in the new 'e-conomy'.[2]

---

1. The two key exceptions to this, i.e. the two key external or global challenges are world environmental interdependency (discussed in Chapter 9) and financial-market interdependence (Chapter 10).

2. There is one other major challenge not addressed in this chapter nor addressed in detail elsewhere in this book – the ageing population. This is clearly a vitally important issue, but it is a product neither of globalization, nor of the changing shape of the economy described in Chapter 2, and it carries no particular implications for the relative success of different modes of capitalism, being a challenge equally to all. It is therefore, though of course important, tangential to the themes of this book. Comments on social security and pension schemes made in Chapter 8 are, however, relevant to that issue.

Rising inequality

'The single most important social change affecting the UK is not the ageing of the population. Nor the breakdown of the family. Rather it is a phenomenon which is still largely unrecognized – a growing dispersion of earnings power.' These words were written not by some die-hard remnant of Old Labour, but by Peter Lilley in 1994, the then Conservative Secretary of State for Social Security. He had immediate practical reasons for focusing on this problem: increasing inequality, resulting from low wages for unskilled work, and high unemployment of unskilled workers, was threatening a relentless explosion in social-welfare expenditures on income support. But the problem he highlighted was not unique to Britain, nor to the particular year in which he wrote. The last twenty-five years indeed have produced in almost all developed societies either (where labour markets are fairly free) a strong tendency towards increased inequality, or (where labour markets are inflexible) a major increase in unemployment levels among less skilled people. The root cause of these effects appears to be the same, and stems from the technological forces described in Chapter 2. The differences between developed economies have reflected simply how they have responded.

In all labour markets where wages have been set in close to free-market conditions, with limited minimum-wage interventions or collective-bargaining distortions, the last twenty-five years has seen an increase in income inequality. That trend to inequality has stabilized or even in some cases reversed slightly during the 1990s, but the long-term shift is clear and large (see Figure 3.1). In the UK median earners gained a 41 per cent increase in real disposable income between 1973–98, but low-income earners gained only 22 per cent and high earners 74 per cent. In the US (see Figure 3.2) the income of the bottom 40 per cent of the population actually fell between 1977–89. In the last five years, rapid growth in the US economy has at last delivered real income increases to almost all income segments, but until then average US real wages had hardly grown over twenty years, unskilled wages had fallen, and almost all the fruits of economic growth had accrued to the richest third of society.

This increasing inequality between the top third and the rest seems to have eased off in the 1990s, but with another more specific phenomenon emerging – huge income and capital-gain increases for those

Figure 3.1 Real wage for low, median and high-paid workers:
UK, 1973–98

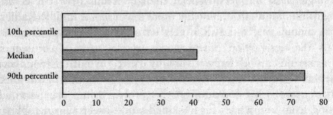

Note: The '10th percentile' earner is one such that 10% of the population earn less than him/her, and 90% more. The '90th percentile' is one such that 90% of the population earn less and 10% more.

Source: Institute for Fiscal Studies.

Figure 3.2 Per cent gain in real income: US, 1977–89

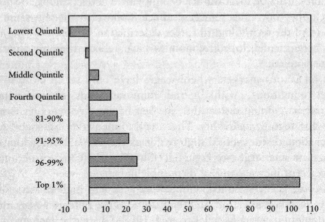

Note: The lowest quintile is the lowest 5th of earners.

Source: Paul Krugman, *Peddling Prosperity*.

right at the top. In fact, the increasing inequality of the 1980s had already included a 'top percentile' effect as Figure 3.2 shows. The top 1 per cent of US income earners gained a 104 per cent real income increase between 1977–89, easily outstripping even the next 4 per cent (a 23 per cent increase) let alone the bottom 20 per cent who suffered a 10 per cent fall in income. What the 1990s have seen, however, appears to be even more specific than that, a huge increase in the earnings and capital gains of the very richest, the top tenths of a per cent. Top football stars now earn massively more than second-rank football stars, and astronomically more than football stars of thirty years ago. Top models the same. Top business executives can earn through stock options serious money previously only earned by entrepreneur-owners. Many US chief executives now receive total remuneration packages worth tens of million of dollars, a few reach into the hundreds of millions. This would have been inconceivable fifteen years ago, but over the last decade packages of this size have increasingly emerged, first in the US, and more slowly in Europe. US chief executives of big companies now earn on average 475 times the pay of their typical employee.[3] And the star information and technology entrepreneurs have made new fortunes at a pace not seen since the great transport, natural resource, and finance fortunes of the late nineteenth century. Bill Gates of Microsoft, Larry Ellison of Oracle and Michael Dell of Dell have made money faster than anybody since Rockefeller, Morgan and Vanderbilt. A long-term trend towards widening inequality between the top 10 per cent and the bottom 10 per cent seems now to have been followed by increasing returns to stardom, and top-level remuneration based on a 'winner takes all' approach.

There are two possible causes for these trends, hotly debated by economists – globalization and the impact of technology. It is highly likely that both forces have played a role, and in terms of social impact and challenges for policy it makes little difference where the exact balance of responsibility lies. But it seems likely that technological change is the more powerful force than globalization.

Globalization, both through increasing ease of trade in those sectors which are inherently tradeable and through the potential migration of skilled people, could well act to increase disparities of income in both developed and developing countries, the former at the bottom end of income distributions, the latter at the top. Unskilled workers in traded sectors in rich countries should, if they are to be employed at all in those sectors, face downward wage pressure as a result of global competition: software developers in India can earn more when they can

3. Towers Perrin Survey, *The Economist*, September 2000.

sell their services in a world market.[4] Some of the trends we see in developed societies almost certainly reflect the former effect. But empirical estimates of the size of these trade effects rarely suggest that they can explain the scale of change we have seen. The exposure of rich economies to global competition is, as noted already, far lower than is often supposed. And while the pay of textile workers in the UK might be held down by global competition, it is less easy to explain on that basis the sharp increase in the pay of a retail-store chief executive relative to the checkout operator, or the phenomenon of strongly increasing income at the very top of the income distribution.

Instead it seems likely that technological progress has been the key driver, ICT primarily, but also the further relentless progress of electro-mechanical technologies. Automation rather than global competition has driven a massive shake-out of manual jobs. British Steel employed 33,000 workers in 2000 versus 120,000 in 1980, not because of markets lost in the face of competition (it actually produced slightly more steel in the latter year) but because productivity has increased over 400 per cent. Productivity in turn has increased because technological advance has made it possible and because a market economy creates incentives to utilize available technologies. A privatized British Steel, seeking to maximize return to shareholders, and facing competition within Europe, would have dramatically cut its workforce even if the low-income developing world did not exist. Our car factories similarly have become relentlessly more productive rather than less competitive in world terms. Britain now produces more cars than in 1980 but with 50 per cent fewer car workers. The application of ICT to interactive functions, meanwhile, has thrown out of work large

---

4. In the classical trade theory of 'factor price equalization' the impact of more intense trade should actually be to increase income disparity in developed countries (as unskilled wages fall due to competition from low-income countries) but to *decrease* income disparities in developing countries because skilled workers there (who previously enjoyed a high income premium due to skill scarcity) face competition from imported goods and services incorporating the abundant skills of richer countries. This classic theory, however, almost certainly fails to capture new features of recent globalization trends which are different in nature from classical trade – the ability of, say, a software developer in India to emigrate to the US, and/ or his ability to participate in the US labour market for software skills through 'down-the-line' work from India, whether employed by an American software company or an Indian subcontractor.

numbers of middle managers and clerical staff – the famous downsizing of corporate staffs – and has done so quite as much in the non-traded sectors of the economy, such as retail financial services, as in traded ones. The information and communications technology which drives the shake-out in turn enables the remaining staff to leverage their skills more effectively. ICT allows business information to flow directly to and from a smaller number of more highly paid business executives, without going through the paper-based manipulations of lower middle management and clerical staff.

Thus ICT, along with the further progress of electro-mechanical technology, appears to be increasing returns to skill and reducing the need for less skilled labour. While most of that unskilled labour does, sometimes after painful delays, find alternative employment in the expanding service sector, it often does so at much lower wage rates. Technological progress seems to be increasing inequality at the bottom end.[5]

The technology leverage factor, along with customer-preference shifts, may also help to explain the phenomenon of increasing returns to very highly skilled people and to 'stars'. Top business talent, whether in manufacturing or commercial companies, professional services or financial services, is both highly remunerated and ferociously busy. Ferociously busy because the mobile phone, the laptop, the email and the conference call have extended work into the home, on to planes, and on to the beach and the ski slopes. Highly remunerated in part because strong skills in information analysis can now be leveraged more intensely since information flows more rapidly to the highly skilled analyst and since decisions and advice can be more efficiently communicated to colleagues across the world. Improved communications technology can thus be expected to increase the returns of those who analyse and decide upon information rather than simply prepare and

---

5. The influence of technological change on earnings relativities are complex and varies with the precise nature of the technology (e.g. the process improvement/ demand creation balance and its speed of diffusion within an economy). It is possible for a technology to have a major impact on inequality well ahead of its discernible impact on productivity. This appears to be true both of the latest ICT wave and of the early phases of the initial Industrial Revolution in Britain from 1750–1850. See Jeremy Greenwood, *The Third Industrial Revolution: Technology, Productivity and Income Inequality*.

transmit it; but above all to increase the returns of those who are very good at such analysis and decision-making. The effect applies not just to analytical skills, however, but also and indeed even more so to creative, physical or intuitive skills and attributes.[6] David Beckham doesn't earn massively more than Stanley Matthews because he is a better player (albeit he may well be with improvements in physique and technique), but for two reasons. First because communication technologies enable his image to reach more people more rapidly. Second, because of customer preference: as people get richer they can spend more money on non-essential goods, and buying merchandised material because it bears the brand of David Beckham or his team is a form of non-essential consumption. Worshipping David Beckham is a high income elasticity category of consumption.

Overall therefore we face in the developed world powerful forces towards increased inequality. Those forces are primarily internal to developed rich societies, but globalization has also played a role. They have driven increased inequality at both the top and bottom end of the income distribution. They may have stabilized in the 1990s at the bottom end, but not at the top. What we should do about this problem, indeed whether we should call it a problem at all, depends on social and political choice rather than the dry calculus of economic success. So far most developed economies have chosen not only to accept the trend, but to accentuate it, reducing tax- and benefit-based redistribution in parallel with these increases in pre-tax inequality. The wisdom of that action, and the issue of whether we should or can do anything to offset inequality trends is addressed in Chapter 8. Whatever the resolution of that question, however, it is clear that the rise of pre-tax inequality also has implications for another highly contentious area of public policy, that of labour-market flexibility.

---

6. See Sherwin Rosen, 'The Economics of Superstars', *American Economic Review*, 71:5 (1981) for the original and classic explanation of this effect. As Rosen points out, the impact of communications is not only to increase the returns to stars, but in some industries to *reduce* total employment while massively increasing the income of a few top performers, e.g. fewer entertainers than in vaudeville days, but top television stars hugely rewarded.

The need for flexible labour markets

Labour-market flexibility is a controversial subject. Many free-market economists see labour-market flexibility as the key to higher employment. But to many trade unionists and continental politicians of the left, 'flexibility' is just a code word for unfettered management power and job insecurity. To some adherents of the 'third way', flexibility is an important concept but best packaged for public consumption under a more acceptable label, such as 'adaptability'.

One of the problems with the debate has been a failure to define terms. People talk of 'flexibility' without specifying what they mean. In fact six quite different dimensions of labour-market flexibility can be identified, some more controversial than others. Functional flexibility relates to the ease with which people move between jobs and functions within a workplace. Skills flexibility means the extent to which people have widely applicable skills and/or the ability rapidly to change or update them. Working-time flexibility encompasses a wide range of part-time, temporary and flexible hours alternatives to the classic permanent full-time job. Numerical flexibility is the right to hire and fire with reasonable ease. Real-wage flexibility exists when wages are set by the market, rather than according to conventional norms, concepts of social justice or relative power in large-scale collective bargaining. Geographical flexibility means the physical mobility of people, both their willingness and ability to travel from home to work, and their willingness to move home in pursuit of work. In addition, labour-market efficiency is affected by the treatment of the unemployed – by levels of benefit relative to wages and by the 'conditionality' of benefit (i.e. what conditions – such as willingness to accept a job when offered – govern its availability). How well different labour markets work overall reflects subtle differences in regulation, convention and behaviour along each of these dimensions.[7]

The changing shape of developed economies has increased the need for labour-market flexibility. Both the rise of the service economy and

---

7. See CBI Report, *Creating a Europe that Works: A Study of Labour Market Flexibility* (1999), for detailed definition of the different dimensions and analysis of degrees of flexibility in six major European countries.

the changing nature of technological change have profound implications for optimal policy.

The increasingly service- and servicing-intensive economy makes inflexible labour markets a greater barrier to full employment than they once were. First and most obviously a service- and servicing-intensive economy requires greater flexibility of working time. A manufactured good is produced at one time, delivered at another, used at another still or over time. Face-to-face services are produced when consumed by customers. If a retail store is to provide a bag-packing service to customers in a cost efficient way, it needs working time patterns which allow staffing to match the peaks and troughs of customer-determined demand.

That need for working-time flexibility and for other dimensions of flexibility is important also because of a second distinguishing feature of many service environments. In most face-to-face services, there is a high degree of freedom to trade off staffing levels with customer service: service quality can usually be improved, at least somewhat, by adding marginal staff. That is not generally so in manufacturing. Tell a line manager in a car factory that you have hired a few extra relatively low-skilled staff so that he can improve product quality, and you will usually just have given him a headache: the precisely engineered machine-driven environment of the factory makes incremental staff often of little extra value, and quality is often improved by taking human interventions and errors out of the equation rather than by adding more. Tell a manager of a pub with five or ten staff that he can have one more staff member, albeit relatively low skilled, and he will still be able to deploy that person to relieve existing staff of mundane duties, improving quality of service as a result.[8] The implication is that service-economy employment levels, far more than manufacturing, are influenced by a myriad of specific labour-market features – the flexibility of working time, the relative pay of unskilled versus skilled labour, the ease of firing staff if after a test run they prove to be of poor quality. French labour market laws make little difference to how many people

---

8. The impact of this factor was illustrated by the take-up of the British Labour government's New Deal programme. New jobs created were almost entirely in face-to-face service environments such as retail. Even where individual CEOs of manufacturing companies were committed to the programme, the ability of their companies to absorb new staff was close to nil.

Table 3.1 Earnings inequality and unemployment

	UK	Germany	France
Ratio of 5th decile to lowest decile earnings (1993)	1.79	1.44	1.64
Unemployment rate among workers with less than upper secondary education (1996)	10.9	14.2	14.8

Source: OECD 1996 *Employment Outlook* for earnings inequality; OECD 1999 *Employment Outlook* for unemployment by education level.

are employed in French factories, compared with American factories: they make a lot of difference to whether French supermarkets match American in providing bag packers.

The need for flexibility, this time in real wage fixing, is also probably increased by the trend to increasing inequality. If the relative economic value of different skills is becoming more unequal, society faces a difficult choice. Either accept the increased inequality, which implies low wages for the unskilled, but at least keep people in work; or respond to offset it, via high minimum wages or collective-bargaining constraints, but at the expense of higher unemployment. In broad terms the Anglo-Saxon response has been to accept the increased inequality, with the consequences we saw in Figures 3.1 and 3.2. Continental countries have tended more to take the interventionist route, contributing to the consequences set out in Table 3.1, a lower level of inequality but higher unemployment rates for unskilled labour.[9]

Finally, technological developments and the rise of the service

9. The importance of this inequality/employment trade-off should not, however, be overstated. All countries (Anglo-Saxon as much as continental European) have much higher levels of unemployment among unskilled rather than skilled workers, and the European economies which have the highest unskilled unemployment typically also have levels of *skilled* employment above those found in more successful job-creating economies. The inequality/unemployment trade-off (sometimes presented as *the* dominant factor in unemployment performance) is therefore simply one factor among many.

economy have combined to increase the need for numerical flexibility and skills flexibility. All economic change requires movement of people from one job or skill to another: all productivity growth requires what Joseph Schumpeter called 'creative destruction', destroying old jobs and creating new ones. But the particular wave of creative destruction we now face has made impediments to numerical flexibility more of a barrier to productivity and employment growth than they were in the 1950s to 1970s.

As Chapter 2 discussed, ICT is different from electro-mechanical technologies in two respects. It achieves a far faster pace of technological advance; and as a result it is, in its direct employment effects, more a job-destroying rather than job-creating technology. Its economic benefit primarily derives not from more people doing ICT-related activities but from less people doing interactive functions and more people working somewhere else entirely, for instance in face-to-face services. To gain its economic benefits big firms have to downsize, and people have to move jobs. The service economy, meanwhile, is characterized by smaller company size and within companies by significantly smaller employment sites (e.g. a pub within a large pub chain is still a small employment site). In the US 25 per cent of service sector employees work at employment sites with fewer than twenty employees, and 38 per cent work for companies employing fewer than 100 employees in total; in manufacturing the equivalent figures are 8 per cent and 22 per cent. Employment in the top fifty UK companies has fallen by over 20 per cent since 1970, while total employment is up over 10 per cent. All employment growth over the next ten years is expected to occur in small and medium companies (less than 250 employees). Since smaller firms have more volatile commercial futures than larger firms this trend to smaller companies makes it more likely that people have to change jobs to stay employed.[10]

---

10. Given the importance of trends in size of company and size of employment site, and given how frequently it is asserted that the employment shift now occurring is from larger to smaller companies and sites, it is frustratingly difficult to find good time series data for the UK or other European countries. The US data (Statistical Abstract of the US, Tables 876 and 877) illustrate, however, the very different company and employment site characteristics of manufacturing versus services, wholesaling and retailing, and this pattern must also apply in Europe. Where major shifts from manufacturing to service-sector employment are now under way (for instance in Germany), a significant shift from larger company and

Together, therefore, changes in technology and consumer preference are making the labour market significantly different from that which existed for much of the post-war period. The essential feature of that change can be summed up simply – more of the employment flow is now from large to small units not small to large. Economic change in the 1950s to 1970s involved creative destruction but much of that took the form of small firms and small shops disappearing and downsizing while bigger companies grew, not big companies downsizing and people finding employment in small- and medium-sized firms. Average company size and the share of employment in the top 100 or 500 companies were on rising trends in most developed countries until the 1970s or 1980s. Those trends made particular labour-relation approaches feasible. Big company promises (implicit or explicit) of security of employment were often deliverable in the 1950s to 1970s because of a particular conjuncture of technology and customer demand: car companies were achieving rapid productivity improvements but volumes were growing faster. Legal and bargaining constraints on downsizing were not major impediments to Schumpeterian creative destruction in the 1950s to 1970s but they have become so today. The changed technological context has changed optimal policy.[11]

---

site to smaller must therefore also be occurring. Equally the very small size of typical agricultural companies and employment sites means that in the period when agriculture was falling rapidly as a percentage of employment and manufacture still rising (i.e. up to about 1970), the average economic unit must have been increasing in size.

The UK company figures are taken from 'The Times 1,000': the measured fall from that source (20 per cent for the top fifty companies) understates the downsizing of large companies, since in 1970 many of the figures were for UK employees only, whereas latest figures are for total worldwide employment.

11. The creative destruction of the 1950s–70s had of course individual and political implications. The economic insecurity of a 1950s small shopkeeper or farmer was no less intense than that of a factory worker or middle manager today, and led to both political protest (e.g. Poujadism) and to a major policy response (large agricultural subsidies). Labour-market regulations were not, however, a constraint on this process of adjustment: neither collective-redundancy laws nor trade-union power restricted downsizing by millions of small units, each shedding just a few (often family) workers. Some big economic units were also downsizing – above all in regionally concentrated basic industries like coal mining and steel – again generating specific policy responses based on transitional subsidies and

One impact of these changes is to undermine the possibility of a 'job for life'. The changes are gradual not sudden and the overall impact on average job tenure is less than sometimes supposed. In Britain average years in job are down from 5.8 in 1975 to 4.9 in the mid-1990s. But this average hides a more significant reduction in tenure for men (down from 7.9 to 6.4), and a significant fall in the number of very long-term jobs (jobs lasting more than twenty years down from 14 per cent of the total to 9 per cent).[12] Moreover, the direction of change is clear, and the implications for required flexibility significant. If there are too many impediments to management's ability to fire people, either productivity improvement can be stymied or, paradoxically, employment creation can be limited, for companies operating in volatile markets will not hire people if the cost of shedding them in a downturn is too high, and firms which are expanding will seek to do so in a highly automated, labour minimizing way. The new economy requires people to move more often between firms and between types of jobs, and requires them to seek individual security in their skills and employability rather than in the job for life. It doesn't make full employment unachievable. Both the US and, through a very different policy mix, the Netherlands are achieving full employment in the face of these developments. But it does mean that the policy mix required to deliver high employment is likely to have changed.

The importance of this dimension of flexibility will increase, moreover, if ICT really is now delivering the spurt in potential productivity growth which US evidence suggests. In order to seize that opportunity greater flexibility will be required. Flexibility to downsize in order to achieve the potential productivity improvements in existing interactive

---

regeneration assistance. What has changed therefore is simply that in many sectors where the 1950s–70s did not pose difficult problems of adjustment – much of manufacturing, financial services, the utilities – creative destruction now requires significant downsizing. In one respect this creative destruction is easier to deal with than in the 1950s–70s – it is less regionally concentrated – we don't have the problem of whole regions heavily dependent on a few basic industries. But it does require changes to the labour-market approaches which developed during the period when many large-scale companies were growing in size, and changes too in the objectives of companies. These are discussed in Chapter 6.

12. See Gregg and Wadsworth, 'A Short History of Labour Turnover, Job Tenure and Job Security 1975–93', *Oxford Review of Economic Policy*, 11:1.

activities; and flexibility to encourage the rapid pace of new job creation, particular in service sectors, which will be needed to offset this downsizing.

In a variety of subtle ways, therefore, it seems likely that the shape of the new economy described in Chapter 2 is increasing the need for labour-market flexibility. That carries implications for the labour-market structures and policies most likely to deliver economic success. Models which were most successful previously may not be the most successful today. Chapters 5 and 6 explore the implications of these changes for the relative success of different variants of capitalism and the challenges they pose in particular to the classic forms of the European economic and social model.

Increased demands on the state

The need for labour-market flexibility means that there are dangers in addressing inequality concerns through labour-market intervention. The implication could therefore be an increased need for the state's role as income redistributor, leaving the market to determine pre-tax wages but taking offsetting action to reduce inequality through the tax and benefit system. But that would increase government expenditure at a time when the changing shape of the economy is also facing the state with other forms of increased demand.

As we have seen, as people get richer they tend to buy more services rather than more physical goods, both because of an innate hierarchy of needs, and because of differential productivity growth rates. Among the services that display the strongest tendency to this high income elasticity are education and health. Wherever health expenditure is privately bought, and therefore free to increase directly in line with customer preference, it grows as a percentage of personal consumption. US personal consumption on medical-care services has grown from 5.3 per cent of the total in 1960 to 10.3 per cent in 1980 to 15.3 per cent today. Wherever health expenditure is not privately bought but paid for via public budgets, either those public budget increase, or there is dissatisfaction with the service level provided. From 1979 to 1997, a British Conservative government committed to reducing the size of the state increased health expenditure in real terms every year, but dissatisfaction with health service quality remained a primary reason for voting against the Conservatives. In every major developed country, indeed, whatever the mix of public and private in health provision, total healthcare expenditure has risen steadily as a percentage of GDP – the OECD average rising from about 4–5 per cent in 1960 to approaching 10 per cent today. Education displays many of the same characteristics. As people get richer their demands for higher education and for high-quality basic education increase, both because education is a desirable social good in its own right and because it is rightly perceived that high skills are a key to high relative income in an increasingly unequal economy.

This relentlessly rising demand has two implications for public policy. The first is that productivity in health and education is as vitally important to national prosperity as productivity in any other sector of the economy, such as manufacturing, or traded services or retailing. Many opportunities for improved productivity exist. Health-service provision is administratively intensive, creating opportunities to use ICT to automate interactive functions, and new technologies of health-care are continually helping us to deliver more for the same resources, to reduce time spent on routine operations freeing up bed space and other resources. Further education and higher education processes can also probably be made greatly more efficient through the use of information technology. But while the pursuit of these opportunities is vital, we would be unwise to assume that they will solve the problem alone. Good health is so central to people's aspirations that it is highly likely that increasing customer demand will continue to overwhelm any productivity improvement. And in some key health and education functions productivity improvement is constrained by the inherently face-to-face and personal nature of the service. The British Government's current commitment to reduce primary-school class size is a commitment to *reduce* measured labour productivity (quite rightly so in this case).

A second implication must therefore be faced, an implication for funding and the nature of provision. Either we accept the increased taxation rates required to fund increased public provision, or we find other categories of public expenditure which can be cut to fund such increased provision, or we accept that increased provision must involve, in education or in health or in both, an increased element of private funding. That choice is explored in Chapter 8 within the wider context of the functions and resources of the modern state.

Regulation – a rising consumer demand

The rising demand for health and education is one expression of the consumer preferences of increasingly rich people. It poses complex challenges because there are good arguments for those services to be funded in part by the state. But the essential required response to this rising demand is clear: if people want more education and health services as income rises, more education and health should in some way be provided. And it is at least possible to solve the problem by shifting to private rather than public supply. Education and health are not *inherently* public goods even if there are arguments for providing them publicly.

Rising income and changing consumer preferences also, however, produce demands for quality of life improvements which are more inherently collective than either health or education, and which pose complex problems of measurement and of public policy choice. Just as richer people want more health services to a greater extent than more television sets, they also want safer and more pleasant workplaces, and a safer and more pleasant physical environment, less polluted air, less noise pollution, less countryside destruction. They want safer food, and are more concerned by food safety issues for precisely the same reasons that they want more healthcare. They want more certain product quality, and demand the right to redress if product quality fails. And they are more assertive about their perceived 'rights': they want to be free from discrimination and to be treated with respect.

From these shifting consumer preferences comes the pressure for regulation and control. Workplace health and safety regulation, transport system safety regulation, environmental and food-safety regulation, planning controls and employee rights: to free-market ideologues these are simply the product of bureaucrats regulating for regulation's sake, but in fact each is essentially a politically organized collective response to the changing consumer preferences of richer people – politically organized and collective because that is the only way that certain consumer preferences can be met. Clean air has to be organized by the state, because we cannot each buy our own individual slice. For every business complaining about the burden of existing regulation there are consumer bodies arguing for more and gaining popular support because they express strong consumer preferences.

As a result the 'problem' of these increased consumer demands is

inherent to all rich societies. It can be expressed and reflected in
different ways. The European model has tended towards more explicit
and predetermined regulation. The US model involves explicit regulations in some areas, but in other areas the pursuit of consumer rights
and preferences is through litigation. The litigation and insurance
burden on American business – in respect to product liability, to
environmental liability and to equal opportunities – is simply the
American variant of the regulatory burden about which European
business complains. And nobody who has filled in American govern-
ment-contract declarations – on equal opportunities, on minority group
subcontractors, or on a drug-free working environment – is under any
illusion that America is magically free of the regulatory version of the
burden either.

The fact that regulation arises from the changing preferences of
richer consumers does not mean that there is not a 'problem'. There is
a problem because regulation does sometimes have implications for
either productivity or employment (though not usually in any meaningful sense for 'competitiveness'). There is a problem because the balance
of benefits and costs is often difficult to measure. There is a problem
because benefits are often focused on specific groups, costs widespread,
and that can bias the system towards higher than optimal regulation.
There is indeed sometimes a problem of bureaucratic momentum for its
own sake. For all these reasons governments are right to worry if they
have the balance correct, right to appoint 'Better Regulation' taskforces,
right to listen to business lobby groups arguing against regulation as
well as consumer lobby groups arguing for. But the fundamental
consumer preference roots of increased demand for regulation must be
recognized, and the trade-off between these consumer benefits and the
cost to measured productivity should be made explicit, not avoided by
reference to the external bogeyman of 'competitiveness'. Chapters 6
and 9 consider some of those trade-offs. Chapter 4 highlights the
inherent uncertainty of prosperity measurements in a world where some
customer preferences are not captured in measured GDP.

Contested goods and environmental trade-offs

The changing pattern of expenditure by increasingly rich consumers has
in general meant a shift from physical goods to non-material or at least
non-durable services. We are in some senses heading towards a more

weightless economy, 'living on thin air'. But among the growing categories of expenditure are two which are deeply physical in their nature and in their consequences: housing and transport. Housing as a share of total UK personal consumption has gone from below 8 per cent in 1970 to 12 per cent today.[13] Total consumer expenditure on transport services has risen from 5.5 per cent in 1970 to 7.5 per cent today. Both these categories of expenditure pose important challenges for rich societies, most severely in densely populated countries. And internationally, disputes over contested goods – the CO_2 absorption capacity of the atmosphere and scarce physical resources such as water or oil – pose global challenges far more difficult than any created by the Internet.

Rising expenditure on housing reflects the dynamics of consumer preference but also a rather special form of the relative productivity growth effect. As people get richer, they devote more of their income to housing. The figures quoted above illustrate this over time, but it is also true as between different income levels at any point in time. The top decile of British households by income devote 25 per cent of

---

13. The correct measurement of 'expenditure' on housing and of 'consumption' of housing is complex. UK figures for 'Household Consumption' (in ONS Economic Trends and ONS Consumer Trends) show consumption of housing services growing from about 6 per cent in 1960 to just below 8 per cent in 1970 and to 12 per cent today: these figures include, however, an 'imputed' amount for the value of the rent which home-owners would have to pay if they did not own their own home, i.e. the value of the benefit they gain from home-ownership. Figures in the Household Expenditure Survey for actual cash payments on mortgage interest, rent, repairs and maintenance show a higher level but less dramatic rise, from 13 per cent in 1970 to 16 per cent today. These figures, however, exclude 'Purchase or alteration of dwellings, mortgages', i.e. own capital commitments to house purchase and alteration as against borrowed (mortgage) capital. They also suffer from the deficiency that the *real* cost of mortgage-interest payments is reduced by inflation. As a result a much higher proportion of mortgage interest is now a real expenditure (rather than an early repayment of capital) than it was in 1970 (when the inflation rate was 5 per cent) let alone than in the mid-1970s, when high inflation (up to 25 per cent) meant that the real burden of interest payments was offset by the rapidly falling real value of outstanding debt. Theoretically at least the 'Household Consumption' figures are therefore a better measure of consumer preference, of the extent to which consumers are choosing to devote available resources (capital + income) to housing rather than to other categories of consumption.

expenditure to housing versus 18 per cent for the sixth decile.[14] Housing may be a basic need but it is also one characterized by high income elasticity, because its perceived quality (defined by size, design and location) varies hugely. Increased housing expenditure is thus partly a consumer-preference effect.

But housing expenditure levels are also determined by limits on supply and by competition for a limited stock of desirable locations. If desirable land were abundant and planning constraints non-existent, increased consumer demands for better housing would be satisfied at a lower price. Some locational competition would still occur – the price of houses in fashionable districts of London is unaffected by whether new housing estates are permitted in Milton Keynes – but across the whole of Britain prices would be lower. In fact, however, in a crowded country, land will never be perceived as abundant or planning controls simply removed. Housing is thus an inherently 'positional', locationally specific good: it is, in economists' terms, highly 'contested'. While software is the least contested of goods (it can be provided at roughly the same cost to 1 million people as it can to one), housing is the most contested: if I own a house you want, not only does it cost real resources to build an equivalent, but in some circumstances it is just impossible to do so.

For that reason, in any densely populated country which limits new housing through planning constraints, housing tends to go up in price not only faster than inflation but faster than average earnings. In the UK the ratio of average house price to average income of borrowers, which averaged about 2.5 from 1955 to 1970, has risen to an average of 2.95 for the 1990s and stood at 3.2 in 2000.[15] Its path from there to

---

14. Family Spending, *Report of the 1998–99 Family Expenditure Survey*, including amounts for 'Purchase and Alteration of Dwellings, Mortgages'. These figures are higher than the 'Household Consumption' figures since they include repairs, maintenance, etc., included elsewhere in the Household Consumption categories.

15. Prior to the mid-1950s prices were inflated by the impact of war destruction and post-war building controls. Pre-war figures were, however, even lower than in the 1950s and 1960s (price to income ratio about 2.1), illustrating the long-term trend. Note that the ratio of average house prices to income of borrowers is a better measure than house prices to average earnings of all people, since trends in the latter ratio have a downward bias in a period when home-ownership levels are increasing and lower-income earners (purchasing cheaper homes) are becoming

here has seen some dramatic ups and downs. It shot massively ahead of its trend in 1973–4, when a unique combination of substantially negative real interest rates and huge tax advantages to home ownership made housing seem not just a desirable good but the only intelligent investment.[16] But the underlying trend is up, despite the progressive removal of tax relief. With the tax advantages now entirely removed, the likeliest future trend is a further increase.

That rising trend reflects the facts of at least partially constrained supply. The ratio is highest in south-east Britain where constraints relative to supply are most severe; it is lowest in regions like the north-east where existing supply is high relative to demand and where new development constraints (in any case less stringent) therefore have no bite. It was lowest in the 1960s following fifteen years in which government saw 'new houses built' as a key measure of success, and during which the major new towns were developed. It is a rising trend with two implications for public policy debate.

The first is that there is an inherent conflict between individual consumer demand and environmental impact. Constraining housing supply limits individuals' ability to turn greater income into one of the most desired forms of consumption; but allowing unconstrained demand destroys value too – the unmeasurable value of our collective desire to preserve countryside, and the measurable value of existing houses whose amenity, and value, is reduced by new ones. The second implication concerns one's attitude towards inequality. The more that goods and services are uncontested, the more valid is the classic conservative philosophy that society should aim to get richer rather

---

owners for the first time. (See *House Prices: Changes Through Time at National and Sub-national Level*, Government Economic Service, Working Paper 110, Department of the Environment, 1990.)

16. Until 1974 mortgage-interest relief was available on the full value of a house without upper limit. The £25,000 limit introduced in 1974 was still twice the average house price. Inflation rose from 10 per cent in 1973 to 17 per cent in 1974 and 25 per cent in 1975, but the mortgage rate rose only to a peak of 12 per cent. Marginal tax rates ranged from 34–83 per cent. The net effect was that home buyers could be borrowing money at effective post-tax rates which were as much as 15 per cent negative in real terms. It is therefore not surprising that the 1970s saw an upward divergence from trend. Apart from this period, however, the pattern is one of a cycle with an underlying upward trend.

than more equal, that only absolute income matters, not relative. But with positional goods that logic cannot hold: what matters is one's income relative to others, not one's absolute income. That is true of all positional goods – fine wines, works of art, antiques – but in most cases the importance of this fact to public policy is slight. But housing matters because it is one of consumers' largest expenditure items and most people's largest store of wealth. The issues of inequality, made more pressing by positional goods, are addressed in Chapter 8.

Transport, like housing, is a high income-elasticity good. As people get richer they want to buy more road and air travel to a greater extent than more television sets – the rising share of consumer expenditure devoted to transport services (up from 5.5 per cent in 1970 to 7.5 per cent today) is the result.[17] And if anything the trend seems to be accelerating. The British government estimates that rail travel will increase by 50 per cent in the next ten years, road traffic by 22 per cent. This rising expenditure creates conflict. For transport, like housing, is an example of a good or service which, in a densely populated country, is highly contested. Demand for personal mobility increases with income, but the more we travel the more congested are the roads and railways. Increased capacity, however, imposes environmental damage without solving the congestion problem, since the moment traffic moves more freely, people and goods make more journeys. The highly contested nature of transportation thus prevents the translation of increased income into increased consumer contentment. We are getting richer, so we want to travel more, but we hate the congestion and some of us at least hate the countryside destruction and noise and air pollution that new roads in particular produce. A resolution of that conundrum is one of the most difficult problems facing governments in crowded countries today. It involves trade-offs and requires political leadership.

---

17. Until 1990 the increase was entirely in motor vehicle running costs, but more recently it is due to rapidly growing public transport use. The motor vehicle running costs included in these figures cover repairs, driving lessons, membership fees, etc., but not motor vehicle fuel costs, which now account for 2.7 per cent of consumer expenditure, similar to 1970 (2.8 per cent). In addition purchase of cars (not included in these figures either) is one of the few physical goods categories which has risen not fallen as a percentage of GDP. In total, transport services, car purchase and fuel costs together have risen from 11.8 per cent to 15.1 per cent of total expenditure.

Finally, at the global level, for all the talk of a weightless economy, physical constraints remain important. Chapter 1 argued that in general nations are not in competition for prosperity. But among the special cases noted was one created by scarce physical resources. Nations can use as much software, consume as much entertainment, and analyse as much information as they want, without that impinging on other nations' freedom to use and consume as much as they also desire: information technology is an almost entirely 'uncontested' good. But in many parts of the world fresh water is an inherently scarce resource, vital to prosperity and a source of potential conflict. And the atmosphere can almost certainly absorb only a finite further quantity of CO_2 without major and harmful climate change. The right to emit CO_2 will need to be recognized as a finite and contested good, and the world will not be able to avoid debates about the distribution of that good and the resulting trade-offs between prosperity and its environmental impact.

Chapter 9 addresses the conflicts created by contested goods and the trade-offs required, both nationally and internationally.

* * *

The need to make trade-offs is indeed a common feature of all the challenges set out in this chapter. Some of them, such as those of labour-market regulation, affect the key indicators of economic performance – productivity and employment creation. Others, those raised by inequality and regulation more generally, relate more to matters of choice – how we divide and spend the cake, rather than how to maximize it. All of them, however, involve society in making choices. Those choices are not constrained, or determined for us, by considerations of external competitiveness. Indeed, external competitiveness has not featured at all in this chapter as a key challenge posed by the new economy, deliberately since it is largely a red herring. We are mainly masters of our own destiny. But we still have difficult choices to make.

Those choices essentially concern which variant of capitalism we wish to pursue. The relative success of different capitalist models in the face of the changing shape of the economy is the subject of the next four chapters.

PART TWO

Europe, the US and the UK: Whose Capitalism is Best?

4. What Are We Trying to Maximize?

The following are all fair statements drawing on respectable data sources.

» The US is richer than Europe and has grown more rapidly over the last five years. The OECD's measure of prosperity ('purchasing power parity income per capita') puts the US 28 per cent above Germany and 35 per cent above France in 1996. The US economy has grown 16 per cent since 1996, the European only 11 per cent. Over a longer period too, the US economy has grown faster, achieving 2.8 per cent growth per annum from 1980 to 1998 versus the European Union's 2.2 per cent. The US created 32 million new jobs between 1980–98, the European Union just 3 million. Its unemployment rate in autumn 2000 was 4 per cent versus the EU's 8.4 per cent. America has weaker trade unions, fewer restrictions on management's right to hire and fire and lower minimum wages. It also has much lower taxes and government spending (government revenues as a percentage of GDP are 31 per cent versus the European average of 45 per cent).

» French and German productivity per hour worked were both higher than the US in 1996. The French level was then 9 per cent above the US and the German level 7 per cent. Over the last nineteen years (1980–99) the European Union has grown prosperity (i.e. per capita income) at almost exactly the same pace as the US (1.9 per cent in both cases) but its output per hour worked and thus sustainable real wages per hour have grown much more rapidly. The growth in US productivity per hour was very poor from the mid-1970s to the mid-1990s and the US only achieved growth in per capita income equal to the EU because of significant increases in total hours worked. Per hour worked Europeans have got richer faster than Americans over the last twenty years. As a result of America's poor productivity performance, average real wage growth in the US over the years 1975–95 was less than

1 per cent per annum, and real wages for those in the bottom tenth of the income distribution actually fell. The vast majority of all the fruits of the US's only modest economic performance over those twenty years accrued to the top third of the income distribution.

» The best country in the world to do business, according to the Economist Intelligence Unit, is the Netherlands. Its macroeconomic indicators also demonstrate excellent performance. Its per capita income in 1999 was (according to the OECD) 11 per cent above the UK's. Its per capita growth rate from 1990 to 1999 has exceeded that of both the US and the UK (Netherlands 2.1 per cent, US 1.8 per cent, UK 1.7 per cent). Its unemployment rate is 2.9 per cent, well below the US's 4 per cent. It has labour productivity about 20 per cent higher than Britain, a large balance of payments surplus, and now has a balanced budget. Its tax burden is in line with the European average and well above UK let alone US levels (government revenues 44 per cent of GDP versus 40 per cent for the UK and 31 per cent for the US), and it has a top marginal income-tax rate of over 50 per cent.[1] It has strong trade unions which play a major 'social partnership' role in the economy: and it has labour-market rules (for instance on employment security and employee consultation) that go beyond any required by the European Social Chapter.

The facts of economic performance could thus be used to support very different conclusions on optimal policy. In part, as we shall see in Chapter 5, that is because there is no single necessary route to economic success, and because different models of capitalism are relatively better at delivering different aspects of economic success. But in part the diversity simply reflects the game of 'pick the measure which proves your point'. Choice of precise time period can make a big difference to apparent rankings of economic performance; the choice of what to measure can make a bigger difference still. For while it is often assumed that economic statistics are definitive facts and that we know the objectives of economic performance – that we know what we are trying to maximize – neither assumption is correct. Economic measures are

---

1. Until 2000 the top tax rate was 60 per cent. Subject to final parliamentary approval it is planned to fall to 52 per cent in 2001.

bedevilled with pragmatic measurement difficulties. But more fundamentally, different economic measures reflect different underlying objectives. Ask which capitalism is better and you can get different answers according to whether your objective is maximizing employment or minimizing unemployment, increasing GDP in total or GDP per capita, and still more different answers if you introduce 'non-economic' concepts like quality of the environment or income distribution. Before assessing the performance of different capitalisms we need to be clear about what the objectives are and how we measure them.

This chapter aims to do that. To do it effectively it cannot avoid introducing some rather technical concepts such as labour, capital and total productivity, and some numerical or graphical illustrations of them. The danger is that the general reader will find that unappealing. Economists' jargon and geometry is not deeply loved by the 'real world'. But the alternative danger is that economists' terms – such as 'total factor productivity' – are used in political debate but neither defined nor understood, used for polemic effect not clarification. The danger too, if we don't explore the subtleties of the measures, is that we assume that there is 'one true measure' of success, when in fact there are important trade-offs which society can make between success on one indicator or another, choices which economists should help clarify but which should not be denied by suggesting that only one measure matters.

Without conceptual clarity we cannot have sensible political discourse on economic matters. Hence this chapter. It deals first with the problems of defining narrowly 'economic' objectives before addressing the still more complex issue of whether those objectives need to be balanced against 'non-economic' ones such as environmental quality or social inclusion. It concludes by drawing out the implications for how we should use economic statistics in public policy debate.

Prosperity and growth: absolute or per capita?

Prosperity and the growth of prosperity would seem to be the most fundamental measures of economic success. The basic proposition of the ultra-liberals is that the US is a better economy than Europe's because it is growing faster, creating more prosperity and more jobs. Growth is good for individuals because they get richer and have more lifestyle choices. Growth is good for governments because even quite

Table 4.1 US and EU growth compared

Growth per annum

	1980–95	1995–99	1980–99
US	2.6	3.8	2.9
EU15	2.1	2.4	2.2

Per capita growth per annum

	1980–95	1995–99	1980–99
US	1.6	2.9	1.9
EU15	1.8	2.1	1.9

Source: OECD *Historical Statistics*, OECD *Economic Outlook*.

small differences in growth rates produce big improvements in government finance. Growth rate and prosperity claims – 'Britain is growing faster than/slower than its major competitors', 'France overtakes Britain', 'Britain overtakes France' (choose according to whether you are for or against the government in power) – are the standard fare of newspaper headlines and politician's speeches, particularly at election time.

But the best measure of economic growth is not agreed. One fundamental choice is whether to talk about absolute growth rates or growth rates per capita. Some commentators typically use the former, others the latter – the answer you get about the relative success of different capitalisms varies a lot depending which you choose (see Table 4.1). Choose absolute growth, the growth in the overall size of the economy, and the US clearly outperforms Europe, not just in the last four years but over fifteen or twenty years. Choose per capita growth as a measure and performance is very similar, so similar that careful choice of time period can decide the argument either way: start in 1981 rather than 1982 to prove a pro-European point, stress the last four years rather than the previous twenty to claim American superiority.

The explanation for these different absolute and per capita results is simple. The US population is continuing to grow at 0.9 per cent per annum, the European grows at only 0.3 per cent. The US therefore needs to be 0.6 per cent ahead in absolute growth to be delivering the same per capita prosperity growth.

The choice between the two measures is not determined by the rules of economics, but is instead a matter of social choice. Absolute growth matters if you are concerned with national prestige for its own sake, or for the long-term geopolitical and military consequences of economic strength. The bigger your economy in absolute terms the more powerful you are in world economic deliberations and, for the same proportionate burden, the more powerful militarily. Per capita growth, however, is clearly the measure of the growth of individual prosperity, and a purely individualist rather than nationalist approach to objectives must pick the per capita measure. The choice is simple: faced with two possibilities – population up 50 per cent with per capita income up 50 per cent and thus GDP up 125 per cent, versus population static with per capita income up 70 per cent and GDP up 70 per cent – which do you think is the better result? I think the latter, both because my approach is individualist rather than nationalist, and because I believe further significant population growth has harmful environmental consequences which are better avoided. The rest of this book will therefore treat per capita growth as a clearly superior measure to absolute growth. But that follows from a personal judgement on a matter of social choice, it is not a given of economics.

Labour productivity and employment

Per capita income and its growth are closely linked to labour productivity and its growth, indeed essentially they are two sides of the same coin – countries are rich because the workers are highly productive. Measurements of labour productivity are therefore key figures in any assessment of different economies, but figures which need to be treated with care. Simplistic use of labour-productivity figures to prove the superiority of one system can be dangerous because it fails to consider employment effects; simplistic adjustments to take account of employment creation can also be equally misleading.

Straightforward measures of labour productivity per hour worked are favoured by supporters of the European model because leading European countries look better on this measure. On average indeed in 1996 French and German workers were probably slightly more productive than American. But the US looks better on the basis of income per capita for two reasons – a higher percentage of its workforce is employed and they work longer hours: as a result hours worked per head of population are 30–40 per cent higher in the US (see Table 4.2).[2] Believers in the superiority of the US model therefore make two criticisms of European performance. First they point out, quite correctly, that French and German average productivity performance is flattered by the fact that France and Germany have excluded from employment the less highly skilled and less productive workers. The US's slightly lower average may therefore conceal 90 per cent of its workers working just as productively or even more productively than French or German workers: the US figure is brought down by the fact that it employs the 'last 5 per cent' of low-skilled people (people simply unemployed in France and Germany), reducing average observed productivity, but increasing total income (see Table 4.3). Like-for-like, the US may still therefore have equal or higher labour productivity than France or Germany. This point is clearly valid.

Second, and more simply, critics of the European system stress that employment creation is in itself a good thing and therefore cite the US's

---

2. The figures for hours worked per person employed are taken from O'Mahony, *Britain's Productivity Performance 1950–96*. This is used as a source for the productivity comparisons in this chapter and Chapter 5 since it gives an integrated and internally consistent picture. It should be noted, however, that other estimates of hours worked per person employed put the American level even further ahead: OECD estimates in *Employment Outlook* 2000 show US hours worked per person employed 27 per cent higher than German, and 22 per cent higher than French, with the divergence growing as US working hours continue to increase. These figures would in turn suggest that the US lead in hours worked per head of population is higher than O'Mahony's 30–40 per cent. O'Mahony's figures for GDP per capita also understate the US advantage slightly relative to OECD figures. In terms of labour-productivity calculations, however, these differences are offsetting.

These different figures illustrate the general point that all the measures used – but particularly measures of GDP on a 'purchasing power parity' basis and thus all measures of labour productivity – should be assumed to the correct only within fairly broad margins of error – say +/–10 per cent. All the different sources, however, suggest the same *pattern* as that presented in this chapter and Chapter 5 – similar levels of labour productivity between the US, France and Germany, but the US working far more hours per capita, France and Germany more capital intensive but achieving lower capital productivity.

Table 4.2 Productivity, hours worked and income per capita

	Employment as % working-age (15–64) population (1998)	Average annual hours worked per person employed (1996)
US	73.8	1706
Germany	64.1	1558
France	59.4	1529
UK	71.2	1597

Indexed to UK = 100 (1996)

	Hours worked per capita*	×	GDP per hour worked	=	GDP per capita
US	113		121		137
Germany	88		129		113
France	80		132		105
UK	100		100		100

* This index is a measure of total hours worked per head of population and therefore reflects three factors – employment as a % of working population, working population as a % of total population, and hours worked per person employed.

Source: OECD *Employment Outlook* for % employed, O'Mahony (NIESR, 1999) for all other figures.

higher hours worked per capita as proof of a superior economy. In 1998 74 per cent of working-age Americans were employed versus only 64 per cent in Germany and 59 per cent in France. The extra income created, it is argued, is doubly good – both because it creates more income and because employment is in itself desirable. This argument is, however, good in parts but in parts only.

The good part is that a low level of *involuntary* unemployment is undoubtedly a 'good thing'. If there are people who want to be employed and can't find jobs, then the economy is both forgoing the

Table 4.3 The impact of employing 'the last 5%': illustration

	High-employment country	Low-employment country
Employment as % of working-age population	95%	90%
Production per employee of 90% highest-skilled workers	100 units per annum	100 units per annum
Production per employee of 5% low-skilled workers	50 units per annum	Not employed
Measured productivity overall	97.4 units per annum	100 units per annum
Output per member of workforce (i.e. prosperity)	92.5 per annum	90 units per annum

The high-employment country has lower measured productivity, but on a like-for-like basis it is just as productive and it is more prosperous because it employs (even though at a lower rate of productivity) 5% of workers not employed at all in the low-employment country.

benefit of extra potential income and condemning people to an enforced and low-income idleness they don't want. And on the basis of standard measures of unemployment, imperfect but still the best we've got, the US clearly does better than France or Germany – 4 per cent in mid-2000 versus about 9.5 per cent in both the major continental economies. Eliminating that unemployment gap should be a key aim of public policy: it would increase European GDP per capita and give the unemployed the dignity of work and the social inclusion which goes with that. We want labour to be as productive as possible, which on the whole means maximizing output per units of input, but unlike with all other factors of production (such as energy, land or capital) we are not solely interested in the output but also, up to a point, with the employment of the input (i.e. people) as an end per se.

In economists' terms labour is a peculiar input because we have some interest in increasing rather than decreasing the level of input. Involuntary unemployment is a bad thing and finding jobs for the involuntarily unemployed is a good thing even if the productivity of employing marginal workers is quite low.

What that does not mean, however, is that maximum employment or even more bizarrely, maximum hours worked should be an aim of economic policy. Individuals and societies make trade-offs between income and leisure. They can choose to take the benefits of rising productivity either in extra income, or in fewer hours worked, and it should be no aim of liberal economics (as against nationalist or statist economics) to tell them what that trade-off should be. The trade-off should simply arise from the free flow of multiple individual choices. If Europe had the same level of involuntary unemployment as the US, and in addition had higher labour productivity, that would be a superior economic performance even if European GDP per capita was lower because of a low level of workforce participation. To the liberal economist interested in maximizing individual choices rather than maximizing national economic strength, labour productivity per hour worked of 110 and hours worked of 80 is superior to labour productivity of 100 and hours worked of 100 even though the latter gives higher GDP per capita (provided only that involuntary unemployment is no higher in the former case). And that is true whether the lower hours worked arise from earlier retirement, from lower female participation rates, or shorter hours worked on average per week. What matters is simply that the hours worked match what people individually choose. If French people are on average less prosperous in per capita income terms than Americans simply because they choose to work less hours, that is not a sign of economic failure but simply a different lifestyle choice, and economists should seek to elucidate the trade-offs of social choice not to deny their validity. Labour is a special case economic input because we are concerned not just with its output, but with the specific problem of involuntarily unemployment. But that does not mean we should turn normal economics (and plain common sense) on its head and make the maximization of an input (i.e. a maximum number of hours worked) an overt policy objective. Much ultra-liberal criticism of European performance implicitly does just that. Citing America's 74 per cent employment rate versus Europe's 61 per cent as proof of a superior economic performance is just plain wrong.

This still, however, leaves employment as well as unemployment rates as a useful *indicator* (rather than objective) of economic perform-ance. What actually matters is involuntary unemployment, but a low level of employment may be a warning signal that standard measures of unemployment are underestimates, that, for instance, over fifty-year-olds have left the active labour market because they think the chances of finding work are too low to bother, or that there are women who would like to participate in the labour market but who find subtle barriers to employment (e.g. rigidities of required hours of work) which make it impossible for them to find suitable jobs or even to register as unemployed. And differences in employment rates by sector (such as those presented in Figure 1.1) can help provide indicators as to the likely solution to unemployment. The fact that the US, along with Denmark and Sweden, the Netherlands and the UK, has a higher employment rate than France, Spain and Ireland, should be a stimulus to analysis. But the definition of a successful prosperous economy at any one time is clear – maximum labour productivity per hours worked combined with a low level of involuntary unemployment.

Capital productivity, investment and growth

The qualification 'at any one time' is, however, a crucial one. In any given year a country is more prosperous relative to effort expended the higher its labour productivity. In that year therefore labour productivity is *the* measure of prosperity relative to effort, and anything that happened in previous years is irrelevant to the measurement of present prosperity. But if we turn from a measurement of this year's prosperity relative to effort, to consider the effort expended in past years, another factor has to enter the equation – capital productivity.

Capital accumulation is vital to economic growth. The key reason why we are richer than two centuries ago is that we have accumulated machines that do things for us. Those machines of course carry within them the benefit of accumulated know-how. If we had simply accumu-lated more of the capital equipment available a hundred years ago, and not progressed in know-how, we wouldn't have become richer to anything like the same extent. Equally, however, if we had simply progressed know-how but not encapsulated it in accumulated machines that do things for us, we would not have made much prosperity progress at all. Knowledge of how to produce electricity would have

*Table 4.4 Capital intensity, capital productivity and labour productivity,
indexed to UK = 100 (1996)*

	Capital intensity (capital employed per hour worked)	× Capital productivity (output per unit of capital employed)	= Labour productivity (output per hour worked)
US	128	94	121
Germany	172	75	129
France	149	88	132
UK	100	100	100

Source: O'Mahony (NIESR, 1999).

made no difference to productivity if we had not built power stations and electrically driven factories, i.e. if we had not invested, devoting resources in past years not to that year's consumption but to accumulating productive capital for future use. Our accounting measurements of this investment are often imperfect. In fundamental economic terms a computer and its software is as much investment as any other machine (together they form a machine which automates away interactive activities), but because of some arbitrary accounting conventions they are not always counted as such either by private companies or by national income accounts. The measurement problems aside, however, the fundamental primacy of investment to economic growth remains. We get richer by investing in 'machines' (widely understood) to do things for us and, if other factors are equal, the more we invest the more rapidly we grow labour productivity.

France and Germany had higher labour productivity per hour in 1996 than the US (and much higher productivity than the UK) because they have much more capital employed per hour worked (see Table 4.4). That reflects higher investment rates in the 1950s to 1980s than seen in either the US or UK. But compared with the US, France and Germany get lower output per unit of capital, as Table 4.4 also shows. On this basis supporters of the American model claim that the European model is less efficient, and that France and Germany's labour productivity advantage is in some sense 'artificial'. As with their points relating to labour productivity and employment, the argument is good in parts, but also easily overstated. For if capital productivity is an important indicator of performance, it is certainly not an objective to be maximized.

What is almost certainly true is that France and Germany's lower capital productivity is a sign of poor capital utilization. American companies typically use their capital stock more intensely, for instance with more night-time and weekend working. For this and a number of other subtle reasons they seem to get more output from any given combination of capital and labour, i.e. to be in some absolute sense more efficient. To the extent that this is so, France and Germany have bought their present prosperity at an unnecessarily high past cost and are now sitting on an opportunity to raise prosperity even without investment. Low capital productivity in no way diminishes labour productivity as a measure of success relative to effort in this year, but it does say that the same labour productivity could be achieved with less previous investment, i.e. less sacrifice of previous years' consumption. Capital productivity is thus a very useful measure of efficiency, past and present, even if not a relevant measure of present prosperity.

But that does not mean that maximizing capital productivity is necessarily a good thing. For another cause of France and Germany's lower capital productivity could be simply that they have set lower hurdle rates for investment, and that they have thus chosen to invest more. Just as in Table 4.3 a higher level of employment tends to be associated, if all other factors are equal, with lower average labour productivity as the least skilled workers are pulled into employment, so in Figure 4.1 a higher level of investment tends to be accompanied with a lower return on investment as lower-return projects are adopted in addition to higher-return ones. And just as ultra-liberals can argue that France and Germany have 'artificially' inflated average labour productivity by labour-market interventions which prevent the employment of lower-productivity workers, it is equally possible for supporters of the European model to argue that the US has 'artificially' inflated its capital productivity by setting unreasonably high hurdle rates which prevent the adoption of somewhat lower but still positive-return projects, and which thus cut growth and future national income. This is indeed precisely the argument which the devotees of the Rhineland/stakeholder model make. To Will Hutton or Michel Albert it is obvious that the superiority of the European model resides in financial structures which

Figure 4.1 Capital intensity, capital productivity and hurdle rates

High hurdle rate country

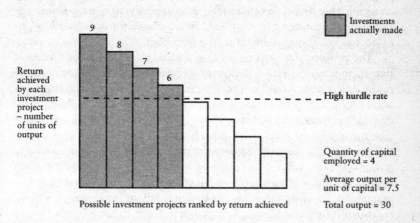

Low hurdle rate country

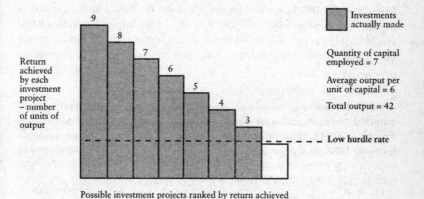

Note: This highly simplistic representation assumes that each project requires the same quantity of capital, and that capital produces outputs without other inputs. It also ignores the complexities of the fact that output is produced from a capital *stock* which is the accumulation of all past flows. The fundamental choice involved in selecting a low or high hurdle can nevertheless be captured by this simplistic representation.

stimulate a longer-term, more investment-oriented culture, while the US is stuck with short-termism and low investment. Far from high US capital productivity being an effective argument against the 'stakeholderist' argument, it is precisely what the stakeholderists expect to see resulting from the short-termism and high hurdle rates for which they condemn the Anglo-Saxon model. Theoretically it is as possible for capital productivity to be 'too high' because investment is 'too low', as to be 'too low' because investment is 'too high'.

The problem for anyone seeking a nice easy measure of success is that there is no definitive answer to this debate, there is no necessarily optimal or 'correct' level of investment. Economic theory and empirical observation can provide some insights and help identify clearly sub-optimal performance, but they don't do more than that. They tell us that the quality of investment matters as well as the quantity – if only the quantity mattered the communist states would have been economic paradises. They tell us that increasing investment levels will tend to depress marginal return, and that neither maximizing investment nor maximizing growth rates nor maximizing labour productivity should be ends in themselves, since few people's desire to save for the future or love of future generations is so great that they would like to go on saving and investing to the point where all positive-return projects have been selected. But economic theory and empirical analysis do not provide a definitive answer to the question of how much investment is optimal, nor do they tell us that only one level of investment is possible.[3] They still therefore leave an important set of public policy issues relating to an economy's total investment level. And they leave

---

3. One attempted way round this problem, popular among ultra-liberals, is to claim that a globalized capital market makes only one cost of capital possible and that, say, German businesses are *bound* in future to seek returns on investment in Germany equal to those available elsewhere (i.e. that hurdle rates are bound to converge). As a description of a convergence tendency likely to occur among larger quoted companies this is probably right, but it in no way resolves the theoretical question of whether previous more nationally specific savings/investment markets produced an overall more desirable result (as the stakeholderists would claim). Nor does it deny the possibility that there could continue to exist German private companies who for cultural reasons are motivated by growth ambitions rather than return to a greater extent than British private companies, and that this could continue to produce over time a higher rate of investment and thus a higher level of labour productivity.

us noting Europe's low capital productivity as a sign of an untapped opportunity for improved efficiency, but not as a denial of the fact that on labour productivity (prosperity per effort expended) some European countries do as well as the US.

Total factor productivity: the one true measure?

People don't like being told by economists that the assessment of economic performance is complex and a matter of trade-offs. They hanker for the one true measure. 'Total factor productivity' sounds like it is that measure. After all, it has 'total' among its three words. So if total factor productivity produces answers which confirm one's own ideological predilections, there is a great temptation to parade it as the answer, the ultimate measure of success. Numerous articles and speeches do precisely that, commenting first on labour-productivity comparisons before bringing out 'TFP' with a flourish, the 'true' measure of productivity. Unfortunately it is no such thing. For total factor productivity, far from allowing us to escape the conceptual difficulties of labour productivity or capital productivity, suffers from both simultaneously.

This is hardly surprising since total factor productivity is simply a weighted average of labour and capital productivity. It is a useful way of summing up in an average fashion the efficiency with which both capital and labour are used, and changes in its level over time are interesting to economic historians because they tell us how much of economic growth is unexplained by simple accumulation of capital or labour and how much must therefore be ascribed to know-how (the 'residual', as it is called).[4] But it is as imperfect as labour productivity

---

4. Differences in TFP can in turn be explained by differences in the skill level of labour or in the quality of capital. Some measures of the residual (i.e. the growth rate of TFP) therefore adjust the measure of capital and labour by incorporating estimates of their 'quality'. If this quality is rising, this adjustment must automatically reduce the measured increase in TFP; if quality is higher in Country A than Country B, then A's TFP advantage over B will be reduced. The methodological problems of measuring quality are, however, severe for both labour and capital and the resulting increase (or difference) in TFP has no specific inherent reason. It is simply a residual, i.e. a measure of what we cannot explain: for if we could adjust *perfectly* for both labour and capital quality differences (including the 'skill'

or capital productivity in dealing with the issues of the optimal level of employment or investment. Average labour productivity can be increased 'artificially' by not employing less skilled employees – the Anglo-Saxon challenge to France and Germany's high labour productivity. Average capital productivity can be increased 'artificially' by only selecting high-return projects, increasing return on capital but at the expense of the investment level and growth – the stakeholderist challenge to the Anglo-Saxon model. Total factor productivity, since it is simply the weighted average of the other two, can be increased 'artificially' by either of these two routes. A country which only employed the highest skilled employees on a small number of very high-return projects would have very high total factor productivity and labour productivity and capital productivity, but it would be poorer than a country which invested more and employed more even though at lower average capital, labour and total productivity rates.

Maximizing TFP should therefore be no more a necessary objective of policy than maximizing capital productivity or labour productivity without reference to involuntary unemployment. And TFP comparisons between countries should not be paraded as 'the answer' which brings all discussion to a close. Instead, and frustrating though it seems, assessment of even the purely 'economic' aspects of a society's success needs to involve looking carefully at a number of different measures:

» Labour productivity per hour worked is the best measure of present prosperity relative to effort, provided that involuntary unemployment is as low as in comparable countries.

» Minimizing involuntary unemployment is a very important aim of public policy: analysing employment rates can help identify causes and possible solutions to involuntary unemployment, but maximizing employment is not an objective.

---

or 'know-how' of management and the technique encapsulated in capital equipment) the rate of TFP increase (or differences between country TFPs) would become by definition nil. The simplest way to measure TFP is therefore arguably the best, i.e. it is the output achieved for weighted *quantitative* inputs of labour and capital, with no quality adjustment to the input figures, but with differences in quality (in particular of labour skill) among the factors to be considered when we try to explain differences in TFP. The TFP figures quoted in Chapter 5 are calculated on this non-quality-adjusted basis.

» Capital productivity is an important indicator of the efficient use of capital assets, and can be used to suggest problems, either of too much or too little investment, but maximizing capital productivity is not an objective.

» Total factor productivity is the nearest measure we have to absolute efficiency, and movements in TFP over time are close proxies for changes in absolute efficiency, but maximizing TFP is not the objective, and a higher TFP level is not always necessarily better.

Frustrating certainly for anyone wanting nice easy answers. But in analysing the relative success of different modes of capitalism nice easy answers are usually facile in both senses of the word.

That would be true even if the key measure of economic prosperity – national income per capita – was a definitive and clearly credible measure of average levels of individual welfare. In fact, however, that assumption too is wrong. National income calculations are the least worst measures we possess of aggregate prosperity, but their profound imperfections and limitations need to be understood and the use of them needs to reflect those limitations.

Some types of national income are more equal than others

National income accounting abhors value judgements. The statisticians who compute our calculations of GDP or GDP per capita do not make judgements about the value of different types of output, they follow simple conventions. The output of the private sector is valued at the price people pay for it: if a McDonald's hamburger sells for $2 that's what it's worth. And the value of public-sector output is valued at the cost to the government: if Britain's defence forces cost £20 billion that's what they are worth. To the national income statistician all types of national income are equally valuable.

These conventions exist because they are the only pragmatic way of proceeding: if we didn't do the calculations this way there would be endless arguments about how valuable different elements of the economy truly are. Nobody who has thought about it, however, can believe that the results give a definitive measure of 'welfare'. The US spends 1.6 per cent of its national income on police, criminal courts and prisons, up from 1.1 per cent in the mid-1980s as the prison population has soared. That spend and the matching output counts as 'prosperity' in national income accounts quite as much as healthcare, or restaurant meals, or home furnishings, or electrical goods or theatre visits. But nobody (just about) would deny that the US would be a better and in some ultimate sense more prosperous place if by some success of economic and social policy it could reduce prison spending and redirect resources to goods and services that people intrinsically desire. Americans would be more prosperous but GDP per capita would be unchanged.

The problem is most obvious when goods and services are provided or purchased collectively, when the state employs people to provide services or when the state purchases services. In these cases we often lack even the external check of a market price as at least an imperfect proxy for value: and in these cases there is a danger that politicians are buying goods and services different from those which consumers truly want. For this reason economic commentators on the right are tempted to discount state sector economic activities, and in some cases with quite specific polemic intent. The recent success of the French economy, for instance, which appears to contradict some of the certainties of the ultra-liberal consensus (France hasn't deregulated or cut taxes enough to *deserve* to succeed), has generated a spate of attempts to explain away apparent French performance, above all by claiming that France's relatively large state production and consumption should not be counted on the 'all types of activity are equal' principle. French citizens, it is plausibly argued, don't necessarily value the large and in some cases inefficient bureaucracy which the French state employs. French technocrats may also have decided to buy more TGV lines and trains than French citizens truly desire. Both the bureaucrats and the TGVs enter national income accounts at the full cost incurred but, claim the ultra-liberals, should not count as equal to the same money spent by individual consumers in the marketplace.

This attempt to discount state purchases and provision is, however, wrong because it is biased. Biased in the sense that it assumes that collective goods and services are always over-provided relative to 'true' consumer preferences, when in fact it is possible for collective-goods provision to be 'too low' relative to consumer preference as easily as 'too high'. The French state may have provided more TGV and other collective or subsidized goods than French consumer preference truly desires (though there is no actual proof of this). But equally the British state may have provided less of some inherently collective goods than consumers want. In my own personal case and, in some very specific areas, that is the case. Even as a purely selfish form of consumer preference (and not out of any altruistic love of my fellow citizens) I would like us to spend more money on subsidized public transport in London to make it a more pleasant, less polluted city, more money on traffic calming measures to make our villages and towns safer and quieter, and more money on noise abatement baffles and tree screens to make our motorways less intrusive in the surrounding countryside. As a purely selfish consumer preference I want all those more than a bigger or more stylish car. I would rather pay more tax to get those benefits than have the extra, personal income available to buy more market goods, and I can only buy these consumer benefits through the tax and government expenditure route since they are inherently collective. If lots of other consumers are like me then Britain is *under*producing this category of public goods relative to consumer preference and it is the final slice of private expenditure which should be discounted in measures of 'true' prosperity, since it has been swollen artificially by people spending privately money they would rather have spent through taxes on collective goods. How many other such fellow consumers/citizens there are I don't know. One of the key roles of politics is to search out through debate and voting the balance of people's preferences for individual versus collective goods. But that debate should not progress on the biased assumption that state provision is always over-provision. It should recognize that present levels of state provision might also be lower than consumers desire. Opinion poll results in which people say they would prefer higher taxes and higher health expenditure at the very least illustrate that possibility.[5]

More generally, moreover, it needs to be recognized that the problem of uncertain inherent value is not a specific public-sector problem, but a general one which can apply to private-sector goods and services

---

5. It might have seemed more obvious in this paragraph to use health spend rather than environmental improvement as the primary example: it is certainly possible that in Britain healthcare has been underfunded by the state relative to customer demand. Healthcare, however, is not an inherently collective good in the same way as environmental quality of public space. It is possible to match increasing demand with greater private provision. The issues this raises are considered briefly in Chapter 8. A purer example of an inherently collective good has therefore been used here.

as well. The fact that the consumption and output category 'prison services' is less inherently desirable than many others is not changed one iota by outsourcing the operation of prisons to private prison companies. And if a society had a choice between resolving all marital disputes amicably (through reconciliation or mutually agreed divorce) versus spending a small fortune on divorce lawyers, and if those divorce lawyer resources could be redeployed to produce inherently desirable goods and services, society would undoubtedly choose the former option and would consider itself more prosperous, even though it would not have higher measured GDP and even though the provision of civil legal services is a primarily private-sector affair.

Overall the conclusion is simple. Measures of national prosperity using the assumption of 'all activities equal' are highly imperfect, particularly when used to compare countries rather than to look at one country over time. There are no simple and agreed adjustments which make the figures 'right'. They are the best we've got and very useful for what they are, but we should not assume they tell us everything we need to know about the economic and social success of our societies. Especially once we bring into the equation three other considerations – the household economy, the environment and income distribution.

The household economy, the environment and income distribution

In his March 1998 budget, Gordon Brown, British Chancellor of the Exchequer, introduced a working family tax credit. Rather than subsidizing people to be unemployed, it aims to subsidize people in relatively low-paid employment. For reasons explored in Chapter 6's discussion of labour-market issues, it is a policy with much merit. But one rather odd side-effect of it, demonstrated in an article by Martin Wolf, the *Financial Times*'s economics correspondent, was that it provided a large incentive for two women, each previously caring for their own child, to go out to work to care for the other's child, using their income to pay for their own childcare. Both children would be looked after, but by the other's mother.[6] The mothers would do the same work as before,

6. Martin Wolf, 'The Mummy State', *Financial Times*, 31 March 1998.

but unemployment would fall, employment would rise, and so too would measured national income. Britain would become, in national income account terms, more prosperous simply because the children had swapped mothers for part of the day.

The article's purpose was to question whether subsidizing mothers to work and then pay for childcare was a sensible policy, compared with, for instance, subsidizing them to look after their own children. But it also illustrated the more general problem that measures of national income are imperfect because they don't allow for 'household' activity. Most students of economics are taught the paradox that marrying your housekeeper reduces measured GDP even if she (or he) then does the same housework as before. Conversely, higher female participation in an economy will increase measured GDP, but part of the increase is offset by lower household value added, more restaurant meals afforded but less home cooking.[7] Longer hours worked per worker similarly increase GDP but if you then have to employ someone to decorate your house rather than do it yourself, real prosperity may not rise proportionately. On a year-to-year basis, for any one country, the resulting imperfections of economic growth measurement are small, but over the long term and when comparing nations with very different employment rates the distinctions can be significant. It is another argument for strongly preferring per hour worked rather than per capita measures of productivity and welfare, and another reason for rejecting maximum employment rates (as against minimized rates of involuntary unemployment) as an objective of economic policy. If French workers get the same income per hour worked as Americans, but work less hours, they may be indifferent to lower measured income either because they enjoy more leisure or because they value household output (and in some cases because of both simultaneously – many people positively enjoy home cooking, DIY and gardening and count them as leisure as well as a means of saving money). Conversely, if part of the US per capita income increase over the last twenty years has come from people working longer hours, it is not surprising that many Americans seem to discount this element of economic success when asked whether they feel better off.

The household activity problem is one of unmeasured benefits. The

---

7. Specifying female sounds sexist, but since more household work is in fact done by women, it's the reality of what actually occurs.

environmental issue concerns both unmeasured benefits and unmeasured costs when those benefits are destroyed. Chapter 9 explores those issues and the implications for policy in more detail, but the essence of the problem is clear. People clearly value peace and quiet, beautiful countryside, and clean air; the fact that house prices or hotel room prices are strongly linked to such amenities would illustrate the point even to an economic rationalist unwilling to accept it as a given. But we don't count negative environmental impact as a negative in national income, and we don't even count the more measurable fall in affected house prices as a cost of, for instance, building a new road even though it clearly is just that. Equally, when new factory processes produce cleaner air or water (either when required by regulation or as a free by-product of technological change) we don't count that benefit. Since people care more about environmental improvement the richer they get (one of the hierarchy of need effects discussed in Chapter 3), our failure to account for environmental benefits and costs becomes more problematic through time.

Finally, and most controversially, there is the issue of income distribution. Most controversially because whereas almost all economists would agree that the other measurement problems cited above are problems (though they might disagree on the severity), there is a straightforward disagreement about whether income distribution matters, about whether the division of the cake matters as well as the size of the cake. Right-wing ultra-liberals argue against any focus on distributional effects both on a fundamental philosophical basis and on the grounds that individuals actually care only about their absolute income, not their relative position. Supporters of the European social model argue for its inclusion on both moral and selfish grounds: we don't want people in a society to be so much worse off than the average as to be 'excluded', and if they are, they will likely act in antisocial criminal ways which carry costs for the rest of society. That issue and its implications for the role of the state are picked up in Chapter 8. Suffice it for now to note that one's point of view has implications for an assessment of the relative success of different modes of capitalism. The last twenty years have seen a trend to greater inequality in almost all mature market economies: but most dramatically in those where the agenda of freeing market forces and reducing the size of state has been most aggressively pursued, and above all in the US. If distributional concerns are allowed to enter the equation, our relative assessment of Anglo-Saxon versus European models of capitalism will shift.[8]

Some implications amid the confusion

The story told above is one of increasing confusion. We started with what looked like concrete measures that meant something – GDP per capita and per hour worked, but we ended up increasingly unsure whether comparisons of GDP per capita between countries are sound and even whether trends in GDP per capita, over long periods of time, are always what they seem. One response faced with such confusion is to seek adjusted measures of economic welfare which will capture all of the appropriate adjustments. The best known of these alternative indices of well-being was constructed for the US in 1972 by William Nordhaus and James Tobin. Their 'measure of economic welfare' sought to add the value of leisure and unpaid household work, and subtracted spending on defence, prisons and other 'regrettable necessities'. Subsequent measures have attempted to include also the impact of pollution, environmental degradation and the depletion of natural resources. A hugely wide range of estimates of 'economic progress' can result from such adjustments.[9]

Tempting though these adjusted indices are – we would all like to know the one true answer – they are not the best response to the confusion. For any 'comprehensive' index rests on so many subjective judgements – how wide to define a regrettable necessity, how to value unpaid work and leisure, how to value environmental quality – that

---

8. One additional imperfection in standard GDP measures not discussed here is the general 'quality' problem – the fact that we may systematically overstate inflation and thus understate real growth because we fail to capture the fact that products and services increase in quality as well as quantity – better cars, better restaurant meals, better haircuts, indeed (in a well-known study) better light bulbs. These effects are undoubtedly significant. But they are not key to inter-country comparison because there is no reason to believe that quality effects are different in importance country to country.

9. E.g. the Californian think tank 'Redefining progress' produced in 1996 an index which suggested that American economic welfare plateaued in the period 1969–74 and has been on a steady downward path since.

you can prove almost anything you want to fit your own social and political predilections. As a result the figures produced usually serve only to rally round a cause – the environment, say, or social inclusion – those people already predisposed to it: they rarely convince opponents and they rarely stimulate informed debate. The huge range of estimates of 'economic progress' produced by such indices usefully illustrates how uncertain our measures of welfare are, they warn us not to fool ourselves that conventional measures tell the whole story, but none of these alternatives provides a certain correct answer.

Rather than hankering after the 'one true measure', therefore, what we should take from the uncertainties of measurement are some implications about how we use measures of economic growth in public policy debate. Taken together with the criticism of the 'competitiveness' theory presented in Chapter 1, these uncertainties carry the following implications:

First, that we should be very wary of attaching importance to minor differences between countries in measured growth rates. We are not 'competing' in the normal sense of the word, so it doesn't matter whether we are just behind or just ahead of some other country. We are not in a race where some win and some lose. What matters is simply our own rate of growth in prosperity or welfare. To calibrate how we are doing relative to potential and to stimulate ideas for change we can usefully observe the performance of others, but in doing so we should concentrate on big differences and big trends. And as we shall see in Chapter 5, the big picture is that the performance of the major mature economies is considerably more similar than different. Political debate focused on claims that one's country has moved just a few places up or down some prosperity league table in a particular year is almost totally pointless.[10] Debate focused on short-term movements up and down tables of 'competitiveness' is even more a waste of breath.

---

10. An example of meaningless comment (and of the imperfections of prosperity estimates) was provided by newspaper articles in spring 2000 commenting on the 'news' that Britain had 'overtaken' France in prosperity. These were based on the publication of the OECD estimates of Purchasing Power Parity GDP for 1999, which showed France slightly behind the UK, versus slightly ahead in 1998. At the same time, however, latest OECD figures showed that France had grown real per capita income significantly faster than Britain in both 1998 and 1999. Clearly these figures are inconsistent – if Britain is growing more slowly than France, it cannot overtake it. In fact what had occurred was a change in OECD methodology which

Secondly, we should recognize that political debate should be about trade-offs and that trade-offs are possible. Since we're not in a race in which a growth rate lower than another country carries any implications for our absolute prosperity, we should accept the possibility that some people may prefer leisure to income and accept the growth consequences of this, not deny choice with a top down growth maximizing objective. We should accept that if people want to trade off measured GDP growth for better physical environment that too is a possible choice. We should pay attention to measured GDP growth, computed according to the classic conventions, because it tells us quite a lot about some very important aspects of total prosperity. But we must not assume that it tells the whole of the story about welfare.

Finally, when we do measure economic prosperity narrowly defined, we should pick our measures with care. Labour productivity per hour worked is the best measure of present prosperity relative to effort, provided that involuntary unemployment is low. Employment rates are important indicators but maximizing the employment rate is not an objective. Capital productivity should be analysed as an indicator of efficiency and to stimulate questions about whether investment levels are too low or too high, but maximizing capital productivity is not an objective. Total factor productivity is the nearest proxy we have to absolute efficiency but maximizing it is also not necessarily an objective.

Which of course makes comparisons of performance rather complex, and judgements on the success of different capitalisms nuanced rather than categorical. But that is simply the way it is. Anything more simple, any approach which latches on to one specific measure and claims that it gives us 'the answer', is a formula for killing useful debate rather than exploring the complexities of the real world.

(together with the growth data for 1998 and 1999) implied that (1) Britain was already ahead of France in 1998; (2) but France was catching up and likely to overtake Britain in 2000 if growth trends continued. If this occurs, however, it will tell us as little as Britain's 1999 'success'. The only sensible thing one can say in comparing French and British economic performance is that in prosperity per capita terms they are very similar, but that France achieves this prosperity with something like 20–25 per cent fewer hours worked because it achieves something like 25–30 per cent higher labour productivity.

5. Which Capitalism is Best?

Given the economic measures discussed in Chapter 4, which variant of capitalism performs better and why? It is striking how rapidly and completely conventional wisdom answers to that question have changed. Only ten years ago Michel Albert's *Capitalism Against Capitalism* was certain that a European or Rhineland model of capitalism was superior, both on the hard economic measures and on the soft social ones. 'Of the two models of capitalism it is the Rhine variant which is plainly more efficient than the neo-American, whether considered from the economic point of view or the social angle.' He seemed to have figures to prove that assertion. Will Hutton's *The State We're In* was equally certain that a stakeholder capitalism (i.e. continental European) was superior to shareholder capitalism (i.e. Anglo-Saxon). Many Americans concurred in a gloomy assessment of their own model. In 1994 Paul Krugman, after recalling that Tom Wolfe had described 1945–70 as the years of America's 'magic economy', could treat it as a 'settled fact' that US standard of living growth had slowed significantly in the 1970s and had not been increased by the deregulations and tax cuts of the Reagan years, that inequality had risen sharply, and that as a result there was a 'pervasive sense that the American dream has gone astray, that children can expect to live worse than their parents'.[1] The magic had gone away and had not come back.

But only four or five years later it seemed the magic had come back, and by the late 1990s most commentators were sure that the US had an inherently superior system, creating more jobs and more prosperity and above all leading in the new economy. European performance looked poor by comparison and it was clear that Europe must embrace America's formula – low taxes, liberalization, deregulation and an overt shareholder value focus – if it was to close its 'competitiveness gap'. As for Japan, whose economic prestige in the late 1980s had been even

---

1. Paul Krugman, *Peddling Prosperity* (1995).

higher than Germany's and which had been confidently expected to overtake America in prosperity as market after market fell to its unbeatable competition, its 1990s performance has been dismal, and everybody now knows for certain that structural reform, liberalization and deregulation (i.e. becoming more American) is the only way forward.

Is this just the flip-flop of intellectual fashion or can we say anything about the relative merits of different policies and of different models of capitalism? This chapter suggests the following answers to that question.

First, that we should be sceptical of any belief that there is one model of capitalism which is 'best' at all times and in all respects. The performance of the American and European economies is greatly more similar than different and the performance of both appears to be affected by autonomous technological factors which have relatively little to do with specific policies pursued.

Second, that we should recognize nevertheless in the American system both some inherent continuous advantages and some features particularly well suited to success given the current phase of technological change.

Third, that the performance of Japan in the 1990s and of the Asian tigers both before and during the 1997 crashes carry few relevant lessons for optimal 'structural policy', illustrating instead that macro-economic policies and global financial-market volatility can have big effects independent of the structural policies pursued.

We begin with the facts on Europe and America.[2] First, a comparison of how well the French, German and American economies now perform on productivity, employment and prosperity. Then a look at growth rates and trends for three periods: 1950 to the mid-1970s, the mid-70s to the mid-1990s, and the last four or five years.

---

2. Two caveats must be made about this Europe versus America comparison. The first that there is no one European model either in terms of policies pursued or in terms of economic performance. This point is picked up in detail in Chapter 6. The second is that France and Germany, used here for comparison, are not in all respects typical of European performance (the Netherlands for instance has performed much better at job creation over the last fifteen years). However, since France and Germany are typically used by ultra-liberals to illustrate 'the European problem' a comparison of them versus the US sets out the terms of the debate.

Productivity, employment and prosperity

The US today enjoys a higher per capita income than almost any other country. According to OECD figures for 1996 it was then about 35 per cent more prosperous than either France or the European Union on average, about 28 per cent more prosperous than Germany: alternative figures presented in Mary O'Mahony's study put the advantage at 30 per cent versus France and 21 per cent versus Germany. The primary reason for this difference is simple. A higher proportion of the American population work and they work longer hours. More work, not higher productivity or superior 'competitiveness' is the primary driver of higher American prosperity when compared with leading European economies.

Figure 5.1 shows the factors which explain the difference in GDP per capita. Income per capita is arithmetically equal to labour productivity per hour worked multiplied by hours worked per capita. On O'Mahony's figures France and Germany had slightly higher labour productivity than the US in 1996 but worked about 30 to 40 per cent fewer hours per capita.[3] Labour productivity in turn can be explained primarily by two factors – first absolute efficiency, the efficiency with which companies use any given quantity of labour and capital, and second the quantity of capital.[4] Relative levels of absolute efficiency are difficult to determine precisely, but total factor productivity is our closest proxy for it, and measurements of total factor productivity for 1996 suggests that the US was something like 3 to 9 per cent ahead of France and Germany, at least in the market sector of the economy. On capital intensity, however, the figures are clear: France and Germany have invested a higher percentage of national income in the past and as

---

3. As in Chapter 4 the source used is O'Mahony, *Britain's Productivity Performance 1950–96*. The 1996 figures are the latest presented in that comprehensive study. The overall picture presented has changed only a little over the last four years. US productivity has grown faster than French or German, but not for long enough to change the comparison significantly. The differences in hours worked have changed only minimally.

4. The determinants of absolute efficiency can in turn be split, though with much less mathematical precision, to distinguish quality of labour (i.e. skill effects), the efficiency with which capital is utilized, and technique or know-how.

Figure 5.1 US, German and French economic performance 1996

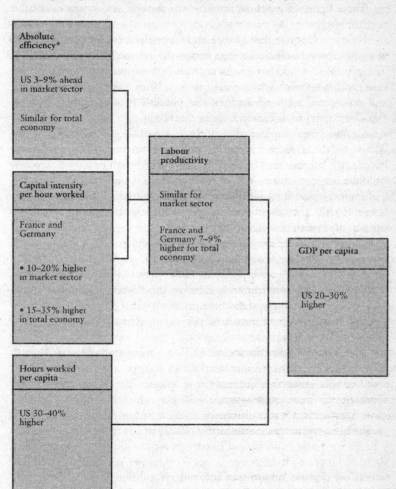

Absolute efficiency*

US 3–9% ahead in market sector

Similar for total economy

Capital intensity per hour worked

France and Germany

• 10–20% higher in market sector

• 15–35% higher in total economy

Hours worked per capita

US 30–40% higher

Labour productivity

Similar for market sector

France and Germany 7–9% higher for total economy

GDP per capita

US 20–30% higher

* Absolute efficiency is output for the same quantity of capital and labour – the nearest measure of it is total factor productivity (TFP).

Note: Figures are estimated in O'Mahony for both market sector and total economy. Both estimates are subject to wide margins of error, rooted in inherent methodological difficulties. Total economy estimates are particularly uncertain because of difficulties in measuring the value of non-market sector output.

Source: O'Mahony (NIESR, 1999).

a result have larger capital stock per worker employed, and an even greater advantage per hour worked.

These figures have three implications for our assessment of relative performance.

First they suggest that France and Germany have an opportunity to close an absolute efficiency gap versus the US in their market sectors. The precise scale of that gap is unclear. It is probably less than 10 per cent, and it is much smaller than it was 30 or forty years ago. But it still represents a US advantage. The possible causes of this 'absolute efficiency' gap are discussed later in this chapter.

Second, they suggest that Europe should look carefully at the issues of labour market structure and performance which could help explain the much lower levels of hours worked than in the US. If many of these missing hours reflect involuntary unemployment or under-employment, and if by reforming its labour markets Europe can reduce unemployment, it has an opportunity to increase prosperity even without an increase in absolutely efficiency.

Third, however, they suggest also that much of the difference in measured prosperity (GDP per capita) may be due to a different social choice in the trade-offs individuals make between income and leisure. If that is true the implication is that we should accept that choice not seek to deny it: that we should simply accept that Europe is less 'prosperous' than the US in measured per capita terms because Europeans choose to work less.

The balance between the second and third implications depends on whether the lower hours worked in Europe are freely chosen or involuntarily enforced. The answer is a mix. French and Germans of working age work on average 25–30 per cent fewer hours per week than Americans. Of this difference about a fifth is due to a higher level of unemployment: this undoubtedly pushes us to the second implication – problems to be addressed in European labour markets. About a third derives, however, from fewer hours worked per person employed and it is likely that the majority of this reflects a different social choice not a labour market failure. The remaining half is due to lower rates of workforce participation, with more people not even looking for work. Part of this lower workforce participation represents a different social choice, but part almost certainly represents hidden unemployment – how much of each we do not know. But the most reasonable overall conclusion is that while there is a significant opportunity to improve European prosperity by reforming labour markets to help create jobs that people want, at least a half and perhaps more of the prosperity gap between France and Germany and the US is a matter of social choice, reflecting the fact that Europeans are choosing to take a significant slice of the gains from increased efficiency in leisure rather than greater income.

If that is their choice, it is an entirely sustainable one. Many opponents of the European model seek to argue that that choice is unsustainable because 'uncompetitive', that in some sense Europeans are 'living beyond their means'. There is, however, not the slightest indication that that is so. As we have seen 'competitiveness' is a close to meaningless concept at the level of a continental economy. Some meaning can attach, however, to the concept of 'sustainability'. If a country or continent consistently ran a large current account deficit and as a result accumulated net liabilities to the rest of the world, the idea that its prosperity might be unsustainable, its consumption running ahead of its income, would have some validity. In fact, however, Europe is not in that position – rather the opposite. In aggregate it has had a strong tendency to run current account surpluses (averaging $76 billion over 1995 to 1999) and to accumulate external assets. Conversely the US has a strong tendency to run current account deficits, accumulating net external liabilities now amounting to about $2 trillion. Large current account surpluses are by no means signs of optimal economic policy: but they should at least give pause for thought to anyone glibly talking of a failure of European competitiveness: and they do disprove completely any argument that Europe's present income/leisure combination is 'unsustainable'. Rich societies are largely masters of their own destiny. They seek to achieve high productivity and low involuntary unemployment. But they can achieve those objectives with different and equally sustainable combinations of total hours worked and total income per capita.

Performance over time

The post-war performance of the US and European economies can best be thought of in three periods: 1950 to the mid-1970s, the mid-70s to the mid-90s, and the last half decade. In the first of these, both continents grew income per capita and productivity at attractive rates, but European countries grew appreciably faster, though from a much lower base. In both continents unemployment rates were at levels which by the mid-1980s would be remembered with envy, but on this dimension too the European economies had the edge (see Table 5.1).

From about the mid-1970s, however, a quite different pattern emerged. Growth slowed in both continents, but important differences emerged on specific aspects of performance, Europe much better at productivity growth, the US at employment creation. On the productivity side the slowdown in US productivity growth was dramatic – from 2.3 per cent in 1950–73 to only 0.8 per cent in 1973–96, and as a result real wage growth in the US was low for the average worker and negative for the lowest income groups. France and Germany slowed down from their very high growth rates of the 1950s and 60s, but still achieved labour productivity growth of 2.8 per cent and 2.6 per cent respectively, taking them above the US in absolute terms during the course of the 1980s. On the employment side, however, the US was clearly the superior performer. After a sharp rise in unemployment in the early 1980s, the US entered a period of rapid and sustained job creation, absorbing rapid growth of the labour force while also cutting unemployment from 9.5 per cent in 1983 to under 5 per cent by the late 90s. Europe, meanwhile, saw unemployment rise from 2.8 per cent in 1974 to 9.8 per cent by 1983, never falling below 8 per cent thereafter.

The mid-1970s to mid-1990s thus allow supporters of either the European or the American model to quote different figures in evidence. On absolute growth the US was ahead (because its population was growing faster); on per capita income (i.e. prosperity) it was a draw; on labour productivity (prosperity per effort expended) Europe did better; on unemployment Europe did worse. Ultra-liberals stress the US jobs record. European model supporters can claim that French and German citizens achieved the same prosperity advances as Americans while also enjoying the benefits of a 15 per cent reduction in working hours. Take your pick. It was in this period that the pattern of Figure 5.1 emerged. In the mid-1970s, America was 25–30 per cent more prosperous than leading European countries because it had a labour productivity advantage; by the mid-1990s, America was ahead by roughly the same amount but primarily because it put in more hours.

From the mid-1990s onwards, however, the pattern changed again, first in America and a little later in Europe. America's productivity growth problem disappeared, then the European job crisis showed the first signs of receding. From about 1993, and more clearly from 1995, US productivity growth took off at rates not seen since the 1960s (2.7

Table 5.1 Growth, productivity, and unemployment rates, 1950–2000

GDP growth per capita: % per annum

	1950–73	1973–83	1983–96	1996–9
US	2.7	0.9	1.7	3.1
France	4.4	1.9	1.5	2.6
Germany	3.7	2.0	2.1	2.1
EU15*	4.0	1.6	2.0	2.3

Labour productivity per hour worked: % growth per annum

	1950–73	1973–96	1996–9**
US	2.3	0.8	2.6
France	4.6	2.8	1.4
Germany	5.2	2.6	1.7

Unemployment rate: %

	1960	1974	1983	1996	2000
US	5.4	5.5	9.5	5.4	4.1
France	1.4	2.8	8.3	12.3	9.6
Germany	1.0	2.1	7.9	8.8	9.5
EU15*	2.4	2.8	9.8	10.8	8.4

* 6 EEC members for figures prior to 1974.

** Per person employed for France and Germany for 1996–9.

Source: OECD *Historical Statistics*, OECD *Economic Outlook*, OECD *Main Economic Indicators*, O'Mahony (NIESR, 1999), *The Economist* (for 2000) and *European Economy*, European Commission, Supplement A, 'Economic Trends'.

per cent on average for 1995–9 versus 0.8 per cent in 1973–96). With job creation still strong, this meant absolute and per capita income growth also not seen for thirty years – growth 4 per cent per annum from 1996 to 2000, prosperity per capita growing at over 3 per cent. The 'magic' seemed to have returned: the triumph of the free market became the latest conventional wisdom. But intriguingly from about 1998, European growth also picked up, per capita income growth growing at almost 2.5 per cent per annum. Still more unexpectedly, growth was accompanied, for the first time since the 1970s, with robust job creation in many countries. Spain has created over 2 million new jobs in five years, France 1.5 million since 1997. The US's overall performance is clearly superior over the last five years, but in both continents performance is improving: America's average income earners are enjoying attractive increases in real wages for the first time in three decades; and the French press is speculating on the prospect of full employment with a confidence unimaginable as late as 1997.

So which capitalism is better?

Do these figures tell us which model of capitalism is better? They throw some light on that question, and carry some implications for policy. But the data also tell us three things which cast doubt on how much difference the choice of model or the fine details of policy actually make: first, that attainable growth rates are strongly determined by whether a country is in a leadership or catch-up position; second, that once adjusted for catch-up versus leadership position growth rates are more similar than different; and third, that there are important shifts in performance, above all in productivity growth, which we do not fully understand but which seem likely to have far more to do with shifts in technology than with even quite significant differences in policy choice.

Whether a country is in a leadership or catch-up position has a huge influence on the sustainable growth rate. Really high growth rates are always associated with catch-up, and once catch-up is complete (i.e. once countries reach the productivity and standard of living of the leader), growth slows down to the more gradual pace of the leader. The leader's pace, meanwhile, seems to be almost inherently constrained within certain limits. Table 1.2 has already illustrated the pattern. Since about the late nineteenth century, since the Industrial Revolution was well advanced and the key institutions of market capitalism were in place, the productivity and prosperity improvement of the leader (i.e. the country which at any given time is the richest and most productive) has moved only within a fairly small band – never more than 3.0 per cent per annum for more than a decade, never much below 1 per cent. Countries in catch-up mode, however, can attain far faster growth rates, and if anything attainable growth rates of catch-up countries seem to have increased over time. Rates of catch-up in the first half of this century (e.g. Sweden's) were gradual, only about 2–3 per cent per annum versus the leader's 1.5 per cent. Growth rates in post-war Europe reached 4 per cent or more per capita, Japan's went higher still to 8–9 per cent and the Asian tigers of the 1990s for a period were close to 10 per cent. The leader's pace is fairly constant, the followers' rate of catch-up seems if anything to accelerate. But once the followers get near to the leader's level, they slow down to something like the leader's pace. That's what happened to Germany and Japan as they approached American standards of living in the 1980s. That's what happened also to Singapore and Hong Kong in the 1990s.

The pattern is clear from the figures and easily explicable too. The leader's pace is set by two factors – the propensity to save (or the ability to import savings) of people already in relative terms rich, and the opportunities for productive investment arising from the technological progress occurring at any time. As we shall see below, those factors vary – but not so dramatically as to take the leader's productivity growth outside the range of 1.0–3.0 per cent per annum. Catch-up countries meanwhile tend to achieve higher growth rates because they invest more relative to their income (funded either by domestic savings or capital inflows) and because they can copy the technologies and techniques already developed in leading countries. As for the acceleration over time, it may also have a simple explanation. Many of the implications often attributed to globalization are, as Chapter 1 described, non-existent. But one real consequence of globalization, indeed the essential defining feature of globalization, is that it has created improved mechanisms for speeding the flow of capital and ideas to wherever there are opportunities to improve productivity and those exist wherever countries are currently behind. Accelerated potential rates of catch-up is the true story of globalization.

For the comparison of Europe and the US the implication is, however, simple. The fact that Europe grew much faster than the US in the 1950s to 1970s does not mean it had an inherently better system; Europe was simply catching up. The fact that Europe slowed down towards US rates in the 1980s doesn't prove that its model had failed – it was simply approaching the position of the leader. Whenever we seek to calibrate economic performance we must first ask whether a country is in catch-up or leadership mode.

Once that adjustment is made, the second striking feature of US and European performance is not the differences but the broad similarities. In terms of prosperity creation (i.e. growth rate of GDP per capita) the US and Europe have been so similar over the last twenty years that if you want to make either a pro-European or pro-American case, you simply have to pick your start and end dates with care. And once you've picked your comparison years, what you end up with is one continent just a few tenths of a per cent ahead of the other. If world prosperity were a 'competitive race' in the normal sense of the world, such differences would matter – first is first in a race and second is second, however small the margin of victory. But since we are not in a competitive race, minor differences, generated by careful selection of dates, prove nothing. Performance of the rich developed economies is greatly more similar than different, implying that there is quite a wide range of policy choices which make relatively little difference to overall economic performance but which may reflect different social choice.

Phases of performance over time are also surprisingly similar. The years 1945–70 may have been those of the 'magic economy' in the US, but the late 40s to the 70s are also 'les trente glorieuses' to the French, and the 50s and 60s the period of the German 'Wirtschaftswunder' (economic miracle). The mid-70s to the mid-90s were difficult on both continents – with slower absolute and per capita growth in both. The 1990s in both continents, however, have seen a turn, first in the US and then later in Europe. The similarities suggest that there is as a common factor at work independent of the specific policies pursued. That factor may be technology.

Long-term productivity growth arises from the application of new technology, primarily encapsulated in our capital investment in machines (including computers and software) which do things for us, allowing us to work more productively. But the technological progress which enables this improvement arises at an uneven pace. The great breakthrough of the Industrial Revolution and the creation of market capitalism took us from a world in which productivity growth was uncertain, very slow and sometimes reversed to a world in which we expect and actually enjoy continual technological and productivity improvement. That growth is seemingly ensured by the institutions,

procedures and cultural assumptions distinctive to the modern world –
science departments in universities, research and development divisions
in companies, product development as the overt aim of marketing
departments, continuous improvement as the explicit aim of management. But while these seem to ensure continuous productivity improvement, they don't mean that it is constant. Some steps in technological
progress are inherently more difficult, some new technologies take
longer than others to progress from idea to commercial application and
from initial commercial application to major economic effect. The
'natural' rate of productivity growth (i.e. the rate likely to occur in a
fairly well-run economy for any given level of capital investment) varies
over time. We don't know with any certainty why American productivity growth slowed so unexpectedly in the 1970s and then accelerated in
the 1990s, but among the most convincing explanations is that put
forward by economists and economic historians who believe that the
biggest cause may have been 'autonomous' changes in technology, i.e.
changes essentially unrelated to the overt policies of government, to tax
rates and subsidies, regulations and market structures.[5]

According to this explanation the 1940s to the 1970s simply
happened to be marked by the intensive application, diffusion and
optimization of key technologies created many years before – in particular the technologies of the electro-mechanical manufacturing environment and of the internal-combustion engine. For a variety of reasons
technological change appears to produce a really strong productivity
effect several decades after initial introduction.[6] Rapid growth in the
1950s to early 1970s may therefore have been a delayed response to
the technological progress of the early twentieth century. By the 1970s,
however, the opportunities for further improvement in the electro-
mechanical environment were beginning to reach declining marginal
returns. Further improvements were achieved but more slowly. Lower
productivity growth in the 1980s was the result, much slower in the
productivity leader (the US), somewhat slower in Europe, where catch-
up potential still existed.

The most likely cause of the 1990s productivity take-off is also in

5. See, for example, Krugman, *Peddling Prosperity*.

6. See David, 'General-Purpose Engines'; Greenwood, *The Third Industrial
Revolution*.

turn technological. For while the 1970s saw diminishing marginal improvements in the electro-mechanical environment, they were the years in which a new technological wave – ICT – was gathering pace in the universities, the space and defence programmes, the R&D departments of high-technology companies and the early steps of the information-technology entrepreneurs. That wave of technological change, for the reasons outlined in Chapter 2, was likely at some stage to produce a period of accelerated productivity growth. But it took until the 1990s before that accelerated growth came through. For just as the full economic benefits of electricity or of the internal-combustion engine took many years to be achieved and reflected in productivity statistics, so too with information technology and for the same reasons. It takes time for us to work out how to use a new technology to best effect, and the first uses of a new technology tend to be isolated islands of automation in which its full benefits cannot be achieved. Swap an electrical typewriter for a word processor and nothing positive may happen in productivity terms: every executive still has a secretary, every memo and letter is still printed and posted or at very best faxed and, because it's easier to make changes, every letter goes through more minor redraftings before dispatch, work expanding to fill the new machine's capacity but with no improvement in valued end product per hour of work. Make the word processor user-friendly enough for the executive to use, add spellcheck and easy formatting tools and link it to an email facility, and true productivity improvement becomes possible. Thousands of different instances of that basic concept – integrated change is massively more powerful than isolated change – could well explain why information technology in the 1980s was everywhere except in the productivity statistics, but then entered the productivity statistics in such a dramatic fashion in the 1990s. The US productivity surge may have relatively little to do with public policy – with tax rates or educational levels, financial structures or regulation – and a lot to do with autonomous technological trends. If so, and given the powerful mechanisms which globalization has created for the transfer of practice across the world, it is quite likely and indeed probable that the productivity surge we have seen in the US will be followed after a short delay by a similar one in Europe almost independently of the precise policies pursued.

The fundamental pattern of catch-up versus the leader, the similarity of performance of different models of capitalism as much as the differences, the vital role of technology as a driver of attainable economic growth, together these three factors caution against any assertion that Capitalism A is better than Capitalism B. There are differences in performance but they are more nuances than fundamentals. We need to keep that perspective in mind as a check against the swings of intellectual fashion. But provided we keep that perspective, the nuances are still worth analysing. For even small differences in growth rates make it far easier for governments to balance competing demands, easier, for instance, to improve public services at acceptable tax rates. Even quite small differences in jobs supplied relative to jobs wanted can produce big swings in unemployment. The differences in performance are relative, not fundamental, but we should still understand them and draw the policy implications.

The US and Europe: relative strengths and weaknesses

Looking through the complexity of divergent measures and different time periods there are still four key differences in performance we should try to understand.

First, Europe's superior labour–productivity performance in the 1970s and 80s, when France and Germany not only completed catch-up but, in West Germany's case, actually overtook the US. It was this superior productivity performance which to writers like Michel Albert and Will Hutton proved the superiority of the Rhineland or stakeholder model. It seemed obvious to them and many others in 1990 that Germany was performing better than the US and in some ways it was.

Second, the apparent superiority of the American economy in both job creation and productivity from the mid-1990s onwards, its lead of several years over the Europeans in grasping the opportunities of information and communications technology.

Third, the more sustained superiority of the US throughout the 1980s and 90s in terms of job creation. Until the mid-90s it was job creation combined with low productivity growth but job creation all the same.

Fourth, the US's apparent advantage in absolute efficiency, the output achieved from any given combination of labour and capital. The scale of this advantage is quite small and has decreased greatly over the last thirty years, but it is still there and the pace of Europe's catch-up now appears to be very slow.

The first three of these seem contradictory and they would be if we assume that one model of capitalism is in all respects and at all times better. But what the facts probably tell us is that the optimal model of capitalism can change over time in the light of changing technologies and economic structures, and that different models can be relatively better at one dimension of the economic challenge than the other, relatively better at productivity growth than employment creation or vice versa.

Different optimal models at different times

To many commentators, including Michel Albert and Will Hutton, it was clear as recently as the early 1990s that the German, Japanese (and to a lesser extent French) models of capitalism were superior to the American model and it was also obvious why. Japan and Germany were both market economies and strong internal competition in the manufacturing sectors was a key platform for external success in both. But they were distinctively different types of capitalism from the American model. They were characterized by patient, long-term relationships between shareholders and management, rather than by a frenetic focus on quarterly financial results: they therefore invested more for the long term and they pursued long-term strategies which achieved the dominance of key markets. The Japanese and German systems were also marked by long-term relationships between committed workforces and managements which invested in their skills, and by systems of industrial relations which avoided the adversarial culture of the US (or even more so of Britain). As a result productivity improved relentlessly in an environment of mutual co-operation. Especially in manufacturing, overall performance seemed to be clearly superior: superior in productivity and in global competitive success in specific sectors, somewhat superior to the best variant of the Anglo-Saxon model (the US), massively superior to a second-rate variant of the Anglo-Saxon model like the UK.

The latest intellectual fashion is to dismiss all of this as nonsense, a set of notions which are not and never were true. To the true believer in the ultra-liberal creed, totally free markets (labour markets as much as product markets) and an overt shareholder value focus are always and in all cases the best system, and if it didn't seem to be so in 1990 that must be because the figures were wrong or because the Japanese and German systems were inherently unsustainable. But that story really doesn't fit the facts. The facts are that the Japanese and German systems performed extremely well and sustainably well over a period of forty years (as indeed did the French). And it stretches credibility to believe that every one of the numerous studies of that strong perform- ance which identified Japanese and German financial and labour-market relationships as advantages were in all respects misguided. Instead the more likely explanation of Japanese and German relative success in the 1960s, 1970s and 1980s – America's in the 1990s – is that the economic context changed: that shifts in technology and the structure of the economy produced a shift in the balance of advantage between different variants of capitalism.

The strengths of the Japanese and German systems were, and indeed still are, peculiarly suited to the management and technological chal- lenges of the engineering world, of a manufacturing sector which as late as 1990 still accounted for 30 per cent of their total economies and about 40 per cent of their private-sector economies. It was an environ- ment characterized by long product cycles and requiring long-term and large capital investments. It was also an environment in which a long- term committed and secure workforce was both peculiarly valuable and feasible. Valuable because productivity improvement was heavily dependent on the endless minor adaptation of manufacturing processes (the classic arena of Japanese superiority); and feasible because while there was continuous productivity improvement it was typically matched by superior volume growth in the cars and television sets and white goods and machine tools produced. In terms of the framework presented in Chapter 2 (see Figure 2.2) manufacturing technology was on the right-hand side of the matrix and productivity improvements typically did not require actual company downsizing: the implicit contract of a both committed and secure workforce was feasible.[7] The Japanese and German systems were thus well designed for success in engineering-based manufacturing, and their economies were successful

---

7. German manufacturing employment as a percentage of total employment as a result hardly changed between 1960–90, falling only from 34 per cent to 32 per cent, and total numbers employed in manufacturing rose in the 1960s and stayed roughly stable in the 1970s and 80s. Only in the 1990s has the fall in manufactur- ing's share of the economy become fast enough (from 32 per cent in 1990 to 24 per cent by 1997) to result in large falls in manufacturing employment (OECD *Historical Statistics*).

overall because manufacturing was a large enough slice of the total economy for superiority in manufacturing to make a big difference. They were never especially good in service sectors (indeed in the Japanese case, productivity in the non-traded sectors of the economy was and remains very poor compared with both US and European standards), but they were very good in a sector which mattered a lot at that time.

Those conditions have changed in the fashion described in Chapter 2 and changed enough to explain why systems which once seemed slightly superior to the American system now seem slightly behind. They have not of course changed radically nor suddenly. As Chapter 2 made clear, the idea that we are all suddenly 'living on thin air' is a massive exaggeration. Quite a lot of the new economy is rather like the old economy; and many old sources of competitive advantage are just as relevant as ever. Toshiba and Siemens, Sony and Saint-Gobain are still successful companies despite not having adopted American ways lock, stock and barrel. But the changed relative performance we are trying to explain is also neither dramatic nor sudden, not a switch from Germany perfect and the US a complete disaster to the vice versa, but a switch from one economy a bit ahead in productivity growth to the other nudging past it. That fairly minor shift in relative performance might well be due to the fact that changes in the shape of the economy have subtly changed the key factors for success. Manufacturing, for reasons explained in Chapter 2, has declined as a proportion of the economy, and that in itself reduces the overall value of system characteristics peculiarly valuable in the manufacturing sector. But in addition the specific nature of the technological wave we now face, the wave of information and communications technology now reaching maturity, seems to have shifted the balance of advantage towards the American model. In three ways in particular the latest technological context may carry implications for optimal policy.

The first derives from ICT's impact on employment. As Chapters 2 and 3 described, information and communications technology is in its direct effects a net job destroyer, its economic benefit deriving not from new jobs created specifically where the technology is applied, but from people freed up to work in other areas of the economy entirely. Partly as a result the flow of workers now created by productivity improvement is to a greater extent from existing big companies to smaller companies, and from large employment sites to smaller, compared with the 1950s and 60s when a significant element of it was from small economic units (farms and corner shops) to large companies. Seizing productivity-improvement potential therefore increasingly requires actual downsizing of large companies; and creating new jobs in new companies is increasingly important to employment creation. Optimal capital and labour-market policies and behaviours have changed as a result. Managers pursuing long-term strategic visions and free of overt shareholder pressure are less likely to improve productivity through downsizing and are constrained from doing so if rules on hire and fire are too tight. The economic benefits of American-style equity-market disciplines and flexible labour markets have therefore increased. And the economic importance of product and labour-market features which facilitate new job creation in entirely new companies has increased also: in this respect too the American model has advantages.

The second reflects the impact of ICT on the nature of business innovation. For information technology's inherent features – in particular its minimal cost of replication – have made it possible for new entrants rapidly to achieve very big economic impact. Relatively more innovation now derives from new entrants doing entirely new things; relatively less (though still a lot) from existing players endlessly achieving improvements in existing processes and products. Microsoft has had a bigger economic impact in a short period of time than any business since those of the late nineteenth-century transport boom. This change shifts the balance of advantage in financial-market structures. It makes an equity culture capable of rapidly allocating capital to new ideas, through venture-capital funding and public issues, relatively more important and the long-term stable relationships of house banks and committed shareholders so beloved by Michel Albert and Will Hutton relatively less valuable.

Third, and finally, information and communications technology increases the importance of competitive conditions in sectors of the economy not previously seen as fundamental to relative economic success. It makes possible major productivity improvements in non-traded sectors of the economy – such as retail financial services and utilities – which have traditionally been defended against the stimulus of competition by state ownership, product market regulation and labour-market rigidities (e.g. employee protection rights in French banks and state-owned enterprises even more rigid than the general national standard). These rigidities always carried a penalty of potential productivity forgone: Japanese productivity in these sectors of the economy was, for instance, always atrocious. But the relative importance of that penalty to overall economic performance increases as manufacturing declines as a proportion of the whole economy.

In a series of inter-related ways, therefore, it is likely that the changing shape of the economy has shifted the balance of advantage between different models of capitalism. We do not know for sure why productivity growth rates ebb and surge, and why one country or continent moves temporarily ahead of another, but as Larry Summers, then the US Treasury Deputy Secretary, suggested in a speech in early 1998 it seems likely that 'the US has lately been extremely successful because the balance of economic advantage has shifted from command and control in favour of motivation and incentive'. That doesn't mean that the strengths of the Japanese or German or French systems are wholly irrelevant in an entirely 'new' economy. It doesn't mean that the American system is right in all respects and for all time – the balance could conceivably, at some future stage, shift back. It doesn't mean Europe's performance is dismal and America's marvellous. It just means that in the mid-1990s the US moved a bit ahead and that for now there are some lessons from the American experience for the European model, lessons implying reform but not rejection of the European model.

The point indeed can be made more generally. Optimal economic models change over time in the light of the changing context of technology and economic structure. Soviet communism was always a deeply horrible political creed but in purely economic terms it was not totally disastrous when a few big tasks – build an electricity network driven by coal and hydro-power – could have big economic pay-offs. It became disastrous economically as well as politically when it came to the next stages of economic development and their more complex challenges – providing a multiplicity of consumer goods and services, motivating people to the endless process improvements which drive forward productivity and quality, stimulating people to link technology to customer value in innovative ways. Similarly French technocratic statism of the 1960s and 1970s – convert the telephone network to digital technology as a top down objective not because profit maximization requires it – may well in some areas and at that time have had advantages over Britain's muddle-through approach. But it contributed little – despite the early success of Minitel – to the ferment of new ideas and new business creativity unleashed, initially in America, by the Internet. Optimal policy mix changes, and the direction of change has recently been towards an increased need for 'flexibility' – in product markets, in capital markets, but above all in labour markets, the area of greatest and most long-lasting European underperformance.

Europe's employment failure: a structural problem

Europe's present productivity growth gap versus the US is recent (since the mid-1990s) and may well disappear as naturally and unexpectedly as it emerged – the globalization of idea and capital flows may well see to that. Europe's employment underperformance is long-lasting, a steady divergence of unemployment rates beginning in early 1983 (when both US and EU unemployment rates were 9.5 per cent) and reaching the point of maximum difference in 1997 with the EU at 10.7 per cent, the US at 5 per cent. Solving that problem is Europe's biggest economic challenge. For that reason, while labour-market flexibility has already been mentioned as one of the dimensions along which the balance of advantage has shifted towards the American model, it is worth exploring this aspect in a bit more detail.

It is important to be clear what the problem is and what it isn't and to calibrate its scale correctly. Quite a bit of it may be cyclical rather than structural and to that extent it may disappear, like the productivity gap, without any great policy initiatives. But much of it seems likely to be structural, reflecting labour-market policies and rigidities. If it is structural it is clearly a different problem in different countries. It certainly has next to nothing to with competitiveness.

Part at least of Europe's unemployment in 1997 was the product of the economic cycle and of the macroeconomic policies pursued to squeeze inflation out of the European economy and to put public finances in good order as a preparation for EMU. Latest assessments suggest that rather more of it was macroeconomic and cyclical (and thus rather less of it structural) than most economists once supposed. In 1995 the OECD estimated that about 80–90 per cent of European unemployment was structural, implying a very limited potential to cut unemployment without either structural reform or inflation. But EU unemployment has fallen from 10.7 per cent in 1997 to 8.4 per cent in 2000 (and Eurozone unemployment from 11.6 per cent to 9.1 per cent), undershooting for many countries the OECD estimates of the structural element, and the OECD now forecasts a further fall in Eurozone

Table 5.2 Employment and unemployment in
European Union countries

	Unemployment rate % (summer 2000)	Employment as % working-age population (1998)
Netherlands	2.5	69.8
Austria	3.1	67.4
Portugal	3.8	66.4
Sweden	4.1	71.5
Ireland	4.8	59.8
Denmark	5.2	75.3
UK	5.3	71.2
Germany	9.4	64.1
France	9.6	59.4
Finland	9.8	64
Italy	10.5	50.8
Belgium	11.5	57.3
Spain	14.5	51.2

Source: *The Economist* for unemployment (except for Portugal, Finland and Ireland – OECD *Main Economic Indicators*); OECD *Employment Outlook* for employment.

unemployment to 7.6 per cent in 2002. Partly this is because some labour-market reforms have indeed started, but partly it reflects the fact that the OECD (like almost all economists) overestimated the structural element. It is at least possible that the next few years will prove Europe's unemployment less difficult to fix than was feared.

It is likely, however, that the structural element remains significant. The most compelling evidence for this is simply the great differences in unemployment and employment rates observed across Europe (see Table 5.2). One clear implication of these differences is that there is

nothing inherent about 'the European approach' which condemns
Europe to high unemployment: the Netherlands, Denmark, Austria,
Sweden and Portugal all have unemployment rates similar to US levels.
A striking feature of these differences, moreover, is that they cannot
be explained by any identifiable macroeconomic or product market
features. There is no sign of a locationally favoured centre leaving
the geographical periphery behind: Belgium and France are both high
unemployment countries; Sweden, Austria and Portugal are low unemployment countries. Nor is there a correlation with recent rates of
growth – Spain's has been only very slightly slower than Portugal's for
the last fifteen to twenty years but its unemployment rate is over three
times as high. Nor is there a correlation with recent fiscal policies. In
the absence of other explanations of these differences, therefore, what
they would seem to tell us is twofold: first, that a large part of European
employment and unemployment differences must be linked to labour-
market structures and policies; second, that the structural problems
are very different in severity in different countries. Belgium and the
Netherlands are geographically contiguous, similar in industrial structure, closely integrated in their traded sectors, and have pursued for the
last twenty years exactly the same exchange rate and monetary policies.
The fact that the Netherlands has an unemployment rate of 2.5 per
cent, Belgium over 10 per cent tells us that something structural rather
than cyclical is going on. But it also tells us that it is something quite
different in the Netherlands than in Belgium.

These structural problems have no impact on any meaningful
measure of competitiveness, but they do seem to have an impact on
the level of job creation, primarily in non-traded service sectors of the
economy. As Table 5.3 (overleaf) shows, the gap between Europe's
overall employment rate and that of the US is entirely explained by
service-sector employment; between the European countries the same is
true. French employment levels are lower than Dutch not because
French companies are less successful in global competition, but because
France has a much lower proportion of people employed in wholesaling, retailing, health, social work and other services.

To solve their unemployment problem European nations therefore
need to identify the different specific labour-market policies which in
different countries and to different degrees are impeding service-sector
job creation. The challenges that might pose for the European model
are considered in Chapter 6.

Table 5.3 Employment by sectors
(% of working-age population employed by sector)

	US	EU15	Neths	France
Primary industries, manufacturing, utilities and construction	19.6	20.7	17.7	18.8
Transport and communications	4.1	3.6	4.0	3.8
Hotels, restaurants, retail, wholesale	17.5	11.6	13.2	10.1
Financial and business services	11.1	6.7	9.4	7.1
Education, health and social work, and other services	18.5	13.2	16.9	14.8
Public administration	3.3	4.6	5.3	5.6
Total	74.0	60.5	66.7	60.1

Source: European Commission, *Employment in Europe, 1999.*

Absolute efficiency: an inherent US advantage?

Many economic-performance measures reflect trade-offs and levels of input: per capita income can be boosted by working more hours; capital productivity rates in part reflect choices on how much to invest. Maximizing any one of these measures is not therefore a sensible objective. But if we knew how much output an economy achieved from a specific combination of labour and capital that would be the measure of absolute efficiency.

Unfortunately, as Chapter 4 discussed, there is no definitive measure of absolute efficiency for a whole economy. But total factor productivity is the nearest proxy we have and overall comparisons of TFP can be supplemented by company and plant level comparisons. Both types of comparison suggest that the US enjoys a small advantage in absolute efficiency at least in the market sectors of the economy.[8] The advantage is quite small – 1995 estimates indicate just 9 per cent versus France and 3 per cent versus Germany, and the gap has closed dramatically over the last fifty years; in 1950 France was about 50 per cent less efficient than the US, Germany about 40 per cent. But the rate of closing appears to have slowed in the last fifteen to twenty years and it is possible that as natural catch-up reaches conclusion we will be left with a small permanent difference.

There are certainly two obvious reasons why we should expect such a difference. One is America's large single market, the other its low population density.

The US economy is a large single market of 275 million consumers with a single currency, one dominant language, a largely common legal system, common product standards, pan-US media networks and a highly homogeneous culture. This uniformity, compared with Europe's diversity, makes high productivity easier to achieve. It creates economies of scale both in manufacturing because companies can produce for a larger market and, perhaps even more significantly, in administrative overheads. A US company operating in several regions of the US can do so with one advertising campaign, one set of sales literature in one language, one set of accounts in one currency, one legal department, one set of personnel records, one payroll system, one PR department, etc. The equivalent company in Europe would have five or six of each even to serve just the major markets.

Quantification is difficult but these advantages in themselves must account for several percentage points of absolute efficiency. They are reinforced, moreover, by the competitive intensity which a large single market makes possible: American companies can be easily challenged by other companies from across America and that fact motivates them to seize aggressively all potential opportunities for productivity improvement.

The US's second advantage was highlighted by a recent report by McKinsey and Company which compared Britain's productivity record

---

8. O'Mahony's TFP estimates for the whole economy, including the state sector, actually put France ahead of the US in 1995. For state sectors, however, productivity comparisons are heavily influenced by differences in measurement technique, and comparisons focused just on market sectors are probably more robust.

with that of the US.[9] The report argued that planning restrictions on new development could impede productivity in several sectors – hotels and retailing as well as manufacturing. The conclusion is indeed obvious to many business people. For the cost and availability of land and ease of development have a pervasive influence on attainable productivity throughout an economy. High retail productivity is easier to achieve in bigger stores, serving wider catchment areas, to which delivery trucks arrive at dependable times, having travelled over uncongested roads. Construction productivity is much higher and costs lower if construction is on greenfield sites: brownfield-site redevelopment imposes a significant cost penalty, refurbishment of old buildings a still higher one. Efficient factory layout is easier to achieve on greenfield sites and manufacturing and distribution economies of scale easier to achieve if large factories are linked via large distribution centres to distant markets by fast-flowing freeways which can be used by large trucks. Several studies of US manufacturing and productivity have found that a large part of any US productivity advantage can be explained simply by longer run lengths, bigger batch sizes and larger overall scale.[10] Cheap, easily developed land is good for productivity, and high productivity is therefore easier to achieve in less densely populated countries where environmental opposition to new business development and new roads is lower. High population density imposes an inherent economic cost which societies have to choose to take either in environmental degradation or in productivity potential forgone. Parts of Europe, of course, are lightly populated, parts of the US densely, but on average the US gains a significant advantage in productivity and measured prosperity from lower average population density.[11]

The US thus enjoys two inherent economic advantages. Indeed, given the extent of those natural advantages what is difficult to explain is not the existence of an absolute efficiency gap but how small it

---

9. 'Driving Productivity Growth in the UK Economy', McKinsey, September 1998.

10. See, for instance, Mason and O'Mahony, 'Capital Accumulation and Manufacturing Productivity Performance: US-European Comparisons' (NIESR, 1997).

11. It is noticeable that the big European country with the lowest population density, France, achieves higher productivity than the UK in retailing and for similar reasons to the US: greater ease of development of large edge-of-town retail stores.

appears to be. One possibility is that America's natural advantages deliver efficiency gains bigger than the difference we observe but with European countries enjoying some other offsetting advantages. One of those offsetting advantages could be workforce skills. For one of the surprising features of US economic performance is that whereas skills are usually believed to be highly relevant to economic success, the US does not score well on comparisons of overall workforce skills. This fact is sometimes used to argue that skills do not in fact matter. But the alternative hypothesis is that skills do matter and that Germany, for instance, has a skill-based advantage over the US which offsets much of the US's natural advantages. One set of calculations indeed suggests that the US total productivity advantage versus Germany would be 12 per cent were it not for a German skills advantage of 9 per cent which reduces the net advantage to just 3 per cent. The figures should be treated as indicative only but serve to illustrate the hypothesis.[12]

The essential conclusion is, however, simple. The US enjoys inherent advantages stemming from a larger more complete single market and ease of physical development. Some of those advantages Europe could never match; some may be undesirable to match. The policies required to pursue the attainable and desirable element of improvement are considered in Chapter 6.

Japan – a case for radical structural reform?

If Europe's performance in the 1990s has fallen behind America's, Japan's has been a real disaster. The eight years 1991–9 produced average economic growth of just 0.9 per cent, compared with Europe's 1.9 per cent and with the 4.0 per cent Japan achieved in the 1980s. Public debt has soared to possibly unsustainable levels (over 110 per

---

12. See O'Mahony, *Britain's Productivity Performance 1950–96*. Note that the calculation of skill contributions to productivity is fraught with both conceptual and measurement problems which should make us wary of any definite conclusion based on quantification.

The distinction between American skill-based high performance and German skill-based high performance appears indeed to be a long-standing characteristic of both economies. See Geoffrey Owen, *From Empire to Europe*, Chapter 1 for a discussion of comparative advantages in pre-First World War industrial development.

cent of GDP versus 60 per cent in 1990) and consumer confidence in the Japanese system is low. Here the record, far more than in Europe, might suggest the need for really radical reform.

If you travelled to Japan in the late 1980s, as a businessman or someone involved in economic policy, you typically came in search of wisdom – you wanted to find the secret of Japan's extraordinary manufacturing performance, to discern whether it was better strategy, or more patient finance, or just more motivated and better-organized workers. Nowadays if you travel with the same status, you are treated as the source of wisdom and above all wisdom on a magic potion called 'structural reform'. Government ministers, employer organizations and business executives all spout the new conventional wisdom – what Japan now needs is structural reform and it must simply find the political will to do it. What precisely structural reform means is often left rather vague, but it is clear to everyone that it is needed. And clear to any true believer in the ultra-liberal orthodoxy that Japan's 1990s failure proves that its once much-praised strengths were always illusions.

The attribution of Japan's 1990s crisis to an absence of structural reform is, however, almost entirely mistaken. Japan's economy could in several key respects benefit from a dose of specific structural reforms and indeed would have benefited from them even in its heyday twenty years ago. But Japan's 1990 slowdown has been primarily caused by something far more simple – deficient demand and bad macroeconomic policies. The lesson of 1990s Japan, far from being that structural reform towards a single ultra-liberal model is the be-all and end-all of economic policy, is instead that really bad macro policy has a huge potential to cause harm and can do so whatever the specific structural model in place.

The case for structural reform in Japan is clear. One of the striking features of Japanese economic statistics has always been a huge difference in the performance of different sectors of the economy. Japanese productivity in certain manufacturing sectors – television production and automobiles, for instance – led the world by the mid-1980s and still does today. But overall Japanese labour productivity per hour worked trailed American, German and French by 35–40 per cent in 1996 and trailed even British productivity by about 12 per cent. Japanese retailing, wholesale distribution, personal services, financial services, transport and telecommunications all showed productivity rates far below British, American and continental levels in the mid-1980s and still do today. Agricultural productivity is almost unbelievably low – a third of European levels and a seventh of America's.[13] Productivity in these sectors matters as much to national prosperity as productivity in traded sectors, and as a result Japan's prosperity trails the US by about 30 per cent and is no better than European levels despite 30 per cent more hours worked per capita per year. Japan's export manufacturing success has always obscured an economy which is not highly productive overall and where prosperity per effort expended therefore lags that of other rich nations.

Changing that pattern requires structural reform. Increased competition in retail distribution and retail financial services could unleash a significant productivity improvement. Free-trade in agricultural products would allow Japanese consumers to benefit from lower world food prices. Further moves to facilitate foreign ownership would provide a capital market stimulus to efficiency throughout the economy. Such reforms would bring with them unsettling social changes and it is for that reason that they have been only slowly introduced. It is for the Japanese themselves to make the trade-off between the benefits and costs of more rapid change. But the fact that structural reform could unleash in Japan a major wave of productivity and thus in measured prosperity growth is incontrovertible.

All that, however, was as true in 1985, or in 1980, or in 1975 as it is today. The relative importance of it has increased somewhat between then and now because the Japanese success story – manufacturing – has declined as a proportion of the whole economy. But manufacturing has not declined enough and the relative importance of structural reform has not increased enough to explain what happened to the Japanese economy in the 1990s. Instead what has happened is simply the first example since the 1930s of a major economy facing the liquidity trap of absolute demand deflation. The tragedy is that the way out is easy – far easier indeed than structural reform – but that the Japanese authorities have resolutely refused to pursue it.

Japan entered recession in the early 1990s because a financial and property price bubble burst. Financial and property-market bubbles are hazards of free market economies, and raise issues as to whether all forms of liberalization are always desirable: these issues are discussed in Chapter 10. For now all that matters is that Japan went into recession not because of any 'structural failure' of its previously successful system,

---

13. See O'Mahony, *Britain's Productivity Performance 1950–96*.

but because of a speculative bubble and bust cycle of the sort which can happen and does happen in many countries or regions (in Massachusetts in the late 80s, in Texas in the early 80s, in Sweden in the early 90s). The oddity was not Japan's entry into recession but its failure to get out of it. For, once in recession, Japan began to suffer from a phenomenon well described by Keynes in *The General Theory* almost seventy years ago – a deflationary spiral in which consumers attempt to save their way to economic security, but in so doing simply make the spiral of falling prices and stagnant output worse. The way out is clear and is one of the few points of economic theory and practice on which monetarists like Friedman and Keynesians (like Keynes) can largely agree. The required policy can be described in two different ways. It requires monetary expansion by the central bank to the extent if necessary of the large-scale purchase of government debt. Described this way it sounds 'monetarist'. But this is equivalent also to an 'unfunded' fiscal deficit which stimulates the economy because the direct fiscal stimulus is not offset by crowding out of private investment or by consumer fears of the consequences of a future public-debt burden. Described this way it sounds Keynesian. But however described it is a certain way of putting a stop to an absolute deflation cycle, which is one of the few problems in economics which we definitely know how to solve and whose solution is close to costless. The key problem in Japan has not been a lack of political will to pursue difficult structural reform, but the government and central bank's continued refusal to pursue obvious and fairly costless policies. Failing to choose policies which involve hard trade-offs and hard decisions may be cowardly but it is understandable. Failing to choose close to costless policies is simply bizarre.[14]

---

14. Some quasi-rational reasons for that failure can be identified. One is that the Bank of Japan has only recently been made independent and is very reluctant to begin its life as an independent central bank by buying up government bonds and thus funding the government's budget deficits with monetary expansion. This reluctance reflects the fact that non-independent banks in high-inflation countries have often contributed to that inflation via monetary financing of government deficits. IMF recommendations/conditions for lending to countries attempting to reduce high inflation therefore frequently include the rule that central banks should *not* fund government deficits by purchasing their bonds. Refusal to fund government deficits with central bank money has indeed become one of the core principles of central banking, and a very sound one as long as the dangers lie entirely on the inflationary side. But it becomes an impediment to sensible policy if the danger

The story of Japan in the 1990s is thus a sad one, but actually somewhat tangential to the key issue explored in this chapter – which model of capitalism is in structural terms and in the long term the best. If Japan had not followed absurd macro policies in the 1990s, we would probably be concluding with a variant of the European story – yes some structural reform is desirable (more indeed than in Europe) but no case for panic action. As it is, the underlying story is obscured by the macroeconomic disaster.

The Asian tigers – a tale with few lessons?

If Japan in the 1990s carries few useful lessons for the debate on what capitalism is best for developed rich countries, the story of the Asian tigers' extraordinary success, the 1997 crash and the subsequent recovery is equally unrevealing. That is not the conventional wisdom of either the pre- or post- crash era. Prior to 1997, it was obvious to many commentators that the Asian tigers' success must be due to some magic elixir of growth. It could be their social habits of trust and mutual family support, or their long-term shareholder structures, or their minimal state and low taxes, but whatever the ideological predisposition of the commentator – and thus the factors most eagerly noted – it was clear that there was something special, some factor which drove Asian growth and which would take Asian countries at some not too distant point soaring past many European nations. After 1997, meanwhile, the fundamental causes of the crash were equally obvious and the long-standing structural weaknesses of the Asian economies plain for many to see. Corruption and crony capitalism, non-transparent corporate governance, poor accounting rules and systematic overinvestment were all structural problems for which deep structural solutions were required: without them recovery would be slow and painful.

In fact, however, almost all of this commentary misses the point. There may be subtle features of the different Asian economies which give them small relative advantages and it is worthwhile trying to identify those. There are indeed in several Asian countries structural

---

is instead nominal demand deflation. Central banks therefore need both the legal independence and the independence of judgement to fight deflationary as well as inflationary risks.

weaknesses of the sort identified and these should be carefully addressed. But the miracle of the Asian economies from the 1950s to 90s essentially illustrates that catch-up can work in a very wide range of different situations. And the crash of 1997 primarily illustrates the dangers of self-fulfilling cycles of irrational exuberance and irrational pessimism in liquid financial markets.

The Asian success story of the 1950s to 90s is essentially an example of the catch-up process examined earlier in this chapter. Countries starting behind in prosperity and productivity enjoy opportunities to achieve growth rates very much higher than those available in the already rich world. Globalization – which above all means greatly improved mechanisms to transfer ideas, know-how and capital across the world – has accelerated the attainable pace of catch-up, but the basic process which Korea went through in the 1970s and 80s was exactly that which Italy experienced in the 1950s and 60s. And when and if Korea and other Asian tigers get to roughly Western standards of living the most likely pattern is that they will then slow down to the leaders' rates of growth – just as Japan and Germany did in the 1980s.

To seize the potential opportunity of catch-up requires some reasonably sensible policies, which we seem to understand, and some cultural characteristics, which we understand less well. Reasonable openness to foreign ideas and capital, reasonable openness to trade and relatively sound macroeconomic policies are all required. If you cut yourself off from the world like Myanmar (Burma) you don't achieve catch-up. If you allow your economy to be afflicted by state profligacy and hyper-inflation, like many Latin American countries in the 1970s and 80s, you catch up only slowly. Asia is catching up, Africa is not, and the complex policy and cultural roots of that divergence merit much careful analysis. But within the ranks of the successful catch-up countries what is striking is not how common they are but how different they are. Taiwan enjoyed catch-up with an economic structure dominated by numerous mid-sized family companies, Korea with complex conglomerates (*chaebols*). Hong Kong caught up with a philosophy of minimal state liberalism, Korea and Taiwan with some elements of statist intervention such as selective protection or promotion of specific industries. Just as Germany's route to catch-up (product-market liberalism combined with labour-market co-operation) was significantly different from France's (a significant dose of technocratic statism) so Asia's paths to success have been varied. There are bad policies which can destroy economic growth prospects, but there is a relatively wide range of different policies, structures and cultures which produce rather similar results. Analysing Asian tiger success for lessons for Africa and other non-catch-up countries is a fruitful exercise; analysing it for lessons applicable to existing rich countries was, even before the crash, largely a waste of time.

The Asian economies crashed in 1997–8. The story of that crash and its implications for the global capitalist system (and in particular the global financial system) will be looked at in Chapter 10. For now three features of that story should be noted. First, while there are certainly many structural features of Asian economies which could usefully be reformed (the standard list of non-transparent corporate governance, poor accounting and corruption, etc.) these had not suddenly emerged in the years prior to 1997 and there is no indication that they had got worse. They were features always present, as much when we were worshipping the Asian tigers in the early 1990s as when we discovered their feet of clay in the late 1990s. They were not therefore the cause of the crash in any meaningful sense. Second, just as the miracle had occurred in countries with very different economic and social structures and practices, so the crash occurred in almost all of them irrespective of precise conditions, policies and practices – in Korea, which had not suffered a wave of irresponsible property lending as much as in Thailand which had. Third, recovery came surprisingly strongly and rapidly in 1999 and 2000 before structural reforms could have time to produce profound effects, and came both in countries which had signed up to the full IMF medicine (including structural reform) and those which had not, in Korea (13 per cent annual growth in the year to 1999 Quarter 4) and also in Malaysia (11 per cent). The implication of those facts is fairly clear. The crash was essentially a financial-market phenomenon of irrational exuberance suddenly reversed: the recovery essentially driven by a rebound from a downward overshoot. Structural reform may well make sense for a lot of Asian countries, and may well become more important as and when they approach the end of catch-up: fine-tuning the system becomes more important once the easy pickings of catch-up are close to exhaustion. But the Asian crash of 1997 is a story largely tangential to that of the need for structural reform, and a story with few useful lessons for economic management in developed rich countries.

*   *   *

This chapter has analysed the economic performance of different countries and thus types of capitalism, using narrowly economic definitions of success rather than some of the wider welfare measures mentioned in Chapter 4. That analysis, combined with conclusions reached in previous chapters, carries a key implication for public policy choice – the implication that we have more freedom to choose our economic and social structures than we are often told. The following four conclusions arise from the analysis presented so far.

» First, that national competitiveness, for the reasons presented in Chapter 1, is a misleading way of thinking about national and certainly continental economic performance, because it implies that beating others at some chosen measure is vitally important, when in fact all that matters is our absolute productivity, prosperity and employment prospects.

» Second, that measures of economic success are not definitive, but can involve social choices and trade-offs between, for instance, leisure and income, environmental quality and measured growth.

» Third, that the performance of the major developed economies is more similar than different and strongly influenced by autonomous technological developments; and that the performance of catch-up countries is primarily driven by the fact of catch-up, a process which works in quite a wide range of different specific situations.

» Fourth, and as a direct implication of the third, that while there are some clearly bad economic policies (such as socialism as we used to understand that term, excessive protectionism and inflationary public finance) there is in both the catch-up and leadership stages of development quite a wide range of different structures and policies which make only a little difference to economic performance.

Taken together these imply that we are to a greater extent than the conventional wisdom believes masters of our destiny. That means in turn that we have trade-offs and choices to make. Those trade-offs and choices are considered in Chapter 6 and subsequent chapters.

6. The European Model –
Reform or Reject?

Europe's economic prosperity and employment are not threatened by global competition and Europe is not a disaster zone faced with an American economic miracle. But the balance of economic advantage has shifted in favour of some aspects of the American system as a result of changes in technology and economic structure. Faced with that shifting balance of advantage how should Europe change? Should it reform or reject its 'economic and social model'?

To ultra-liberals the answer is clear: Europe must reject its traditional model, privatize, liberalize, deregulate, cut taxes and dismantle its 'unaffordable' welfare states. If all that is unsettling and places desirable social objectives at risk, so be it, that is the price of staying competitive in the global economy. The answer given in this book is different. Europe should liberalize its product, capital and labour markets but can do so without sacrificing essential rather than incidental features of a distinctive European approach, and should do so without turning deregulation into a dogma rather than a means to an end. And while European governments must focus their role to achieve desirable objectives within constrained means, European welfare states are not unaffordable and there is no need to reduce tax and government spend to American levels. Socialism is over and many traditional social democratic means of pursuing objectives are now ineffective or impossible, but Europe can still choose to pursue a distinctive path, one summed up best, perhaps, in Lionel Jospin's phrase 'the market economy but not the market society'.

Before arguing that case, however, a caveat is essential. There is no one European and social model but many different national models common only at the level of objectives and broad approaches. In corporate governance Germany's traditional system of two-tier boards and co-determination is quite different from the traditional French model. German financial structures with big banks holding both debt and equity stakes in public companies were always different from Italy's complex mesh of corporate and private cross-shareholdings. Trade unionization rates range from 10 per cent in France to 90 per cent in Scandinavia. Statutory minimum wages are national in some countries, regional or sectoral in others, non-existent in Germany. Hire-and-fire rules vary significantly by country. Tax and spend levels vary from 33 per cent of GDP in Ireland and 36 per cent in Spain to 56 per cent in Denmark. The nature of the state's role in the economy has differed too. France has had a tradition of active state involvement in economic development including the state ownership of normal commercial companies. Germany's post-war economic system has been based on a rigorously liberal approach to competitive markets. In philosophical terms too Catholic Christian democracy, French technocrat statism and German liberalism have very different roots.

A patchwork quilt, therefore, not a uniform blanket. But despite diversity there is enough similarity of objectives pursued for the concept of a distinctive European approach to have some validity and with the distinction above all versus the US. In essence that distinction is simple: much less willingness to accept as given that the outcome of free competition between individuals is by definition right, attractive and unchangeable; much greater willingness to accept that there is such a thing as 'society' which can and should modulate the outcomes of individual competition. That broad philosophy has been expressed in different ways in different countries. In some it has been reflected in corporate objectives which speak of a wider group of stakeholders rather than shareholders alone; in others in an unwillingness to treat the price of labour as a 'price like any other' to be determined by market forces alone. In all it is expressed through provision of health-care irrespective of income as essential to equality of citizenship. The means differ and some of them are outdated and will have to change, but the common objectives remain both attractive and attainable.

The changes required in different aspects of Europe's models are set out below. The general direction of change should be towards market liberalism. In product markets this is largely accepted, in capital markets inevitable, in labour markets it is still controversial but particularly important. This needs to be balanced, however, by a still large but focused social role for European states. Market liberalism but not the dismantling of European welfare states: the good news is that this is largely the path on which Europe is increasingly embarked. The Euro-sceptic myth of Europe as incapable of change is just that, a myth. Europe should be confident that it can change while preserving desirable features of its traditional approach – it is already on the right road.

Product-market liberalization

Product-market liberalization and privatization are core mantras of the ultra-liberal creed – luckily they are in most instances desirable. Europe is already well embarked on the liberalization and privatization road and the key policy priority is simply to stick with it. Fortunately that path does not in general entail any sacrifice of essential rather than incidental features of the European model and where it does we can choose to make exceptions without losing the benefits of the broad direction. For liberalization and privatization should be seen as powerful means to achieve desired ends, not religious dogmas incapable of pragmatic exception.

Market liberalization is a term loosely used and entails many constituent elements. Its simplest form is trade liberalization, absence of internal tariffs within a market area, low tariffs and few quota restrictions versus the rest of world. But it also implies the possibility of intense competition within markets, created by strong anti-cartel regulations, by the absence of legal or de facto monopolies and by the removal of subsidy distortions arising from either direct grants or the operation of state-owned companies in a loss-making or low-return fashion. Privatization is not absolutely essential for market liberalization – you can run a state-owned company on a fully commercial basis independent of day-to-day government intervention – but in practice it usually accompanies liberalization and for a good reason. It is very difficult for governments to own companies but resist the temptation to direct or subsidize, and if they do resist that temptation the supposed rationale for state ownership largely disappears.

The general case for market liberalization and privatization is strong and in many ways always has been. Intense internal competition, policed by a strong cartel office, was a vital driver of Germany's postwar recovery. Trade liberalization resulting from the establishment of the European Economic Community was the key to rapid European economic growth in the 1950s and 60s, and almost certainly more important to France's '*trente glorieuses*' than all the clever plans and interventions of the Commissariat du Plan.[1] Conversely, Britain's failure to enter the free-trade area of the Common Market in the 1950s, which

---

1. See Owen, *From Empire to Europe* – discussed further in Chapter 7.

would have exposed its industry to the beneficial effects of competition, was probably the biggest cause of Britain's post-war relative decline. Much play is often made of Japan's interventionist industrial policy (orchestrated by MITI) but in the sectors where Japan has been most successful – such as automobiles and consumer electronics – ferocious internal competition was always equally if not more important. And as Chapter 5 has argued, one key explanation of the US's absolute-efficiency advantage is its large single market which makes possible economies of scale and which ensures strongly contested markets. The case for market liberalization has therefore always been there and opposition to liberalized product markets (whether via tariffs, subsidies, cartels or nationalization) was always wrong and confused.

But if the case was always a good one it has become stronger still under the impact of globalization and structural change, most obviously in respect of privatization. Nationalization of the 'commanding heights' of the economy was always a mistake but at least an understandable one when national companies operated primarily in national econo-mies. When 'what is good for General Motors is good for America' was a true statement, the concept of 'national champions' had a surface appeal. But when major companies operate with employees, activities and shareholders spread throughout the world, the rationale collapses completely. In the late 1980s and early 1990s Credit Lyonnais, then owned by the French state, went on a lending spree throughout the world. The stated rationale was to build a French bank of global scale and the proposed route to that ambition included lending at lower than cost of risk to, among others, Hollywood film producers and British property developers. What looked good temporarily for Credit Lyon-nais was fun while it lasted for top management but it was from start to finish a disaster for the French taxpayer, without even the side benefit that the beneficiaries of its pricing largesse were all French. The whole concept of national champions collapses once companies and banks become transnational and global in scope.

Changes in technology and economic structure have also reduced the case for state ownership even of what were once 'natural monopo-lies'. Until but a few decades ago, the challenge for telephony and electricity companies seemed simple, strategic and social – to achieve national coverage of relatively undifferentiated services as an under-pinning both of economic growth and social inclusion. That task could be performed by a regulated monopoly (such as AT&T) but well-run public companies (such as France Telecom) appeared to do it just as well. In both industries, however, conditions have changed. Telecoms services have ceased to be a natural monopoly as long-distance capacity costs have fallen and radio technology and cable TV have made possible local access competition. Product innovation and product differentiation in telecoms, meanwhile, have become crucial to seizing the potential of information technology. There is now an overwhelmingly strong rationale for liberalization of telecoms services which was missing only twenty years ago. In electricity distribution developments have been different. There is no product proliferation, the industry is mature and on the whole electricity is just electricity. But the period of building capacity and distribution coverage is over too, universal service is in place. The economic efficiency challenge is simply to run a mature network at the lowest possible cost, and the best route to achieve that is probably to have privatized distribution companies facing pressure from both regulators and the threat of takeover.

The case for Europe to privatize and liberalize product markets is therefore strong. That fact, however, produces two sets of fears: Euro-sceptics and ultra-liberals fearing that Europe is incapable of change, opponents of globalization and liberalization fearing that these changes threaten desirable aspects of the European model. The first fear is simply wrong. The second feature need not be true as long as we use liberalization as a means to defined ends, not as a god to be worshipped.

In Britain, though not elsewhere in Europe, ultra-liberalism is a strange bedfellow of Euro-scepticism and the European Union is believed to be a determined agent of state intervention and a barrier to liberalization. In fact quite the opposite is true. The broad thrust of European Community and European Union policy has always been in the direction of market liberalism, and the latest and most ambitious project, the single currency, is in its microeconomic effects a further step in that direction.

The European Economic Community was from the outset (except in the agricultural sector) a force for market liberalization, and indeed was opposed as such by British socialists with good reason given their then policies (and thus with considerably more ideological coherence than right-wing Euro-scepticism now displays). Internal tariff elimination followed directly from the Treaty of Rome in 1957. Free movement of labour and capital were objectives from the start but only completely achieved with the Single European Act of 1987, fully implemented by 1992. External tariffs versus the US and the rest of the world have been continually reduced and most industrial products now enter Europe duty-free. But trade liberalization is not itself enough if Europe is to match the large single-market benefits which the US enjoys. In the US conditions for a large intensely competitive single market exist as a natural by-product of political union; in Europe they have been imperfectly created by European-level action while still preserving the ultimate sovereignty of individual states. If you want open competition in products and services you need either common standards or (as a second best) a regime of mutually agreed recognition of different standards. If you want to achieve economies of scale in automobile manufacture you need a common law on environmental emissions. To create competitive conditions you need a European level of competition law, action to restrict state subsidies and Commission pressure on countries to take liberalization steps which upset vested interests. You need in other words the whole panoply of European powers which Euro-sceptics so hate. The process involves endless trade-offs between the benefits of standardization, the costs of transition, and the dangers of public reaction, and sometimes the Commission gets it wrong. The process is also often frustratingly slow. But in the long run the achievements are startling. If anyone had predicted fifteen years ago that Europe would have in place by 2000 an open market in telecoms services and that the French government would have privatized France Telecom he would have been dismissed as a deluded dreamer. But both changes have occurred.

The process is incomplete. Further liberalization is needed. Competition in local telephony access needs to be ensured; postal services should be liberalized. Energy markets and retail financial services are still sectors with inadequate competition. But that list defines precisely the current priorities of the European Commission. Market liberalization, far from being impossible, is already in hand.

In hand too is the creation of a single currency. In macroeconomic terms there are important arguments for and against a single currency (discussed in Chapter 10). But in its microeconomic effect the nature of a single currency is clear – it is a market liberalizing measure which creates more intense competition in a manner closely analogous to trade liberalization. It is one of the key features of the US's inherent efficiency advantage. Monetary union will create and already is creating more intense competition across Europe for three reasons. Transparency and stability of price comparisons will directly stimulate price competition in both business-to-consumer and business-to-business markets. The absence of internal exchange-rate risk will create the potential for companies to build pan-European production and logistics networks, no longer needing to hold assets in different countries simply in order to achieve natural currency hedges: rationalization and productivity improvement will result.[2] Finally, the emergence of a pan-European equity market in which French equities are as likely to be held by German individuals or institutions as French, and vice versa, will increase the pressure on companies to perform, direct savings to highest return on investments wherever in Europe, and foster a pan-European market in corporate control, i.e. stimulate mergers and takeovers. Many of these effects are indeed visible already: the total value of mergers and acquisitions activity in Europe increased almost six times between 1995 and 1999, the cross-border element seven times. Contrary to British Euro-sceptic pessimism that Europe is incapable of change and that the euro is an anti-liberal project, Europe is changing in precisely the direction required and the euro is a positive stimulus.

The alternative fear is that liberalization and privatization will occur, but that they threaten distinctive and desirable features of the European social model – that privatization will undermine public service levels and that further trade liberalization will undermine the particularities and quality of culture or indeed cuisine. Whether it is the French farmer Jose Bové attacking McDonald's in opposition to the perceived threat of '*malbouffe*' or Ken Livingstone winning a landslide victory in London while opposing tube privatization, the fear that the liberal creed will undermine quality of life provokes significant political reaction.

Those fears could be justified if we turned market liberalism into a rigid dogma rather than a means to an end. For if applied as dogma, market liberalism can undermine desirable objectives. In most cases it does not. In many cases indeed, opposition to market liberalizing measures on the basis of 'quality of life' or 'public service' is simply a

---

2. It is sometimes asserted that the benefits of exchange-rate certainty can be gained by hedging on the forward foreign-exchange markets. This is based on a complete misunderstanding of the most important benefits of exchange-rate stability and of the capacities of the forward exchange markets. It is possible to hedge a specific foreign-exchange receipt for a specific future date. But it is not possible to hedge an uncertain stream of future sales receipts which will arrive in uncertain amount and at uncertain times over a number of years: without that possibility floating exchange rates within a business's potential markets increase risk in investment decisions.

smokescreen for the defence of vested interests. Many French socialists resist moves to privatize electricity distribution on the grounds that universal service obligations would be threatened. This is complete nonsense. Local electricity distribution remains a natural monopoly, privatized electricity distributors will always be regulated, and regulation can ensure universal service levels as effectively as state ownership and management. Britain has a universal electricity service to households despite privatization, and electricity privatization (unlike rail privatization) has provoked no concerns about the quality of that service. What is threatened is not universal service but staffing levels and employee perks (such as pension terms massively more favourable than those enjoyed by the average French citizen). Inefficient working practices and the privilege of one segment of workers compared with others are accidental by-products of Europe's economic and social model and neither essential to Europe's distinctive approach nor desirable.

In many other cases the appropriate design of regulatory structures can defend desirable social objectives as well if not better than public ownership. If Britain wants to privatize the British Post Office and preserve the extent of the network of rural post offices it can.[3] If countries want to privatize railways but still subsidize elements of the network for social and environmental reasons they can, and operating subsidies to franchise holders may prove a more efficient way of buying social and environmental benefits than the more hidden subsidy of public ownership. As for the environmental consequences of water and waste management, the clear separation of business management from standard setting achieved by Britain's water privatization has proved a better model for achieving improvements than was the previous regime in which environmental improvements were traded off against other government priorities year by year, with necessary capital investments cut in the face of short-term financial pressures.

In most cases, therefore, market liberalization is not only fully compatible with wider social objectives but can actually help achieve

---

3. Indeed the irony of British opposition to Post Office privatization – from both Labour and Conservative members of Parliament – on the grounds of a threat to sub-post offices, is that sub-post offices form the one part of the UK network which is already private – effectively a sub-post office is a privately owned franchise.

them more cost-effectively. To ensure this we need simply a pragmatic rather than religious approach to both privatization and market liberalization, using these tools as means to ends not as ends per se. If they don't deliver those ends or if they conflict with other desired objectives we should make exceptions.

Pragmatism and realism are needed in privatization. British rail privatization may in the end deliver improved service, but two features of its implementation have undermined it. The first was rush – too much change at once, all levels of the system privatized simultaneously, no fixed points of continuity, no experiment with new and untested relationships (between track owner and rail-operating companies, between operating companies and equipment providers) before committing to the whole design. The almost total investment vacuum in the British railway system during the transition years of 1996–7, coming on top of years of under-investment was one inevitable consequence (rolling-stock investment fell in 1996–7 to one-tenth of its early 1990s level); large individual gains made not from improved performance but from under-pricing of privatized assets was another: both have undermined public support and railway-company credibility. The second mistake was to assume that privatization of public transport systems is a route to eliminate or greatly reduce public subsidy – committing most of the rail system to the elimination of public subsidies by 2005.[4] In fact, as Chapter 9 will argue, the environmental and social case for subsidizing public transport remains sound even if private companies own and manage the assets involved. The idea that all markets can operate entirely on the basis of the free competition of unsubsidized operators is a delusion. Privatization is a means to an end, but the ends still need defining. As Gerald Corbett, at that time the Chief Executive of the UK's Railtrack, declared in autumn 2000, what went wrong in British rail privatization was not the principle of regulated private ownership but the fact that the specific form of privatization was designed to maximize revenues to the Treasury rather than to facilitate increased investment in a high-quality rail network.

Pragmatism and a clear focus on objectives is needed also in market

---

4. A policy now reversed, but which undermined investment levels in the initial years. The large rise in public investment in the railways now planned (£14.7 billion for 2001–10 following £0.2 billion 1996–2000), reflects the reality of the need for major subsidized investment.

liberalization: if market liberalization conflicts with desirable social objectives we should not be afraid to make exceptions. Two examples can illustrate the point. The first is the French attachment to 'cultural exception'. The French government insists that measures to preserve the vitality of French language and culture should be exceptions to Europe's normal free-market rules. It pursues those objectives through quotas on English-language films shown in cinemas and on television and through subsidies to its own cultural industries. The objectives and effectiveness of such policies are a legitimate subject for debate. Many people, including many French people, might doubt the value of the objective, wishing simply to be able to watch as many American films as possible as cheaply as possible. Others may argue that the measures could in principle be justifiable but in practice don't work. France's European partners may wish that France would sacrifice cultural exception in world trade negotiations to gain benefits for all European citizens. All of those are valid arguments. But it is quite invalid to argue that cultural exception is inadmissible even as a subject for debate, and it is unhelpful to exaggerate the importance of the issue. The total prosperity penalty introduced by a French cultural exception either in France, in her fellow European countries, or in trading partners like America is trivial, and if we want to take a small productivity hit to protect cultural diversity we can choose to do so.[5]

The second example concerns planning and the physical environment. Chapter 5 has already mentioned the McKinsey and Company report of 1998 which argued that British planning restrictions on business development have a negative impact on productivity, especially in sectors like retailing and hotels. For the reasons discussed in Chapter 5 the McKinsey team was probably right. Plentiful land and few planning restrictions allow easy greenfield development, increase competitive intensity and make economies of scale and efficient layout easier to achieve. Some positive productivity effect from looser planning rules is therefore almost inevitable. But in densely populated countries

---

5. One argument against such exceptions advanced by those involved in world trade negotiations is that of the 'slippery slope' – i.e. the economic impact of any specific exception may be unimportant, but if any country is allowed any divergence from free trade principles then the whole structure of world trade liberation will 'unravel'. This argument is discussed in Chapter 11. There is no sign that it is valid.

the benefit of slightly higher productivity would come at the cost of countryside destruction which some people would not want to pay. If we don't want to pay that cost we don't have to. We have a choice. We are not liberalizing as a 'no alternative' necessity in order to win in a winner-takes-all competitive race: we are liberalizing to achieve specific benefits. We should liberalize when benefits outweigh costs, which they do in most cases, but not if they do not.

Capital markets and corporate objectives

Product-market liberalization is contentious because of feared social effects but the economic benefits are largely accepted. Stakeholderists such as Hutton and Albert made no case that Europe's product markets were distinctive from or superior to America's. They did, however, see Rhineland financial structures and corporate objectives as defining characteristics of the stakeholder model and inherently better than Anglo-Saxon alternatives. Long-term committed managers free from the tyranny of short-term results were seen as the key to higher investment, high productivity and workforce security. Changes to these features therefore seem a bigger challenge to the European model than further progress down the product-market liberalization road.

Change, however, is close to inevitable, already happening and on the whole desirable. That does not mean that the case for Rhineland financial structures was necessarily without merit: simply that whatever's one conclusion in principle on the Rhineland/Anglo-Saxon debate the balance of advantage has shifted in the American system's favour.

Continental European corporate financial structures have always varied greatly between countries but some common features of distinction from the American system are striking and were even more so ten years ago. Equity markets have played a much smaller economic role: in 1990 German equity-market capitalization was 23 per cent of GDP versus America's 54 per cent. French fund-raising from equity markets via rights issues and initial offerings (IPOs) was about one-tenth as important as in the US. Venture capital was and is less developed (American funds raised in 1999 about $50 billion, German about $5 billion). Pensions are (except in the Netherlands) primarily pay-as-you-go, not funded, and funds under management is therefore a less-developed business, with the role of pension funds and other professional fund managers as holders of corporate equity much smaller.

But as important as the figures have been the attitudes. Ten years ago very few continental executives would have stated shareholder-value maximization as an overt aim, but many British and American managers did. Ten years ago contested takeovers were almost unheard of on the continent, as were stock options.

To the stakeholderists these continental features were causes for celebration not concern. To Albert and Hutton it was precisely the equity-market fixation of British and American managers – the performance tables, fear of takeover and stock options – which condemned them to short-termism. The case was probably always overstated. Undemanding shareholders can result in weak, inefficient management or in wasteful expansion for its own sake as much as in strategic long-term vision. The success of the US high-tech companies – Microsoft, IBM, Hewlett-Packard – with price-earnings ratios which attach a huge value to future growth, showed that an overt shareholder culture can support long-termism. And the superiority of the German and Japanese systems should never be overstated – most of their faster growth was simply catch-up. But these arguments notwithstanding, the stakeholder arguments appeared to have some validity. In the early 1990s a reasonable person could argue the case either way. What has changed is the economic context.

The argument has already been stated in Chapter 5. Some continental European and Japanese companies may well have gained some advantages from the financial structures which Albert and Hutton praise, but they did so, in particular manufacturing industries with particular characteristics at a particular time. Two factors have reduced whatever advantages those financial systems had and increased the advantages of the American equity-driven model.

The first is the changing nature of productivity improvement potential described in Chapter 2. Productivity improvements now more frequently require radical restructuring and actual downsizing of large sites and companies, with the economic benefit deriving from the fact that people are released to work in other sectors of the economy entirely. Pressure for high shareholder return and the threat of takeover have therefore become more important to the attainment of maximum potential productivity. The American system is thus better designed to ensure that companies rapidly seize the productivity potential of information and communications technology.

The second is that the economic importance of start-ups and rapid-growth companies has increased. The latest wave of technological change (ICT) provides greater opportunities for important innovation by small-scale operators. Funding the innovation and growth of new companies has therefore become more important to overall economic success. Venture-capital funds to support start-up and rapid growth firms and liquid equity markets to support IPOs and rights issues are increasingly vital to economic performance. In 1998 and 1999 US high-tech firms raised $48 billion from venture capital; the equivalent European figure was $11 billion. Long-term stable financial structures of the Rhineland variety were good for funding long-term companies enjoying gradual growth; the Anglo-Saxon system is better for achieving rapid re-allocation of capital (out of downsizing companies and into fast-growth companies), which is what the present technological conjuncture requires.

If Europe is to seize the opportunities of the new economy its capital market structures and behaviour should therefore evolve in the American direction: because of globalization they will whether governments plan it or not. For one of the true effects of globalization is that capital can move easily across borders and that corporate-ownership structures are cross-border. In a world where Daimler-Chrysler has assets, employees and shareholders across the world and where 33 per cent of French corporate equity is owned by non-French shareholders (up from 22 per cent in 1993), financial structures and corporate-governance approaches are bound to converge towards the presently more successful American model.

A great deal of change is indeed already occurring. Equity-market capitalization as a percentage of GDP has soared across Europe during the 1990s – from 23 to 71 per cent in Germany, from 32 to 116 per cent in France. Contested takeovers, such as Olivetti's of Telecom Italia and Vodafone's of Mannesman, are now accepted. So too is talk of shareholder-value maximization. Germany's planned abolition of capital-gains tax on corporate shareholdings (to take effect in January 2002) will unleash corporate restructuring to create companies more focused on core businesses and on shareholder return. Corporate cross-holdings of shares have already fallen from 44 per cent of the German total in 1990 to below 30 per cent today: financial company and institutional investor holdings have increased from 24 per cent to 37 per cent. Funded pension schemes are – slowly – being developed in almost all European countries. European venture capital in high-tech firms may be well behind the US but it increased three times between 1998 and 1999. IPO markets for high-tech firms have rapidly developed in France (the Nouveau Marché) and in Germany (the Neue Markt). Further change needs to come, above all through the creation of pan-European equity exchanges with the liquidity and depth of their US equivalents. But the direction of change is clear.

Overall the change should be welcomed. But its implication for how Europe achieves the objectives of a good society must be faced. For in an equity-market-driven economy the definition of corporate objectives will play a decreasing role in the achievement of the European model's distinctive and desirable objectives. Stakeholderist corporate objectives have sometimes in the past included an implicit or explicit commitment to security of employment. The argument presented in Chapter 5 and again here is that those objectives were only deliverable without efficiency penalty because of the particular technological context of the 1950s and 70s. They were and still are, however, seen as key elements of the European model. When Renault announced the closure of its Wilwoorde car plant in Belgium in 1997 as part of its inevitable rationalization programme, it was condemned for acting in an Anglo-Saxon fashion and trade unions put pressure on the European Commission to introduce new restrictions on restructuring. When Michelin announced a rationalization programme in 1999 the French Prime Minister Lionel Jospin publicly attacked it for planning employment reduction in pursuit of profit maximization rather than because of absolute competitive necessity. But if we want to maximize productivity potential in the current technological context we will sometimes have to cut workforces because that is possible and profitable, not always because it is necessary. In turn we will have to pursue the desirable European objectives of social inclusion and economic security through other routes. Corporate objectives and capital-market pressures will drive economic efficiency: the good society will need to be achieved by other means.

A similar shift in approach is required also in labour-market regulation.

Labour-market flexibility

On 19 January 1996 John Major, then the British Prime Minister, gave a speech to the Institute of Directors in Birmingham. In it he warned of the dire consequences of European labour-market policies and cited Britain's opt-out of the European Social Chapter (negotiated by him at

Maastricht in 1991) as a key factor in Britain's superior economic performance, its superior 'competitiveness' and, above all, its low unemployment rate. 'If I had signed the Social Chapter' he said 'I could never have looked the unemployed in the eye again.' The speech was typical of many of that era and of an enduring strain in British Euro-sceptic and ultra-liberal opinion. European labour-market rigidities are the key driver of European unemployment: the transmission mechanism is through the 'burden' which regulations impose on businesses and thus on their 'competitiveness', and the problem is Europe-wide, expressed primarily through the European Union's Social Chapter.

But only a little of this is true. There are rigidities in several European labour markets which inhibit job creation. But the problem is not a Europe-wide one: it is not a problem of competitiveness and the role of the Social Chapter in creating the problem is nil. It is against that reality that the nature and scope of required changes in European labour markets needs to be assessed. The changes needed would shift European labour markets in a more free-market direction but do not require that European countries abandon entirely the pursuit of desirable social objectives via labour-market regulation.

Continental European labour markets are in general more regulated than American; the UK's lies in between. The precise details of regulation vary greatly by country and with no simple pattern: a country which is more flexible on one dimension (such as working-time regulations) may be less flexible on another (such as hire-and-fire rules). The major differences versus the US can, however, be generalized as follows:[6]

» All continental countries have wage-determination systems in which unions play a larger role than in the US. Most wages are collectively bargained in some way rather than simply set by management and in many countries there is an element of national collective bargaining (or at least 'co-ordination') as well as bargaining at company or plant level.
» Minimum wages are not a general point of distinction. Most European countries have statutory minimum wages, but then so

---

6. See CBI, *Creating a Europe that Works*, for a factual description of labour-market features in six major European countries.

does the US, and some European countries do not (e.g. Germany).[7] Continental minimum wages tend, however, to be somewhat higher as a percentage of average earnings than in the US and particularly so for young workers (e.g. in France). Taking collective bargaining and minimum wages together, continental European labour markets have more powerful mechanisms than those in the US to prevent low-skilled wages falling to very low levels.

» There are considerably more restrictions on making workers redundant. All countries specify required consultation procedures ahead of collective redundancy (indeed this is one area where there is a European-wide regulation). More importantly, several countries (e.g. France and the Netherlands) require administrative approval of collective redundancies and there is a cultural assumption in some countries that these should be justified by economic 'necessity' rather than by the pursuit of profit and productivity improvement as ends in themselves. Restraints on dismissing individual workers are also typically tighter.

» Rules on working time exist in most countries, whether via legislation or through collectively bargained contracts. Until recently these included restrictions which made part-time work less common (and which reinforced the assumption that only full-time permanent employment was 'real work') but these have tended to disappear. Limits on absolute number of hours of work remain (with a European-wide dimension – the forty-eight-hour working week). Restrictions on temporary-contract terms are also common.

» Maternity-leave rights and pay, parental-leave rights and gender equality of opportunity requirements are more developed.

» Unemployment benefits are in general higher as a percentage of average earnings and less conditional upon search for work, although in this area there is huge variety – conditionality in particular varies greatly and Italy is an outlier with almost no unemployment-benefit system.

Overall, therefore, and despite huge national variety at the detailed level it is possible to define a European approach to labour markets which has been clearly distinct from that of the US. There is less

---

7. Germany does, however, have regional and sectoral minima established not via law but via collective bargaining.

willingness to accept that the labour market is a 'market like any other' in which both quantities demanded and prices set can be left simply to free-market forces; and there is greater willingness to use labour-market interventions in an attempt to pursue desired social objectives, such as poverty prevention, economic security, equal opportunity, or easier balance of work and family life.[8]

For many years this labour-market approach did not impose an unemployment penalty. In the 1960s and 1970s, indeed, European unemployment rates were, on average, lower than US levels and, while some of the rigidities have grown over the decades, the essential distinctions between the European and American approaches already existed then. But Europe's key problem is now unemployment and much of that is structural rather than cyclical. We therefore have to explain deterioration in performance despite largely unchanged policy: the most likely explanation is changed economic context.

The changes in technology and economic structure outlined in Chapters 2 and 3 pose challenges to traditional European labour market approaches. The rise of the service economy is creating the need for more part-time jobs, making the assumption that all jobs must be full-time an impediment to job creation. Fortunately this is largely accepted; fortunately too this change does not threaten desirable objectives – indeed part-time jobs serve to increase lifestyle choice rather than decrease it.[9] The latest phase of technological change, however, has two more troublesome effects: it increases income inequality between different levels of skill and thus makes it more likely that minimum wage or bargaining constraints on free movement of wages will create unemployment for low-skilled workers; and it creates an environment in which more of the employment flow is from large companies to small, making restrictive hire-and-fire policies greater impediments to productivity growth and to employment creation. Given these trends, it is possible that Europe's

---

8. The refusal to accept the labour market as a 'market like any other' is indeed an overt and central element of Christian Democratic philosophy drawing on a tradition of Catholic social thought which goes back to the papal encyclical *Rerum Novarum* of 1893.

9. Survey evidence shows that in countries where part-time work is most developed and accepted, the clear majority of part-timers positively prefer the part-time option rather than seeing it as a second best to full-time work, e.g. survey by European Foundation for Improvement of Living and Working Conditions (1993).

worse unemployment record than the US since the mid-1980s reflects the fact that features of its labour markets which were not previously impediments to high employment have become so as the economic context has changed. If that is true then some European countries will have to reform labour markets in order to reduce unemployment. All should certainly look with care at all aspects of existing labour-market regulation and all should consider alternative ways to pursue desired social objectives – low-income problems, for instance, addressed through in-work benefits rather than through minimum wages. The likely trend will be for European labour markets to become to a greater extent markets like any other; with social objectives pursued by other means.

But while that is the probable trend it does not mean that Europe must simply copy the American model or reject entirely the use of labour-market regulation to achieve desirable ends. For while changing technology and changing economic structure provide a general justification for greater liberalization, detailed analysis suggests three qualifications: it reveals that more liberalization is not limitlessly better; it shows us that different countries have achieved equally good results with different policy mixes; and it tells us that while some types of labour-market regulation are likely to cause employment problems others do not.

Logic and the overall comparison of Europe and the US suggest that wage determination and hire-and-fire rules need to become more flexible in the light of changing economic structure, but detailed empirical analysis reveals a more complex story. Numerous studies have attempted to establish statistically robust relationships between unemployment or employment and specific labour-market rules:[10] the results caution us against any belief that deregulation is a sure and universal solution to Europe's unemployment problems. They reveal, for instance, that while minimum wages can in theory cause unemployment most have in practice been set at levels where the effect is minimal. Specific

10. See Stephen Nickell, 'Unemployment and Labour-Market Rigidities: Europe Versus North America', *Journal of Economic Perspectives*, summer 1997, for a good summary covering all the key possible factors. Also Richard Layard, *Tackling Unemployment*, OECD *Jobs Study 1994*, OECD *Employment Outlook* (June 1999). The correlations in the latter study show, for instance, no link between the strictness of employment-protection rules and unemployment, but weak correlation evidence that employment of young people and women is decreased by tight employment laws, while employment of prime-aged men is slightly increased.

countries (e.g. France and Spain) should consider lower rates for young people but there is no reasonable conclusion that minimum wages should be abolished or radically reduced throughout Europe. Similarly on hire-and-fire rules, very strict limits on firing permanent workers can act to distort labour markets, keeping market outsiders (such as young people and women with children) out of the labour market or forcing them on to temporary contracts. The Spanish labour market before reforms in the mid-1990s is a clear example – employment 'protection' laws so strict that they were in fact employment destroying. But there is no evidence that easier hire-and-fire rules are always limitlessly better whatever the starting point. Very strict regimes should be reformed but in several European countries existing regimes can be left in place.

Different countries, moreover, have achieved equally successful outcomes via different routes. The UK has a better employment record than the continental average, but the Netherlands, Denmark, Sweden and Austria achieve similar or even lower unemployment rates. In most of these examples there are some common features. Part-time work has been vital to creating high employment in the Netherlands as much as in the UK. Fairly tight conditionality on unemployment benefit (i.e. requirements on benefit claimants to look for work and to accept work when available) are found in most successful examples. But there are also striking differences particularly in wage bargaining. The UK has achieved low unemployment with a highly decentralized labour market in which national collective bargaining now plays almost no part in the private sector; the Netherlands has a national collective bargaining approach which co-ordinates the overall level of pay rises but leaves scope for variation. It is striking that the co-ordinated approaches seem to work best in smaller countries (e.g. the Netherlands, Ireland) where the problem of required regional variations is more limited. It is also likely that the direction of change in future, under the impact of changed technology and changed economic structure, will be towards decentralization. The German labour market is now experiencing a significant breakdown of national collective bargaining with much greater use of regional and plant-level variations. But the overall conclusion still stands. Different countries have found different routes to success. There isn't a European-wide problem and there doesn't need to be a common European solution.[11]

---

11. Both empirical analysis and theory indeed have led some economists to the

Different types of labour-market regulation, moreover, have a very different capacity to create unemployment problems. This fact is obscured by competitiveness-speak in which labour-market regulations create 'burdens' and 'burdens' create unemployment by increasing labour costs, making European countries 'uncompetitive' in world markets. According to this theory, onerous labour-market regulation is no different from a high average wage cost or higher taxes on labour and all three can make Europe's economy uncompetitive. This is, however, a quite mistaken description of how labour-market rigidities (or indeed taxes) can create unemployment.·

The confusions of the 'competitiveness burden' approach to tax levels (and by analogy regulation) are dealt with in detail in Chapter 8. They derive from two key fallacies. The first is to imagine that 'competitiveness' is a meaningful concept at the level of a continental economy and that high labour costs in Europe could or in fact do create an overall competitiveness problem. In fact high average labour costs (whether resulting from high wages, high taxes or regulation) cannot create 'competitiveness' problems for economies with externally floating exchange rates because the exchange rate can move to achieve a competitive equilibrium. And Europe's balanced current account position (and until recently its large surplus) is prima facie evidence that at the current external exchange rate Europe's traded sector is not uncompetitive and thus that Europe's total wage costs are not 'too high'.[12]

The second is to assume that taxes on labour necessarily increase the total cost of labour. In fact across-the-board taxes on labour, whether income taxes or employer payroll taxes, have no necessary

---

hypothesis that the best bargaining systems for employment creation lie at the extremes: either full decentralization or extensive co-ordination between employers and responsible trade unions. The halfway house, i.e. strong trade unions but without responsible co-ordination, is believed to be the worst possible combination. Or as Professor Stephen Nickell puts it 'unions are bad for jobs, but these bad effects can be nullified if both the unions and the employers can co-ordinate their wage bargaining activities'.

12. An individual country within a fixed exchange-rate regime can, however, suffer from labour costs which are too high if it enters the system at an uncompetitively high exchange rate, while other countries in the system enjoy a super-competitively low rate. The implications of this special case are considered in Chapter 8.

long-term impact on the total cost of labour and indeed no likely impact provided that labour markets are fairly efficient. Higher income taxes reduce post-tax individual income by diverting money to collective government expenditure and the most likely long-term impact of employer payroll taxes is the same – higher nominal labour cost passed on in prices, real wages as a result lower than they would otherwise be.[13] But this reduction in post-tax real wages leaves total labour costs to the employer unchanged (and set by the productivity achieved by companies in that country). High levels of tax can still have harmful economic effects if they harm incentives (a possibility considered in Chapter 8) but they are not effects usefully described in terms of 'competitiveness'.

Across-the-board 'labour standards' – such as a right to paid annual leave or to parental leave or the French thirty-five-hour week – have a similar economic effect to across-the-board proportional taxes. They amount to a diversion (in some cases forced) of potential post-tax income towards greater leisure but they have no necessary long-term impact on total labour costs per hour let alone on competitiveness. Such rights raise a number of legitimate issues – whether people truly want extra leisure rather than extra income, whether society wants to suffer the potential income effect of parental-leave rights (in this specific case very small) in return for the benefits of expanded choice for parents and better parenting for society. But the idea that such rights will have any sustained impact on employment levels is wrong. If they did we would see countries with the most generous rights of this sort facing high unemployment: in fact we see Scandinavia and the Netherlands with amongst the lowest unemployment rates in Europe. High unemployment is not in general created by 'competitiveness burdens' on business.

Instead unemployment can be caused by very specific labour-market rigidities which prevent the matching of specific categories of labour potentially supplied and demanded. Lack of skills flexibility can mean that potential demand is not matched by the relevant skills required. Minimum wages can create unemployment by making the total cost of employing low-skilled workers too high relative to their specific

---

13. Chapter 8 discusses also an important exception to this general rule, when labour markets are inefficient and the normal real wage effect of taxes or regulations is resisted.

productivity.[14] Collective bargaining which increases the wages of low-skilled workers can have the same effect, so too can over-generous unemployment benefits too easily available (individual unemployed people setting as it were their own minimum wage since they have the option of not working and still receiving income). Part-time work restrictions can prevent the cost-effective matching of peak-time labour supply with peak-time customer demand. European countries need therefore to consider carefully whether such rigidities are present and whether they should eliminate them, pursuing desired social objectives – such as income maintenance – through other means. But they should not be driven by the fear that all regulation of labour standards produces unemployment through an impact on competitiveness.

Europe should therefore reform its labour markets, but with the confidence that this does not require simply copying American approaches nor sacrificing all scope for important aspects of social choice. Or rather not 'Europe' but the individual countries of Europe should pursue these reforms. For the problems are essentially national, the solutions also lie almost entirely in national hands, and the useful role of European-level initiatives in the labour markets is relatively small. European initiatives can be justified to facilitate free movement of people, or to make possible pan-European incorporation of companies, enabling European business to achieve the economies of scale in legal and tax administration which American companies enjoy. But there is no need for the same law on parental leave to apply in Sweden and Portugal or for workforce consultation procedures in companies operating purely within the British market to be harmonized with Dutch ones.

For these reasons opposition in principle to some aspects of the European Social Chapter is quite justified. But the idea that the Social Chapter is a key driver of European labour-market performance or a threat to Britain is a myth. Measures introduced so far under the Social Chapter and applied to Britain since we joined in 1997 have had no discernible impact on British employment or productivity performance. Nor are they likely to in the future, since the Social Chapter quite

---

14. Payroll taxes on workers receiving the minimum wage or close to can also produce unemployment because the minimum wage prevents the incidence of the tax taking the normal form of lower earnings: this is important to the reform of tax systems discussed in Chapter 8.

rightly excludes from European competence the labour-market policies which really matter – minimum wage rates, trade-union bargaining and strike rules, unemployment-benefit rates and eligibility rules. It is still reasonable to argue against some Social Chapter rules: the fact that European initiatives are not doing positive harm is not good enough, we should only be taking at European level initiatives which are positively useful. But John Major, whose election defeat in 1997 led directly to the introduction of the Social Chapter to Britain, can risk looking Britain's unemployed in the eye.

The 'burden of regulation'

The 'burden of labour-market regulations' is simply a specific variant of a more general complaint. For Europe, it is frequently asserted, has burdened its business with so many regulations – environmental, public health and safety-related as much as employment – that this has damaged its 'competitiveness' in world markets. Europe must deregulate across the board if it is to compete effectively. There is, however, next to no evidence that this is true. The challenge of achieving cost-effective regulation is a continual one for all governments of modern societies and there are specific areas of regulation where some European nations need to focus specific attention, but the idea of a general 'burden of regulation' as a key driver of European economic performance is based on conceptual confusion and a failure to look at the facts.

Richer societies demand regulation as mechanisms to achieve desirable ends. Richer people want not just more physical goods and services individually owned and enjoyed but a cleaner environment, safer workplaces, safe food, and to be treated with 'respect' in their employment whatever their personal characteristics. Those are 'consumer demands' quite as much as more washing machines, more Internet usage, or more restaurant meals. They are demands which can only be met by regulation, or by granting people 'rights' in defence of which they can litigate.

Those regulations or rights may carry economic cost. But those economic costs are not well understood by reference to 'competitiveness' since national competitiveness is a close to meaningless concept. Instead the costs are usually similar in form to those imposed by general labour-market standards – they represent the diversion of potential real wages from monetary income to social benefit (for instance by limiting our ability to achieve higher productivity). The scale of such costs is often extremely difficult to calculate. It is often far less than initial 'shock horror' estimates because these fail to capture the way in which costs can be minimized by redesigning entire business processes in line with the new regulation. Conversely costs can sometimes be considerably more than first seemed because of the hidden expense of administrative complexity, the record keeping and reporting activities which companies need to undertake to comply with the regulation: when the European Union's working-time directive was introduced to Britain it was the pointless record keeping which caused greatest annoyance among businesses not the actual limits on hours worked. The challenge of public policy is continually to balance demands for the benefits of regulation with the costs incurred. In striking that balance legitimate lobby groups play legitimate roles. Consumer and environmental groups stress the benefits; business lobby groups stress the costs. And in striking a balance governments should use all the methodologies and tools at their disposal. Better regulation task forces, formal processes to ensure that all costs are identified, continual review of existing regulations, 'sunset clauses' to require regulations to be re-justified or otherwise lapse: all should be used by governments attempting to best balance the costs and benefits.

The balance struck can, however, differ by country and certainly by continent. There is nothing unsustainable about Europe having, if it wants, higher environmental standards than the US even if those are at the expense of a productivity penalty. In fact, however, with the exception of land-use planning rules already discussed, there is no prima facie evidence to suggest that the panoply of non-labour-market regulation in Europe represents a larger 'burden' on European business than the combined cost of regulation and litigation on American. And within Europe there is no evidence that countries known for the quality of their environmental standards or their broadly defined social rights, such as Scandinavia or the Netherlands, are suffering an economic penalty in either productivity or employment creation. The case for making 'deregulation' an all-encompassing theme of European reform is totally unproven.

Rather than pursuing the delusion of across-the-board deregulation, what European countries should launch are programmes focused on specific identifiable problems. For just as with labour-market regulations the real problems are created by specific types of regulation (such as minimum wages set too high) which interfere with the matching of potential supply and demand, so in regulation more generally. Some environmental rules may carry greater productivity costs than the benefits are worth, but they will not, except in extreme circumstances, impact aggregate employment. But regulations which deter business creation can prevent the matching of potential entrepreneurial activity with potential new demand and the importance of that has increased in a technological environment where employment creation is increasingly dependent on small-company growth. It is calculated that twenty-five bureaucratic procedures (legal and tax registrations, etc.) are required to establish a new business in France versus five in the US. Many of these steps are the consequence not of desirable social objectives pursued by regulation but of bureaucratic inertia and vested interest. The details of business-registration procedure, the tax treatment of entrepreneurs and the details of bankruptcy law are all fruitful areas on which several European governments should focus attention: the case for simplifying tax returns and for exempting small companies from some labour-market regulations is strong. But changes in this area have few if any implications for the attractive rather than accidental features of the European social model.

European nations can make social trade-offs on the balance between regulatory costs and benefits without fear that global competition constrains that choice.

The European social model: preserving the essence

The changes required in Europe's economic policies and thus models are often exaggerated and the extent of change already in hand often not adequately perceived. Product-market liberalization is not a new story for Europe, it has been an integral objective of the European Community for many years. Privatization programmes are already far advanced. Capital-market change is occurring whether governments plan it or not. Labour-market change is at least beginning. The across-the-board 'burden of regulation' story is largely a red herring. But the impact on the European model of the required changes, whether already achieved or yet to come, is still significant. In total the changes mean a significant shift towards a more liberal free-market economy, and that European nations' capacity to pursue desired social objectives through interventions in markets will be diminished. European companies will increasingly define objectives in shareholder value rather than stake-holder terms, and European labour markets will increasingly be markets and decreasingly expressions of social solidarity. Liberalization and free markets must not become dogma, but the direction of change is and will be and should be towards freer markets.

That does not mean, however, that the distinctive European social philosophy needs to be abandoned. For that philosophy need not be expressed solely or primarily through interventions in markets. It is also expressed by the role of the European state as a provider of collective goods and services and as a redistributor of economic outcomes to a far greater extent than in the US. The provision of free healthcare to people unable to afford it is a fundamental feature of the European model; state ownership of businesses was always an incidental feature which can and should be changed to meet new circumstances. If new technology and changed economic structure make market liberalization desirable that does not threaten the essence of the European model. But if globalization made it essential for European countries to match the US's low levels of tax and government expenditure, Europe's distinctive approach would be truly threatened.

Polemicists of the right, however, argue precisely that: that Europe must match America's low-tax, low-spend combination to be competitive; that high taxes on labour and capital are a severe burden on the European economy and that Europe's high marginal tax rates are disincentives to enterprise; that globalization and the Internet will make tax revenues disappear. Those arguments are considered in detail in Chapter 8. For now the three key conclusions of that chapter can be summarized as follows.

First – the need for the state to play a role as a provider of collective goods and as a redistributor of outcomes has not diminished but rather increased as a direct consequence of the changes outlined in Chapters 2 and 3 and the market liberalization urged in this chapter. A more flexible labour market will help achieve low unemployment but probably at the expense of greater pre-tax inequality: if we want to ensure that low-income families are above poverty levels more in-work benefits are likely to be required. A more fluid labour market with more rapid movement between jobs and careers is essential to deal with technological and structural change, but that means insecurity unless people have the skills needed to flourish in a more fluid economy: increasing pressure on education and training budgets will be the result. Increasing wealth means higher demand for healthcare, but healthcare is provided free because it is essential to equality of citizenship. That means higher government spending. Increasing wealth also means more demands for environmental goods, for high-quality public space, and for high-quality public transport. The demands on the state are going to increase as our markets become freer and as our incomes rise.

Second – the changing shape of the economy does place some constraints on government resources. Globalization, the Internet, free movement of capital and of highly skilled people all place some limitations on the ability of governments to maintain high tax rates. And marginal tax rates above certain levels do have disincentive effects. Some European states probably should reduce their tax and public-expenditure levels. All governments will have to look radically at how they achieve efficiency in public spending, at the balance, for instance, between administrative and market mechanisms in the provision of healthcare. All governments will have to consider radical options for redesigning tax structures to reduce adverse incentive and avoidance effects – more taxes on property and energy, more road pricing and fewer taxes on labour is likely to be a sensible mix.

Third, however, these constraints on the aggregate size of the state are often overstated and for deliberate polemic purpose. Some tax rates may have to fall for specific reasons but the idea that a lower overall tax burden in some general sense makes countries more competitive is wrong and it is likely that there is a range of tax and public spend 'burdens' – certainly up to 40 per cent of GDP, probably somewhat higher, across which the precise level makes relatively little difference to economic performance. Provided we design well how the state raises taxes and manages public expenditure, modern societies retain significant degrees of freedom to make their own trade-offs and social choices. People who want minimal states as ends per se should argue on that basis: they should argue that lower taxes and lower spend are what people actually want, and in some cases they may be right. But they should not use the phoney logic of competitiveness to deny that we have a choice.

Europe is already changing

The overall shape of change required in Europe is therefore clear. Liberalization of markets but not to the extent of dogma, governments' social roles reformed and focused, but not dramatically reduced. Reform but not rejection of the European model. Common themes at European level but precise actions primarily at national level. The good news is that much of that change is already in hand. National policies, to different degrees in different countries and from different starting points, are evolving towards a more liberal approach; and the thrust of the European Union's interventions, far from opposing liberalization, has been in favour of extending it. These assertions will surprise some British readers, for there is a prevalent Euro-sceptic belief that Europe is incapable of change and that the European Commission is committed to resisting it. But the evidence is clearly to the contrary.

Market liberalization has always been a key objective of the European Union and before that of the European Community. The Union's single-market vision is essentially a liberal capitalist one and expressed in a relentless programme to create more competitive and open European markets. That programme was intensified still further by commitments made at the Lisbon summit in March 2000. Telecoms liberalization is already well advanced but has now been reinforced by measures to ensure competition in local access. Postal services will increasingly be liberalized. All barriers to non-financial services are to be removed by 2002 and barriers to financial services by 2005. More open competition in public procurement was also agreed. The progress is sometimes frustratingly slow but over the long term the achievement is clear and indeed dramatic.

Privatization has progressed in parallel with liberalization, the arguments presented in its favour earlier in this chapter now accepted by all European governments. Christian and social democratic governments in Germany and Netherlands have privatized their post offices – in the US it remains in government hands. Fifteen years ago the French state held majority control stakes in thirty-seven of the top fifty enterprises in France; it now controls twelve and the number will fall further. No one fifteen years ago would have predicted that the French state would execute a huge privatization programme exiting such commanding heights of the economy as banking and telecoms but under governments of both right and left it has done just that – $40 billion of assets privatized since 1995 alone. Capital markets are changing rapidly with aggressive takeovers and increasing pressure on management from institutional investors. Europe is already far closer to replicating America's competitively intense single market than it was ten years ago and it will get closer still in the next few years. In product and capital market liberalization Europe is already doing most of what is required

Progress in labour markets is slower because change there is more contentious. But there too change has occurred. The Netherlands was among the first to change, pursuing labour-market reforms from the mid-1980s onwards which have helped drive unemployment down to only 2.9 per cent through entirely predictable means – more benefit conditionality, more part-time jobs, more face-to-face services. Spain's reforms of its employment protection laws have helped cut its unemployment rate from 22 per cent to 14 per cent. France may in headline terms have gone the other way with the imposition of the thirty-five-hour week, but to the surprise of politicians, trade unionists and employers this has been the catalyst for the introduction of more flexible working contracts such as annual-hours agreements. Further change remains essential. There is still too much wishful thinking that structural and unemployment problems can be solved entirely by skills initiatives, and too facile an assumption that high-tech jobs will be the main key to job creation: the blunt facts that if we want full employment we need bag packers in supermarkets and that the French minimum wage is a barrier to their employment are still in the too-difficult file. But the direction of change is the appropriate one and unemployment levels are falling throughout Europe.

In other areas of regulation, meanwhile, the approach is increasingly sensible. There is no appetite for a wholesale assault on environmental, health and safety, or consumer protection legislation nor on social legislation such as maternity and parental-leave rights or equal opportunities. But there does not need to be. Instead what was agreed at Lisbon was a specific focus on the procedures involved in setting up companies. And where active European Union-level involvement is needed to create single market conditions, appropriate action is also in hand – the take-off of electronic commerce across Europe will be facilitated by the proposed e-commerce directive, allowing firms to provide online services across Europe while normally complying only with the laws of their home country.

Finally, on tax and spend levels Europe is also changing. France's socialist government is committed to slow but steady reduction of taxation as a percentage of GDP and is cutting its corporate tax rate from 40 to 33 per cent. Germany is cutting the top rate of income tax from 51 per cent to 42 per cent, its corporate tax rate from 40 per cent to 25 per cent (effectively about 35 per cent once local levies are added). The Netherlands is cutting its top income-tax rate from 60 per cent to 52 per cent. No government, it is true, is committed to radical dismantling of its welfare state, to tax competition with America by cutting tax and spend levels below 35 per cent of GDP. But that is just as well for that would be, as Chapter 8 will argue, both unnecessary and undesirable.

None of this implies that everything is rosy. Further reform of labour markets is almost certainly needed in some countries. Reduced taxation burdens on labour may be desirable, and more radical redesign of tax systems may be necessary to make that possible. But change is already under way, and that change is likely to offset the balance in America's economic favour which the evolution of technological and economic structure appears to have produced. Europe's performance is not that of a disaster zone faced with American perfection: much of its present performance gap is likely to close naturally as autonomous technological developments produce their impact: and much of the change required is in hand already. Europe should have the confidence to see reform not rejection of its model as the way forward.

7. Cool Britannia or Still the Sick Man of Europe?

Opinions on Britain's economic performance relative to continental Europe have been as extreme and volatile as those on Europe's performance relative to the US. For several decades a pessimistic view dominated. One of its strongest expressions was Will Hutton's *The State We're In*. Writing in 1995, he recorded as a simple fact that 'The country's great industrial cities are decaying and listless, while in the new industries and technologies Britain is barely represented.' Britain was poorer than the continent, less productive, less competitive. But within only a few years a very different picture of Britain was being painted, and a very different picture of the continent. To the Conservative Party Britain was 'The Enterprise Centre of Europe' and with increasing hysteria as Britain approached the 1997 election the story was told of a Britain freed by Thatcherite reforms to soar ahead of a sclerotic, unreformed, uncompetitive, high-unemployment continent. In February 1997 the satirical magazine *Private Eye* ran a spoof article, 'exclusive to all Tory newspapers', which described how 'The German man in the *strasse* now looks with hungry eyes towards Britain's economic miracle' while 'starving toddlers roam the autobahns begging for scraps of liverwurst'. The really funny thing about the article was that it was only a mild caricature of some of the more extreme articles appearing in Britain's more Euro-sceptic newspapers.

In May 1997 the British Labour Party – New Labour indeed as it had now become – returned to government after eighteen years of opposition. Some might have expected them to talk down Britain's economic prospects on the basis of their inheritance from the past – that, after all, is what new CEOs of major public companies usually do if the previous leadership has been removed abruptly – large write-downs and a gloomy but determined initial statement providing a good basis for 'recovery' thereafter. But while there was an element of this in the new government's assessment of public finances the overall story remained one of confidence and at times superiority. Tony Blair's appearance at the European Union's Amsterdam conference shortly after his election victory was not as one come to learn from superior French or German models, but as the self-confident leader of a country that was on the right track. Britain had led the way in 'structural reform', others must follow. Britain was 'Cool Britannia', continental Europe rather passé. Britain was better placed to grasp the opportunities of the new economy. French public opinion appeared mired in '*morosité*' and change in France seemed to be blocked by public-sector strikes. Germany looked exhausted by the burdens of reunification. At conferences of business people and politicians it was the British speakers who were listened to with the greatest attention because they had experienced 'structural reform' and could tell others how to do it. Lower taxes, more flexible labour markets and privatization had made Britain more successful than the continent and the only issue was whether the continent could be persuaded to follow suit. New Labour said it would win the case for reform in Europe; Euro-sceptics claimed that task was impossible. But the fact that Britain has a lot to teach the continent was a shared assumption of British opinion in the late 1990s.

So what is the truth and what light does it shed on the choice between variants of capitalism, between an ultra-liberal model and some reformed version of the European approach? The answer is simple. During the 1980s Britain put an end to three decades of relative economic decline and caught up some lost ground versus continental leaders and that achievement reflected the benefits of market-liberalization measures introduced under Margaret Thatcher. But Britain's absolute productivity and prosperity performance is still below the European average and its pace of catch-up has been slow. As for employment, Britain's flexible labour markets have helped deliver unemployment rates below the European average but some other European countries have achieved equal or better performance with a different policy mix, illustrating that Britain's model is not the only route to job creation. On some key social indicators, meanwhile – quality of healthcare, levels of poverty – Britain scores badly. The Thatcher years achieved important beneficial changes which it would be unwise to reverse. But the idea that Britain has a clearly superior economy to the continent is a delusion which serves its national interest ill since it stymies intelligent debate about how to achieve further improvement.

As in Chapter 6 for the comparison of France, Germany and the US, the facts are most easily understood by looking first at the static picture, then at changes over time.

Britain, France and Germany – the picture in 1996

The essence of Britain's economic position in 1996, at the end of seventeen years of Conservative rule and significant structural change, is captured in Figure 7.1. In prosperity per capita terms Britain was similar to France and only 10 to 15 per cent behind Germany, but in labour-productivity terms (i.e. in prosperity per hour worked) Britain was about 20–30 per cent behind both. That deficit in labour productivity in turn was explained by two factors: primarily by capital intensity, with France and Germany both having much higher capital stock per hour worked; but also by a low level of absolute efficiency – our nearest proxy for efficiency showing Britain something like 8–18 per cent behind France and Germany.[1] Given these productivity deficits Britain was only able to achieve prosperity similar to France and within 15 per cent of Germany by working more hours on average per person per year; 14 per cent more than Germany and 25 per cent more than France on O'Mahony's figures. These higher hours per head of population in turn reflected two factors: a higher employment level (71 per cent versus France's 61 per cent in 1998); and longer working hours for those in employment – 4 per cent more than France on O'Mahony's figures, 8 per cent more on latest OECD figures.[2]

The British economy in 1996 was thus better at creating jobs than the French or German but significantly less productive. Since 1996 our productivity deficit may actually have widened slightly and job creation on the continent has improved, but Figure 7.1 still captures the essence of the comparison today.

---

1. The figures are slightly different according to whether we look at the total economy or just the market (i.e. non-state) sector. France was 8 per cent ahead in market sectors, 18 per cent for total economy; Germany 15 per cent ahead in market sectors, 9 per cent total economy. O'Mahony, *Britain's Productivity Performance 1950–96*.

2. These differences in average hours worked per employed person hide bigger differences in hours worked by full-time workers, since the UK has many more part-timers (about 25 per cent of all workers versus 17 per cent in France). If we assume that part-timers work on average half-time, then the OECD figures imply that British full-timers work 13 per cent longer hours than the French.

Figure 7.1 British, German and French performance 1996

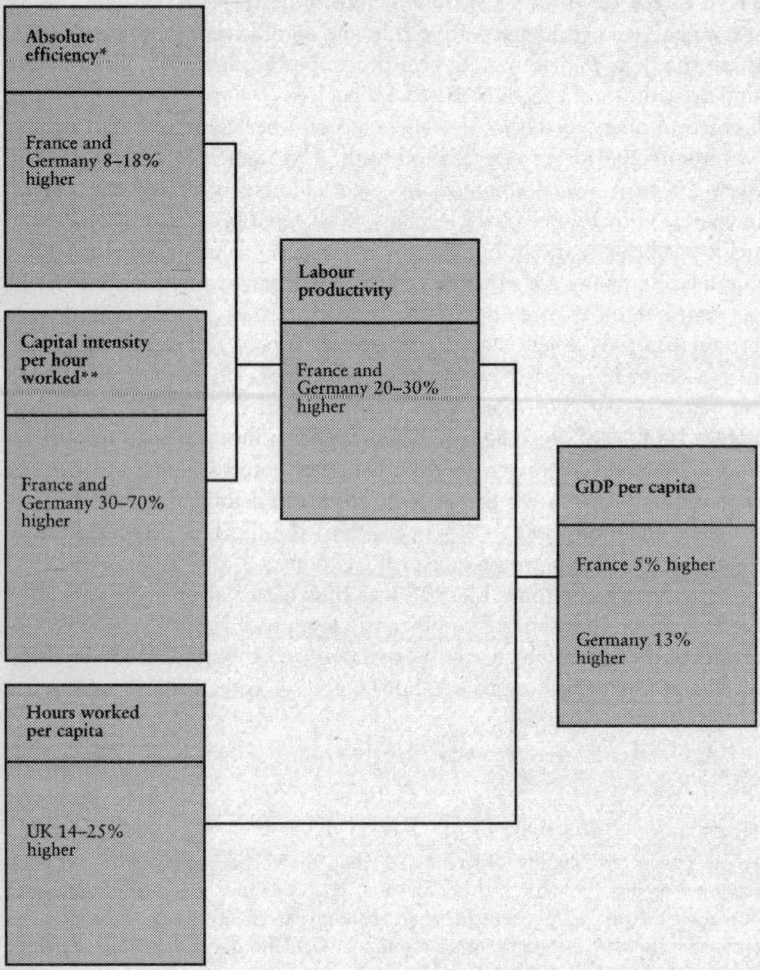

| Absolute efficiency* |
| France and Germany 8–18% higher |

| Capital intensity per hour worked** |
| France and Germany 30–70% higher |

| Labour productivity |
| France and Germany 20–30% higher |

| Hours worked per capita |
| UK 14–25% higher |

| GDP per capita |
| France 5% higher |
| Germany 13% higher |

* Absolute efficiency is output for the same quantity of capital and labour. The nearest measure of it is total factor productivity (TFP).

** Measures of capital stock advantage per hour worked vary from 33% for the French economy in total to 72% for the German market sector. The advantage is smaller, but still considerable, on a per person employed basis.

Source: O'Mahony (NIESR, 1999).

Relative decline and relative catch-up

From 1950 until the 1970s Britain suffered a period of relative economic decline (see Table 7.1.). It was not absolute decline, indeed absolute growth rates per capita in that period compared well with the inter-war years and with the period of British leadership in the nineteenth century. But France, Germany, Italy and Benelux all grew much faster: they achieved catch-up, closing most of their productivity gap versus the US. Britain did not: it grew only slightly faster than the US despite all the opportunities which a lower starting position allows for copying of technology and know-how. As a result Britain fell behind leading continental countries in productivity and in prosperity. Only on employment creation did it perform as well – with continental Europe, the US and Britain all achieving in the 1950s and 1960s unemployment rates which by the 1980s were to look unattainably low.

Between 1980 and the mid-1990s relative economic decline was halted and some catch-up occurred. Germany's lead over Britain in manufacturing productivity fell from 47 per cent in 1979 to 26 per cent in 1996 and its lead over Britain in total factor productivity fell from 14 per cent to 9 per cent overall and from 27 per cent to 15 per cent in market sectors of the economy. British per capita growth exceeded France's, Germany's and the European Union average. Unemployment, after severe setbacks in 1981 and 1991, had by 1997 fallen to under 7 per cent versus a European Union average of 11 per cent. By the mid-1990s the description of Britain as the sick man of Europe was clearly in the past.

But while relative economic decline had clearly been halted the scale of catch-up in productivity and prosperity was still small. Britain's per capita growth from 1979 to 1997 was 1.9 per cent, the European Union average was 1.75 per cent – at that pace of catch-up it takes about sixty years to close a 10 per cent gap.[3] In 1979 Britain was ranked ninth among the current fifteen members of the European Union in OECD measures of prosperity. In 1980 it fell to tenth, and by 1995

---

3. Starting from 1980 you get a slightly larger UK advantage: 2.1 per cent versus 1.8 per cent. But that illustrates a key point – Britain's performance in the last two decades is so close to the European average that careful choice of dates is key to relative ranking.

Table 7.1 The end of Britain's relative decline

Growth in GDP per capita (% per annum)

	1950–70	1970–79	1979–97
US	2.0	2.3	1.5
France	4.5	3.3	1.4
Germany	5.1	2.8	1.7
UK	2.3	2.1	1.9

Growth in labour productivity per hour worked (whole economy) (% per annum)

	1950–73	1973–79	1979–96
US	2.3	0.6	0.8
France	4.6	4.1	2.4
Germany	5.2	3.7	2.2
UK	3.0	2.1	2.3

Unemployment %

	1960	1974	1983	1997
US	5.4	5.5	9.5	4.9
France	1.4	2.8	8.3	12.5
Germany	1.0	2.1	7.9	9.8
UK	1.3	2.1	11.2	6.8

Source: OECD *Historical Statistics*, O'Mahony (NIESR, 1999).

it had fallen one position further. By 1999 it had climbed back to tenth. Productivity gaps versus Germany (in both the overall economy and in manufacturing specifically) have closed somewhat since 1979 but hardly at all against France. And while employment performance was clearly superior to French and German, by the late 1990s the Netherlands, Denmark, Austria, Portugal and Sweden all had similar or lower unemployment rates, proving that Britain did not have some unique formula for creating jobs. Britain ceased relative economic decline in the 1980s and 1990s but the idea that it had emerged by the mid-1990s as the economic superstar of Europe was a total delusion.

Nor have the last four to five years changed that assessment in any significant way, indeed if anything they should make us less triumphalist about UK economic performance than in 1995. In manufacturing the years 1995–8 saw extremely low productivity growth in Britain, rapid growth in Germany, the gap widening again. Overall EU growth has exceeded Britain's in the years 1997–2000. Partly this is just a cyclical effect (other European countries being at a lower point in the cycle in 1997) but that in turn suggests that Britain's growth up to 1997 was flattered by cyclical effects, making the conclusion that catch-up until then had been very slow still more valid. Britain's employment-creation advantage, meanwhile, is eroding as other European economies have moved on to a robust job-creation path. As for the new economy, Britain has undoubtedly generated more dotcoms than other European countries. A *Sunday Times* list of the 100 most promising European dotcoms published in June 2000 included sixty-five whose headquarters are in the UK. But as Chapter 2 stressed, the rate of dotcom emergence is the least important indicator of success in the new economy. On the really crucial issue, whether we are achieving the acceleration of productivity growth from the application of ICT which the US seems now to be enjoying, there is no sign that Britain is doing better than France or Germany or other continental countries.

Britain ceased relative economic decline during the 1980s and 1990s: it is now a reasonably successful economy growing roughly in line with other European countries, but it is not a superior economy and on the key measures of productivity and prosperity it has caught up at only a very slow pace. To draw lessons for future policy in Britain and elsewhere we should therefore ask two questions. Why did Britain cease relative decline? Why has catch-up not been more rapid?

The end of relative decline

To understand why relative decline was halted in the 1980s we need to understand why it occurred in the first place. The issue is greatly debated by economic and social historians. One prominent school of thought asserts that the roots of Britain's relative decline in the 1950s and 1960s lie much earlier, that Britain's relative decline began in the late nineteenth century and that it had deep sociological causes. Martin Wiener's *English Culture and the Decline of the Industrial Spirit* and Corelli Barnett's *The Audit of War* tell different aspects of a story in which Britain's social values and institutions became unfavourable to economic success. An anti-industrial culture and the experience of empire made society value administrators and scholars more than industrialists. The cultural values of the old universities could support pure scientific endeavour but were inimical to its practical application. Industrial management was dominated by a mixture of gentlemen amateurs and self-taught practical men lacking either the technical engineering excellence of the Germans or the professional management skills of the business-school-educated Americans. Capitalist values were thus under attack from the pre-industrial values of public schools, old universities and landed wealth, to which new industrialists themselves aspired. But they were also under attack, according to this account, from a peculiarly luddite trade-union movement, beloved of strikes and restrictive practices and general obstreperousness, which was in turn, however, almost the inevitable consequence of poor management. Finally, Britain's financial system, the City in particular, looked to the opportunities of trading and foreign investment, keeping itself distant from industry. To this school of thought Britain's relative decline from 1945 onwards was an almost inevitable consequence of what Britain had already become by 1939.

Several of these arguments strike a chord. But an important counter-view has been provided by Geoffrey Owen's recent book *From Empire to Europe* (1999). Basing his conclusions on detailed studies of specific industries, Owen argues persuasively that Britain's relative decline prior to the Second World War has been overstated and that the deep cultural factors were less important than post-war policy mistakes. In particular, he focuses on the lack of internal market liberalization of the sort the Germans pursued under Ludwig Erhard's command of the Economic Affairs ministry, but even more on Britain's failure to grasp the trade-liberalization benefits which could have come from early Common Market membership. To Owen some of the traditional arguments have some merit – technical-education deficiencies mattered in the engineering sector, and trade-union relations became a problem as relative decline progressed – but 'the biggest single mistake was to opt out of European integration in the 1950s'.

A synthesis of Owen's views with those of Wiener, Barnett and others is possible and may indeed be needed to explain why 1980s catch-up was not more dramatic and definitive. Arguably indeed a synthesis is required to explain why the policy mistakes were made. If Britain's bureaucrats and politicians were wrongly convinced in the 1950s that Britain's economic future lay primarily with the Empire, the reasons for that failure of judgement may have lain in the cultural assumptions and educational approaches which Wiener and Barnett criticize. But Owen's conclusion remains a compelling one. Under the impact of Common Market trade liberalization France went from 42 per cent reliance on former colonial markets in 1952 to 13 per cent by 1968. Britain reoriented more slowly and later. In industry after industry which Owen analyses, failure to face the stimulus of open competition from other advanced economies was a major cause of decline. As decline progressed and became the subject of increasing national debate it generated failed attempts at industrial intervention which only made the problem worse. But the major initial cause of relative decline was a failure to open up to competition in the 1950s and 60s.

It is against that context that the 1980s turning point is best understood. Essentially what Thatcherism did was to liberalize the British economy in both an internal and external sense. Paradoxically, given Thatcher's subsequent political beliefs, the first key step in the process had already been taken with Britain's belated entry to the European Economic Community in 1973 and a further key step was Thatcher's own commitment to the Single European Act which became law in July 1987. These steps ensured the external liberalization effect of a large single market. Domestic liberalization was, however, equally important – Britain pursuing ahead of many continental countries the changes for which Chapter 6 has argued.

Labour-market liberalization was one key change. Chapter 6 made the point that there is more than one route to labour-market efficiency and that particularly in wage bargaining two quite different but equally feasible models can be identified – the Dutch and the American. It is therefore an interesting historical speculation as to whether Britain could have progressed down a path towards a co-ordinated labour market with more influential but responsible trade unions. That choice died, however, with the defeat first of the Labour Government's proposals for a new industrial relations framework ('In Place of Strife') in 1968 and then subsequently of Edward Heath's Industrial Relations Act. The changes of the Thatcher years therefore took Britain instead in the American direction to decentralized pay bargaining and limited trade-union power. That reform was successful in three respects. It broke Britain's reputation for industrial-relations strife and thus helped attract inward investors; it made easier the industrial rationalization which drove productivity improvements; and after the macroeconomic setbacks of 1979–81 and 1988–92 it put Britain on a path to lower unemployment.

Privatization and the end of industrial subsidy were also important both in fully competitive markets and in utilities. Unlike the French, Britain had never had a self-confident philosophy of statist intervention but increasingly in the 1960s and 1970s, as a response both to relative decline and to short-term crises, it had wandered into a muddled industrial policy and a rather random set of nationalizations. Geoffrey Owen argues that French industrial intervention was never particularly effective even in the 1950s and 1960s and that France succeeded despite rather than because of its grand strategies, and overall that appears right. But it can at least be said that French intervention tended to be better (i.e. less bad) than British. Ceasing that intervention through the privatization of commercially competitive companies in the 1980s was a wholehearted success. British Steel went from being a byword for inefficiency to a world-class company and from a major drain on public funds to a major tax payer; British Airways and Rolls Royce similarly flourished in the private sector. Privatization of British Telecom in 1984 and liberalization of the telecoms market delivered large cuts in telecoms prices and an explosion of new services. More controversial and in some senses less central were the privatizations of pure utilities, such as electricity, but here too the rationale was sound. Britain's electricity industry now employs 60 per cent fewer people than in 1980 without any diminution in quality of service and that represents productivity improvement as important to the economy as equivalent achievements in manufacturing.

The Thatcher years also saw tax cuts, though more so in marginal rates than in the overall burden of taxation. Chapter 8 will discuss the issue of tax burdens in more detail and question the ultra-liberal orthodoxy that lower tax is always better. The idea that there is something economically beneficial in a standard rate of tax of 20 per cent rather than 25 per cent is at best massively overstated and arguably quite wrong. But marginal tax rates of 83 per cent cannot but distort and blunt incentives and reducing top rates from 83 per cent to 40 per cent was a powerful symbol of a shift of culture in favour of enterprise, a shift in culture which, despite Owen's questioning of the Wiener and Barnett school of thought, was probably an element in changed performance.

Finally, 1980s Britain welcomed inward investment and did so at a time when other countries resisted it, believing that national owner-ship of key business assets was essential to economic success. That investment, in particular by big Japanese manufacturers but also by American and continental investors, had clearly beneficial direct and indirect effects. The direct effect of 'jobs created' was a somewhat spurious basis for celebratory speeches at ribbon-cutting ceremonies. The real impact was more profound. The new factories proved that high productivity rates could be achieved in the UK; they pioneered new forms of trade-union relations and workplace involvement; they acted as stimuli to productivity improvement by competitors; and they improved performance throughout their supply chains by being demanding purchasers.

The inward-investment story is thus an important part of the whole but also an illustration of a wider point – that what essentially happened in 1980s Britain was that the impediments to success were removed. The impact of globalization, as Chapter 1 argued, is often overstated and misunderstood. But globalization is a powerful mech-anism for transferring capital and know-how to wherever there is opportunity, and opportunity exists wherever existing productivity and wage rates are lower than elsewhere. If you can achieve world-class productivity in a country where others do not and where wages reflect competitor's lower average productivity, you make big profits. The investment resulting is a key driver of catch-up. Countries can prevent catch-up by pursuing protectionism in trade or capital flows, through bad macroeconomic policies or via high tax rates, or if they have disastrous industrial relations or very poor workplace skills, but as long as those impediments are absent a country behind will tend in an open global economy to catch up. A large part of what happened in Britain in the 1980s was that the impediments to catch-up were removed.

Why not better?

But while Britain stopped relative decline and achieved some catch-up, the 1980s turnaround was less stellar than propaganda suggested. In some senses it was disappointing. For Britain has completed ahead of continental countries most of the product and capital-market liberalization for which Chapter 6 argued. But the return from that ahead-of-the-game liberalization has been limited to British growth per capita of 1.9 per cent versus the European average of 1.75 per cent, and from a lower starting point. Why not better and what policies are now required to do better?

The reasons why British labour productivity lags French and German are in arithmetical terms simple and clear from Figure 7.1. It has considerably lower capital stock per worker and achieves somewhat lower absolute efficiency, i.e. lower output for any given quantity of labour and capital. That absolute efficiency disadvantage could in turn reflect either lower-quality inputs – such as low skills – or structural factors such as lower intensity of competition and a failure to achieve economies of scale. All three factors – quantity of capital, quality of skills and intensity of competition – should drive future policy.

Capital investment is, as Chapter 5 argued, essential to economic growth and capital stock (i.e. accumulated capital investment) is a prime determinant of productivity and prosperity. That assertion needs to be balanced with several caveats: that efficient use of capital matters as well as quantity; that investment in computer hardware and software is in economic terms as much capital investment as is factory machinery; that investment in research and development and know-how has a vital role to play alongside physical investment. But these caveats do not deny the fundamental fact: we get richer by devoting some of this year's economic activity not to present consumption but to devising new processes and products to be used and delivered in the future, and the greater part of this investment takes the form of building machines (widely defined) which automate previously manual functions. If other factors are equal, the more you invest the richer you get.

Britain has in the past invested less than France or Germany and therefore has a smaller capital stock. It has invested less in public infrastructure and less in privately owned plant and machinery. The arithmetical roots of that lower investment are once again easy to describe. British business invested a lower percentage of national income than France or Germany between the 1950s and 1970s and therefore fell behind in absolute capital stock and in absolute income. Over the last fifteen years capital investment by business as a percentage of GDP has increased (from 10 per cent in 1985 to 14 per cent in 1999), while continental levels have decreased, and as a result Britain now invests roughly the same percentage of GDP as France and Germany. But once you have fallen behind in capital stock you only catch up if for a period of time you invest a higher percentage of income than others rather than just the same percentage. So far Britain has not done that even though its lower present productivity and wages should make investment in Britain more attractive than on the continent. And Britain continues to invest a lower percentage of national income in research and development – 1.8 per cent in 1997 versus 2.3–2.6 per cent in France, Germany and the US.

The mathematics are simple, the causes of past under-investment more difficult to discern. To Will Hutton and other stakeholderists the culprits were clear – City short-termism, too much shareholder-value fixation, lack of the long-term financing structures and strategic focus which the continent enjoyed. To Geoffrey Owen this financial-structure explanation is a total red herring. Personally I am not quite so sure. For an accumulation of survey and anecdotal evidence suggests that the relationship between Britain's industrial and financial systems was at times an impediment to investment by some types of business. CBI and Bank of England surveys in 1994 illustrated that British industry appeared to demand quite irrationally high financial returns, a sign of apparent risk aversion. And during my years as Director-General of the CBI, while I encountered little anecdotal evidence that the biggest British companies were constrained by their financial relations, I was continually struck by the number of mid-sized engineering companies which had struggled to survive as UK public companies but had flourished when acquired by continental owners or after going private. The managers of those companies certainly argued, sometimes apparently with good reason, that equity-market pressure made it difficult for mid-sized companies to take a long-term approach.

It is thus possible that one of the factors which slowed Britain's catch-up was a subtle mix of financial relations and managerial assumptions that generated a more short-term approach than found either on the continent or indeed in the US.[4] But it is possible in turn that those attitudes were a rational reaction to macroeconomic instability. The British economy was subject for several decades prior to the 1990s to greater instability than most other developed countries, higher and more volatile inflation and interest rates combined with major periods of exchange-rate volatility (such as the dramatic swings against both the dollar and continental currencies in the period 1979–81). British managers of small and medium-sized companies may have been more short-termist than in other countries simply because the ones who were long-termist didn't survive to tell the tale. If this explanation is correct macroeconomic stability rather than changes in financial structure and behaviour are the key to closing the investment gap.

Britain's deficiency in capital stock is numerically obvious. The facts of its performance on skills are less easily expressed in summary figures and their significance is debated. International comparisons are inherently difficult, and the links between skills and economic performance are not straightforward and agreed.[5] But it is almost certain that a low

---

4. The oddity of the British system indeed is that it seems to have been less effective at supporting long-term investment than *either* the continental model (more free of short-term equity pressures) *or* the US model, which always had overt equity-market pressure but which has fostered the creation of major new companies (in particular the ICT leaders) where a long-term approach was essential. The possible explanation is that it is the interreaction in the UK between an equity-driven system and macroeconomic instability, which made it difficult for managers to take a long-term approach. In the US system, while the value of the dollar has been as volatile as the pound, exchange-rate volatility is much less important because of the more closed nature of the US economy. US mid-sized growth companies can reach a size which would put them in the 'big' category in Europe before exchange-rate volatility has any significant influence on their activity.

5. The conventional wisdom is that skill needs are bound to increase in the 'knowledge-intensive economy of tomorrow', and in its more simplistic forms, the implication seems almost that everybody will be working in 'IT'. That picture needs to be balanced with two considerations at least. First, some technological progress actually results in *reduced* not increased skill needs: clever machines enabling us to achieve high productivity despite low skills. Second, future skill needs will certainly not be all 'hi-tech' and IT intensive. For instance, given trends in consumer expenditure towards more restaurant meals, improved cooking skills will also be important. The general conclusion that higher skills are conducive to high productivity nevertheless stands – and is supported by data on correlations between earnings and skill level, by employer judgements and by comparisons

level of workforce skills contributes to Britain's productivity gap versus leading continental countries. The UK government's National Skills Taskforce identified three key deficiencies. First, Britain has more people with very low basic skills. OECD figures for 1997 put it eleventh out of twelve participating countries in terms of the proportion of people with inadequate levels of literacy and numeracy.[6] And in a 1996 survey of multinational companies, asking them to assess the basic skills of different workforces, Britain scored considerably worse than France, and far below Germany. Second, Britain has a low level of advanced mathematical skills, which are believed to be particularly relevant to problem solving and thus productivity improvement in many contexts. Less than 10 per cent of British eighteen-year-olds gain an A level in mathematics; the equivalent figures for France and Germany are higher, 16 per cent and 27 per cent on some estimates. Third, Britain suffers from a more general deficiency in the proportion of its workforce educated and trained to intermediate levels of skill (see Figure 7.2): 55 per cent of the UK workforce is skilled to 'level 2' versus 73 per cent in France and 83 per cent in Germany; 37 per cent are skilled to 'level 3' versus 74 per cent in Germany (with France scoring similarly to Britain on this measure for the whole workforce, but ahead in terms of twenty-five to twenty-eight-year-olds). In traditional industry terms, this gap reflects the long-observed fact that the German workforce has higher technical engineering skills than the British. But it is a gap which remains equally important in a world of high-tech IT and high-touch face-to-face services: Britain's hospitality industry compares poorly with the French in terms of staff qualified in key catering and customer-service skills.[7]

---

between the UK and leading continental countries. The empirical evidence which runs counter to this is that the US, while scoring very well in terms of elite universities and research skills, *does not* have high levels of basic workforce skills, performing almost as badly as Britain in measures of literacy and numeracy. The probable explanation of this and the implications of this for Britain's choice between an American and continental model are addressed later in this chapter. See: UK National Skills Taskforce – *Final Report* (2000). Also Alison Wolf, 'Education and Economic Growth', *IPPR New Economy*, March 1999, for a summary of important caveats and counter-arguments.

6. OECD, *International Adult Literacy Survey* (1997).

7. See CBI Reports, *Filling the Gaps – Skills for Tourism* (July 1995), *World Hosts – International Benchmarking of the Hospitality Industry* (November 1995).

Figure 7.2 Intermediate-level skills in UK, France and Germany

Qualifications held at 'Level 2'

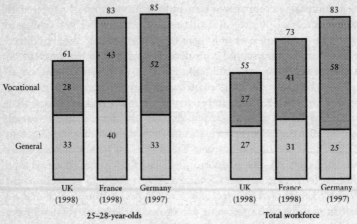

'Level 2' is defined in UK terms as O level, GCSE or equivalent (5+ grades A–C); NVQ (level 2).

Qualifications held at 'Level 3'

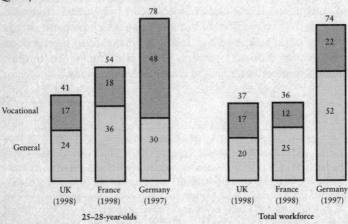

'Level 3' is defined in UK terms as A level and equivalent (2+); NVQ level 3.

Note: Britain's performance among 19–21-year-olds is relatively better. This reflects in part, recent improvements in performance, but also the fact that more 21–25-year-old French and Germans continue to train towards improved qualifications.

Source: UK National Skills Task Force, *Final Report 2000*.

The relevance or robustness of any of these individual statistics can be debated, but the overall story they tell is compelling: Britain's workforce has on average inferior skills to those found in leading continental countries. And these statistics and their implications for productivity are supported by the judgements of business executives operating across several countries. Ask one of the American companies operating car plants in both Germany and the UK to explain the differences in labour productivity which exist despite common ownership, common top management, common know-how and opportunities to transfer best practice, and the answer you typically get is twofold: less accumulated capital equipment in Britain and lower skills, especially at the level of supervisors and first-line management. Estimates in O'Mahony's productivity study for the NIESR suggest that of Germany's 15 per cent total factor productivity advantage versus the UK, up to 11 per cent could be explained by skill differences.

The most likely driver of higher French and German labour productivity is thus simply that they have invested more in both capital and skills. Britain's skill deficiency argues for actions within Britain's education and training system: these are discussed below. The capital deficiency argues above all for economic stability. But it is also possible that the skills deficiency has itself contributed to low capital investment; and possible also that this reflects the impact of labour-market structures. For the point was stressed in Chapter 1 that there are two quite different challenges of economic performance – high productivity and high employment creation – and that different policy mixes can tend to favour one or the other. Britain's low productivity may in part be a consequence of the flexible labour market which has helped to drive down its unemployment.

A story, I believe not apocryphal, is told of Mrs Thatcher in the mid-1980s speaking to a group of major industrialists with interests across Europe. Urging them to invest in Britain she stressed the benefits of a flexible labour market, with easier rules on firing workers, fewer restrictions on hours, no minimum wage and lower payroll taxes. That must mean, she asserted, that Britain is the place to invest. Not necessarily so answered one business leader present. For, if investment aims to automate away labour costs, investment will be skewed to where labour costs are highest and where the return from automation is therefore highest. The point was made to me by a Dutch industrialist operating plants in the Netherlands and in the UK: into the Netherlands went the big capital investments for the long production-run big volume

lines; into the UK, with its more flexible labour markets, the labour-
intensive processes that could not be easily automated. Businesses
respond to economic incentives, and the economic incentives in
Germany and France – from inflexible labour markets and a tax system
favourable to investment, and in Germany's case from a rising Deutschmark – pushed continental businesses towards high investment, high
skill and high productivity but with the downside by the 1980s of lower
employment creation.[8] From the position Germany and France now
occupy, greater flexibility and employment creation are the priorities.

But Britain's balance in the 1980s may have been too far the other
way, too many companies relying on low wages and flexible labour
markets to remain competitive, rather than on investment in capital
equipment and technique. Certainly CBI benchmarking studies in the
mid-1990s found evidence that while British companies included many

---

8. The application of the thirty-five-hour working week in France may also turn
out to be another example of a regulation which stimulates productivity increase,
through increased investment in capital, skills and, crucially in this case, greater
flexibility of workplace organization. Indeed it is interesting to note that in this
case the arguments of both proponents and opponents of the law seem to be being
proved false. The thirty-five-hour law (introduced by the socialist government
following its election in 1997) was proposed as a route to increase employment on
the basis of 'lump of labour' logic – the fallacy that there is a fixed amount of
work to be done which needs to be shared out. But while French unemployment is
now falling almost all respected analyses conclude that this has little if anything to
do with the effects of the law. The law was opposed by French employers as a
threat to competitiveness but all the signs are that French companies have been
well able to offset its effects through productivity improvements, and indeed have
used it as a catalyst to introduce valuable new dimensions of workplace flexibility.
The detrimental effect of the thirty-five-hour week is likely indeed to have nothing
to do with competitiveness but to be limited to an adverse impact on the
employment prospects of low-skill, low-pay workers, arising from the fact that the
application of the law drives an automatic increase in the SMIC (minimum wage)
per hour payable to full-time workers. A law proposed as a solution to unemployment and opposed as a threat to business competitiveness may thus actually end
up simply accentuating both the strengths and weakness of the French economy –
an economy of extremely competitive companies but with a structural problem of
high unemployment amongst lower-skilled workers. See also Richardson and
Rubin, 'The Shorter Working Week in Engineering: Surrender Without Sacrifice',
New Perspectives in Industrial Disputes, Metcalf and Milner (eds.) (1993) for an
analysis of a similar productivity impact from a shorter working week in the
British engineering industry.

world-class competitors, there was also a higher proportion than on the continent of rather poor-performing and low-aspiration companies whose competitive advantage lay entirely in low cost.[9] And it is possible that the presence of that long tail established a low-pay/low-skill equilibrium which made it rational even for the best-run companies to invest less in Britain than was required rapidly to close the productivity gap.[10] From Britain's current position, greater investment not greater flexibility is now the priority.

Whatever the precise pattern of root causes and subsequent interactions, therefore, insufficient capital and inadequate skills are certainly part of the story of Britain's low labour productivity. But a major report on Britain's productivity in 1998, by former colleagues of mine at McKinsey and Company, argued that the third possible factor – insufficiently competitive markets – was the most important culprit. While they did not deny the arithmetic that if Britain is to achieve French, German or US levels of productivity it will have to invest more, the report saw low capital investment as a consequence of low competitive intensity and played down the importance of workforce skills to productivity. It argued also that restrictions on competition such as planning laws have an adverse impact on efficiency quite independent of the amount of capital invested.

The focus on competitive markets rather than capital and skills followed from the fact that McKinsey's primary comparator was the

---

9. CBI National Manufacturing Council report, *Fit for the Future* (1998).

10. The possibility of a rational low-pay/low-capital equilibrium works as follows. A multinational company operating with the same level of expertise and the same motivations in several different countries will make decisions on relative capital/labour balance in the light of the relative cost of capital and labour in those countries. If capital (as is likely) is equally available to it in each country (in terms of both physical availability and cost) then the multinational's capital/labour balance decisions will be driven entirely by the relative costs of labour. The cost of labour is set, however, not only by the demands of multinationals operating in several countries but by the demands of all companies, including purely domestic ones. If Country A's purely domestic companies, for whatever reason, invest less on average in capital and skills than in Country B, then both productivity and as a result wages will be lower in A than in B. This lower cost of labour in turn makes it perfectly rational for even world-class competitors, operating in different countries with the same management approach, to pursue a lower investment strategy in A than in B.

US rather than France or Germany. There is little if any evidence that European product, capital or labour markets are more liberalized than in Britain, indeed rather the contrary; Britain is a member of the same single market and has taken domestic liberalization further. Greater competitive intensity cannot therefore be an explanatory factor of the French and German productivity advantage. But productivity comparisons (whether of Britain or France and Germany) versus the US do, as Chapter 5 discussed, suggest an inherent US advantage based on two factors – a large more complete single market which makes possible economies of scale and more intense competition; and lower density of population which enables easier greenfield development, higher productivity layout and again more intense competition. As Chapter 5 argued, the inherent US advantage is actually rather easy to explain, the key question is how and in some cases whether to respond to it.

Policy priorities and policy choices

The different possible causes of Britain's only adequate economic performance suggest different policy priorities. The key choice can be highlighted with some illustrative figures. In 1995 Germany enjoyed a 27 per cent labour-productivity advantage over the UK, the US a 21 per cent advantage. But the reasons for those advantages differed. Germany's advantage derived significantly from better skills (5 per cent), largely from capital (17 per cent) as well as from an absolute-efficiency advantage (6 per cent); the US's advantage derived hardly at all from skills (2 per cent) less than Germany's from capital (7 per cent) and largely from absolute efficiency (12 per cent).[11] The figures should be treated as judgemental estimates only but they serve to make the policy choice clear. The UK could pursue productivity enhancement primarily by emulating the US model, deregulating in the hope that the absolute-efficiency advantage would disappear, with capital intensity and skill levels growing but as consequences rather than causes. Or it could see continental models as more instructive and define capital intensity and skills as important per se, further intensification of competition as valuable but not as the one magic answer.

The latter is the better approach for Britain. Under either approach,

---

11. O'Mahony, *Britain's Productivity Performance 1950–96*.

however, three common themes and policies make sense. There should be a caution against magic formulae, a strong commitment to macro-stability, and a strong commitment to the European single market, including the single currency.

The caution against seeking a magic formula, and against too much policy tinkering, follows from points already made in this and previous chapters. The role of autonomous technology change appears to be large: globalization is a powerful force for the transfer of capital and know-how to wherever opportunity exists, and while Britain's catch-up has been slow it has been occurring and Britain's investment rate has already risen. Britain's economy is therefore likely, even with no changes in policy, to keep pace with leading continental economies, and may automatically achieve further catch-up. The levers available to increase that rate of catch-up are, moreover, few and uncertain. Governments should certainly seek to pull them to best effect. The tax treatment of smaller companies can make a difference, disseminating and encouraging best-practice management techniques can be useful, decisions on the appropriate use of selective industrial assistance need to be well made. The initiatives outlined in successive DTI Competitive-ness White Papers are therefore valuable, even if one can quibble with the title. But equally we have to recognize that the total impact of such initiatives on sustainable growth is likely to be small. Boring though it appears, continuity in most aspects of policy has a lot to commend it and government's potentially beneficial role is limited.

Macroeconomic stability is also important whatever overall philos-ophy is being pursued. For while the causes of Britain's past under-investment are debated, the one clear conclusion is that economic volatility is bad for long-term investment. Ensuring a stable macroecon-omy – low and stable rates of inflation – is one policy likely to increase Britain's investment rate and within government's power to deliver. Considerable progress was made during Kenneth Clarke's years at the Exchequer. But that progress has been reinforced by Gordon Brown's fiscal policy and through the independence of the Bank of England. Britain already enjoys a more stable and better managed macroeconomy than for decades and keeping that stability should be a foremost policy priority.

Sound domestic policy cannot, however, deliver one important aspect of stability – exchange-rate stability. For as Chapter 10 will argue, all liquid financial markets are subject to periodic irrational volatility and overshoots which can cause real harm to the real economy. An undervalued exchange rate can make life too easy for traded-sector businesses, reducing the pressure for productivity improvement; an overvalued exchange rate can drive out of business companies which would otherwise be sustainable; and instability of any sort increases risk, which must tend to deter investment.[12] These effects provide the macro-economic rationale for entry into the single currency. That rationale has to be balanced against the risks created by one interest rate across the Eurozone. This book is not going to argue in detail the macroeconomic pros and cons of the single-currency project, but a reasonable judgement is that they are at least balanced provided certain economic convergence conditions are achieved.[13] If the macroeconomic balance is either even or in favour, Britain should enter the single currency to enjoy the microeconomic benefits which will accrue from this further step in the creation of the single market.

For the single currency is in essence a continuation of the market-liberalization process which has been creating a European single market and which is essential to closing the productivity gap versus the US. The US's large and close to perfect single market is one key cause of its inherent productivity advantage. Its perfection stems from many features – from free internal trade and from common language, currency and accounting practices, common technical standards and media and fairly common legal system and culture. Some of these features (e.g. internal free trade) Europe has already matched. Some, such as mutually recognized standards and freedom of establishment, are objectives of the European single-market project which Britain, through the European Union, should continue vigorously to pursue. Some of them Europe can neither replicate nor should want to – if the last 5 cent productivity improvement required total cultural and linguistic homogeneity it wouldn't be worth the sacrifice even if it were feasible. If the last 5 per cent depended on widespread environmental damage it wouldn't be worth having. But where characteristics of the American single market can be achieved without sacrificing inherent desirable diversity they should be. Language, culture and the beauty of preserved

---

12. The impact of an undervalued exchange rate in reducing pressure for productivity improvement may help explain why Britain's productivity catch-up versus leading continental countries stopped and indeed reversed in the mid-1990s.

13. See Layard *et al.*, 'The Case for the Euro' (Britain in Europe, June 2000). See also Chapter 10's discussion of the macro-case.

landscape are essential aspects of national identity and desirable diversity; different notes and coins, multiple accounting systems and activities of bureaux de change are not. If by sacrificing different currencies we gain increased efficiency we should do so.

For reasons already discussed in Chapter 6 it is highly likely that the single currency will drive further productivity gains across Europe.[14] Price transparency will increase competitive intensity. Absence of exchange-rate risk will allow businesses to redesign production and logistics systems on a least-cost pan-European basis. A single European capital market will drive accelerated industrial rationalization and restructuring. Those effects indeed are already visible in mergers and acquisition activity across Europe. If Britain stands back from that process it risks forgoing the benefits. For while Britain may well catch up further on continental leaders provided simply that existing market-liberalization measures are left in place, the one thing that could prevent that is if the rest of Europe enjoys benefits of market liberalization from which Britain is excluded. In its microeconomic benefits the single currency has an impact closely analogous to trade liberalization. It was the trade liberalization of the Common Market which played a major role in unleashing German and French growth in the 1950s and 60s, and as Geoffrey Owen says, 'the biggest single mistake [of Britain's post-war economic policy] was to opt out of European integration in the 1950s'. Failure to enter the euro once reasonable macro-convergence conditions are in place could be a repeat of that self-inflicted wound.

Continuity of much of the existing policy mix without too much tinkering, sound fiscal and monetary policies to deliver macroeconomic stability, and entry into the single currency – those are the common features of sensible policy whether one's guiding light is the German or the American route to high productivity. Beyond that, however, we face choices. With America as a model we might search for yet further opportunities to liberalize and deregulate markets or to stimulate our economy through reduced tax rates. With the best in continental performance as our guide we would focus on increased investment

---

14. The scale of effects is difficult to quantify but one study by Professor Andrew Rose, University of California Berkeley, suggests it could amount to 20 per cent additional British productivity growth over twenty to thirty years. See Andrew Rose, *EMU's Potential Effect on British Trade* (Britain in Europe, July 2000).

in capital and in skills. The deregulation route on closer inspection is either a delusion or less attractive; the increased investment route is more desirable on both economic and social grounds, though the levers by which we achieve it are by no means straightforward.

Still more deregulation?

The case for more deregulation is often presented in general terms but the most concrete and controversial proposals focus on the labour market and on land-use planning for the simple reason that product-market liberalization (other than entry into the single currency) is already far advanced and its principle generally agreed. Telecoms liberalization should be taken to its full conclusion with adequate competition in the local loop: but that is already in hand at pan-European and national level. Laws against anti-competitive practices should be rigorously enforced and there may be some potential to improve both UK and European competition law to foster more competitive markets, but there is no evidence to suggest that the performance benefits attainable from such action would be more than minimal.[15] Increased competition in postal services would be beneficial and the privatization of the Post Office logical but it is difficult to argue that failure to privatize Britain's Post Office has been a key cause of the productivity gap versus the US when the US Post Office remains in federal government hands. Privatization and liberalization in other product markets are important but in Britain they have reached the point of diminishing marginal returns and throughout Europe they soon will. There isn't much left to privatize in Europe and very little indeed in Britain. If there is a deregulation trick being missed in British economic policy it must either lie in the labour market or in planning. In neither area is significant deregulation desirable. (Nor is there a case

---

15. See Irwin Stezler, 'Why Britain Should Jail Businessmen', *New Statesman*, 20 November 2000 for the case for strengthened competition law. While this and other articles restate the generic (and sound) case for effective competition law, none of them provides evidence that less effective competition law is a key driver of the productivity difference versus the US. Greater competitive intensity in the US is far more likely to be a product of inherent structural factors – in particular the size and homogeneity of its single market.

for the ultra-liberal argument that a lower tax burden would produce beneficial economic effects. The arguments for and against that proposition are, however, left till Chapter 8.)

The case for labour-market deregulation even from Britain's present flexible position has been put most intelligently (and also tentatively) by David Smith, Economics Editor of the *Sunday Times* in his book *Will Europe Work?*[16] The general thrust of the book is the need for continental countries to deregulate their labour markets and much of the analysis is consistent with the view of European labour markets presented in Chapter 6, though with greater pessimism as to both the extent of present problems and the potential for change. In relation to the UK, however, Smith questions whether its labour market is not 'stranded in no man's land', being neither as flexible as America's nor a coherent continental model like the Dutch. If it is so stranded, Smith's implication is that a full-blooded American model would be preferable. The cruder case for deregulation from current UK levels rests on a simpler and more political analysis. Britain, it is argued, had achieved by 1997 an attractively flexible labour market. The Labour government is now undermining that flexibility by 'a whole raft of regulatory burdens', the minimum wage, trade-union recognition, parental-leave rights, etc. These burdens will destroy employment and must therefore be reversed. Britain needs deregulation simply to get it back to where it was in 1997. Patrick Minford and Andrew Holdenby's pamphlet for the Centre for Policy Studies, *The Price of Fairness*, is representative of this argument, which finds frequent echo in several newspapers.

It is very difficult, however, to support an argument for deregulation from Britain's current position either on the basis of sound theory or of the empirical facts. Smith's description of the UK as in some senses halfway between US and continental models may be true, but there is no clear reason to say that such a position is untenable. On the one key policy dimension where economists have argued for a clear either/or choice – between decentralized or fully co-ordinated wage bargaining – the UK is clearly at the decentralized end, and there is no reason why highly decentralized wage bargaining on the US model cannot be combined with greater social rights (such as maternity and parental-leave rights) on the continental model. The labour-market legislation

16. Social Market Foundation, 1999.

introduced by the Labour government, meanwhile, is extremely unlikely to undermine Britain's employment performance to any significant extent. The minimum wage has been introduced at a sufficiently prudent level that the Low Pay Commission can find 'no measurable impact on overall employment'.[17] Hire-and-fire rules have not been changed in a significant fashion.[18] The European part time directive effectively had no bite in the UK since a previous House of Lords judgement had already established the principle of equal treatment of part-timers without adversely impacting the beneficial growth of part-

---

17. See Low Pay Commission Report, February 2000. This review was produced after only eight months of operation of the minimum wage and was therefore only able to make tentative conclusions on the impact. But no evidence has subsequently emerged to challenge the conclusion that the British minimum wage has had a negligible effect on employment.

The impact or 'burden' of the minimum wage is sometimes expressed, however, not in terms of employment effects, but of the increase in the total wage bill. Estimates of £4.5 billion are sometimes cited. But these figures totally ignore the issue of the true incidence of these costs. As Chapter 6 argued, the most likely incidence of across-the-board taxes is to decrease post-tax real wages leaving total labour costs unchanged, and the primary impact of a minimum wage is a variant of this effect. A minimum wage increases the income of those who receive it and increases the nominal costs of businesses paying it, leading them in turn to increase prices, slightly decreasing the real incomes of everybody who does not receive it, e.g. we all pay marginally more for restaurant meals and waiters are paid a bit more. But it has no necessary or indeed likely impact on business profits. Its potentially harmful effect therefore derives not from competitiveness nor reduced profits effects, but solely from the danger that a higher relative price for unskilled labour will lead to higher unemployment, with capital substituted for labour, or marginal levels of service simply not provided. The sole correct measure of any detrimental effect is therefore its impact on unemployment; in the British case the evidence suggests minimal impact. And more generally, financial estimates of the 'burden of regulation' which quote a gross *cost* impact, rather than an estimated *profit* impact (after allowing for price pass-through effects) are misleading and of little value.

18. The time period within which an individual can be dismissed without recourse to unfair dismissal claims was reduced from two years to one year. No significant business lobby group believed, however, that this would make an appreciable difference to labour-market behaviour, and none indeed had urged on the previous Conservative government the increase from one to two years. A reduction from one year to six months, or even more so to nil (as urged by some trade unions) would, however, be a significant tightening of policy.

time employment. And the European parental-leave directive, for the reasons discussed in Chapter 6, is not the sort of employment regulation which can be expected adversely to affect job creation. The only one of Labour's new initiatives which had the potential seriously to harm the performance of Britain's labour market is the new law on trade-union recognition. If wrongly designed, this could have shifted Britain towards an untenable halfway house on wage bargaining. But it is difficult to argue that the law actually introduced is inimical to American-style labour-market flexibility when its core procedures (on union recognition ballots) are largely modelled on America's industrial-relations legislation.[19]

The proof of the pudding, however, must be in the eating, in the empirical facts. Usefully one of the clearest statements of the 'too much regulation' school of thought provided a precise prediction of the damage that Labour's new regulations would cause and we can use this to calibrate what has in fact occurred. According to Minford and Holdenby's calculations, the measures already introduced or planned by June 1999 would produce 565,000 more unemployed within one year and 1,050,000 within two. In fact, unemployment has fallen since June 1999 by a further 200,000 to reach the lowest absolute figure and the lowest rate since the late 1970s.[20] There is simply no good evidence to suggest that the mild re-regulation introduced by the Labour

---

19. One adverse effect of recent changes in British employment law has, however, been a big increase in individual claims before employment tribunals – up 25 per cent in two years, partly as a result of higher maximum compensation payments. These claims – including many which are little short of blackmail – divert management time to unproductive activities and generate significant legal costs. Action to weed out frivolous claims, e.g. by facing unreasonable litigants with full costs, are essential and planned. It is extremely unlikely, however, that the net economic effect is other than negligible at the macroeconomic level. The real issue is rather the simple injustice which arises when small companies in particular pay up against unjustified claims as the cheaper alternative to legal fees and management time diversion.

20. Where we are in Minford and Holdenby's predicted time-line is a little unclear (trade-union recognition rules only applied from April 2000, the minimum wage became law in April 1999), but by autumn 2000 we should certainly on Minford and Holdenby's calculations have seen a job destruction impact of several hundred thousand, and by spring 2001 job destruction of about 700,000.

government has had any significant adverse impact on Britain's ability to create jobs.

The labour market aside, the other key area where deregulation is frequently urged is in planning rules. The most striking conclusion of the 1998 McKinsey report on Britain's productivity gap was that planning rules play a major part in restricting productivity potential in many sectors – including manufacturing, retailing and hotels. Unlike with labour-market arguments, this conclusion raises few issues of fact but important issues of social choice. For as Chapter 5 has already discussed, it is indeed likely that part of America's absolute-efficiency advantage is simply the product of cheaper and more easily developed land, more greenfield sites and lower building costs. These in turn are the product of lower population density. Population density imposes costs which we can choose to face in either a productivity penalty or environmental degradation. Chapter 9 will argue that the penalty is often overstated and that there are specific policies which can help to achieve the best trade-off possible. But if at the end of the day more relaxed planning rules are required to close the last few percentage points of the productivity gap it is a matter of social choice whether we take the environmental cost to get the benefit. My personal choice would be to say no; others would argue in favour. But the key thing to realize is that we have a choice. Liberalization and deregulation are in general good things but if they conflict with inherently desirable objectives we must not make either liberalization a dogma, or increased productivity an objective above all others.

Increased investment?

The 'deregulation in all things' route to increase prosperity is either a delusion or undesirable. The alternative vision for Britain's economy – combining a largely liberalized economy with a high level of investment – is inherently more attractive. Indeed for Britain – as for France and Germany – it is likely to be the only feasible route to come close to US levels of productivity. Higher investment is undoubtedly essential – Britain could only achieve continental and American levels of labour productivity on the basis of its existing capital stock if it magically achieved capital productivity 20 per cent *above* US levels, and there is no reason to believe that this is possible. Higher skill levels are also almost certainly essential. That conclusion is sometimes rejected on the empirical grounds that the US achieves high productivity despite workforce skills apparently as poor as Britain's. But that in no way proves that skills are unimportant. Instead the likely explanation is that the US's inherent advantages of a large single market and easy availability of land make a bigger difference to absolute efficiency than the productivity figures first suggest, with part of that bigger difference being offset by France and Germany's superior average skills. High capital investment and high skills are the routes by which European countries offset some at least of America's inherent advantages. Higher investment and better skills are therefore vital objectives for Britain. To achieve these objectives there are no easy levers. But there are some clear implications for public policy.

The key policies to stimulate sustained business investment have already been mentioned – macroeconomic stability and entry into the single currency once conditions are appropriate. Tax changes may also play a useful but subsidiary role. The tax treatment of capital investment appears to play only a limited role in the investment decisions of large multinational companies but it is far more likely to influence the decisions of smaller companies where cashflow can be a constraint on investment levels. More favourable tax treatment of investment by small and medium enterprises may bear some fruit. Equally there is some merit in using the capital-gains tax system to nudge investors towards a long-term investment approach and some dangers indeed that the British government's latest revisions of CGT (tapering down to 10 per cent after just four years) may fail to encourage that long-term perspective. But we would be unwise to assume more than small but useful incremental benefit from such tweaks of tax-system design. Private investment will increase if there are sound prospects for business in a large competitively intense market enjoying reasonable macro-stability, and government's key role is to ensure those conditions, not to micro-manage.

Government has a bigger role to play in investment in infrastructure, both of the physical and intellectual variety. The key difference between British and continental investment levels now lies not in business investment in physical plant, but in research and development and in public infrastructure investment. British investment in all transport infrastructure has significantly lagged the European average for several decades, and dramatically so in rail, running at only a third to a quarter of European levels.[21] Good transport infrastructure can improve both business productivity and the efficiency of the labour market. It also raises environmental issues discussed in Chapter 9 and important issues about who pays (the answer should include road tolling). But whatever the environmental trade-offs struck and payment mechanisms used, transport strategy is clearly one area where good government policy can make a big difference. Britain's under-investment in transport infrastructure in the 1980s and 1990s was bad policy; the commitments now made to substantially increased investment are a major improvement.

On research and development too, the UK has lagged behind – with France and Germany both investing about a third more on research and development as a percentage of GDP. Closing that gap is primarily up to private business. But the quality of the public-supported science base is also important. Business R&D is sometimes closely linked to university research, and a high-quality science base is relevant to the special case of competitiveness discussed in Chapter 1, the success of leading-edge technology-based industries being one of the few instances where national competitiveness theory makes any economic sense. British public expenditure on science, engineering and technology research fell 13 per cent in real terms between 1986 and 1998. The 10 per cent increase made since then is a sensible government contribution to a high-investment economic strategy.

Government also has a major role to play in the improvement of workforce skills. What it does not possess, however, is a precise understanding either of the specific skills likely to be required or the economic payback from different policies. Simple trend observations, e.g. that more jobs are being filled by graduates, need to be treated with great care before being used as the base for expensive public policies, and the fact that companies use educational qualifications as a discrim-

---

21. Between 1985–93, transport infrastructure investment in Britain was 25 per cent lower per head of population than in France (and 60 per cent below German levels – where, however, the development of East Germany creates somewhat of a special case). Investment was also much lower over the previous decade, and was cut further in the mid-1990s. Rail investment per head was particularly low, a third of the level of the Netherlands and Germany and a quarter that of France in the period 1987–93. See CBI transport strategy reports, *Missing Links* (1995) and *Moving Forward* (1995).

inator in recruitment selection does not prove that the skills delivered by that education were essential to the jobs performed.[22]

But amid the uncertainty three public policy priorities can be identified. The first is the need to improve basic skills, for social reasons as well as economic. Very low levels of basic skills – low literacy, low numeracy and poor work discipline – are highly correlated with poor individual employment prospects and almost certainly increase overall unemployment and constrain productivity. Fixing that deficiency, through improvements in schools and also through adult education and training, is the highest priority: it will require additional public investment. The second priority is to improve Britain's performance in 'intermediate' level skills – especially of the vocational rather than academic variety. Growing numbers of jobs do seem in some intrinsic sense to require skills at the 'intermediate' and 'associate professional' level, and Britain has typically underperformed other European countries in training people to this level: it simply has fewer people training to a high level of technical competence, whether the industry is engineering or hospitality. A key recommendation of the National Skills Taskforce was to give all young people up to their twenty-fifth birthday an entitlement to free education and training leading to a 'level 3' qualification. That is an expensive commitment, but a sensible one. Third, and finally, government needs to continue to invest in the elite end of education, in the research and teaching base of the country's top universities. For the one part of the education system in which the US appears to be superior, not just to the UK but to much of continental Europe, is the quality of its top universities, and that in turn is highly relevant to its current leadership both in information technology and biotechnology. Governments should not pick technological winners but they should aim to make their countries attractive locations for whatever are the high-technology industries of the future. Excellent teaching at elite universities is important to this as well as the excellent research base already mentioned.

---

22. See Alison Wolf, 'Education and Economic Growth'. If companies believe that selective entry *into* a graduate course is a reasonable discriminator of relative talent they will tend to recruit the output of that graduate course even if the specific skills learnt are largely irrelevant to the job subsequently performed.

The good society: it's not the economy, stupid?

The best economic policy mix for Britain can be summed up as follows. We should maintain the product-market liberalization of the Thatcher years, maintain the stability we have more recently achieved, deepen liberalization through further development of the European single market and encourage higher investment in capital equipment, research and skills but without fooling ourselves that we possess either easy or precisely targeted mechanisms to achieve these investment effects. We should recognize Britain as a moderately successful mid-sized economy which has put relative economic decline behind it, but not pretend that we are performing better than the rest of Europe. We should hope to achieve a gradual catch-up with leading European levels of productivity, and a slightly higher trend growth rate than in the past, but without getting fixated on minor movements up and down league tables.

We should recognize, moreover, that some of our most urgent priorities are not those of economic performance. For while expanding the size of the economic pie is important it is not everything. Larry Summers, US Treasury Secretary 1999–2000 and before that Deputy Secretary, commented in a speech in 1997 that: 'as a model for making the economic pie as large as possible American capitalism is second to none. But as a means of creating a stable society and addressing the concerns of our citizens the Americans model's superiority is far from clear'. Child poverty indices are worse in America than in all European countries:[23] the prison population is four times higher per head of population than the nearest European country, levels of inequality are higher and 44 million Americans are not covered by health insurance and receive medical care worse than almost anyone in Europe despite the fact that the US in total spends a far higher percentage of its national income on health services. Or as Larry Summers graphically illustrated the point: 'a child born in New York today is less likely to

---

23. E.g. children living in households below 50 per cent of national median income: US 23 per cent, UK 20 per cent, Germany 11 per cent, France 8 per cent, Sweden 3 per cent. *The Economist*, 23 June 2000. The disputed issue of whether such measures of relative income (rather than absolute income) matter is discussed in Chapter 8.

live to five than a child born in Shanghai. A young American black man is more likely to go to jail than to go to college'.[24]

Britain also scores badly on some of these non-economic indicators. On child poverty it is, with Italy, the only European country close to US levels. On healthcare a recent report found the quality of our output among the worst in Europe. Our prison population relative to total population is the highest in Europe apart from Portugal's. And although more difficult to quantify, it is clear that the quality of much of Britain's public infrastructure is poorer too, with more congested roads, poorer-quality public transport and less investment in environmental measures such as traffic-calming schemes and sound screening. Resolving those problems may be more difficult than managing the economy: making the trade-offs involved may require more hard choices than choosing the best economic policy. In terms of public policy priorities the motto should perhaps be 'it's *not* the economy, stupid'.

The solutions to these problems are not mechanically linked to overall prosperity nor to levels of government spending (much of Britain's crime problem seems to be the crimes of the relatively affluent not of the destitute). They would however, be impossible to resolve if there were an economic imperative not only to keep government spending under control but to reduce British and European levels of tax and spend towards an American level in the pursuit of competitiveness. Fortunately, as Chapter 8 will argue, no such imperative exists.

24. Larry Summers, speaking at World Economic Forum, 1997, quoted in Anatole Kaletsky, 'No Easy Answers', *The Times*, 7 February 1997.

PART THREE

Implications for Policy

8. Choosing the State We Want

In March 1999 the *Sunday Times* published an editorial on flexibility and supply-side reform in Europe.[1] It noted with approval Tony Blair's insistence, at a meeting of European socialists, that Europe must learn lessons from the success of the US economy. But it attacked him for failing to match words with deeds, pointing out that the British government 'is content with public expenditure at 40 per cent of GDP' while 'a truly flexible strategy would reduce it to 30 per cent as in America'. The assertion is a commonplace of the conservative right: an efficient market economy requires also a minimal state. But it is halfway between massively overstated and simply wrong.

The idea that government tax and expenditure levels must fall in a global economy is pervasive and combines polemicists of right and left, the former in triumph, the latter in pessimistic despair. To William Hague, speaking in November 1999, it was clear that: 'Britain must cut taxes if it is to become a leader in the new global economy'.[2] Indeed, he warned bluntly: 'if we do not cut taxes, then Britain will fail'. The *Sunday Times* in another editorial asserted that: 'British tax levels must come down if we are to have a fighting chance.' In numerous other articles and speeches it is accepted as self-evident that Europe's high tax burden imposes a significant economic disadvantage and that radical cuts in tax and welfare levels are therefore essential. Three propositions underlie this belief. First, that a high tax level imposes a 'competitiveness burden', making the country's businesses 'uncompetitive' in world markets and cutting employment as a result. Second, that higher taxes blunt incentives, and that lower American taxes are a key driver of superior enterprise and higher productivity. Third, that high tax rates are unsustainable in a globalized and information-intensive economy

---

1. 7 March 1999.

2. Speech to CBI National Conference, November 1999.

because tax bases will migrate and erode – skilled people and corporate activity moving to low-tax regimes, and the Internet allowing cross-border tax-free shopping. For all three reasons tax rates must and will come down and governments must cut expenditure to make that possible.

These assertions are key weapons in the polemic armoury of the right. But they are accepted too by many on the left as part of a wider pessimism about the impact of globalization. John Gray's book *False Dawn: The Delusions of Global Capitalism* sees the 'Washington consensus' of global free markets as a dangerous threat to welfare states and cultural diversity. Comparing the way in which the excesses of late nineteenth-century capitalism were offset by social reform with today's need to manage global capitalism's social consequences, he warns that: 'it will be harder now than it was then to moderate the social costs of free markets. The leverage of national governments over their economies is much weaker'. Global financial markets have diminished the potential for Keynesian full-employment policies; privatization and deregulation have unleashed a rapacious capitalism which ignores and overrides social responsibility; and tax bases – as the right triumphantly asserts – will be eroded through tax competition in a relentless race for the bottom. The latter theme, in particular, finds frequent echoes across Europe, but also a proposed response. The European Union must harmonize taxes and labour standards within Europe and use trade barriers to prevent 'social dumping' (i.e. 'unfair' competition) from outside. 'If business taxes are not harmonized, competition for inward investment will mean competition to bring tax rates down to the extent that even a modernized welfare state could prove unsustainable,' writes one proponent of this view,[3] only to draw forth the right-wing response that tax harmonization within Europe will make Europe uncompetitive in the wider world.

This chapter evaluates these propositions. It argues four points in turn. First, that governments should and largely do accept that their role as active managers of the economy is now reduced, but that this does not threaten desirable objectives provided the state's social role is still affordable. Second, that that social role remains vital – and indeed has become more important – as a result of the trends identified in this book, trends which unless well-managed can fracture the social compact

---

3. Donald McIntyre, *Independent*, 12 June 1998.

on which modern capitalism must be based. Third, that while migration and incentive effects put some limits on governments' ability to tax and spend, and while they argue for tax reduction and tax reform in some European countries, they do not require radical downsizing of European welfare states. Fourth, that the European Union can and should play a limited role in preventing harmful tax competition but that the required scope of that action is likely to be small and would in no way limit the freedom of individual European countries to make significantly different choices about tax and spend levels.

We are therefore to a great degree free to choose and polemicists on all sides should face that fact. Right-wingers who believe individual consumption is always best and who dislike redistribution or extensive public-goods provision should argue their case on those grounds and not by reference to the phoney economics of competitiveness. Pessimists of the John Gray mould should cheer up – the biggest threat to desirable social objectives comes not from external circumstances but from a lack of intellectual coherence and self-confidence among those who support those objectives. Euro-federalists should cease telling us that a race for the bottom requires wholesale tax harmonization; Euro-sceptics should cease fearing that any element of tax harmonization would open the floodgates to harmonization in all respects. There are alternatives and we can choose, and the essence of politics is about the making of choices. No politician should ever be allowed to say that there are no alternatives.

Government's limited economic role

In one sense the right-wing polemicists and left-wing pessimists are right. The possible and appropriate role of governments in the management of the economy has declined because the economic context has changed. That is true whether we look at micro- or macro-policies and whether our concern is narrowly defined economic performance or the attainment of social objectives through interventions in product, capital and labour markets. We should head and are heading towards more free-market approaches. But that in itself does not remove our ability to pursue desirable social objectives.

The case for a more free-market approach in product capital and labour markets has already been made in Chapter 6. Trends in technology and economic structure, along with globalization, have shifted the balance of advantage towards more liberalized markets. The case for privatization grows as the concept of national champions becomes untenable and as productivity improvement in utilities becomes increasingly important to overall prosperity growth. More explicit shareholder-value approaches to corporate governance have economic advantages when creative destruction requires movement from big companies to small, not from farms and small shops to big companies. Labour markets need to be more flexible in the service-intensive economy. The state's ability to play a useful developmental role declines as the economy becomes more complex. And this shift to freer markets does reduce the extent to which desirable social aims can be pursued through market interventions or corporate objectives. The implicit employment promises of large companies will be decreasingly valid bases for personal economic security and the role of minimum wages as primary anti-poverty tools will decline. To some extent the left-wing pessimists are right.

Where they go wrong is in overstating the scope and scale of the effect. Some shifts to freer markets have an impact on the pursuit of desirable social objectives but many others do not. There is absolutely nothing about water privatization which threatens environmental standards, indeed the evidence in Britain is that they have improved since privatization. There is nothing inherently desirable about inefficient staffing levels in electricity-distribution companies and nothing about the ending of them which threatens desirable rather than incidental features of the European model. Rail privatization can be used as a technique to enable society to buy public service and environmental benefits at least cost, but can be accompanied by greater rather than reduced public subsidy if society wishes to purchase more of those benefits than before. European labour markets should be reformed in a more flexible direction but there is no case for limitless deregulation, for the complete dismantling of employment-protection laws or for the abolition (rather than reform) of minimum wages. And if countries want to make exceptions to market liberalization they can. The French can keep cultural exception while sacrificing only a trivial part of the benefits of free markets, Britain can subsidize the BBC to achieve whatever cultural objectives we want without any serious economic detriment, and if we want to keep tight planning rules at the expense of the last few percentage points of productivity potential we can make that choice. The shift to freer markets poses some challenges for the pursuit of desirable social and economic objectives, and it moves more of the burden of that pursuit on to the social rather than the economic function of the state but, provided we use market liberalization as a means to an end, not an end in itself, it does not make the pursuit of those objectives impossible.

The shift to freer markets has in most cases been accompanied by a shift to 'sound money' (i.e. formal inflation targets and constrained borrowing). There is nothing inherent about that coupling either in theory or empirical experience – the Reagan administration was a deregulating tax cutter but also fiscally irresponsible. But usually they have gone together, and the rejection of 'Keynesianism' is bemoaned by left-wing pessimists as much as market liberalization. Global capital markets and currency speculation have, it is feared, undermined governments' freedom to provide high levels of social welfare and removed their ability to achieve full employment by demand management. And, as with their fears of market liberalization, there is the grain of truth lurking here, but also a great deal of confusion. At least for developed rich societies the limits imposed on freedom of action by global capital markets are slight.

The pessimists' attitude to public borrowing is one confusion. Most well-run countries now aim to limit government borrowing. In some emerging economies those limits exist because of global capital-market discipline, and that does raise issues about the efficiency of global financial markets and their impact on developing countries.[4] For developed rich countries, however, the impetus for control of borrowing has been essentially internal and totally compatible with progressive social aims. High levels of government borrowing can crowd out private savings and investment and impose burdens on future generations: there was never anything progressive about either of those effects. Ending high public borrowing, moreover, need not mean rejecting high levels of public expenditure. Sweden is now running a budget surplus with government revenues at about 57 per cent of GDP, expenditure at 55 per cent, while the UK achieves the same effect at 40 per cent and 39 per cent, and the bond markets make no distinction between them in terms of creditworthiness.[5] Left-wing attachment to sustained high

---

4. This issue is discussed in Chapter 10.

5. The figures quoted are for 'General government total outlays' and 'General government current tax and non-tax receipts' for 2000 (see OECD *Economic Outlook*). Figures for *current* outlays (excluding capital) and for tax receipts

levels of borrowing to pay for high public expenditure was always a triumph of economic irresponsibility over political courage. If we want a high level of government expenditure we should have the honesty and confidence to argue the case for the taxes to support it.

The rejection of high sustained borrowing has been accompanied by a move to rule-driven approaches to demand management. Formal inflation targets have replaced high employment and growth as the objectives of fiscal and monetary policy. But this shift has very little to do with the constraints of global capital markets. It reflects instead our better understanding of how demand-management levers work and of their inherent limitations. The 1960s belief that faster long-term growth and higher sustained employment could be achieved via demand stimulation was both a perversion rather than true expression of Keynes's own theories and simply wrong. It ignored the long-term supply-side determinants of growth and failed to recognize that excess demand generates inflationary expectations which undermine any temporary stimulus to activity. As a result it helped to create the 'stagflation' of the 1970s – a combination of high inflation *and* high unemployment. Getting out of that stagflation required the deflationary and painful policies of the early 1980s – driving inflationary expectations down is far more difficult than driving them up. It is far better to prevent inflationary expectations rising in the first place and the policies through which governments achieve that – constrained borrowing, central-bank independence and formal inflation targets – are, as we have discovered in the late 1990s, no barriers to high employment. Sound money is neither a dogma nor an imposition of global capital markets: it is simply a more sensible way to run an economy and one likely over the long term to deliver both a lower rate of inflation and a lower average rate of unemployment.

Nor is sound money in any sense anti-Keynesian. For Keynes's essential insights remain valid and highly relevant to policy. High inflation is difficult and painful to eradicate, but Keynes's greatest insight – that demand deflation is also a danger to which there is no automatic free-market cure – remains as vital as ever and has important implications for how sound money should be implemented. Inflation targets should be positive and symmetric, not zero and asymmetric (e.g.

(excluding non-tax) are slightly lower in both countries. Ten-year bond yields in September 2000 were UK 5.27 per cent, Sweden 5.21 per cent.

'less than 3 per cent but greater than 1 per cent', rather than 'at or below zero').[6] Countries should eschew sustained high levels of borrowing which reduce their future freedom of manoeuvre, but should still allow borrowing to vary with the economic cycle as an automatic fiscal stabilizer – naturally higher taxes in booms helping to slow the economy down, lower taxes and high welfare spending in slumps helping to stimulate the economy. And if despite such safeguards (or because of the absence of them) a country still falls into an absolute deflation trap, as Japan did in the 1990s, we should preserve and use the freedom to stimulate the economy by combined fiscal and monetary means in the fashion which both Keynes and Friedman would recommend. There is nothing about the global economy which is limiting developed countries' freedom to pursue sound money in such sensible Keynesian ways.

Overall, therefore, the fears of the left-wing pessimists are, at least for developed rich countries, overstated. In macro-policy we have not lost real freedom of action but merely delusions we are better off without. In micro-policy we still have the freedom to make exceptions to market liberalization if we want. But the pessimists' proposition still remains partially valid. The move to market liberalization limits our ability to achieve desirable social objectives through direct market interventions. It therefore throws an increased burden on to the social role of the state.

Government's social role: an increasing challenge

Totally laissez-faire capitalism is unworkable socially. Modern capitalism is inevitably managed and modulated by government's social role. The laissez-faire economy of mid-Victorian Britain was humanized by a series of government interventions which began with the earliest factory acts of the 1830s, but gathered pace from the 1870s onwards

---

6. The move to a rule-driven approach is often wrongly described as a rejection of 'fine-tuning'. In fact symmetric inflation targets commit central banks to a continual process of monetary fine-tuning to prevent both under and overshoots. The difference compared with thirty years ago is not that we have rejected demand management but that demand-management levers are now focused on appropriate and attainable objectives and as a result are more effectively used.

and developed into a full philosophy of social liberalism in the decade
before the First World War. Regulation of working conditions, social
insurance schemes to cover against unemployment and ill-health, universal education as an underpinning of opportunity and skill development, and increasing social investment in the urban environment, water
and sewage systems, new roads and street lighting, public parks and
slum clearance: these were the essential mechanisms which averted the
Marxist prediction that capitalism would consume itself in its own
excesses and collapse under the tensions of cumulatively increasing
inequality. Those mechanisms remain as important as ever – capitalism
still needs to be regulated and moderated by social interventions if it is
to succeed as a social system. In some ways, indeed, the need for those
interventions is increasing as well as changing.

Governments do three things to make capitalism work as a social
system. They ensure the provision of collective goods and services
which individual consumers cannot purchase in individual slices –
defence and law and order, environmental protection, subsidized public
transport and water systems, attractive public space. They do not need
to own or manage all the assets involved and many of these collective
goods are delivered by regulation rather than direct provision – food
standards, workplace health and safety and pollution control are all
regulated, not provided. But government has to decide how much, and
consumer preferences have to be expressed through the political process
since they cannot be expressed in individual purchase decisions.

Second, governments subsidize or provide for free services which
could be privately supplied and bought but which are particularly
important to equality of opportunity and equality of citizenship –
healthcare, education and access to legal services being the most
important.

Third, governments redistribute both outcomes and opportunities.
An element of redistribution is usually implicit in collective-goods
provision. It is more explicit in the provision of the services which
deliver equality of citizenship. But it is most obvious in money transfers
– from employed to unemployed, from people who have adequate
private provision for old age to those who do not, and from rich to
poor.

The demands on government to perform these roles are increasing
rather than decreasing as a result of trends in economic structure,
technology and consumer preference. Demand for inherently collective
goods is likely to increase as we get richer. Environmental quality is a

high income-elasticity customer preference – the richer people get the more they want cleaner air and water and better preserved countryside. But the more they also want to travel, and transport poses some of our most difficult environmental challenges. Richer people want safer workplaces and care more about food hygiene and quality. The natural development of an economy getting steadily richer includes more regulation to achieve collective benefits and more subsidized public transport to try to square the circle of competing demands for mobility and environmental improvement. And one of the observed realities of richer societies, though the demand here is less inherent, is more expenditure on law and order.[7]

Demands for goods and services vital to equality of citizenship are also increasing both because the goods and services involved are highly income elastic – richer people want more of them – and because they are often not susceptible to productivity improvement. As people get richer they want more healthcare and there may be no limit to that preference. As the population ages too healthcare needs rise. The more that medical science can improve our health, the more we will demand better health as a good more precious than any other. Some healthcare activities are susceptible to productivity improvements – via keyhole and remote surgery, for instance – but some rely on unautomatable face-to-face service. Britain now spends about 7 per cent of GDP on healthcare, France 10 per cent, the US 14 per cent and there is no reason why in fifty years' time spend levels could not be much higher still.[8] If we are to maintain equal access to healthcare, government expenditure will rise.

---

7. Nor indeed should we forget defence. Although there is no inherent tendency for rich countries to wish or need to spend more on defence, there is equally no natural inverse correlation. The world remains a dangerous place, and Europe would be naive to believe it can forever rely on the surprising but welcome willingness of America to shoulder a disproportionate share of NATO's military burden, especially in situations where there is no American self-interest involved. Squaring the circle of other competing demands by cutting European defence spending is not an option: instead we should be increasing it.

8. The UK figure will soon rise. Government plans for the National Health Service announced in the *Comprehensive Spending Review* of July 2000 will take public expenditure to about 7.8 per cent of GDP and total healthcare (public and private) to above 8 per cent.

Education is another high income-elasticity good – richer people want more of it. It is also becoming more important as the guarantor of social inclusion. Liberalization of capital and labour markets is desirable but it makes it less likely that economic security will derive from employment security in existing jobs: individual skills and attitudes which ensure employability will be increasingly important. The case for excellent basic education freely provided is therefore overwhelming. The means of delivering it are, moreover, expensive, for while there is certainly opportunity for technologically based productivity improvement in some aspects of education, in primary education there are probably two key drivers of quality – smaller class sizes (i.e. more teachers) and high-quality teachers (which probably requires more pay).

Finally, the demands on the social role of the state have increased because inequality has increased. The scale of that increase and its likely causes have already been discussed in Chapter 3 – technology and globalization acting together to increase the dispersion of free-market earnings. That trend may now be slowing down or stopping, but it is not reversing and its impact is reinforced by three other factors. The first is the need for labour-market flexibility. We cannot intervene too strongly against inequality in the labour market, for instance via high minimum wages, without creating unemployment: the case for tax credits or in-work benefits for low-income households has therefore increased. The second is the rising importance of positional goods. The classic conservative response to discussion of inequality is simple: 'don't worry about equality, worry about prosperity; don't covet your neighbour's house, go out and earn enough money to get an equally pleasant one yourself'. It is an argument with considerable appeal, but most applicable when positional goods are least important and above all that means when population densities are low and land plentiful. If you live in Phoenix, Arizona, and aspire to the housing of the already well-to-do, the political ideology which says 'don't get equal get richer' is underpinned by the real possibility of carving out of the desert another equally attractive community. If you live in London you are involved in a competition for a limited supply of locationally specific desirable houses. Relative income and wealth matter and will matter increasingly in future.[9]

_____

9. One implication of this is that even a non-socialist, interested only in opportunity

The third and final reason why inequality will remain an inescap-able issue is genetic science. One reaction to rising healthcare expendi-ture could be to 'privatize' some of the redistribution. Private health insurance effectively performs part of the redistributive function – not the element from rich to poor but the element from those less liable to illness to those more liable. But it can only do that because of our ignorance – the fact that we do not know in advance who has a cancer-liable gene and who not. The more that genetic science can tell us in advance who is liable to illness and who not the more we will have to be explicit about redistribution and the less available will be the option of redistributing through blind pools of insurance.

The social role of the state is therefore not going to wither away. But precisely how large that role should be is not determined by economic science but instead by one's personal preferences for collec-tive versus individual goods and by one's philosophical approach to inequality. There is no science by which to judge between the social effects of Denmark's state taxing and spending 53 per cent of GDP and America's taxing and spending 30 per cent. The key issues indeed are what people want and whether their choices are economically affordable.

In 1996, however, Kenneth Clarke, then Britain's Chancellor of the Exchequer in a Conservative government, expressed the belief that it would probably be both difficult and undesirable for any European nation to push government's tax and spend significantly below the 40 per cent level which Britain was then on target to reach. Personally

---

and not in equalization of outcomes, can support redistributive taxation of high income and wealth as an end per se rather than simply as a means of raising revenue. It is possible, moreover, to support that taxation for long-term economic as well as social reasons. Inequality if not offset by some element of redistribution is cumulative: rich people can save more and accumulate faster. And it becomes more rapidly cumulative the greater the importance of positional goods – unres-tricted inheritance of positional goods leads to rising asset prices generating capital gains for the already well-to-do. Nil redistribution would therefore produce a class system of steadily increasing inherited inequality. Paradoxically, therefore, the dynamism of capitalism needs to be preserved by some element of redistributive taxation. If America goes on getting richer and more populous and if Republicans get their way and abolish inheritance taxes entirely they will over time destroy some of the most attractive features of American society – its democratic spirit, its sense of universal opportunity, its absence of an inherited class system.

I concur with that judgement. From where Britain stood in 1996 further attempts to reduce the role of the state would almost certainly have made it a less pleasant place; if anything we needed instead a slight increase in that role.

The rationale for that judgement is inevitably personal and highly subjective. It has both selfish and altruistic aspects. Part altruistic but largely selfish is my personal preference for better-quality collective goods, for cleaner streets, less congestion and better public transport. London is a wonderful, dynamic city: it would be better still if we invested a bit more in our common rather than individual wealth. Largely altruistic is my concern for poverty and equal opportunity. Britain has become a much more unequal society. Over the last twenty years the top fifth of income earners have seen their share of post-tax income grow from 37 per cent to 44 per cent, while the share of the bottom fifth has fallen from 9 per cent to 7 per cent; 20 per cent of Britain's children live in poverty, 23 per cent in the US, 3 per cent in Sweden: we would be a better society if we were closer to Sweden's figures.[10] The latest report from the Joseph Rowntree Foundation,

---

10. See *The Economist*, 17–23 June: UNICEF figures for percentage of children living in households with below 50 per cent of national median income. Conservatives object to such measures of poverty on the grounds that relative definitions are irrelevant – all that matters is absolute income. Even on absolute figures, of course, Sweden would look better than Britain since median income is similar. The wider dispute remains, however, an important one. This book will not consider it in detail but my attitude is best summed up by Sir Samuel Brittan in a recent article: 'there seems no escape from the notion that poverty is in part a relative and in part an absolute concept'. That can be argued on theoretical welfare-economics grounds, but more simply on the commonsensical basis that defining it in entirely relative or entirely absolute terms produces absurdity. If we define it in entirely relative terms we have to conclude that the average earner on a stable real income gets poorer if the number of people able to fly first class rises from 1 per cent to 3 per cent of the population. If in entirely absolute terms, we have to believe that a family with two children living in Britain today on £5,000 a year is not poor since £5,000 in India today or the real equivalent in Britain in the 1930s would afford a middle-class lifestyle. This ignores the cost of positional goods (rents are higher the higher is average income), the non-availability of low-income, low-price goods (the option of third-class railway tickets doesn't exist) and the fact that access to the common experience of the vast majority of one's fellow citizens clearly matters – not to be able to afford a television is to be in some meaningful sense poor in a society where 95 per cent of one's fellow citizens have one. A concept of 'equality

Poverty and Social Exclusion in Britain, suggests that the proportion of households living in poverty rose from 14 per cent to 24 per cent between 1983 and 1999. Britain's National Health Service fails to deliver the quality of care we should aspire to and however radically it is reformed it will need more money. So too will our education system if we are even to approach equality of opportunity. A non-socialist uninterested in equality of outcome and concerned solely with poverty and opportunity could argue for more state spending and for progressive taxes to pay for it given Britain's position at the time of Kenneth Clarke's 1996 speech.

Present levels of spending at least (and certainly no reduction to US levels) may also be desirable on more purely selfish grounds. For there is probably some level of state provision below which we undermine social cohesion and foster crime and antisocial behaviour. That sounds like a tentative conclusion and deliberately so. Many other writers are more categorical, and certain too that free markets themselves, not just a minimal state, rupture social cohesion. To John Gray it is obvious that free markets and greater inequality are the reasons why America has four to five times as many prisoners per head of population than Britain, and obvious that Britain's explosion of single-parent families, unmatched by continental countries, stems from Thatcherite laissez-faire economics. 'The effects of freeing up markets on marriage, the family and the incidence of crime are clear.'[11] Many of the effects, however, are either not at all clear or clearly linked also to other factors. The most important reason why the US has more murders is that it has more guns because it has absurd gun laws. Relatively affluent young people are not indulging in alcohol-fuelled rowdiness on Friday and Saturday nights in Britain's major cities because they are now employed by private companies whereas their fathers worked for state-owned ones. The rise in single-parent families may have far more to do with the breakdown of traditional moral values than with any economic factor. We should not fall into a simple economic determinism or

---

of citizenship' requires a concern for relative income at the low end of the income distribution. Defining poverty by reference to the relationship between low and median incomes is therefore sensible. See Sir Samuel Brittan, *The Poor Need Not Always Be With Us* (Joseph Rowntree Foundation, spring 2000).

11. Gray, *False Dawn*.

conflate all aspects of economic liberalism with minimal state levels of income support and public-goods provision.

Those caveats made, however, some links probably do exist. John Gray's argument that New Zealand has experienced in the last twenty years a radical experiment in economic liberalization, including a large-scale dismantling of its welfare state, and has seen at the same time the emergence of a significant underclass and increasing crime in a society previously noted for the relative absence of such features should at least give minimal statists pause for thought.[12] America's high crime rate and prison population may not have been caused primarily by the increasing economic inequality and insecurity of the 1980s, but the possibility that some of it was has more prima facie credibility than the hard right's alternative assertion that it was due to welfare dependency. Welfare dependency in Scandinavia may perhaps have reduced economic dynamism but it notably has not produced an underclass on anything like the American scale. Even without a moral concern for inequality, capitalism's beneficiaries should in their own self-interest be willing to invest in measures likely to create social cohesion – in excellent schools, in high-quality public space which people feel an incentive to respect rather than vandalize, in working-family tax credits which give people greater incentives to work, and in what Gray and others refer to as the 'auxiliary agents of social control' – the park keepers and bus conductors and school caretakers laid off in cost-efficiency drives as being unnecessary to economic success but who performed important roles in enforcing society's rules. In some countries capitalism's beneficiaries have a self-interest in these investments more than in further tax cuts.

Or at least they have this self-interest if they are not able to escape. For one further implication of America's low population density, in addition to the productivity and positional-goods effects already mentioned, is that the American upper middle class can literally escape.

I am writing this paragraph while staying with friends in a delightful ocean-side town with white clapboard houses on the New England coast. When our hosts take us down to the beach they leave the house

12. See Jane Kelsey, *Economic Fundamentalism* (1995). The economic results of New Zealand's liberalization project have also been poor. Between 1984–98 New Zealand's per capita income grew only about 5.4 per cent, or 0.4 per cent per annum, well below the EU average and one of the lowest rates of increase among all OECD countries. See OECD *Historic Statistics* and OECD *Economic Outlook*.

unlocked, also the car and their bicycles – a behaviour almost unimaginable anywhere in Britain. And the town is in many ways a strong and caring community: there is a collection being raised to ensure adequate healthcare for a townsperson who has suffered a bad accident. The town library is a delight. Elsewhere, many miles from here, there are neighbourhoods of America as crimeridden as any in the world but they seem simply irrelevant to me and my hosts. And throughout America there are many people with inadequate healthcare to whom long-distance collections, through taxes, are not being transferred. This community is a strong one but it can be defined and is defined in very local terms. That is not an option when I return to my house in Kensington. I live there in as well-to-do an area as this, but in Kensington I lock my door and I have to define my community, whether thinking about crime, or quality of public space, or pollution, or public transport, in terms at least of all of London if not the whole nation. America's physical space creates the option of a very local definition of community and thus of a very limited role for government, an option not available in most of more densely populated Europe. By some estimates 10 per cent of Americans now live in 'gated communities' or other privately guarded buildings where the quality of their public space and indeed of law and order services is effectively privatized; many more live in suburbs sufficiently distant from the inner-city ghettos that they can if they want wash their hands of the ghettos' problems. You can do that in the small towns and spread-out suburbs of Middle America, but not in central London or indeed New York – one reason why support for minimal state politics is usually highest in sparse suburbs and lowest in densely packed cities, even among the city's rich.

Kenneth Clarke was probably therefore right. European states are unlikely to be able to push government tax and spend burdens much below 40 per cent of GDP without rupturing the social compact and losing popular support. Even to manage it at that level indeed is likely to require the radical approach to efficiency and focus discussed later in the chapter. Some increase from 40 per cent may indeed be what people want. One key reason why the Conservatives lost in 1997 was that even those who welcomed the economic dynamism the Conservative government had helped create were worried that it had tipped the balance of the state's role too much in the low-tax, low-spend direction. Ultimately the people decide and their choice in Britain in 1997 was for a bit more tax and a bit more spend.

But the quotes with which this chapter started were concerned not with social choice but with economic necessity, with the belief that whatever our preferences there is some economic imperative demanding that we reduce tax and spend towards US levels. 'If we do not cut taxes, then Britain will fail.' The good news is that this is not true.

Tax and economic performance

Right-wing proponents of minimal states sometimes argue against European levels of collective-goods provision and redistribution on principle. More often they argue that the high taxes needed to pay for them will have harmful economic effects, and as a polemic strategy that is clearly wise. 'You can't fight poverty unless you create wealth' appeals to more people than stating that you don't think poverty very important. And clearly the argument is at some level true. There is a level of taxation which would destroy the dynamism of capitalism and reduce the prosperity on which all government spending must be based. In itself, however, that proposition takes us hardly anywhere.[13] The vital empirical question is: at what level and with what trade-offs?

Three economic arguments are put forward for lower taxes. First, high taxes undermine competitiveness; second, high taxes destroy incentives to work and save; third, high taxes will be avoided and evaded by migration and capital flight, especially in the era of the Internet.

The first argument is the largely nonsensical product of conceptual confusion. The second and third are important possible effects which argue for tax cuts or tax reform in some European countries, but which are not sufficiently powerful to require radical downsizing of European welfare states towards American levels.

---

13. The most polemically successful expression of the economic case for the minimal state was the famous Laffer curve, Arthur Laffer's demonstration, apparently first traced out on a paper napkin in a New York restaurant, that tax revenues will be zero at a tax rate of 0 per cent and zero also if tax rates are 100 per cent, describing a first upward and then downward sloping curve as we progress from 0 to 100 per cent. It is difficult to imagine an equally famous proposition stating such a blindingly obvious, and in practice useless, insight. The fact that tax revenues will be zero at a 0 per cent rate and zero at 100 per cent tells us nothing: what matters is the slope of the curve at all the intermediate values, over what range it rises and over what range it falls, as well as the wider economic effects of taxes, not just the point of maximum revenue collection.

To many people it is obvious that high taxes produce high labour and capital costs and therefore make a country 'uncompetitive' in global markets. Germany has high employer payroll taxes therefore Germany has high and uncompetitive labour costs. But for the reasons set out in Chapter 1 and elsewhere in this book that proposition, though apparently compelling, is in almost all respects misleading: the 'almost' included here, as in Chapter 1, because there are a few special-case exceptions.

Taxes represent a diversion of pre-tax income from individual to collective consumption and their impact is essentially just that – people have less money to spend on private consumption but the government spends more on their behalf on defence, or healthcare, or education, etc. They have no necessary impact on pre-tax real income or total wage costs, and that is true of consumption taxes, such as VAT or employer payroll taxes, as much as of personal income taxes where the point is more intuitively obvious.[14] Indeed, provided labour markets are efficient, high labour taxes will definitely not increase total labour costs, the impact instead falling on post-tax real wages, with companies increasing prices to offset the tax increase and real wages falling as a result.[15] High Swedish taxes mean that Swedes enjoy lower post-tax private consumption and more government-provided services or transfers, but they have no necessary influence on Swedish labour costs. And if they did temporarily, because, for instance, Swedish trade unions successfully resisted the impact of increased taxes by demanding and receiving higher nominal wages, the Swedish krona could fall over time to compensate, bringing Swedish labour costs into a new competitive equilibrium. The real issue for Swedes is whether they want the collective/private divide which their high taxes imply, not the impact on competitiveness. Over the long-term competitiveness is a quite meaningless concept for a country with a floating exchange rate, and the idea that high taxes

---

14. Under some circumstances it may also be true of corporation tax – the incidence of which can fall, through increased prices, on post-tax real wages instead of on post-tax shareholder returns.

15. The same effect can be also, and sometimes is, produced by a lower level of nominal wage increases. In the case of consumption taxes, the effect is produced via higher tax-inclusive prices unmatched by nominal wage growth.

can produce a competitiveness problem is simply a specific absurdity within a wider confusion.[16]

But the reference to a floating exchange rate points us towards one of the special cases, that of countries within a fixed-rate currency union. For it is possible that a country could enter a fixed-rate regime or currency union at an exchange rate which is 'uncompetitive', and which therefore requires real labour costs to rise for a time by less than productivity to bring about a new equilibrium. The problem is not caused by high taxes, but by the wrong exchange rate of entry: and the solution can lie in lower real wage increases (or cuts) as much as in lower taxes. But a country in this position may find it easier to get out of it via tax reductions than via nominal wage-rate freezes and real wage cuts; the people who supported and voted for a high tax regime before the exchange-rate mistake was made may prefer to reduce collective consumption rather than private consumption in order to correct it. In that special-case sense, tax reductions could be relevant to a competitiveness correction if a country had entered a fixed exchange-rate regime at too high a rate. Some economists believe Germany is in that position. But if it is, the specificity of the case must be stressed. A specific country or region of the Euro zone could have this problem, but the total Euro zone, with a floating external exchange rate, cannot: indeed to the extent that one region within the zone is 'uncompetitive' some others must by definition be 'super-competitive' (i.e. have total labour costs below equilibrium levels). As a justification for a generalized reduction in the size of all European states, arguments based on a tax-driven competitiveness problem are without merit.[17]

––––––––

16. Floating exchange rates can of course fail to move in a rational fashion and can thus either fail to compensate for higher taxes (producing a temporary problem of uncompetitiveness) or overcompensate (making the country super-competitive). This potential irrationality is, however, a problem quite independent of tax policy – it can afflict low-tax countries as much as high tax, countries raising taxes as much as those cutting them, and can lead either to uncompetitiveness or super-competitiveness. It therefore in no way undermines the arguments 1) that there is no essential link between high taxes and competitiveness problems, 2) that national competitiveness is, except temporarily, a meaningless concept for a country with a floating exchange rate.

17. For a more detailed discussion of these tax-incidence arguments, including all the possible special cases (none of which invalidates the general point that

The second special case can arise if labour markets are not efficient. In efficient labour markets the incidence of consumption taxes or taxes on labour will fall on individuals, leaving total labour cost to business unaffected. In inefficient labour markets, however, trade-union bargaining might be able to resist the impact of rising taxes on post-tax income: as a result it could produce a rise in the cost of labour, provoking in turn substitution of capital for labour and consequent unemployment. A study by two Italian economists has found evidence of this effect.[18] In common with previous studies they found little or no correlation between absolute levels of tax and employment creation. And they found no evidence that rising tax burdens correlated with rising unemployment in labour markets which were reasonably efficient, whether this efficiency was achieved (as in the US or UK) via decentralization and flexibility, or (as in Scandinavia) through strongly unionized but also co-ordinated arrangements. But in countries with strong but unco-ordinated unions (such as France, Italy or Belgium) they found evidence that the impact of rising tax burdens in the 1970s and 80s was successfully resisted, and that a higher total cost of labour drove businesses to substitute capital for labour, creating unemployment as a result.

This finding has three important implications. First, it provides a further rationale for efficient labour markets: the more flexible and efficient are labour markets, the easier it is for societies to choose their level of taxation and public expenditure without fear of adverse economic effects. Second, they argue, especially where labour markets are not efficient, against significant or sudden *increases* in tax rates.[19] Third,

---

competitiveness is largely a red herring in this debate), see the author's lecture 'Choosing the State We Want', LSE, 31 October 2000.

18. Francesco Daveri and Guido Tabellini, 'Unemployment, Growth and Taxation in Industrial Countries', CEPR Discussion Paper, No. 1681 (1997).

19. The key correlation in Daveri and Tabellini relates not the *level* of tax but to the pace of increase, since it is this which generates the real wage-resistance effect. It is likely, moreover, that over time the effect wears off, i.e. that even in 'inefficient' labour markets, the tax incidence eventually falls on post-tax real wages. It is noticeable, for instance, that the deterioration (i.e. unsustainable increase) in French labour costs which occurred in the 1970s and 80s (which Daveri and Tabellini ascribe to rising taxes successfully resisted) has been reversed in the 1990s, with French wage costs growing significantly more slowly than productivity.

they highlight the importance of popular consent. Provided people are willing to accept the implication that higher taxes and public expenditure mean lower post-tax real wages and private consumption, taxes will not have any adverse impact on total labour costs, on competitiveness or on unemployment: the problems arise because the natural impact is resisted. That in turn may imply that if governments wish to raise taxes on labour, they are better to do so openly and honestly rather than stealthily – through income taxes rather than through the apparently costless route of payroll taxes – since the more open route is the one more likely to command overt public support.

This 'real wage resistance' special case is therefore important. But it actually has nothing essentially to do with competitiveness. The effect described could occur in a totally closed economy not trading at all with the rest of the world, competing with no one. And in an open economy the impact on external traded competitiveness could be offset by movements in the exchange rate even if the internal impact on capital/labour substitution occurred. Nor does the effect imply any inherent limit on the economically feasible size of the state, provided other aspects of policy are well designed.[20] If there are inherent limits on the feasible size of the state they must instead derive from incentive effects or from migration/avoidance effects. Both could be important. Neither justifies the assertion that Europe must match American tax rates to be economically successful.

Tax rates can clearly affect people's propensity to work and save. But the nature of these effects is far more complex, and the empirical evidence for them far more tentative, than the assured rhetoric of ultra-liberal conservatism suggests. The case for avoiding very high marginal rates, say above 50 per cent, is strong. The proposition that 30 per cent is necessarily better than 40 per cent, or 20 per cent better than 22 per cent, is unproven and uncertain. A bit of economic theory is required to understand why.

---

20. One final important special-case effect should also be noted. Employer payroll taxes can increase the total labour cost of workers receiving the minimum wage, since in this case the minimum-wage law prevents the tax incidence from falling, as normal, on the individual. As a result employer payroll taxes on low-income workers can create unemployment, though for reasons quite unrelated to 'national competitiveness'. This argues for reforming the structure of taxation rather than necessarily for reductions in the total level.

Whether people work and how hard people work will be affected by tax rates, but the total impact is the product of two offsetting factors, sometimes labelled by economists the 'income' and 'substitution' effects. The 'income effect' describes a process by which the more you tax me, the *more* I may work. A simple example can illustrate. Suppose I start with a weekly income of 100 units, reflecting forty hours of work at 2.5 units per hour. If a lump sum tax of 10 is then imposed (for instance to pay for unanticipated defence needs) I will almost certainly choose to work more (say forty-three hours for 107.5 units leaving me 97.5 for private consumption) since I am unwilling to live on only 90 units of private consumption and wish to replace some of the lost income even at the expense of more hours of work.

Such 'income effects' will always be positive (i.e. higher taxes result in more work) provided taxes are lump sum in nature. In fact, however, most taxes, for reasons of equity, are either proportional or progressive. I am not taxed 10 lump sum units to pay for defence, I am taxed at 10 per cent of my income. As a result in our simple example, when I consider replacing my 10 units of lost income with extra work, I am faced with a post-tax wage per hour of only 2.25 units not 2.5. This reduced rate at which leisure and income are substituted can be shown logically to make me less likely to work the extra three hours than if taxes were lump sum in nature: it may indeed make me work less. So income effects with lump-sum taxes produce more work; substitution effects (i.e. increases in marginal tax rates) produce less work if income effects are absent. The net effect in practice is a balance, the direction of which is unpredictable by theory and reflects the preferences of all the individuals involved. The impact of taxes on work should therefore be an empirical question, not one where we know in advance that lower taxes always mean more or harder work, that lower income taxes are always economically better.[21]

---

21. The fact that the impact is a balance between income and substitution effects has some intriguing and perhaps unexpected implications for types of tax burden which have different effects. Thus a proportional tax on the better off from which the better off benefit (e.g. a tax used to pay for healthcare provision from which the better off derive a benefit roughly equal to the tax they pay) will be bound to produce less work (because there is no income effect to offset the substitution effect). But the same tax used entirely to redistribute to others could produce either more or less work depending on the balance of income and substitution effects.

Note also that at the level of the overall workforce, though not for individuals

Numerous studies over the years have therefore attempted to measure empirically the direction and scale of taxation effects on work incentives. Specific results vary considerably. But overall they suggest two broad conclusions: first, that for most labour-force categories tax effects, while tending to be negative (i.e. lower post-tax earnings – arising from higher taxes – produce less work), are rather small; second, that there is one category of labour – women with children – where incentive effects are significant. And the explanation for the latter is simple. Those women are not actually trading off work versus leisure, they are trading off more paid work against the extra expenses incurred when the value of their household work is sacrificed (childcare costs rather than looking after their own children, cleaners rather than doing their own cleaning). Lower marginal tax rates probably make appreciably more women with children work; their measurable effects on other categories of work quantity are relatively small.

That in turn means that the economic benefits accruing from even quite large tax cuts could be small. If for example the overall elasticity of labour supply (combining income and substitution effects) is 20 per cent (a figure within the range of the different estimates)[22] this would

---

within it, income effects must have some tendency to cancel each other out. Redistribution of income from rich to poor, for instance, would tend (if taken and given in a lump sum way) to increase the work of the high-income earners but decrease that of recipients.

22. In fact, estimates of elasticity vary hugely between studies. Some studies actually show positive overall elasticity with respect to tax rates (i.e. higher tax rates and thus lower post-tax wages produce more work) for prime-aged males and in particular for low-income earners. Most estimates tend, however, to show negative but small effects from tax rises (and positive but small effects from tax cuts, i.e. lower taxes produce more work) though often significantly smaller than the 20 per cent example used here. (See Brown, *Fiscal Studies*, 9 (4), November 1988, Triest in *Economic Effects of Fundamental Tax Reform*, Aaron and Cale (eds.) (1996); C.V. Brown, *Taxation and the Incentive to Work* (OUP, 1983). Estimates for the UK by Ashworth and Ulph (1981), however, are a bit higher, closer to 30 per cent, as are US estimates quoted in Jerry Hausman, 'Taxes and Labor Supply' in Auerbach and Feldstein (eds.), *Handbook of Public Economics* (1985). Twenty per cent is a reasonable 'within range' figure for men in a range stretching from below 0 to 30 per cent. Estimated effects also vary considerably by country: Atkinson and Mogensen (eds.), *Welfare and Work Incentives: A North European Perspective* (OUP, 1993), find very low prime-age male effects but much

mean that a 10 per cent increase in post-tax income (requiring cuts in tax rates from, say, 30 per cent to 23 per cent) would produce an increase in work and thus in measured GDP of (roughly) 2 per cent. In absolute terms this would be a big number, but it is a one-off increase not a repeated one and equivalent to just one year's average growth. Even this 2 per cent, however, is a significant overestimate of the true prosperity effect since the leisure forgone had value as leisure, and all workers, not just mothers with children, place some value on household work. Once allowance for that is made the impact of this very large tax cut would be just a 0.6 per cent increase in true prosperity, achieved at the expense of huge reductions in public expenditure including possibly on infrastructure or skill investments themselves relevant to GDP growth.[23] The ultra-liberal idea that there is some magic elixir of growth and prosperity to be found in lower taxation whatever the starting point is a delusion.

There is nevertheless a good case for reducing very high rates of taxation. Most of the empirical studies consider the impact of tax-rate variations around the sort of rates paid by average earners – 20 or 30 or maybe 40 per cent – rates which typically can only be varied by a few percentage points. They fail to identify the impact of movements in tax rates from say 80 to 40 per cent because in most countries only two categories of people ever paid these really high rates – a minority of quite rich people (who have some very particular motivational characteristics and whose work volume is difficult to define) and a minority of poor people caught in combined tax and benefit traps. It is therefore possible that whereas movements in rates from, say, 30 to 28 per cent show minimal impact, movements from 80 per cent to 40 per cent have more significant effects. Indeed that is likely both because the total movement is much larger and because of an obvious but rarely

---

higher elasticities for women, except in Denmark where elasticities are only 10 per cent for both men and women.

23. The value of leisure and household work forgone can be calculated fairly precisely if we assume that the tax payers are making rational decisions. If a worker declines marginal work when the tax rate is 30 per cent but takes it at a tax rate of 23 per cent, that worker must be placing a value on leisure and household work forgone equal to between 70 per cent and 77 per cent of the pay they receive for work. At least 70 per cent of the increase in measured GDP achieved is therefore not a true increase in prosperity.

emphasized fact about tax rates and incentives: that the power of the incentive effect is determined not by the tax rate but by the proportion of income left after tax. As a result cuts in very high rates of tax are likely to have much larger incentive effects than equal cuts in lower rates. Cutting a tax rate from 90 per cent to 80 per cent (which doubles the marginal income employees keep for themselves) can be expected, for instance, to have an effect on incentives equivalent to cutting a 50 per cent rate to nil. Cutting tax rates is therefore a policy subject to declining marginal benefit relative to revenue forgone the more we cut. Some British conservatives are attracted to American flat tax ideas and would like to cut Britain's top marginal tax rate from 40 to 30 per cent: one justification proposed is that this would unleash further incentive effects. But a cut from 40 to 30 per cent (increasing marginal income retained by a sixth) could only have an incentive effect equal to one-fifteenth of that produced by the 1980s tax cuts which reduced Britain's top marginal rate from 83 to 40 per cent (an increase of 253 per cent in marginal income retained). It is therefore quite possible to believe that the cut from 83 per cent to 40 per cent had significant beneficial incentive effects, but to be unconvinced that the move from 40 to 30 per cent would make more than the most trivial difference.[24] And there is a danger indeed that such a further reduction would take us into a range where income effects outweigh substitution. I cannot imagine a single high-income professional or business executive of my acquaintance rushing out to work more hours because their marginal tax rate has been cut from 40 to 30 per cent, but I could imagine some who might consider retiring earlier if the lower rate enabled them to achieve a target wealth level sooner.[25]

---

24. Empirical evidence of the effect of very high tax rates (e.g. 50 per cent and above) is also provided by studies of Sweden. Sweden is one of the very few countries where a large proportion of the workforce has in the past paid tax at these rates. See Hansson and Stuart, 'Sweden: Tax Reform in a High Tax Environment', and S. Blomquist (1983) quoted in Hausman, 'Taxes and Labor Supply', *Handbook of Public Economics* (1985).

25. One reason why they might not retire earlier is that since every other high income earner would also enjoy the tax cut more money would pursue positional assets such as desirable houses, pushing up their prices and increasing the target wealth required for any given standard of living. The significant role of positional goods in the consumption patterns of higher income groups is indeed a good

Cutting very high income-tax rates therefore makes sense. But the conservative proposition that lower income-tax rates are always economically better is a dogma not a balanced judgement.

That is true also of another article of faith of the ultra-liberal creed – that lower taxes on savings always produce more savings. It is a credo often repeated: lower capital gains tax will produce more investment; lower tax on investment income will increase personal savings. But it is theoretically uncertain and contradicted by many observable facts. Savings rates do not necessarily rise with investment return: indeed if people are motivated to save by target levels of wealth which they believe essential to a secure and pleasant retirement, they will tend to save less if their return on investment increases. And that is not just a theoretical possibility but a frequently observed fact of economic life. Every employer running a defined benefit pension scheme knows that the lower the post-tax rate of return the higher the contributions the company needs to make on future pensioners' behalf. The American personal savings rate has fallen almost to zero over the last five years: this is not because of higher taxes and low post-tax returns but because the stock market has risen so rapidly and generated such high returns that many Americans feel no need to make further savings out of current income in order to achieve target wealth levels. The nice easy theory of an always upward sloping supply curve for savings (i.e. a higher return produces a higher savings rate) is taught in year one Economics but typically contrasted with real world complexity in year two. But it has lodged as an absolute and immutable truth in the polemics of some ultra-liberal conservatives.

There are nevertheless good reasons for avoiding very high rates of tax on savings. Above some level they probably do discourage savings and they can certainly distort investment decisions especially if different categories of savings and investment are treated differently. Tax rates of 40 per cent on business investment but 0 per cent on housing capital

---

ground for concluding that both income and substitution effects may be blunted for high earners. Essentially high income earners are engaged in a competitive struggle focused almost entirely on relative rather than absolute post-tax income, and tax rates therefore may make little difference to how much or how hard they work, affecting instead simply the equilibrium price of positional goods. See Layard, 'Human Satisfactions and Public Policy', *Economic Journal* (1980), for other implications of positional goods and 'status' competition.

gains will push the rational tax payer towards purchasing as big a house as possible. Arguments for low tax rates and wide tax bases (i.e. few loopholes) are therefore especially applicable in the taxation of personal savings and business investment. But assertions that lower taxes on savings always give significant economic advantages or that the US has a superior economy because it taxes savings and investment less cannot be sustained by the facts.

The third weapon in the conservatives' armoury is migration and avoidance effects. We might wish to have generous welfare states, and if we were a closed economy we could afford them without killing incentives to work or save, but in the world of mobile capital and labour we need to compete with low tax rates and in the world of the Internet tax bases will erode whether we want it or not. On this issue, moreover, left-wing pessimists tend to agree with the conservative diagnosis.

But while migration and avoidance effects undoubtedly limit somewhat the government's ability to raise taxes, both conservatives and left-wing pessimists are almost certainly overstating the case. Three main tax bases might be affected: business taxes, personal income taxes and consumption taxes. On each both logic and evidence (or rather lack of it) suggests less dramatic impacts than hoped for or feared.

Business taxes can be avoided either by legal shifts in tax 'domicile' or by real shifts in business activity. The former danger, much debated in Britain in 2000, argues for careful consideration of the details of multinational tax regulations, but its potential impact on total tax bases is small. Changing domicile is, even for sophisticated multinationals, less easy than often supposed: it is simply not an option for large numbers of mid-sized and small companies operating entirely or primarily in one national economy and it does not change the fact that profits actually generated in a country are taxable in that country. While domicile-related issues (and all the minutiae of double taxation, transfer pricing and remittance rules that underlie them) are thus important ones on which Treasury and corporate-tax experts are bound to lock horns, they do not have the potential to unleash major erosion of business-tax bases. Large-scale erosion could only result from big shifts in actual business activity. But here too there are important constraints. Some manufacturing activity could indeed shift to low-tax environments, but much could not or will not since many other factors are also vital to locational decisions – quality of infrastructure and skills, established clusters of suppliers able to make just-in-time deliveries, closeness to market for rapid response. And as value added shifts to service and servicing activities – to the inherently local economy – a growing proportion of the economy becomes unshiftable. If you want to service cars in Germany, run restaurants in France, retail stores in Britain or residential care in the Netherlands, you will have to pay business taxes in those countries. The actual potential for migration and avoidance therefore reflects a balance of factors and it is not at all clear that the balance is shifting to make migration and avoidance easier. The empirical facts indeed provide no evidence of an erosion effect. European corporate taxes as a percentage of EU GDP were 2.2 per cent in 1970 and 3.0 per cent in 1997, and corporate taxes in the OECD have fluctuated around 3 per cent with no particular trend from the late 1970s to the 1990s. An Institute for Fiscal Studies report in 1997 could find no evidence whatsoever that effective corporate-tax rates were collapsing in a race to the bottom.[26] Perhaps we are on the brink of a sudden erosion not previously apparent but it is unclear why that should be so. There is nothing suddenly new about globalization likely to make the next ten years dramatically different to previous decades.

A similar 'not proven' verdict must be returned in respect to personal taxes. Highly skilled labour can migrate for tax reasons and if differences in the tax rate are very large, will: if Britain still had a top

---

26. *Taxing Profits in a Changing World* (Institute for Fiscal Studies, 1997). See also Kitty Ussher, *The Spectre of Tax Harmonisation* (Centre for European Reform, 2000).

While 'effective' corporate tax rates (measured by tax as a percentage of GDP) are not falling, marginal tax rates are falling and, in Europe, converging. Germany is cutting its federal rate from 42 to 25 per cent (effectively in the mid-30s once local levies are allowed for), France from 42 to 33.3 per cent, Sweden, Finland and Norway have all converged on 28 per cent. Britain cut its marginal rate earlier (in 1984) from 52 to 35 per cent and now has a 30 per cent rate. But the 1984 British corporate-tax reform actually increased total tax take since rate cuts were offset by a widening of the tax base, and Britain has had since then a higher effective tax burden than the European average – 4.3 per cent of GDP in 1997 versus 3.0 per cent for Europe overall. The case for lower business tax *rates* and wider bases is a strong one, and the European marginal tax-rate cuts now occurring need not reduce total tax take. As this reform and convergence process completes, Europe has a sensible and sustainable corporate tax regime which it would be best now to leave well alone.

tax rate of 83 per cent (as it did in 1979) it probably would face a serious 'brain drain' to the US. But at the actual rates now existing in Europe the scale of the effect may be minor. French government ministers get worked up about French companies – 'taxation tourists' – decamping to Ashford in Kent, and some reduction in France's top tax rates probably makes sense (and is now happening). Major Swedish companies have moved some corporate functions to the UK to facilitate hiring of high-skill individuals. But while anecdotes abound there is actually no evidence that the French or Swedish or Netherlands economies (with top tax rates of 54, 58 and 60 per cent respectively) are suffering economic harm from shortages of skilled labour large enough to register at the level of overall economic statistics.[27] The Netherlands indeed is regularly rated very highly in world competitiveness rankings for skill and management ability despite its tax rates.

This lack of mobility reflects the fact that many people rather like their own country, even if tax rates are a bit higher. Vermont suffers no identifiable economic disadvantage from having a state income tax up to 7 per cent above that of geographically contiguous New Hampshire, and if that is true between two culturally and linguistically homogeneous American states it will be even more true of the nation states within Europe.[28] It also reflects the fact that with highly skilled people, as with capital, there are powerful cluster effects – skilled people moving to where there is a critical mass of companies demanding their skills – which limit the sensitivity of location decisions to small differences in tax. If Germany introduces a top tax rate just a few percentage points below the UK's, that is not going suddenly to reverse the self-reinforcing advantages which the City of London enjoys over Frankfurt as a financial centre. Personal migration and avoidance effects, like incentive effects, provide a good case for reducing very highly marginal tax rates but the idea that globalization has suddenly created an impetus for rapid and limitless erosion of income-tax bases is more a figment of right-wing wishful thinking than an established fact.

Nor is the Internet likely to erode consumption-tax bases as radi-

---

27. The Netherlands top tax rate is planned to reduce to 52 per cent in 2001, and the French to 52.5 per cent.

28. Vermont charges a state income tax which is 24 per cent of the federal income-tax charge: for higher ratepayers paying federal tax at 30 per cent, this is equivalent to a 7.2 per cent of marginal rate. New Hampshire has no state income tax.

cally as many commentators seem to think. Some consumption-tax bases are undoubtedly susceptible to erosion from Internet-based forms of service delivery. Betting can be delivered offshore; if digital music download takes off it would be very difficult to tax; CDs delivered from the US by Amazon.com could escape VAT. But the vast majority of personal consumption is going to be taxed in the same way as before whether or not consumers use the Internet to gather information and place orders. Taxation of face-to-face services – restaurants and hotels and sports centres, cinemas and rail travel and healthcare – will be unaffected whether the booking is made physically or over the Internet. Household appliances and cars are not going to be delivered transatlantic and tax-free by DHL. If online supermarket retailing takes off the delivery will be from local warehouses and the goods taxed exactly as if picked up at the supermarket. As Chapter 2 stressed, the idea of an entirely new economy free from the physical reality of warehouses, just-in-time delivery and face-to-face service is, except in some specific sectors, a myth. And in the one major sector where it is not a myth – entertainment and information services – consumption taxes have never been significant since the 'old economy' form of provision, broadcast TV, was paid for by advertising and free to the user. The Internet's impact on the tax base is therefore likely to be far less than recent breathless accounts suggest. Britain's betting levies (£1.5 billion) are vulnerable, but council tax (£12.8 billion) is not, since you cannot actually live on the Internet. VAT on CDs and tapes (about £0.6 billion) may be vulnerable in part but the vast majority of VAT (£54 billion) is not. The £23 billion from road fuel duties may now be limited by popular opposition, but certainly not by the Internet – you cannot download diesel. An illustrative analysis of the consumption tax base (Table 8.1) suggests indeed that even a pessimistic estimate of the Internet's impact would not exceed 1 per cent of government revenues, or 0.5 per cent of GDP. Erosion on that scale would still be a major development to which finance ministries would need to respond but even if replacement with other revenues was impossible it would not require a wholesale dismantling of European welfare states.

Overall, therefore, the idea that European states are bound by some economic necessity radically to reduce levels of tax and spend is hugely overstated. The competitiveness effect of tax burdens is largely a delusion. Incentive effects are important and argue for avoiding high marginal rates but not relentless tax reduction from whatever the

Table 8.1 UK consumption tax vulnerability to Internet-based erosion

Consumption category	£ BN tax revenues* 1998	Vulnerability to Internet-based erosion
Road and other fuel and power	24	Nil
Alcohol and tobacco	20	Nil/minimal
Betting and gaming	1.5	Significant
Air passenger and insurance	2	Minimal
Vehicles and other durables	8	Nil/minimal
Motor vehicles repair and running	3	Nil/minimal
Household good, chemists, opticians etc.	4.5	Nil/minimal
Catering	7	Nil
Household and misc. services	4	Nil
Books, newspapers, magazines	neg.	Already zero rated
Clothing and footwear	4	Small
Misc. goods	4	Small
Records and CDs	0.6	Significant?
Communications	1.5	Significant?
Recreational, educational and other services	4.0	Significant?
Total	88	

Illustrative calculation of impact
– assume 'small' = 5%
– assume 'significant' = 25%

Total erosion = £2.3 bn
= 0.7% of total tax revenues
= 0.3% of GDP

* Revenues include both VAT and excise and other duties. Estimates of VAT by category are based on consumption expenditure multiplied by 17.5% minus reductions for zero-rating, lower rates and exemptions.

Source: HM Treasury, *Budget 1999*; ONS, *Consumer Trends 1999*.

Figure 8.1 GDP per capita growth and public expenditure 1960–95

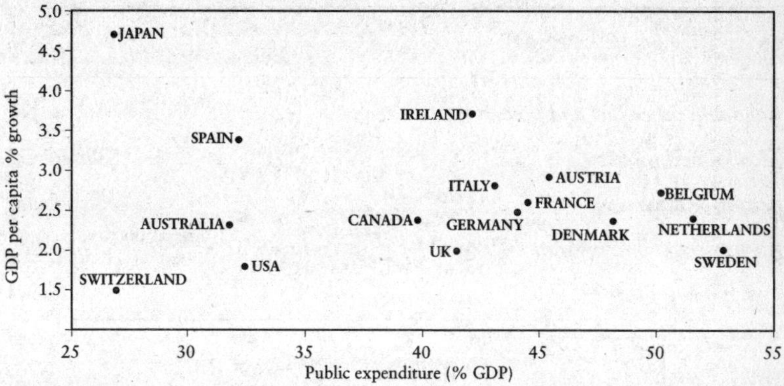

Source: OECD *Historical Statistics*.

present level. Migration and avoidance effects could be significant in specific circumstances but are unlikely, even in the age of the Internet, to mean the massive erosion of tax bases so welcomed by the right and feared by the left. Clearly there are tax levels above which economic dynamism is harmed, but there is no logical support or specific evidence for the sort of simplistic 'lower taxes always better' mantra so often heard.

These conclusions are confirmed by the macro-evidence. Rather than thinking through the logic of and empirical evidence on the specific possible effects, we can look instead at the relative performance of different economies with different tax and spend burdens. Figures 8.1 to 8.4 set out the data. In Figure 8.1 growth rates per capita from 1960–95 are compared with public expenditure as a percentage of GDP. There is no statistically significant correlation between the two variables, and while the most rapidly growing country – Japan – happened also to have a low public-spend burden, another low-tax country – Switzerland – had the lowest growth rate of all. Figure 8.2 repeats the exercise for 1994–9, but this time comparing per capita growth rates with the tax burden. Here again there is no significant correlation. Ireland stands out as a low-tax, high-growth country, and it can be argued that part of Ireland's success stemmed from its

Figure 8.2 GDP per capita growth and government receipts 1994–9

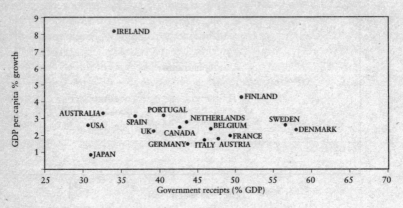

Source: OECD *Economic Outlook*.

Figure 8.3 Government receipts and employment 1994–9

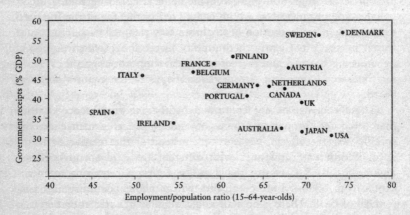

Source: OECD *Economic Outlook*.

ability to attract investment with low corporate taxes. But there is no overall pattern. Low-tax Australia and the US grew faster over this period than high-tax Germany and France, but the Netherlands,

Figure 8.4 Gross national savings and government receipts 1994–9

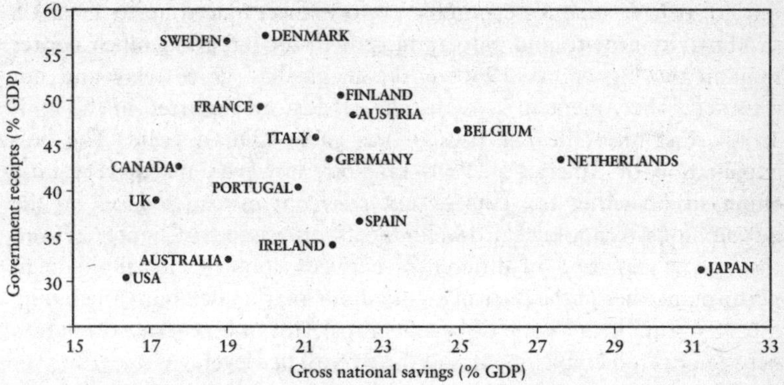

Source: OECD *Economic Outlook*.

Finland and Sweden performed well despite high tax burdens, and Japan in this period combined low growth with low taxes. More detailed analysis, excluding 'special cases' and selecting other time periods, can be used to suggest some mild correlation, but any reasonable person looking at this data would deliver a 'not proven' verdict on the charge that taxes above American levels inhibit growth, and would conclude that many other factors must be more important in explaining differences in performance. That conclusion is confirmed by Figures 8.3 and 8.4, which show no correlation either between lower tax rates and higher savings or between lower tax rates and higher employment rates. Higher taxes must have some economic effect at some level but at the levels currently seen there is no clear evidence of significant effects. And the performance of Denmark and the Netherlands – high-tax, high-spending countries which have performed well on both the employment and prosperity dimensions – shows clearly that European levels of government spend are not incompatible with strong economic performance provided other aspects of policy are well designed.

Changes over time confirm this complex rather than simple picture. The Netherlands and Scandinavian countries – strong performers of the late 1990s – have indeed been taking steps to trim their tax rates and reform their welfare systems and that may have been important in their specific cases. But in the US the correlation of tax cutting to economic take-off simply does not exist. The tax cuts of the early Reagan years did not deliver superior economic performance: indeed up to 1993 US productivity growth and per capita growth looked poor, much poorer than in the higher tax 1960s – the magic had gone away and not returned. The American growth take-off instead occurred in the mid-1990s, just after the tax rises of the early Clinton years. The best explanation of America's 1990s take-off, however, places very little emphasis on either tax cuts or tax rises but instead focuses on the autonomous technological developments discussed in Chapter 2. And the best explanation of differences between countries in employment performance lies in the intricacies of labour-market flexibility (including the very specific tax issue of benefit traps), not in a general correlation between overall employment and the overall tax level.

We are therefore left neither with a nice easy one-directional rule ('lower taxes are always better') nor with an absolute numerical rule ('taxes above X per cent of GDP cause economic harm'). We are left with judgement. My own judgement would go as follows. There is clearly a level above which tax effects could be significant and several European states are probably at or above that limit. It is also likely that that level will fall somewhat (but not dramatically) as migration and avoidance effects become more important. It is likely in addition that the level varies by culture and language: for both cultural and linguistic reasons British people are more likely to migrate to the US for a tax advantage than French. But there is no evidence that the overall European level is substantially above sustainable levels. As a stab at some numbers I would suggest the following: somewhere about 45 per cent we are probably getting 'too high', and European states above that level may be wise to reduce towards it; but at 40 per cent there is no reason to believe that further reductions will deliver major economic benefit. That is of course just a personal judgement. Others might look at the data and suggests different precise figures. But no one looking dispassionately at the data or the logic can conclude that there is some economic necessity driving the size of our states down to 30 per cent GDP, or that a country at Britain's current 40 per cent level must reduce taxes 'if we are to have a fighting chance'.

The whole language of external economic necessity is, however, the wrong way to think about this issue. For the biggest constraint on the size of the state is not competitiveness, or incentives and migration effects, but popular support, what people want. The best argument for reducing the size of the French state is not that some major competitiveness benefit will result but that French governments have pushed the balance of collective versus individual spending, of redistribution versus individual reward, beyond the point which French people desire and are willing to support. British opinion polls, taking in a country taxing and spending about 40 per cent of GDP, tend to suggest public support for a bit more tax and a bit more public spending.[29] French polls, taken in a country taxing 52 per cent of GDP, tend to show support for tax cuts. That popular demand provides a very good reason for reducing the size of the French state (the current strategy indeed of a French 'socialist' government) but it is a reason rooted in liberal political philosophy, not in economic necessity.

States need to live within taxation limits that command popular support. During the 1980s many European states seem to have reached or crossed over that limit. Up until the 1970s rising public expenditure in Europe was largely matched by rising tax revenues (Figure 8.5).[30] Beyond that point structural budget deficits began to emerge. Structural deficits are an indicator of tax going beyond acceptable limits: when states are raising expenditures which have popular support they have the political courage to tax; when they are going beyond the point of acceptance they borrow, throwing a burden on to future generations. Popular will rather than economic necessity limits the size of the state.

Empowering that popular will, moreover, provides a far better rationale for overt promises on the size of the state than the demands of external competitiveness. The CBI, when I was its Director-General, proposed for Britain an upper limit of 40 per cent for the tax burden. The rationale of that limit was expressed partly in terms of competitiveness. But the valid rationale is different. It is that unless governments commit to some rule, however debatable the precise figure, popular will

---

29. See *The Economist*/MORI poll, May 1997. At that time 74 per cent of respondents favoured higher taxes and higher spend, 14 per cent no change and 7 per cent tax cuts. An equivalent poll for France, published in *Le Figaro* on 4 September 2000, found 62 per cent favouring lower taxation and 34 per cent 'other priorities'.

30. See Robert Skidelsky, *Beyond the Welfare State* (Social Market Foundation, 1997).

Figure 8.5 Government outlays and receipts of major industrial countries
as % GDP, 1960–94

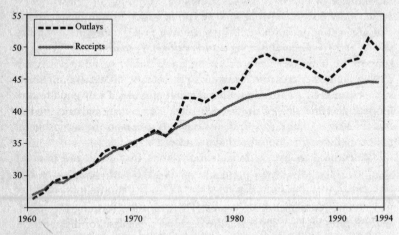

Source: IMF *World Economic Outlook*, May 1996.
Primary source: OECD *Historical Statistics*.

cannot be enforced and expenditure will tend to grow relentlessly.
Government spending levels partly reflect inherent public demands but
they also reflect three other factors. One is the power of public-sector
lobby groups (whether public employees or recipients of specific public
goods and benefits) who care more passionately about each specific
proposal than the general public and whose influence in arguing for
greater spending therefore faces an inadequate countervailing force. The
second is electoral bribery, the fact that public borrowing allows
governments as elections approach to bribe electors with their own
money, presenting the bill later. The third is simple inertia – once
spending programmes are in place they tend to remain unless rigorous
zero-budgeting rules are enforced. All three factors combine to create a
ratchet effect, a tendency for public spending to rise beyond levels
of public support. To offset that ratchet effect explicit promises to
which governments can be held accountable – e.g. tax to be no higher
than X per cent of GDP – are valuable; and explicit debate on the level
of X is valuable too because it can raise the quality of debate on public
spending and tax, making clear the differences between the parties,

rather than muddying them with competing claims that maintained spending and lower taxes can simultaneously be achieved. But they are valuable because we have choices, not because our choice is severely constrained.

Focusing expenditure, reforming taxes

We should, however, avoid swinging to the other extreme. If our choice is not as severely constrained as sometimes supposed it is equally not limitless. Incentive effects argue for reducing high marginal tax rates in some countries. Migration and avoidance effects may be sufficient to make reduction of some of Europe's highest tax burdens essential. Living within even a 45 per cent limit and certainly within a 40 per cent constraint would, as demands on the state increase, require a rigorous focus on essential objectives. Ensuring a sustainable tax base may require redesigned tax systems. The case for reforming European welfare states and tax systems is strong even if the case for dismantling welfare states and slashing taxes is not.

Government's threefold social role has already been described – the provision of inherently collective goods, ensuring free or subsidized provision of goods and services which define equality of citizenship, and redistribution to offset poverty and to support opportunity. To fulfil those roles adequately European governments will need to be pragmatic as to means and focused on these essential objectives.

Pragmatism requires, above all, a non-ideological attitude to the power of the market. If public healthcare is most efficiently provided by internal markets, rather than via centralized planning systems, we should utilize them. If the French system of significant private and charitable supply but close to universal state insurance turns out to be superior, Britain's attachment to healthcare 'free at the point of provision' should not be treated as sacrosanct. If competitive contracting or private finance allows more efficient provision of public services they should be utilized. What matters is end results not means. The confusion of progressive objectives with non-market means was one of socialism's great mistakes. Equally there should be no presumption that private-ownership solutions are axiomatically best. If a publicly owned and managed service happens to be efficiently run we should not privatize it for dogmatic reasons. Some capital expenditure projects are better financed publicly than through overly complex private schemes: whether London's Underground modernization is one remains a moot point. Totally free markets in healthcare work badly because of the asymmetry of information and knowledge between consumers and producers.[31] The US, spending 14 per cent of GDP on healthcare versus France's 10 per cent but without commensurately superior results and with 44 million Americans not adequately covered, is not a system to emulate. What matters is simply what works.

Pragmatism as to means, however, is unlikely in itself to be sufficient. Straight efficiency savings though valuable will only make a minor difference to government expenditure levels. The increasing demands placed on states will also require more rigorous focus on essential objectives. In healthcare that may mean making a distinction between essential and non-essential provision. If healthcare demand truly is limitless we cannot simply increase spend without at some stage passing the point where tax levels have major disincentive effects. Equality of citizenship requires that a person with the cancer gene is not also disadvantaged by the burden of healthcare expenditure – but it may not require access to cosmetic surgery, to drugs which improve sexual performance, or to free treatment of sport-induced injuries. In education likewise distinctions will increasingly have to be made. Universal free provision of high-quality primary and secondary education is essential to a society of equal citizens. But increasing private contributions to tertiary education will be essential if education budgets are not to grow relentlessly as a percentage of GDP, and are justified by the private returns which university education delivers to the individual. We can afford to achieve our essential objectives of social inclusion but only if we focus on that specific aim.

Focus will be essential above all in the arena of social security. It is expenditures on social security which explain – far more than health and education – the difference between US and European levels of tax and public expenditure (see Table 8.2). Those expenditures hide within them two conceptually quite different categories. In part they are inherently redistributive systems – from better off to poor, from those unlikely to be unemployed to those likely to be. In part, however, they

---

31. See Kenneth Arrow, 'Uncertainty and the Welfare Economics of Medical Care' and other related papers in *Collected Papers of Kenneth Arrow* (1985), vol. 6: *Applied Economics*.

Table 8.2 Public expenditure by category* (% GDP)

	US	UK	France
'Social security' and welfare	9.2	16.4	19.5
Health	7.1	5.8	10.8
Education	7.5	5.4	6.0
Other	10.3	16.8	17.7
Total current expenditure	34.1	44.4	54.0

* 1993 figures for US and France; 1995 figures for UK.

Source: OECD *National Accounts*, IMF *Government Finance Statistics*.

are true insurance and savings schemes – the payment, for instance, of pension-fund contributions and the receipt of pensions – redistributive only to the extent that insurance always redistributes from, for instance, pensioners who die early to those who die old. There is a strong case for removing from the activity of the state as much of the latter category as possible, for moving across Europe to privately funded pensions. For whenever governments perform functions which they do not absolutely need to perform, functions which are neither inherently collective nor redistributive, they are using up limited tax capacity on non-essential objectives, endangering our ability to pay for the essential social functions of the state within tax levels which avoid economic damage and which are acceptable to public opinion. States should as far as possible get out of the business of 'churn' (of receiving and making payments to and from the same people).[32] Recent estimates of the size of churn

---

32. The counter-argument on churn is that if middle- and high-income earners are recipients of benefits as well as payers of taxes, this creates commitment to welfare states which would erode if they were stripped back to their more purely redistributive role. Essentially this asserts that higher-income earners will accept redistribution if it is disguised by churn. The danger in that argument is that it increases marginal tax rates, and that it comes close to assuming that people can be fooled into redistributive policies they would not otherwise support. It is better to argue the case for the state's essential roles – including redistribution – directly and honestly.

Figure 8.6 Government expenditure levels and 'churn' 1993–5

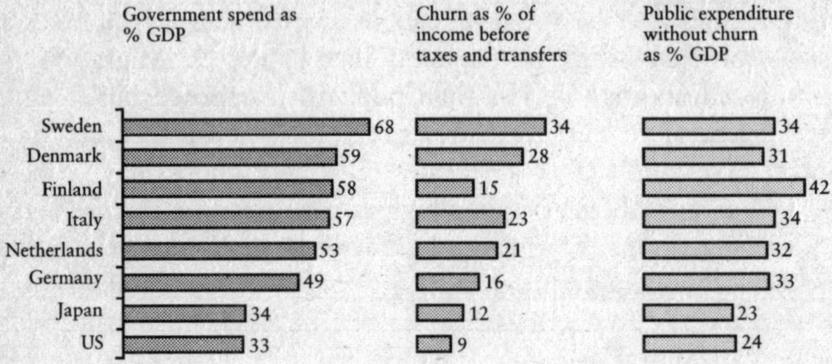

	Government spend as % GDP	Churn as % of income before taxes and transfers	Public expenditure without churn as % GDP
Sweden	68	34	34
Denmark	59	28	31
Finland	58	15	42
Italy	57	23	34
Netherlands	53	21	32
Germany	49	16	33
Japan	34	12	23
US	33	9	24

Note: The figures for total government spend are higher than those used elsewhere in this chapter because of different dates and definitions.

Source: OECD *Economic Outlook* (June 1998), quoted in *Public Spending in the 20th Century*, Tanzi and Schuknecht (2000).

illustrate the very large potential to reduce the size of the state sector in some countries without reducing either public-goods provision or true redistribution (Figure 8.6).[33]

On the tax side too the case for reform is in some countries strong. Competitiveness concerns focused on the overall level of payroll taxes and labour cost are usually confused, but payroll taxes combined with minimum wages do increase the total cost of low-skilled labour and can create unemployment. They should therefore be reduced or rebalanced from low to high income as in Britain in 1998. The disincentive effects of income taxes are often overstated but they can be significant at very high rates. Cutting the highest rates on high earners in France

---

33. Vito Tanzi and Ludger Schuknecht, *Public Spending in the 20th Century* (2000). The potential for removing churn clearly varies hugely by country. In Britain it may be small, since the social-security budget is significantly smaller than in some other European countries and a large proportion of it is already of a fundamentally redistributive nature. In Britain therefore there may be limited potential to cut social security, rather than simply constrain it, without making poor people poorer. The comparative figures calculated by Tanzi and Schuknecht and shown in Figure 8.6, do not unfortunately include figures for the UK.

and Sweden probably makes sense; cutting the very high marginal rates which arise at low income from the combination of tax and benefit systems is an even greater priority. Increased energy taxes and other environmental taxes balanced by cuts in income and payroll taxes are sensible for reasons to be explored in Chapter 9. Migration and avoidance effects may be less than popularly supposed but it makes sense in general to aim for lower tax rates and broader tax bases. Property taxes and higher VAT rates on luxury goods may be better ways of taxing the better off than high income-tax rates.[34] Europe does not need to slash taxes in pursuit of American or Asian levels. But the highest tax countries should trim their total tax burdens and all should consider carefully how to make the tax burden less distortive in a world of slightly more mobile capital and skilled labour.

Provided they do that there is no reason to believe that the key features of the European social model need to be discarded as tax bases relentlessly erode. Countries are far freer to choose their own social balance than much rhetoric suggests. And within Europe most of that choice can be exercised at nation state rather than at European level. To the extent that it cannot, some European harmonization of taxes is both possible and justifiable.

European tax harmonization: a limited, non-threatening role

European tax harmonization generates enormous passions. To some Euro-federalists it is the essential 'next step' in the construction of Europe and the only way to prevent a relentless race for the bottom of lower taxes and public spending cuts. To Euro-sceptics it is the unavoidable concomitant of monetary union, the death of national sovereignty and the nightmare route to inevitably higher taxes which will make all of Europe uncompetitive. In fact it is none of these. Tax harmonization is neither inevitable nor a great threat. It is instead a

---

34. In Britain, in particular, higher property-value taxes have much to commend them. They tax the better off without distorting work incentives, and they help to offset positional goods inflation. In other European countries property tax rates are in general higher. Britain's level is now significantly below what it was before the poll-tax debacle.

potential development of limited but still useful scope which would in no way threaten European competitiveness or restrict the freedom of national governments to make significantly different social choices one from another.

Tax harmonization is not a necessary or automatic concomitant of monetary union. There is nothing about the macroeconomics of a single-currency area which requires the same tax rate in each region or the same aggregate level of tax as a percentage of GDP. State income-tax rates, sales taxes and property taxes all vary significantly between states in the US and nobody has ever proposed that a federal law is required to limit the extent of that variation. Economic adjustment within a single currency area is eased if 'fiscal stabilizers' are free to work (i.e. if deficits can increase in recessions and reduce in booms) but that can be achieved with tax and spend at 42 and 44 per cent of GDP respectively as easily as at 32 and 34, or 52 and 54: what matters is the difference, not the absolute level. In terms of macroeconomics, the idea that a single-currency area requires tax harmonization is nonsense.

What a single currency might do is increase the possibility of migration and avoidance effects and thereby increase pressure for tax harmonization. Savings tax evasion may get marginally more likely when Germans and Luxembourgeois both hold accounts in euros. But only marginally: Germans were able to hold DM accounts in Luxembourg long before currency union. Corporate-tax migration effects may also get somewhat more intense because absence of exchange-rate risk makes it easier to design business systems on a pan-European basis, and businesses themselves may argue for a pan-European corporate tax system to maximize the efficiency benefits they can achieve. Cross-border shopping may increase slightly. But those minor impacts aside, it is difficult to see why the single currency is going to unleash migration and avoidance effects significantly greater than those that already exist in a single market of free movement of capital and labour. If there is a danger of a race for the bottom, it exists already because of the single market and of the wider forces of globalization.

The threat, however, is still greater in potential and in anecdote than in observed and quantifiable reality. The absence of evidence for significant migration and avoidance effects has already been described. A reasonable judgement today would be that judicious reform of marginal rates and tax structures, voluntarily agreed measures to close obvious tax loopholes, and some modest reduction of overall tax levels in the highest-taxed European states might well be sufficient to offset the danger of tax-base erosion.[35]

If they are not sufficient, however, there is no reason why some tax measures should not be co-ordinated at European level. For if the case in favour is greatly overstated by the race-for-the-bottom pessimists, the arguments presented against *any* harmonization are equally poor. Opponents argue that if Europe harmonizes taxes within Europe to prevent 'unfair' competition it will simply make itself uncompetitive externally, its cost bases too high for success in world markets, capital leaving in pursuit of lower taxes elsewhere. But this is simply another variant of the forever confused competitiveness theory. At the level of Europe, competitiveness is close to meaningless and the idea of tax effects on competitiveness is meaningless also. As for migration and avoidance effects, if the likelihood of these occurring between European countries is less than often supposed the possibility between continents is very slight indeed. French entrepreneurs frustrated by French corporate taxes are not going to decamp in large numbers to New York State even if they were given the right to emigrate there. Manufacturers requiring proximity to market for rapid customer response might choose *between* European countries on the basis of tax (though the evidence is they largely don't) but their potential to move out of Europe entirely is much less. A pan-European alcohol excise tax would in principle be enforceable. Cross-border shopping across the Channel is eroding the UK's alcohol tax base, but a pan-European excise duty, unless set at absurdly high levels, would not induce similar-scale effects. Whether European tax harmonization is desirable or necessary is highly debatable but for many taxes it is feasible and would have no adverse economic effects.

Nor would any level of tax harmonization likely to be proposed place any restriction on a nation's freedom to choose its own aggregate level of tax and spend. A case for a minimum European rate of corporation tax can be constructed. The case for a pan-European approach to industrial energy taxes is (for reasons discussed in Chapter 9) very strong indeed. Minimum rates of excise duty on alcohol would be useful if the different approaches of different countries to different

---

35. Potential voluntarily agreed measures include those arising from the EU Code of Conduct discussions on tax loopholes (1999) and the recent OECD paper on tax havens (2000).

types of alcohol could ever be resolved. But even if minimum rates for all of these were agreed, the total 'unavoidable' level of taxation would still be far less than 10 per cent of GDP, leaving it quite open for one country to set all other taxes at 25 per cent of GDP, another to set them at 35 per cent. Sensible harmonization of rates where tax competition and avoidance are threatening to erode tax bases would have no implications for aggregate tax and spending levels.

The only valid case for opposing European tax harmonization in principle rather than in detail is therefore the fear that once started it will prove an unstoppable process, that intelligent limited forms of harmonization, such as a European approach to energy taxes, will lead inevitably to wide-ranging harmonization without any rationale. The barrier against that slippery slope is, however, simple. European Union decisions on tax measures can only be decided unanimously and should remain so. Provided we keep that discipline there is no reason why we should not unanimously agree limited but still useful measures of tax harmonization. Nor should we be at all concerned if there is an unlegislated but de facto tendency for some of the most politically sensitive rates to move towards natural convergence – for top personal tax rates to cluster about the 40–45 per cent level or for corporation-tax rates to cluster around 30–35 per cent. In the case of corporation taxes indeed this is precisely what is already occurring.

In other words we should all calm down and we should all argue honestly. Ultra-liberals who want intra-European tax competition as a forcing device to drive taxes lower are probably indulging in wishful thinking but they should at least state their desire directly, not hide behind phoney competitiveness arguments. Euro-federalists who propose wide-ranging tax harmonization should think out more clearly why and which taxes specifically and not go on scaring themselves with the belief that we are on the verge of a limitless downward spiral of taxation and expenditure levels which requires a blanket tax-harmonization response. Euro-sceptics should stop asserting that intelligent limited harmonization is impossible. We are free to choose.

Liberal managed capitalism: a choice we can make

The common belief of ultra-liberal conservatives and left-wing pessimists is that developed economies face severe constraints on social choice, that either (in the conservatives' version) we must accept the economic imperatives of the global economy or (in the pessimists' version) that we are doomed to do so unless we break entirely from the philosophy of free market. But in fact we are freer to choose than either suppose: free to limit the application of free markets in specific instances where they are undesirable and free to combine flexible market economies with European rather than American levels of provision of collective goods and redistributive welfare nets.

That freedom to choose rests on two facts. The first is that the impact of different social choices on economic growth – whether through environmental standards, labour laws or taxation levels – is less than often supposed. This chapter has argued that case with reference to the detailed logic of specific taxation effects but the case can equally be made by the most broad brush of comparisons. The Netherlands, according to the Economic Intelligence Unit, is the best place in the world to do business. Its per capita growth rate across the 1990s exceeded that of the US. It has sound public finance, low inflation and unemployment lower than the US. Its tax and spend level is about 43 per cent of GDP, its top tax rate has been 60 per cent (now reducing to 52 per cent). It has an extensive though intelligently reformed welfare state. It is prosperous and successful on the basis of a very different set of social choices from America and there is not the slightest sign that those social choices are unsustainable. The link between economic success and the minimal state either doesn't exist or is greatly overstated.

Even if it did exist, however, we would still be free to choose since we are not in a competitive race in which some win and others lose. This chapter may be too optimistic: the effect of high taxes on economic prosperity may be larger than I have suggested. But even if that is so social choice still remains. If Sweden is condemned by its large government sector to be somewhat less prosperous than America, Swedes can choose to accept that if they consider it a worthwhile sacrifice in return for better collective goods and more redistribution. Being 10 per cent less prosperous than another country in measured GDP carries no implications for future further relative decline nor for employment. It simply means you are 10 per cent behind in measured GDP and probably less behind in true prosperity once leisure and household work effects are taken into account. If a country wants to make that trade-off, it can.

The key constraint on the size of state is therefore not external and economic but internal and political. It is what people want. This chapter has suggested that what we should want lies in the pragmatic middle. High-quality collective-goods provision but not so high as to require very high tax rates. Excellent 'equality of citizenship' goods but with a need to define clearly the limits of this commitment. Redistribution to prevent poverty and to prevent cumulative growth in inequality but not so much as to deny individuals their legitimate and natural desires to better themselves. Some readers will reject this as lacking principle. Where's the vision in believing in equality of opportunity 'up to a point'?

But the political philosophy of this book lies unapologetically in the pragmatic middle for three reasons. First, because the pragmatic middle reflects human nature. People have a mixture of selfish and altruistic motivations. Liberal managed capitalism reflects human nature in a way that neither socialism nor laissez-faire conservatism ever can. Second, because the pursuit of pure principle produces disaster. Dreams of absolute equality produced the disaster of communism. The laissez-faire capitalism of the nineteenth century almost destroyed itself through the inequality and insecurity it created: it was saved by the interventions of social liberalism, social democracy and Keynesian demand management. Liberal managed capitalism lacks the beautiful intellectual certainty of either socialism or laissez-faire conservatism but it has the advantage that it works. All capitalist countries today indeed actually operate somewhere in the pragmatic middle – the choice is simply whether we are a bit more towards the laissez-faire end (as in the US) or a bit more towards the managed.

The third reason for tentative conclusions, for conclusions 'up to a point', is that that is all that the empirical evidence can support, and it is the empirical evidence that should guide us. Free-markets are not right because they are revealed truth: they are right if they work and because they work. Liberal managed capitalism is right if it works and because it works. I have suggested that a government sector up to 45 per cent of GDP may make little difference to economic performance. Perhaps I am wrong and the level is lower; perhaps, however, it is higher. Perhaps it will become lower through time in the face of changing circumstances. If so we should change our conclusions. Policy should derive from an iterative process of experiment and observation, not from dogma. The danger of the ultra-liberal creed today is that it has gone beyond the intelligent application of the insights of market economic theory and become dogma. Lower taxes are always better, and freer markets are always better: these are asserted as universal and incontrovertible truths, not as testable hypotheses.

The *Sunday Times* was wrong in its March 1999 editorial. A flexible economy, a dynamic market economy, does not require a minimal state along American lines. We can revitalize European social market economies provided we embrace the power of the market while managing and moderating its effects. We can have a market economy without a market society.

9. Green Capitalism:
Market Economics and the Environment

This book has three main themes. First, that societies enjoy much greater degrees of freedom to make their own social choices than the rhetoric of competitiveness suggests. Second, that the market economy is a powerful tool for achieving desirable ends. But third, that laissez-faire markets, unmanaged and unmoderated by political intervention, are incapable of satisfying the full range of human aspirations or of dealing with important distributional issues. In no area of public policy are these themes more relevant than in relation to the environment.

Environmental issues, moreover, are growing in importance, because for all our talk of a knowledge-based economy, of 'living on thin air', in fact both the environmental impact of economic growth and consumer demands for a better physical environment are becoming more pressing and in greater potential conflict. Richer people care more about clean air, clean rivers and preserved countryside than poorer people, but the richer we get the more our demands for mobility and houses in the suburbs or countryside destroy the very things we increasingly value.

Market economies, correctly understood, can play a crucial role in resolving those conflicts, clarifying the nature of the trade-offs we face and helping us achieve benefits at least cost. But bad market economics, misunderstood and used for polemic purposes, often gets in the way. Confused arguments about competitiveness are used to suggest stark 'no alternative' conflicts between environmental improvements and prosperity, rather than trade-offs of benefits and cost. Policies which aim to make markets work better, such as charges for road use ('congestion pricing'), are rejected as limitations on economic freedom. Attempts to reflect environmental benefits and costs in economic decisions are derided as the concern of anti-market dreamers. Sensible proposals for a European approach to energy tax are attacked as bad for competitiveness when in fact they would address legitimate competitiveness concerns. Just as minimal-state conservatives misuse the language of market economics to justify policies whose essential purpose is simply conservative, so vested interests abuse free-market rhetoric to oppose the application of market principles to environmental policy. And just as left-wing pessimists play into the minimal statists' hands by accepting their analysis while bemoaning the implications, so many 'green' groups harm their cause by defining market economics as the problem rather than a key element in solution.

Clear analysis of the economics is therefore vital. But so is political leadership. For many environmental improvements are inherently collective in nature and many involve distributional trade-offs between different groups. Political leadership is essential to create support for the multiple individual sacrifices and changes in behaviour required to achieve benefits collectively enjoyed by all. Political leadership is also vital to ensure long-term approaches to long-term problems. Markets are powerful tools to achieve environmental ends, but they cannot reflect the full range of human aspirations or the future consequences of present actions unless governments intervene to offset their inherent imperfections.

This chapter therefore starts with the economics and ends with the political challenge. It begins with economic principles and theory because until we have those clear we cannot think straight. It then applies those principles to three of the most difficult environmental issues we face – global climate change, the impact of personal transport mobility, and the conflict between physical development and countryside preservation.[1] On each more radical policies will be required if bad market economics is not to make us worse off. The chapter ends by arguing the need for greater political leadership on environmental issues, leadership essential if the market is to achieve its full potential in helping us resolve these issues.

Principles and theory: competitiveness, prosperity and the power of the market

To think straight about environmental economics, we need to do three things. First, to be clear about competitiveness arguments: often they

---

1. With the exception of global climate change, the focus of this chapter is on environmental problems faced by the developed rich world and the appropriate policy responses. The issue of the links between global capitalism and environmental destruction in the emerging economies is considered in Chapter 11.

are confused but in specific circumstances they can be valid. Second, to recognize that the fundamental issue has nothing to do with competitiveness but is a matter of social choice, a trade-off between the value of environmental improvements and their costs: both have to be considered to make good decisions. Third, to recognize that the market is a tremendously powerful tool which can help us make that trade-off in the most cost-effective fashion, getting us as close as possible to win-win results.

The economic costs of environmental regulation or taxes are usually described in the language of competitiveness. If Britain or Europe is burdened with regulations or tax it will become uncompetitive and jobs will be lost – the standard refrain of business lobby groups. And in some instances they are right, but only in some and for a specific reason which carries implications for the detailed design of policy.

As a general proposition the belief that 'burdens on business' create a 'competitiveness' problem is confused. Chapters 6 and 8 explored that confusion in relation to the general level of taxation and across-the-board labour-market regulations: neither has any meaningful effect on competitiveness. The same arguments apply to environmental taxes whose impact is cross-sectoral in nature or which primarily affect non-traded sectors of the economy. If an environmental regulation or tax was introduced which affected all sectors equally, the extra cost would have no impact on any meaningful measure of competitiveness or on employment. If the tax burden was offset by lower taxes on, say, labour there would be no necessity for any other adjustment – total business costs would be unchanged. If the tax burden was not offset, or if the regulation imposed real costs, the adjustment would come through lower real wages – price increases unmatched by nominal wage increases – and/or through a fall in the exchange rate. The real issue would be whether people valued the environmental benefits pursued and/or whether they valued the government expenditure paid for by higher tax, but not competitiveness.[2]

---

2. It is worth noting that all environmental taxes and regulations ultimately entail costs for individuals and that in general and in the long term taxes and regulations (whether environmental or of any other nature) have minimal implications for business profitability, the costs typically being passed on in higher prices and thus lower real wages (the true tax incidence can fall on either consumers or shareholders, but in most cases the vast majority will fall on the former; both shareholders

Many environmental regulations or taxes are either cross-sectoral in nature or affect primarily non-traded sectors and as a result have no meaningful competitiveness effects. Regulations on packaging recycling, workplace parking taxes, or taxes or regulations on the quarrying industry fall into this category. There are real costs involved and important social choices about costs and benefits to be made, but they have nothing to do with competitiveness.[3]

The problem with some environmental regulations or taxes, however, is that unlike taxes on labour or labour-market regulation they are not across the board, but affect different sectors differently. If these are traded sectors, regulations or taxes can as a result have the terms of trade effects identified in Chapter 1 as a valid special case of competitiveness theory. If Britain introduces a tax on industrial use of energy, this falls disproportionately on energy-intensive sectors, including some important traded sectors. That in turn can have two effects,

---

and consumers are, however, individuals). This truth is, however, obfuscated both by governments and some environmental lobbyists who prefer to suggest that business is facing the costs of its own pollution (and thus by implication that taxes and regulation are costless to consumers). It is not surprising that in turn business lobby groups resist environmental (and other) taxes and regulations as a threat to their margins. The essential issue is always, however, whether the benefits to individuals are worth the costs they will also face, and the quality of environmental policy debates would be improved if that was more openly and honestly recognized.

3. The precise criteria for determining if a regulation or tax can have a competitiveness effect are threefold: (i) whether the measure is cross-sectoral or sectorally skewed in its effect; (ii) its indirect as well as direct effects; (iii) whether sectors directly or indirectly affected in a disproportionate manner are traded or not. Regulations falling directly on non-traded consumer sectors (e.g. retailing) do not have competitiveness effects even if they are sectorally specific – the issue is simply cost versus benefit to consumers. Regulations falling on a largely non-traded sector which supplies traded sectors could have a competitiveness effect but only if the output was skewed towards a specific traded sector. It is because quarry aggregates enter the supply chain of other sectors in a roughly proportionate manner (there are no traded sectors *peculiarly* dependent on aggregates) that regulations and taxes here are also unlikely to have competitiveness effects. Freight and business-car costs also have a largely across-the-board rather than sectorally skewed effect: arguments that high fuel duties (even if offset by lower taxes elsewhere) can create a competitiveness problem for freight users (rather than for the freight industry itself) are therefore largely invalid.

one permanent and on prosperity, the other transitional and on employment.

The prosperity effect occurs because of changes in sectoral balance within the economy. Movements in the exchange rate in response to sectoral competitiveness problems will over time achieve a new equilibrium; in that sense a competitiveness problem cannot exist in the long term. But the new equilibrium may well entail smaller energy-intensive sectors than before balanced by growth in other sectors. And it is possible that the new equilibrium will involve less favourable terms of trade than the old – that more labour resources will have to be employed in the new export industries to pay for desired imports, labour resources which are then unavailable to serve other consumer needs. Or to put it in concrete but illustrative terms: if we make our chemical sector less competitive, the exchange rate will fall to make more of our textile industry competitive, but we may need to employ more workers in textiles than in chemicals to afford the same level of imports.[4] Regulation or taxes which have a sectorally specific effect can thus cut long-term prosperity by bringing about a sectoral balance different from that which would exist in the absence of tax and regulation. The effect should not be overstated. It is one-off, not cumulative (i.e. the level of GDP is lower by a given percentage in any year but that percentage does not grow larger over time). It is equal to the terms of trade effect multiplied by the scale of sectoral shift and both percentages may be small.[5] And it has no effect on long-term attainable employment. But it is worth worrying about, and worth taking into account in the design of environmental regulation and tax, especially since the same sectoral shift which produces the prosperity effect may undermine the intended environmental benefit, activity moving to other countries with less stringent environmental standards.

The transitional employment effect also follows from changing sectoral balance. In the long run sectoral change has no consequence

---

4. The labour resources in both cases could be either in the sector itself or in the companies which supply that sector with either current inputs or capital goods.

5. For example, if energy-intensive exporting industries' accounting for 5 per cent of GDP shrank by half as a result of an energy tax, and the alternative exporting industries had terms of trade characteristics which were 20 per cent less favourable, the long-term impact is that GDP in any year is 0.5 per cent lower than it would otherwise be.

for overall attainable employment level (indeed, depending how we use the proceeds of a tax, long-term employment might under some circumstances rise). But in the short term the shift will cut jobs in specific sectors and cut the relative income of some workers and the profits of some employers. And that, though short term, is an important effect. If it is true that higher fuel taxes make British truckers uncompetitive relative to French drivers exercising their single market 'cabotage' rights, it is of only limited consolation for them to know that economists can demonstrate conclusively that the long-term rate of attainable employment is totally unaffected.[6]

That example leads us directly, however, to a vital point about these special-case competitiveness effects – that they diminish the wider we make the economic unit to which the regulation or tax applies. At the level of a small country, say Finland, a regulation or tax with a sectorally skewed effect could have a significant prosperity as well as a transitional employment effect. At the level of the world it could have no such effects. At British national level the effects will be much less than for Finland, and at European level much less still. Indeed, on average we can say how much less. Britain trades 29 per cent of GDP, while the European Union trades in total 11.5 per cent of GDP with countries outside the EU: at least 60 per cent (17.5 out of 29) of all valid rather than phoney competitiveness concerns therefore disappear if environmental regulations or taxes are introduced or harmonized at European level.[7] And 100 per cent of the more specific competitiveness

---

6. 'Cabotage' is the term used for the right of lorry drivers in one European Union country to ply for trade in another. Given the very large capacity of lorry diesel tanks this right makes it possible for, say, a French lorry driver to compete in the UK haulage market on the basis of fuel purchased in France. How important this problem is in practice is debated. Estimates suggest that less than 1 per cent of domestic freight traffic in the UK is carried by foreign operators exercising cabotage rights. If this percentage grew significantly that could create a rationale for proposing a European approach to fuel duty; if it stays at the current level, a purely national approach remains tenable for Britain and there is no reason why British fuel duties should not significantly exceed continental levels.

7. The percentage of the competitiveness problem eliminated is actually likely to be significantly in excess of the 60 per cent suggested by trade exposure numbers. Many manufacturing plants, for instance, could conceivably relocate across boundaries within Europe while still being close enough to market to achieve just-in-

problems produced by the cabotage right would disappear if fuel duty was harmonized across Europe, since truckers outside the European Union have no rights to come and ply for trade within it.[8]

Overall, therefore, while blanket competitiveness arguments are as confused in respect to environmental issues as they are more generally, the sectorally specific nature of environmental regulation and tax makes some competitiveness concerns valid. They must not be overstated, and cannot be knockout factors against essential environmental measures. But they do argue for careful design of tax regimes and provide an overwhelming rationale for pursuing most environmental regulation at European rather than national level.

Competitiveness effects are not, however, the only economic consequences of environmental policies: indeed because they can be offset by careful design of policy they are not the most important. Instead the essential economic issue raised by environmental policies is one which would exist even in a totally closed economy – a trade-off between the value of environmental improvements achieved and the costs in terms of productivity and thus measured prosperity sacrificed.

A simple example illustrates the point. If we introduce an environmental regulation aimed at producing, say, cleaner air, which requires the diversion of 0.5 per cent of productive resources to achieving that objective, that measure will reduce productivity and measured GDP by 0.5 per cent. Effectively what has occurred is a governmental decision to divert 0.5 per cent of consumption from 'more products' to 'cleaner air'. The impact of this on true prosperity depends entirely on how much people value cleaner air. If they value it more than 0.5 per cent of GDP, true prosperity will rise, and the fall in measured GDP reflects simply a measurement deficiency – the fact that while people value cleaner air they don't buy it in individual slices and so we don't count it in national income accounts. If they value it less than 0.5 per cent of

---

time-delivery; the ability to move outside European Union boundaries is for many far more constrained.

8. The sector competitiveness problems created by cabotage are indeed an example of how a single-market freedom might in theory become incompatible with the total absence of tax harmonization. Note, however, in relation to Chapter 8's discussion of European tax harmonization, that the case for harmonization is created by single-market rules, the existence or not of the single currency being on this, and almost all other tax issues, irrelevant.

GDP, true prosperity will fall as well as measured GDP, though by a smaller amount. The essential questions of environmental economics are therefore simple: how much do we value environmental improvement, and how much does it cost in terms of other (measured) aspects of prosperity forgone? It is on these issues, rather than on competitiveness, that environmental policy debates should primarily focus. If we don't place a value on environmental improvements or degradation we will make ourselves poorer in true prosperity terms even while maximizing measured GDP. If we don't think through the costs of environmental improvement we may both sacrifice significant increments of prosperity for only small environmental gain and fail to identify how those costs can be reduced.

The unvalued costs of environmental degradation are pervasive and large. They derive from two different categories of market failure. In one, measured prosperity for some is being achieved at the expense of the measured prosperity of others, but there is no mechanism to face the former with the consequences of their actions. Even on a measured GDP basis, CO_2 emissions today are likely to impose huge costs on future generations, but because the costs lie both far in the future and in some cases at the other end of the world, they are not caught in our estimates of national prosperity today, let alone in the costs, profits and decision-making of individual businesses. In the second, measured prosperity is achieved at the expense of unmeasured prosperity detriment – noise and pollution, and congestion and countryside destruction which we will never capture in any GDP measurement, because no one has individually defined property rights to those benefits, and because we don't purchase them individually. Estimating the first category of costs is in practice immensely difficult; estimating the second close to impossible because of their inherently collective nature. We may often therefore have to make decisions on the basis of a description rather than quantification of environmental benefits balanced judgementally against more quantifiable costs in measured GDP. But the inherently difficult nature of such judgements cannot be an excuse for not making them. Without those judgements and resulting policy interventions the market economy is incapable of producing an optimum result: we need to intervene in the market to correct for its inherent failures.[9]

---

9. The process of estimating costs in quantifiable terms and comparing them judgementally with benefits is indeed an indirect way of placing a value on

Achieving those environmental benefits typically, however, requires some sacrifice of productivity and thus of measured prosperity. Three different types of productivity effects can be distinguished. The first has already been illustrated in the simple example. If an environmental improvement requires resources to be dedicated to achieving it, attainable productivity is reduced. If we deal with global climate change, for instance, not by reducing energy consumption but solely by developing more expensive renewable sources, the adverse productivity effect derives from the extra resources we need to commit to the energy sector.

An alternative response to climate change, however, would be to reduce total energy consumption: this would have a different type of impact on labour productivity. Reduced energy consumption is likely to make high labour productivity more difficult to achieve in sectors throughout the economy. Energy, along with capital (i.e. machines), is a fundamental driver of productivity – we are more productive and prosperous than 300 years ago because we perform many functions with machines driven by energy. If we use less energy we will need to increase other inputs, e.g. more and better capital investment, or improved technique, if labour productivity is to be maintained; if we don't increase those other inputs labour productivity must tend to be lower.[10]

The third effect also stems from constraints on the availability of a key economic input – but in this case not energy but land. For as Chapters 5 and 7 have already discussed, cheap and plentiful land, free

---

environmental benefits. Most people find it very difficult even to think about how much they would precisely value, say, less congested, less polluted cities, but are willing to make judgements of the form – if the costs are less than £X million it's worth it, but if the cost goes above £Y million it's not. Structuring such debates is an essential function of politics, without which we cannot arrive at an efficient reflection of the full range of customer preferences.

10. The mathematics of productivity with respect to different levels and types of input can be described in what are known as 'production functions'. Production processes can be modelled such that the level of output is a 'function' of the levels of input (e.g. land, labour, capital, energy). In general it holds true that if the quantity of INPUT 1 is reduced, the productivity with respect to INPUT 2 (i.e. output per unit of INPUT 2) must reduce unless either INPUTS 3 and 4 can be increased or unless 'technique'/'know-how' or the quality of inputs (e.g. the skills of the labour) can be improved.

from development constraints, has a pervasive effect upon obtainable productivity levels in many industries – retailing and hotels, manufacturing and distribution among others. One of the fundamental reasons why the US is more productive in measured GDP terms is simply that it has a lower population density and as a result fewer constraints on development. The advantage is finite and one-off, not cumulative, and if Britain sought to match it by relaxed planning rules it would do so at the expense of environmental damage which might reduce true prosperity even while measured GDP increased. But it needs to be recognized as a category of productivity effect, an inherent implication indeed of population density.

Environmental policy debates should therefore be focused, not on the 'no-alternative' rhetoric of competitiveness, but on a social choice we can and must make between the value of environmental improvements and the cost of productivity potential forgone. Both sides of that equation need to be recognized. It is bad market economics to refuse to place a value on consumer preferences simply because they are expressed collectively rather than via individual purchase. And it is wishful thinking to imagine that all environmental improvements can be achieved at nil or trivial cost. But three features of the cost side of the equation need to be stressed if the costs are not to be exaggerated. The first is that they are finite, not cumulative. We are not in a competitive struggle for national survival, so 'coming behind' another nation by 5 per cent carries no implications other than that 5 per cent; if we want to make controlled sacrifices of measured GDP for environmental benefits we can. The second is that the cost of environmental constraints is almost entirely in the form of a productivity penalty, not an employment penalty: a low-energy input makes achieving high labour productivity more difficult, but has no necessary implications for jobs.[11] The third is that we have available an immensely powerful tool for minimizing the productivity impact of environmental constraints. That tool is the market economy.

The long-term costs of environmental improvements are usually far less than initial estimates suggest. That is because initial estimates fail to capture the power of the market economy to provoke myriad second,

---

11. An important possible exception to this general rule is discussed later in the chapter under the heading of 'Physical development and countryside preservation': it relates to the development of economic clusters.

third and higher order effects. A new air pollution standard met by retro-fitting filters to existing plant processes will usually cost many times more than one implemented through fundamental redesign of the whole production process, incorporating a higher standard into each process step, and into each item of capital equipment. But the cost will be still lower over the very long term, over timescales long enough to provoke changes in priority in the research and product development departments of both final manufacturers and equipment suppliers, new materials emerging to make processes more efficient, new products emerging which meet inherent customer demands in new ways. A rise in the price of petrol or diesel produces in the short term only a small change in the number of miles people travel, but over the long run it affects whether people buy fuel-efficient cars, whether manufacturers make fuel-efficiency a priority in product development, whether manufacturers' suppliers research new lightweight materials, and how intensely distribution companies concentrate on fuel cost minimization in their decisions about warehouse location. As a result estimates of the price elasticity of demand for petrol and diesel range from −0.1 for very short-term effects (i.e. a 10 per cent price increase produces a 1 per cent fall in demand) to over −1.0 (10 per cent increase generates 10 per cent fall) in some estimates of total long-term impact.[12] The essential superiority of the market system over planned economies indeed is that a combination of price signals and profit-maximizing incentives produces an infinite and continuous process of optimizing adjustments which no planned economy could ever conceivably replicate and which we can never precisely predict. Its superiority lies in its invisible rather than visible hand.

That in turn has two implications for public policy. One is that we should announce environmental policies as far in advance as possible. The other is that we should use the power of market instruments – such as taxes and schemes to allow the trading of rights to emit ('emission trading schemes') – to achieve environmental benefits at least possible cost, recycling the tax revenue to reduce taxes on labour.[13]

---

12. See Barker, Ekins and Johnstone (eds.), *Global Warming and Energy Demand* (London, Routledge, 1995).

13. The issue of whether reduced labour taxes have a 'doubled dividend' economic effect and their role in the politics of environmental taxes are discussed under 'Radicalism, tax and political leadership' later in this chapter.

Or to put it all in blunt and concrete terms, the case for high and steadily rising energy taxes is in economic terms overwhelmingly strong. And the case for avoiding competitiveness effects by harmonizing them at European level extremely strong also. Hardly a set of policies likely to appeal to any politician faced with the fuel-duty protests and Euro-scepticism of Britain in autumn 2000. But that illustrates the essential point. The economics of how we reconcile environmental responsibility and a prosperous economy are much easier than the politics. This chapter will therefore return to the political challenge after considering how these economic principles apply to three of the most pressing environmental problems we face.

Specific policy issues

On many environmental issues developed capitalist economies have already achieved a lot. In particular, where pollution effects are local – and thus where the beneficiaries of employment and profit and the sufferers from pollution overlap – great progress has been made and will continue to be made. Industry has achieved dramatic reductions in many damaging pollutants – in the UK discharges to water by the chemical industry of 'red list' substances (the most noxious of pollutants) are down 96 per cent in ten years, emissions of SO_2 are down by 56 per cent, NO_2 down by 38 per cent. Water and air quality in Europe and America are in most localities far better than thirty years ago let alone than in the pre-1950 period of London smogs or the Victorian age of London's 'big stinks'. There are salmon in the Thames; we've taken lead out of petrol; quarrying and gravel-extraction processes are much less noisy than they used to be.

That record illustrates two points. First, that existing policy levers and social pressures work. Environmental regulation and taxation produce effects. Corporate environmental responsibility is a key stimulus to action. Pressure groups stimulate response. Profit maximization within the constraints of clear regulation, influenced by well-designed taxes, and subject to the pressure of public opinion can produce good environmental results – far better indeed than the planned economies of the Soviet era which bequeathed widespread environmental destruction. On many issues of local pollution we do not need a radical shift of gear, we just need more of the same.

Second, that improvements can be achieved without significant economic detriment. There is no evidence that increasing environmental constraints have slowed overall growth rates, and no evidence that higher environmental standards in some developed countries have disadvantaged them economically versus others. Nor evidence that environmental standards have had any impact on our ability to create jobs. What has been achieved so far should give us confidence that there is little conflict between prosperity, employment and environmental improvement provided we consider carefully at each stage the balance of benefits and costs. Economic theory tells us that the market is an immensely powerful mechanism for minimizing the long-term cost of environmental improvements – and the empirical record confirms that that is so.

But despite that optimism we face at least three issues – global warming, the impact of personal transport mobility, and physical development of greenfield land – which are inherently more difficult either because of their uncertain, future and non-local effect or because they primarily concern issues of lifestyle choice rather than business efficiency. Each illustrates the need for a true understanding of market economics if bad market economics is not to make us poorer. Each illustrates the need for market-based interventions if the market economy is to fulfil its potential and serve the full range of human aspirations.

Global warming

Global warming, almost certainly caused by man-made greenhouse gas emissions, is almost certainly going to have a huge environmental and economic impact to which the world must respond. If we respond soon and radically and using market instruments to achieve improvements efficiently, we can solve the problem at only a small cost to measured prosperity.

Opponents of radical action disagree with that paragraph for four reasons. They object to acting on a probability not a certainty, they deny that the probability is high, they deny that the costs of climate change are significant and they claim that the 'economic constraints' limiting possible policy responses are severe. Each argument is wrong.

There is no absolute certainty that global warming is occurring, that its causes are man-made, or what its effects will be. But there is no certainty in any business or public policy decision, only probabilities.

Some of the same large companies which, in America more than in Europe, have argued against effective action on the grounds of no certainty would consider it idiotic if someone suggested that they should not invest in a new product, in exploration of a new oil field or in a new technology because the economics were probable rather than totally certain.

The probabilities, moreover, are high, for while we do not understand the full picture we know some things with reasonable certainty. We know that there is a 'greenhouse effect', indeed without it human life on earth would probably not exist, for CO_2 and other greenhouse gases in the atmosphere almost certainly make the earth something like 30 °C warmer than it would otherwise be. We know also with close to certainty that in the last 200 years (i.e. since the Industrial Revolution) human generated emissions, primarily from burning fossil fuels, have increased concentrations of CO_2 in the atmosphere from about 280 parts per million (p.p.m.v.) to about 370 and that a further increase to 550 p.p.m.v. or more is almost inevitable even if we now take significant offsetting action. At the very least, therefore, we know that we are conducting an enormously risky experiment – doubling the volume of the crucial input to a chemical process whose outcome has a huge effect on our environment.[14]

The evidence suggests, moreover, that the world is warming up and from a starting point close to the top end of the fluctuations in temperature that have occurred over the last 400,000 years. What we lack is a robust understanding of why past fluctuations have occurred and it is possible that the initial exogenous driver of those fluctuations has been variations in the intensity of the sun's radiation. But our best scientific understanding suggests that greenhouse gas concentrations have played an important reinforcing role in previous warming phases and the best assessment is therefore that whatever the initial trigger of the latest warming phase it will be more severe the more greenhouse gases we emit into the atmosphere. Nothing is certain but the best estimate of the scientific commissions established to look dispassionately at the data, in both Britain and internationally, is that if we take no offsetting action atmospheric concentrations of greenhouse gases

14. UK Royal Commission on Environmental Pollution, *Energy – The Changing Climate* (June 2000). The findings of the Royal Commission are similar to those of the UN International Panel on Climate Change, Second assessment, 1995.

will by 2100 be two and a half times pre-industrial levels, that global mean surface temperatures will rise by 4.5 °C and some land temperatures by considerably more – 'a combination of magnitude and rate of change [which] would exceed anything species and ecosystems have experienced in the last half million years'.[15]

The environmental and economic effects of that climate change are likely to be hugely detrimental. This of course is not absolutely certain and is contested. Some opponents of policies to limit climate change point indeed to potential positive effects from a warmer earth, in particular rising agricultural yields in temperate zones. But any such positive effects are likely to be far offset by negatives. Higher agricultural yields in some zones are likely to be offset by desertification elsewhere. Rises in global sea levels will impose huge economic costs. Tropical diseases – malaria in particular – will likely become more widespread as temperatures rise.[16] And arguments which attempt to offset negative impacts with positive in any case miss the fundamental point that it is almost certain that any major climate change, whatever its precise pattern, will have huge economic costs. For the present pattern of human habitation, of architecture and capital equipment, of agricultural skills and methods, of leisure facilities, reflects the existing pattern of the climate. People live on deltas which may flood with rising sea levels: if the climate had always been different they wouldn't live there but they do and moving them would be either enormously expensive or, in poor and densely populated countries, impossible. Other people live in areas which may turn to desert: the fact that somewhere else crop yields may rise due to a warmer climate will not offset the huge economic costs and human suffering created, or the resulting political instability. Alpine skiing resorts have invested hugely in capital equipment, in transport links and hotels: if the lower resorts become unsustainable that investment is lost. British homes have neither

---

15. UK Royal Commission on Environmental Pollution, *Energy – The Changing Climate*. Latest estimates from the UK's Hadley Centre (November 2000) suggest that the temperature increase could be higher still.

16. David Landes in *The Wealth and Poverty of Nations*, Chapter 1: 'Nature's inequalities' makes the point that one key reason why industrialization occurred first in temperate zones was the inherent climatic disadvantages (in particular tropical diseases) suffered by parts of the world with hotter and more extreme climates.

air conditioning nor the natural cooling design of Mediterranean architecture – redesigning them would be hugely expensive (and air conditioning would make CO_2 emissions worse).[17] In myriad ways – some apparently trivial, some matters of life and death – climate change is likely to impose massive economic costs. Even on the narrow calculus of economics and excluding the danger of very large and continuous climate change, the case for being prepared to spend huge resources to limit climate change is clear. And clear on both altruistic and selfish grounds. The developed rich world does not have the moral right to increase the risk of flooding in Bangladesh, and European business executives worried about the cost of action should consider it the necessary price for preserving at least some skiing in the Alps.

Action is therefore essential and the likely required scale of change is huge. Present levels of emissions are causing rising atmospheric concentrations of CO_2; to stabilize concentrations even at levels well above those already reached – at levels which would still make a 2–3 °C warming unavoidable – will therefore require total global emissions to be brought below present levels. But the 4.5 billion people of the poor and developing world currently produce emissions per capita a quarter or less of those of the 1 billion rich. The only equitable and politically feasible vision is one in which eventually each country in the world has a roughly equal right to emissions per capita. That means that emissions from the developed world will ultimately have to fall not by the 5–10 per cent targets agreed in the Kyoto Protocol but by 70 per cent or more.[18]

Developed country climate change strategies need therefore to be designed around the assumption that reductions of that magnitude will eventually be required. That assumption may of course prove wrong.

---

17. Anybody responding to this by claiming that the redesign would 'create jobs and thus wealth' is guilty of one of the oldest fallacies of misunderstood economics – the 'lump of labour' fallacy in which there is a shortage of jobs which has to be solved either by rationing real jobs or by 'creating' new ones artificially. In fact there is no shortage of work, and investing to overcome the capital destruction consequences of climate change will therefore simply divert employment from other truly prosperity-creating activities.

18. The Kyoto Protocol commitments by the developed nations amount in aggregate to a reduction of 5.2 per cent in greenhouse gas emissions below the 1990 level by 2010; the EU commitment was 8 per cent.

New scientific evidence may lead us to revise previous assessments. If so we may not need to complete the later and more difficult stages of reduction. But if they are needed, failure to take action soon will greatly increase the total cost of adjustment. On the basis of hard-headed economic assessment amid conditions of unavoidable uncertainty, developed countries should be aiming to achieve reductions of the scale recommended for the UK by Britain's Royal Commission on Environmental Pollution – 60 per cent by 2050 rising to perhaps 80 per cent by 2100.

That will be a huge challenge, but almost certainly manageable without unacceptable economic cost. Technically it is manageable because there is no world shortage of energy, and there are huge opportunities to improve our efficiency of energy use. Total solar energy reaching the earth is about 10,000 times greater than total human energy consumption; total wind, wave and tidal power are also massively greater; and the technologies to convert those sources of power to electricity are proven and will become economically viable over time. Average car fuel-efficiency could be doubled if people selected the most fuel-efficient models already becoming available, let alone future generations of vehicle. Personal transport mobility is compatible with greatly reduced fuel consumption, even if driving vehicles with an off-road capability which 99 per cent of drivers will never use probably is not. Fuel cell technology will within twenty years allow us to use renewable energy sources (converted to hydrogen) to power vehicles as well as stationary applications.[19] Light bulbs are already in the shops which turn electricity into light four times more efficiently than the standard bulbs in use. Home fuel-efficiency can be dramatically improved by better insulation. In technical terms there is no long-term problem. We will be able to have a growing economy and enjoy rising consumption while producing 60–80 per cent less CO_2 emissions than today.

---

19. Fuel cell technology will enable a car engine to run on hydrogen, which is converted to electricity when combined with oxygen from the air. The only emission is water vapour. Major car companies are aiming to have fuel cell cars on the road by 2005. This will produce immediate benefits in local air quality. Initially, however, the hydrogen will be derived from hydrocarbon sources and no reduction in CO_2 emissions will result. But the opportunity will be created for the subsequent development of hydrogen extraction from water using renewable energy sources such as solar or wind power, etc.

The problem therefore is not technical but one of costs, the potential costs to labour productivity of lower energy consumption in industrial activities, or the extra resource costs required to provide non-polluting forms of energy. Those costs are bound to exist and should not be denied. But because we have time and provided we use the power of the market, they are unlikely to have an unacceptable impact on attainable growth rates and thus future prosperity. Detailed studies by Cambridge Econometrics suggests that the total economic cost of achieving a 17 per cent reduction in Britain's CO_2 levels by 2010 (as compared to 1990) will amount to 0.28 per cent of Britain's GDP in that year. That is equivalent to a 0.02 reduction in the annual growth rate from 2000 to 2010, and would mean that Britain would attain in mid-February 2011 the prosperity level it would otherwise have reached a month and a half earlier.[20] Estimates of cost over longer-term periods are inevitably more judgemental – beyond a certain time horizon the techniques of econometric analysis simply cannot work. But at least some order of magnitude can be indicated as a counterweight to scare stories of the 'end of growth'. Britain currently devotes about 4–4.5 per cent of GDP to producing or importing energy. If energy costs stayed constant in real terms and present trends in energy intensity continued, that percentage would fall to below 2 per cent by 2050.[21] If instead energy costs have to rise three times in real terms as fossil fuels are replaced with renewables, and if that increase provoked no additional improvements in energy-use efficiency, the total effect on GDP in 2050 would be about 4 per cent, reducing the annual growth rate from now to then by less than one-tenth of a per cent and implying that we could attain in 2052 the standard of living otherwise attainable in 2050. The actual cost could well be considerably less, since most

---

20. Forum for the Future, *The 20% Solution* (Insights Publication Series, November 1999).

21. Figures for energy use are taken from the *Digest of UK Energy Statistics*, 'Basic Value of Inland Consumption', i.e. at wholesale level and excluding taxes. The percentage share of GDP varies considerably with the oil price – 4.9 per cent in 1997, 3.7 per cent in 1999. The average for 1997–9 was 4.15 per cent. Estimates in the Royal Commission report (*Energy – The Changing Climate*) show energy intensity on a long-term downward trend now running at about 1.8 per cent per annum: this would reduce energy intensity as a percentage of GDP to 40 per cent of its current level by 2050.

indications are that renewable technologies will by then become economic even if energy prices are well below three times present levels. But the calculation at least illustrates the point. This is a trade-off we can afford to make.

The difficult challenge indeed is not making reductions of the scale required, but achieving them as cost-efficiently as possible. To do that a range of policies are required, each aimed at compensating for market failure, for the failure of current prices and behaviours to reflect future environmental and fuel costs. Better government funding for energy-related research is essential: British government spending on renewable energy fell 81 per cent between 1987 and 1998 – it should have been rising to compensate for the impact of a falling oil price on private-sector funding decisions. Subsidies to renewable energy sources are justified to help them achieve cost economies of scale at an earlier date – several of the new techniques, such as solar cells, have economics heavily dependent on achieving large production volumes. Subsidies and encouragement to domestic fuel-efficiency are justifiable – they are a more cost-effective solution to low-income fuel poverty than income transfers and they compensate for failures of information and incentive in private decision-making. Emissions trading schemes have a major potential role to play, especially between large industrial sites.[22]

But of all our market instruments available, the most powerful and flexible is price. A rising price for fossil fuels, delivered by deliberate taxation policy and declared far in advance, is the development most likely to generate the myriad market-driven adjustments which will minimize the total cost of adjustment. If we do not use the price instrument as a complement to other policies, everything we know about economic logic tells us that the cost of adjustment will increase. And past experience illustrates both the powerful influence of energy

22. Emissions trading schemes can play a valuable role within a mix of policy levers, both domestically and internationally, and have the potential to ensure that emission-control actions are concentrated on sites where the cost/benefit ratio is highest. But it is important to realize that they are not magic means to avoid adjustment costs, and that they will tend to generate price rises. Those price rises indeed are probably essential to achieving a cost minimizing solution, since the *most* efficient solution may lie not in any of the sites and processes covered by the trading schemes but among their customers economizing on the use of inputs and/or meeting customer needs in different ways.

prices on demand and the compatibility of higher energy prices with economic growth. As Figure 9.1 shows, the oil price shock of the 1970s did produce a rapid and significant change in world energy demand, energy demand per person ending its steep upward trajectory, major improvements in, for instance, car fuel-efficiency being achieved between the 1970s and 1980s only to peter out as oil prices fell in the late 1980s; average new car fuel-efficiency in Britain improved 18 per cent between 1978–86, and not at all between 1986–97.[23] And while the shock rather than steady nature of that change produced major economic disruption in the 1970s, by the early 1980s the world had learnt to live with high energy prices. Between 1979–85 real oil prices in current terms averaged about \$50–5, well above the levels which caused such consternation in autumn 2000. But from 1981 onwards the economies of America, Europe and the Asian tigers were all growing at robust rates.[24]

The really difficult challenge of global warming is therefore neither technical nor even economic but political – how to achieve global action when a world government neither exists nor is going to, and how to secure domestic support for change. The first step has to be action by developed countries taken either alone or as a bloc. Against such action two arguments are put forward. The first is competitiveness. If the US imposes energy taxes (or equivalent cost-increasing regulations) but China does not, it will harm US competitiveness; if the UK imposes energy taxes but Europe and the US do not, British competitiveness

---

23. Since 1997 fuel efficiency seems again on an upswing, up 3 per cent 1997–9 as fuel duty increases began to influence decision-making.

24. The one thing that government policy cannot of course secure is a *steady* rate of price increase in fossil fuel prices rather than a fluctuating one, given the inherent volatility of the world oil price in particular. The instability of the world oil price is indeed a major and inherent problem, since a fluctuating price signal – alternatively shaking people into panic energy-saving action and then lulling them back to false security – is less likely to generate an optimal cost-minimizing process of adaptation than a steady upward trend. Other energy prices are, however, less volatile, and governments have at least some degree of freedom to deliberately vary their oil-taxation policies in a counter-cyclical fashion. The failure to develop a political strategy to deal with the volatility problem, and to communicate a long-term strategy which establishes long-term expectations irrespective of short-term swings, is one of the issues returned to under 'Radicalism, tax and political leadership' later in this chapter.

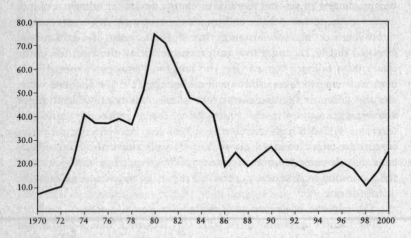

Figure 9.1a Real oil price 1973–99*

* Deflated by US Consumer Price Index.
Source: IMF *International Financial Statistics*, OECD *Economic Outlook*.

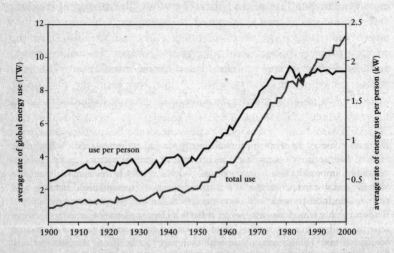

Figure 9.1b Growth in global energy use

Source: UK Royal Commission on Environmental Pollution, *Energy – The Changing Climate*.

will suffer. But at the level of continental economies these arguments, as with most competitiveness arguments, are very poor. The impact of higher energy prices on the US economy would be almost entirely domestic, the terms of trade and transitional unemployment effects very small in an economy which only trades 13 per cent of GDP. At the level of the UK, the argument has greater merit but the best solution is clear and a fallback is possible. The case for a European approach to industrial energy taxes is compelling and the case for fuel-duty harmonization could become strong if cabotage activity grew significantly above current levels. Even without a European approach, however, careful design of British energy-tax systems can mitigate the effects on energy-intensive traded sectors. Industrial energy taxes can and in Britain's case do include special rebates for competitively exposed sectors: road fuel taxes could if necessary allow for commercial-user rebates, distinguishing between freight uses where competitiveness considerations apply and passenger transport where they do not.[25]

The second argument is that there is 'no point', that if China and India have not committed to CO_2 emissions targets, the world is going to warm up in any case, so why should we face the costs of fruitless action? This is a poor argument for two reasons. The first is that 60 per cent of all emissions currently come from the developed rich world: getting the rich world's act in order is, at least today, disproportionately important and likely to remain so for several decades. The second and more fundamental has to do with technological leadership. If America and Europe and Japan committed to stretching emission-reduction targets and rising energy prices their huge economies would support the creation of new products and processes – cheaper renewable energy, more fuel-efficient car systems, better home-installation systems – capable of being applied elsewhere. In the long term the developing world has as great or greater an interest in limiting climate change as

---

25. In the case of Britain's industrial energy tax, to be introduced in 2001, the reduced-rate approach is used for energy-intensive traded sectors. Some environmentalists opposed these reductions as loopholes which undermine the tax's environmental impact, but this is not true since the sectors involved must instead put in place industry-wide voluntary agreements to achieve emissions reductions. Without such exemptions, moreover, there is a danger that some energy-intensive activities will migrate to neighbouring countries, undermining the environmental benefits of tax. This danger, along with competitiveness effects, is also massively reduced if the tax is agreed at the European level.

the rich – those most vulnerable to flooding and desertification live there. If rich countries drive the technologies and show commitment to an equitable division of emissions rights, the chances of action by developing countries are hugely increased. America and Europe and Japan can certainly act alone and should. Even Europe alone can act. A market of 370 million consumers is enough to drive technological development. The failure of America to deal responsibly with climate-change issues is concerning in environmental terms and bizarre in geopolitical: it is harming the world environment and increasing American reliance on oil imports from the world's most unstable region for fear of economic consequences which are hugely exaggerated. Responsible American leadership on this issue will at some time be vital. But its present absence can be no excuse for a lack of action at European and UK level.

The domestic political challenge of creating support for that action is the subject to which this chapter returns at its conclusion.

Mobility, congestion and pollution

Personal mobility is a high income-elasticity good – as people get richer they travel more, spending an increasing share of their income on transport services. It is also a good where economic 'externalities' abound, where my behaviour imposes costs on other people which I am not made to face. My mobility causes congestion for others; my mobility causes pollution for which I am not required to pay. It is therefore a good where optimal economic results can only be attained via government intervention (whether via taxes, regulation, or the definition of new property rights) and where the need for that intervention will increase through time. Without collectively agreed actions to make these markets work we are all poorer. At present – in two crucial respects – our failure to compensate for market failure produces a bias in favour of mobility and environmental degradation.

Personal mobility is increasing, one illustration of the overall truth that for all our chatter about the e-conomy, large and growing elements of the economy are as deeply physical as ever. Public transport use is booming, up by 17 per cent in Britain since 1996 and forecast to increase by 50 per cent by 2010. Car usage is relentlessly increasing – passenger miles travelled up 50 per cent in the last twenty years.[26] Some of the causes are inherent, some the product of self-reinforcing cycles. Richer people travel further on holiday, further to get to the shop they prefer, and further to have lunch with a friend, but they do that partly because new roads and motorways make the journey feasible. Richer societies are more fixated on the safety of children so more people drive their children to school, and once some do, most do, both because social mores are influential and because more cars on the road make the journey to school more dangerous for the minority who still walk. The result is congestion.

The problem is made worse by two forms of market failure. One is the fact that drivers do not face the cost of congestion they are imposing on others. If I join an already crowded road I slow down the traffic marginally yet more, but nobody charges me for the economic costs and waste of time thereby imposed on others.[27] The other cause is that choices between public and private transport are skewed by differences in the balance to consumer of fixed and marginal cost. Most people will always want to own a car to give them at least the option, when necessary, of private rather than public transport mobility; but if public transport recovers in its fares fixed as well as marginal costs it will almost always then make sense to make marginal journeys by car. That fact in turn can push public transport volumes below economic levels except on key routes, in turn making us all more likely still to make the journey by car. This is a vicious circle from which a crowded country cannot escape simply by building more roads, or through the exercise of individual marketplace rights.

The challenge is to break the circle without creating highly unequal access to mobility. The key policy initiative required is clear – congestion charging for crowded road space (both in city centres and on the most congested stretches of motorway) with the proceeds used for a

---

26. UK Department of the Environment, Transport and the Regions (DETR), *Transport 2010, the 10 Year Plan* (July 2000), Chapters 3 and 6.

27. At the CBI someone once worked out that the economic cost of congestion on British roads, let alone the frustration cost, was £15 billion, and the estimate continues to appear as a sort of gospel truth in many newspapers accounts. When I was Director-General I always treated the estimate with great caution – we could never find the audit trail of who had done the work and with what methodology. Most estimates of congestion cost, however, produce a figure of that sort of magnitude.

mix of two purposes – subsidy of public transport and a general reduction of taxes, the latter focused particularly on lower-income groups to offset the otherwise regressive effects of non-income related charges.[28] The case for such congestion charging is in terms of economic theory and potential benefit overwhelming: congestion charging is essential to make markets for mobility work.[29]

Transport (and in particular road transport) also imposes external environmental costs. The global dimension of these (CO_2 emissions) has already been discussed. The local impact is equally important and more obvious – air pollution in the city, noise pollution in the city and countryside, visual destruction of the countryside. These costs are sometimes dismissed as vague, judgemental and therefore arguably non-existent. But such dismissal flies in the face of price evidence, and in a market economy prices always incorporate information. Houses further away from road noise in cities, suburbs or the countryside sell for higher prices: the price differential is a measure of value destroyed. Restaurants with terraces overlooking quiet streets can charge higher prices than those overlooking road junctions, another hard economic

---

28. Devoting transport taxes *entirely* to other transport uses ('hypothecation') is an attractive political device to overcome people's distrust of government – their fear that without it the money simply disappears into higher overall expenditure which they do not specifically support. It has the disadvantage, however, that it forces us to subsidize other forms of mobility and removes the option of using the transport taxes to reduce taxes elsewhere. Such a direct tax offset may in consumer preference terms be more efficient: those who value mobility highly making net payments to those who value it less. It is worth noting that such a transfer makes congestion charges and offsetting tax reductions functionally equivalent to defining property rights, with one group of consumers 'selling' their rights to others.

29. The same principle may also at some stage have to be applied to some congested destinations such as national parks or major historical/artistic sites. At present most countries 'redistribute' outcomes by ensuring that these goods are not privately owned and are allocated either for free or with relatively small charges designed only to cover costs of operation and maintenance. Free or highly subsidized allocation, however, degrades the good for all, creating a level of congestion which destroys everybody's ability to enjoy these highly positional goods. If societies moved from free allocation to much higher access charges, however, they would need to redistribute charges in a progressive fashion if they are to keep the distribution approach equivalent to that which they have previously, implicitly, been pursuing.

measure. Build a road through beautiful countryside and house prices nearby collapse – a measure of part of the environmental impact but not all, for the value of those who enjoy the countryside without owning houses in it should also be counted. These are real economic costs, which increase with population density. The Eurostar route across the Pas-de-Calais was planned and built with far less public opposition than the route through Kent. That is not because the citizens of Kent are a bunch of impractical tree-huggers untouched by economic rationality. They are instead defending their essential economic interest in the only way possible (i.e. political protest) in a situation where property rights are neither defined nor compensated. France's lower population density means new transport projects tend to affect less people. France can therefore afford more generous compensation for property values affected – and not just for properties in the direct line of the railway or autoroute but those nearby. South-east England faces inherent costs of population density; we can argue about how to face these and how to allocate them between different citizens but we cannot escape them.

These large environmental costs of transport – local as well as global – provide a strong argument for high taxes on the transport sector, and especially on road transport. The precise level can be and is hotly debated, but the case in principle for road transport to bear a tax burden well in excess of what the government spends on road transport is undeniable. There are also strong arguments for increasing our focus on environmental impacts in our economic assessment of new transport schemes, and indeed for changing our approach to compensation. The principle, however difficult to implement, should be that all negative effects on property prices should be compensated or at least taken into account, along with still more judgemental assessments of the value of countryside amenity destroyed.

The counter-argument will be that this would greatly increase the cost of road (or indeed rail) building. In fact it will not increase it, all it will do is recognize it and distribute it differently. If we build a bypass for £50 million and house prices in the surrounding area fall by an aggregate £10 million the true cost of the road is £60 million – we have simply chosen as a society to impose £50 million on the general taxpayer and £10 million on those specific citizens who live nearby. Recognizing this cost is in principle right and equitable, but also an incentive to efficiency. If another £5 million on tunnels, or deeper cuts, or more noise baffling and less noisy road surfaces could reduce compensation payments by £5 million or more, that would be a more efficient, more value-creating solution as well as more environmentally responsible.

We cannot have efficient transport markets without congestion charging and full recognition of external environmental impacts. Two arguments are presented against the specific application of these principles. One relates, as always, to competitiveness. Business competitiveness, it is claimed, will be hurt if we have congestion charges, while other countries do not. But on congestion charges, even more than on industrial energy tax and fuel duty, this is a concern both greatly overstated and easily countered by efficient charge design. For the impact of congestion charging is far less sectorally skewed than an industrial energy tax, and the specific problems of cabotage-based competition simply do not apply, since all users of a specific stretch of road pay the relevant congestion charge. Since congestion charges thus have a sectorally across-the-board impact, their likely impact on prosperity through competitiveness effects is minimal or nil. And if we want to skew the charge regime in favour of freight we can: high charges for private cars using the M25 but relatively low charges for lorries would help make it what it always should have been – an efficient freight route for exporters to reach the channel ports, rather than a enticement to junction-hopping to get to the supermarket.

The other argument is more valid, relating simply to customer preferences and to the measurement of external effects. For some people believe that fuel duties in Britain and elsewhere already reflect full external effects and that the cost of congestion is less than suggested; others disagree. And while we can attempt some quantification the decisions will ultimately be judgemental. We will never be able to capture in calculations how much more pleasant a place central London would be if we significantly cut traffic and pedestrianized more streets and squares. That is why we have politics, for the essence of politics is a debate about the level of provision of inherently collective goods and about our attitude to redistribution. Ultimately the people of London, not the calculus of any economist, should decide whether we have congestion charges. In May 2000 the people of London voted for a mayor who proposes to introduce one.

Physical development and countryside preservation

Physical development of greenfield space is one of the most fundamental environmental issues. It is fundamental because it reflects not industrial efficiency but lifestyle choices – how many children we have, whether and how rapidly the population grows, and whether we live in dense cities or spread out. It is fundamental because the demand for higher-quality housing rises with rising income in developed countries and explosively so in developing ones. And it is fundamental because unless we constrain physical development we ultimately cannot preserve our environment whatever other measures of environmental protection we pursue. However much better business gets at producing goods with less pollution, and however more energy-efficient cars and homes become, if every year we pave some more of England's countryside in concrete, eventually we will have little left. And however many anti-poacher programmes are introduced to preserve the tiger, if the percentage of the earth's surface covered by human houses and roads does not at some stage cease growing, eventually there will be no tigers left except in zoos.

Because physical development reflects lifestyle choices opinions on appropriate policy differ greatly. Some people care about countryside and wildlife preservation, others do not. Some have moral objections to family planning; others consider opposition to family planning equally morally wrong. Some believe that constraining housing in south-east England represents an unacceptable defence of privilege, that Hampshire rural dwellers have no right to constrain the migration rights of northerners; others disagree for a mix of self-interested and altruistic, environmental reasons. Where one stands on these issues is more a matter of personal preference and politics than of economics.

But that fact – that these are to a significant degree matters of personal choice not economics – is itself important. For the language of economics and competitiveness is often introduced into these debates to suggest that we have 'no choice' that 'economic necessity' constrains us. In fact the choice is ours to make. Bad market economics should not be used to deny choice.

The blanket and wrong argument of absolute economic necessity was given extensive airing in Britain in 1999, when a government-commissioned report called for 1.1 million new houses to be built over the next twenty years in south-east England, despite the fact that

Britain's population is roughly stable.[30] The report's conclusions were rejected by both government and opposition, but its argument is still worth considering for it reflects a strong strand in developmentist thinking, the supporters of which wrongly believe is rooted in hard-headed economics. 'If the expansion of towns into the countryside is to cease,' said the chairman of the panel, Professor Crow, 'this can only come about through the south-east ceasing to be an area of economic growth. It is a mere pretence, indeed a cruel delusion, to suppose otherwise.' Far from being either a pretence or a delusion to suppose otherwise, however, it is simply wrong to suppose that the assertion is true. For economic growth is not inherently dependent on physical expansion, and if the expansion of towns and countryside in south-east England ceased entirely, growth would not cease. If London, for instance, were an island totally surrounded by water, incapable through absolute physical limit of absorbing any more greenfield land – a sort of Singapore of the North Sea – it would still enjoy economic growth, it would still invest and improve productivity, innovate new products and services, improve quality of existing goods and services and develop and improve the efficiency of existing buildings. It would experience a different shape of growth and perhaps slightly lower growth than if it could expand geographically, but there is no economic logic whatsoever which says it would have no growth. And the same is true for the whole South of England. If the South of England allowed not a single further acre of greenfield land to be used for development, it would still experience GDP per capita growth through investment in skills, R&D and physical equipment within the constraints of the present developed land. Expansive physical development makes achieving economic growth easier, but nil potential for greenfield physical development does not mean nil growth.

Equally, however, the existence of economic trade-offs should not be denied. For restrictions on land use can have implications for productivity and, in specific circumstances, for employment. Restricted availability of land must make it harder to achieve higher labour productivity since land, like capital, labour and energy, is a crucial input to most production processes and the more we curtail the supply of any one input the more difficult it is to achieve high productivity with respect to any other. As a result, and as discussed in previous

---

30. Panel Report on *South East Regional Planning Guidance* (October 1999).

chapters, cheaper land and greater ease of development are one of the two key drivers of America's inherent productivity advantage. How big that advantage is is unclear. Chapter 5 suggested that the US performs about 5–10 per cent better than the best European countries in terms of absolute efficiency: ease of physical development accounts for part of that advantage.[31] What we do with such estimates is a matter of social choice – a choice indeed of how (not whether) societies face the inherent economic costs of population density. If we relaxed planning laws in southern England and other densely populated parts of Europe we probably would close some of this gap, but we would do so at the expense of unmeasured environmental destruction.[32] Faced with that choice, I personally would simply accept the measured prosperity disadvantage in return for the unmeasured benefits of preserved countryside; others would differ. But it is a choice we can make.[33]

The second potential impact of planning restrictions poses greater difficulties for people who care about preserved countryside since it concerns one of the few ways in which environmental constraints can have an impact on employment levels rather than simply imposing a one-off productivity penalty. For tight development rules may constrain the development of clusters, and it is clear that physical clustering sometimes plays an important role in the processes by which business sectors grow and create employment. Northern Italian firms in leather

---

31. It is possible, however, as Chapter 7 noted, that the US inherent advantage – resulting from a large single market and ease of land development – is actually greater than the observed 5–10 per cent, with higher European skill levels reducing the net advantage.

32. The reason why we could only close some of the gap is that however much we relaxed planning restrictions and built roads we would not overcome traffic-congestion problems, with the new roads simply generating greater traffic. Road congestion affects productivity through its influence on economically feasible economies of scale (in both manufacturing and distribution centres) and on the predictability of delivery times.

33. Whatever the precise choice we make, it is clear that the *optimal* trade-off is bound to entail the country with a higher population density having a lower measured labour productivity (or higher level of other inputs such as capital and skill) for two reasons. First, because some of the productivity gap will be impossible to close for the reasons discussed in footnote 31. Second, because the consumer value of preserved countryside is bound to be higher the less there is left.

and fashion goods cluster together in specific towns – if they could not they would be less efficient and less competitively successful. More striking still, even the most sophisticated users and developers of ICT in the world, even those clearly 'living on thin air', cluster together in Silicon Valley. And the explanations are increasingly well understood: clustering reduces the risks for individuals with specific skills to sell and for businesses with specific skill needs, and in some sectors that's important, even when proximity for physical supply purposes is not. Restricting the development of a cluster once it begins to develop can therefore have a more significant economic impact than restrictions on non-clustering industries such as retailing. If Britain restricts hyper-market development, it may suffer a small productivity gap versus the US, but there will be no implications for long-term growth rates or employment levels. If planning laws restrict science-based industry development clustering around Cambridge University this may have a bigger effect – still finite, still not catastrophic, but bigger and more difficult to define. Developmentalists should drop their scare stories that any constraints on physical development kill growth, but environmentalists need in turn to recognize real economic trade-offs where these truly exist.

That recognized, the role of economics in most physical-development debates remains subsidiary, the issue of social choice dominant. Cluster-effect arguments can be valid in specific circumstances, but in the vast majority of cases where new physical development is proposed and opposed they are not. The strongest argument for less restrictions on housing development in attractive but densely populated regions such as south-east England is that those who already live there have no right to prevent others moving there. It is a legitimate argument which needs to be balanced against environmental concerns. But it has nothing to do with competitiveness and economic necessity.

We need therefore to debate that social choice and to recognize it as a choice. And we need to pursue policies most likely to produce win-wins, the best possible trade-offs. We should invest in urban quality of life: the more we make major cities pleasant living environments – less polluted, less noisy, less littered, less congested and with better public transport, better quality of public space and better schools – the less people feel driven to escape either to the countryside or the suburbs. And we should use the tax system to make market prices better reflect environmental impact. New houses impose environmental costs which refurbishments do not, but in Britain the former attract a zero rate of

VAT, the latter are charged at 17.5 per cent. The rates should at least be equalized, arguably the relativity should be reversed. The case for tax incentives to develop brownfield sites and not to develop greenfield is also strong. The incentives of the market economy are immensely powerful tools. Britain certainly is not using them to anything like their potential.

And we need also to establish a principle on greenfield development, for without one the destruction of our countryside is simply a matter of when, not whether. Arguably that principle should, in rich densely populated countries, be one of no net greenfield development, if not immediately then soon. We cannot without significant detriment freeze entirely the dynamic of clustering effects, but we could establish the objective that except in exceptional circumstances we will redevelop entirely within the confines of already developed land, and that for each acre of countryside over which we pour concrete we aim to restore to countryside or park another acre elsewhere. We can decide against applying the principle immediately, on the grounds that a final phase of housing development is needed to house all people in the sort of housing the lucky already enjoy. But unless at some time we apply it we are really not serious when we use the standard definition of sustainable development – a development which does not prejudice the ability of future generations to enjoy the same quality of environment we enjoy.

We can also choose never to apply it – if we place little value on preserved countryside and would rather achieve further increments, however small, in measured prosperity. But if so we should recognize that that is our choice, not something required by economic necessity or competitiveness, by some inherent link between economic growth and expansive physical development.

Radicalism, tax and political leadership

The politics of environmental issues are more difficult than the economics. There are trade-offs between environmental improvements and economic growth, between measured and unmeasured aspects of prosperity, but they are less severe than often supposed and market instruments are tremendously powerful tools for achieving the benefits at minimized cost. We can respond to global warming and preserve our countryside without sacrificing more than a small element of economic growth, and we have alternatives to the lose-lose solution of rationing road space by congestion.

Among the most powerful tools to minimize costs and maximize benefits are taxes and charges. Tax incentives can play a role in preserving greenfield countryside and encouraging brownfield development. Road-usage charges are the key instrument for tackling traffic congestion. Taxes on fossil fuels are our most powerful lever for unleashing the multiple unplannable adjustments which will improve energy efficiency and develop alternative energy sources. Taxes should certainly not be the only tool – in almost all areas of policy an integrated package of measures is required – but unless taxes and thus the price system are key elements within the policy mix we are almost bound to pay more for environmental benefits that we need to.

There is therefore a strong economic case for being bold in our use of tax instruments to achieve environmental aims. And a strong case too for making an overall shift towards the taxation of environmental 'bads' and away from the taxation of labour a key theme of tax policy for two reasons. First, political: reduced income and payroll taxes ought to make it easier to gain acceptance of environmental taxes from both individuals and business. Second, economic: because the case advanced by environmentalists that the shift can have a 'double dividend' effect (increasing employment as well as curbing pollution) is partially true. It should not be overstated: in general a shift from income taxes to consumption taxes has no necessary employment-creating effects. But payroll tax reductions specifically focused on lower-income groups could increase demand for labour, and a small increase in employment may therefore be an additional benefit of taxes introduced to achieve environmental policy aims.[34] In theory, a win-win-win of

---

34. A shift from income taxes to consumption taxes has in general no necessary consequences for the supply of labour because the 'tax wedge' (the difference between total cost of labour and post-tax disposable consumption power) is not changed and thus incentive effects should not (if people are acting rationally) be changed. Similarly a shift from payroll taxes (e.g. employers' national insurance) to consumption taxes has no necessary consequences for demand for labour since tax-incidence theory suggests the equilibrium level of real wages will tend as a result to be higher, leaving total labour cost unchanged. However, reducing payroll taxes on low-income earners can reduce total labour costs of those earners if minimum wages or trade-union bargaining have created wage rates already above

political support, economic benefit and environmental responsibility is attainable.

But it certainly didn't feel that way to governments across Europe in autumn 2000. In almost all countries there were protests against fuel taxes introduced at least notionally for environmental reasons. In France these resulted in a surrender to tax cut demands. In Britain they resulted in a sudden fall in the popularity of a government which had previously seemed to walk on water (and a partial surrender two months later). The lesson most European politicians will take from autumn 2000 is the need for caution, not boldness.

The true lesson, however, at least in Britain, is the need for greater honesty in debates on taxation, for more imagination in the detailed implementation of environmental taxes, and for more political leadership on the most important environmental polices.

In the British case four factors help to explain the dichotomy between the rosy possibility of popular support for a sensible taxation shift and the crisis of autumn 2000. The first is that people don't trust governments on tax, and with good reason, for governments rarely tell the whole truth. The British road fuel duty escalator was introduced in 1993. It was designed to achieve environmental benefit, and it did so – CO_2 emissions were cut as a result by at least 1–2.5 million tonnes on the government's best estimates.[35] But it was also one of the tax measures which during the course of the 1990s closed a gaping hole in Britain's public finance – taking tax as a percentage of GDP from 33 per cent in 1993 to 37 per cent in 1999, and public borrowing as a result from 8 per cent to 0 per cent. Those tax rises, pursued first by Norman Lamont and Kenneth Clarke and finished off by Gordon Brown, were essential to good macroeconomic policy, laying the basis for the more stable and low-inflation economy Britain now enjoys. But one reason why they were essential was that tax revenues had been cut unaffordably in the years before 1992, and one of the uses to which fuel duties and other indirect tax rises were put was to finance further

---

equilibrium levels; this lower cost of low-skilled labour can make more employment economic.

35. UK Government, *Draft Climate Change Programme* (2000), Chapter 5: 'Transport'. The figure of 1–2.5 m.t.c. is the government's best estimate of the impact of the increases introduced between 1996–9. Since the earlier increases from 1993–6 were of equivalent magnitude, the total savings could be double this estimate.

cuts in income-tax rates even while the overall tax burden was increased. (Between 1987 and 2000 the standard rate of income tax was cut from 29 to 22 per cent, cutting government revenue by about £19 billion. Road fuel duties, meanwhile, increased from £8 billion to £23 billion.) Increases in road fuel duty and other indirect taxes financed a dramatic cut in income taxes. But that is not how the story was told. Tax increases in budget speeches are rather technical things that simply happen; tax decreases are the product of sound economic management. Public support for high fuel duties would be greater if the truth had been clear.

And looking forward, popular support for a shift to environmental taxes will be increased if governments make clearer the uses to which those taxes will be put. If they are to finance a further increase in the level of public spending, the tax burden rising higher, that needs to be clearly stated and support for that policy overtly sought. If they are to finance more income-tax cuts within a stable tax burden that too must be made clear and must be made credible by stated policies towards the overall size of the state.[36] We cannot have a mature debate on environmental taxes outside a more mature and honest approach to tax and spend levels in general.

The second problem is inherent – oil price volatility. For, ironically, the tax protests of autumn 2000 in Britain and elsewhere were not provoked by tax increases but by the soaring price of crude oil (up from $10 a barrel in February 1999 to $33 by September 2000). In Britain, indeed, the policy of automatic increases in road fuel duties had been abandoned in 1999 and the 2000 budget saw the lowest increase in fuel duty for over ten years. Market price movements triggered resistance across Europe to taxes which had previously been largely accepted, and which indeed had only just returned real price levels to those of the early 1980s – the retail price of petrol in the UK in autumn 2000 was in real terms almost exactly the same as in 1981; in 1999 it had been 14 per cent lower. This sensitivity of public opinion to sharp

---

36. Chapter 8 made the point that clearly expressed limits on the size of the state ('taxes no more than X per cent of GDP') are valuable not because of the dangers of competitiveness burdens but because without them popular will cannot be empowered, and tax and spend choices cannot be debated sensibly. They are also the only means by which governments can be held to promises that new environmental taxes will be recycled in a 'tax neutral' fashion.

movements in price is, however, entirely understandable, for sudden rises have distributional and real income effects far more severe than a steady rise.[37] The implication is not, however, that environmental tax policies are politically unfeasible, but simply that they need to be implemented with imagination. There is no reason why the pace of shift from taxes on labour to environmental taxes should not vary with the oil price, fastest when oil prices are low, ceasing entirely when they are high. And there is no reason, other than convention, why we should not respond, even in the middle of the financial year, to dramatic rises in the oil price with at least partially offsetting cuts in fuel duty, matched by rises when prices fall. Such a policy could be better in macroeconomic management terms.[38] It would be better in environmental terms, since the ideal price signal is a steady upward trend, not sudden surges followed by sudden collapse. And if put in place in advance, as an overt and well-communicated strategy, rather than as a reaction to street pressure, it would be good politics – better by far than abandoning the long-term principle of rising fuel duties in the face of

---

37. Distributional and real income effects can be severe when prices suddenly change, even in markets where they are minimal in the long term. The most obvious examples relate to administered prices. Taxi drivers are made significantly poorer by sudden increases in oil price if meter charges are not immediately adjusted. But even where prices are not administered, volatility can produce significant temporary income losses. Freight-carriage contracts may not respond immediately to higher prices, especially if purchasers have significant market power. And individuals' abilities to take offsetting action are limited if effects are sudden: people who purchased cars in 1998 and 1999 did not anticipate the petrol prices of the autumn of 2000 in their approach to fuel efficiency trade-offs. Sudden movements are therefore bound to produce more severe public reactions than steady ones.

38. The policy might be better in macro-demand management terms because while some fuel taxes are fixed per gallon (e.g. excise duties) others (VAT) are proportional, and in Britain at least Petroleum Revenue Tax is more than proportional with the oil price. As a result when the oil price rises tax revenues rise in an unanticipated fashion, producing an unintended tightening of fiscal policy. (The rise in VAT on oil products is partially, but only partially, offset by a fall of VAT revenues on other categories of consumer expenditure.) Reducing duty in these circumstances to (as best possible) offset the unanticipated tax rise would therefore keep demand-management policy more stable, as well as offsetting accusations that governments are treating oil price rises as an excuse for 'stealth' increases in the total tax burden.

short-term pressure. Governments need to be imaginative in the details of environmental taxes and to respond to legitimate concerns.

Imagination is needed also to deal with the third problem, longer-term distributional effects. Some of these are overstated – in overall terms increased road fuel taxes are reasonably progressive, since car ownership is lowest among the lowest-income groups.[39] But some problems are real and do need to be managed. High petrol and diesel costs do impose a bigger burden on rural dwellers than on other groups in society: a slowdown in fuel-duty increases and a shift to encouraging fuel-efficiency through vehicle-registration taxes differentiated strongly by fuel-efficiency of engine may therefore make sense: owners of small cars in rural districts would gain; owners of petrol guzzlers in the city would lose. If the charges for fuel-inefficient cars were high enough, the overall effect could be better environmentally as well as in terms of equity.

The fourth and final problem is competitiveness and the British attitude to Europe. Industrial energy taxes applied in one European country and not in others can create real competitiveness problems in some sectors. So too could high road fuel duties if cabotage effects became large. The long-term case for a pan-European approach to energy taxes is therefore strong. But in the week after Britain's September 2000 fuel crisis, the Minister for Transport confirmed Britain's total opposition to any exploration of European solutions, confident that a European perspective would inflame protesters rather than be seen as a potential long-term solution. In Britain in 2000 he was probably right. But until we are able to consider European-wide approaches we will be trying to achieve environmental benefits at least economic cost with one hand tied behind our back.

Britain's use of fiscal instruments to achieve environmental benefits thus hit the buffers in September 2000 in part at least because the government failed to deal imaginatively with the details. It also failed to make the case. It is difficult to remember a single speech in which a British chancellor of the Exchequer has attempted to link a vision of environmental responsibility to the economics of how it is to be achieved. It is certainly impossible to remember one in which a British chancellor or prime minister has dared even whisper the possibility that

39. Institute for Fiscal Studies, *The Petrol Tax Debate*, Briefing Note No. 8 (July 2000).

a European dimension might in principle help. And in autumn 2000, amid extensive flooding which may itself have been a by-product of global warming, the government never once sought to rally public opinion against the fuel protestors with a robust statement that high fuel taxes are good for the environment, and that they have enabled the government to set income taxes far lower than they would otherwise be.[40]

But without that leadership it is difficult to achieve the optimal solutions which market economics make possible. Market economics correctly understood and well used can help us make the best trade-offs possible between environmental quality and measured aspects of prosperity. But totally free markets, unconstrained and unmanaged by government interventions, are often inefficient, incapable of dealing effectively with the full economic costs of global warming, or reflecting the full range of human aspirations and preferences. Capitalism can be green, far greener indeed than planned economies ever could be, but governments have to make it so.

---

40. The oddity indeed of the British government's autumn 2000 stance was its insistence on using phoney arguments against fuel-tax reductions rather than good ones, e.g. the argument that tax cuts were in some absolute sense unaffordable, or that reductions would drive interest rates higher (despite the fact that the oil price rise had generated an unanticipated tightening of the fiscal position).

10. Global Finance:
Engine of Growth or Dangerous Casino?

Fashions in economic commentary change rapidly and memories are short. Amid the confidence of year 2000's new economy it was difficult to recall how gloomy was the prognosis for global capitalism in autumn 1998. The tiger economies of East Asia had crashed the previous year, Malaysia's GDP down 6 per cent, Thailand's 8 per cent, Indonesia's 14 per cent. Indonesia, in particular, seemed to be heading towards economic and social 'meltdown'. The Russian experiment in rapid liberalization collapsed in August when the government defaulted on its debts. The US stock market fell 20 per cent in August and September, many commentators predicted still further collapse, and the newspapers were full of comparisons with 1929. In late September the hedge fund Long-Term Capital Management threatened to collapse with net positions of $200 billion and potential losses of $14 billion, and on Wall Street and in the City talk of a 'global credit crunch' was rife. Paul Krugman penned his book *The Return of Depression Economics*. George Soros wrote *The Crisis of Global Capitalism*. Henry Kissinger wrote an article entitled 'Global Capitalism is Stoking Flames of Financial Disaster'. Lobby groups attacked global capitalism in general and the IMF in particular as threats to the Third World poor and to the global environment. Even capitalism's high priests and greatest beneficiaries – the heads of central, commercial and investment banks – warned that financial instability was potentially catastrophic and gathered together for weighty discussions on the need for a 'new financial architecture'. The case for the latter was pressing and the speed with which our political leaders responded impressive. On 3 October 1998 the *Guardian* reported that Gordon Brown was urging that a new world super-regulator should be in place by Christmas.

Two years later it just seemed like a bad dream. The Asian economies bounced back far more rapidly than anyone dared hope. The global financial system did not collapse. Left-wingers and environmentalists still did battle with global capitalism on the streets of Seattle but among capitalism's technicians, believers and beneficiaries confidence was restored. The Washington consensus of free-market capitalism today seems more dominant than ever. John Gray's 'false dawn' seems to have given way to bright confident morning. Market fundamentalists – believers that free markets are always and everywhere right – walk tall and proud again.

But we would be unwise simply to forget the events of 1998 and the debates they then unleashed. For while this book has played down the impact of globalization on rich developed countries, its impact on the developing world and on the stability of financial markets raises more debatable issues. In these arenas left-wing pessimists present at least a serious case to answer. For while capitalism is good for the developing world, totally free markets in all things are not. The benefits of global capitalism must be embraced but the dangers of market fundamentalism rejected.

The benefits of global capitalism

Chapter 1 argued that globalization is often overstated. Trade intensities in the developed world (trade as a percentage of GDP) are not on a relentless upward trend. Capital flows as a percentage of British GDP are no higher than they were in the late nineteenth century.[1] But the phenomenon of globalization is still a real one, especially for developing countries. Trade intensities of developing countries have been rising as trade liberalization has reduced tariff and non-tariff barriers: India now trades 9.9 per cent of GDP versus 6.8 per cent in 1980. Barriers to capital movement have come down rapidly and the nature of capital flow has changed. Total net inflow to developing countries is up only marginally from the levels of the mid-1970s, from 4.9 per cent of GDP to 5 per cent, but the private element is up from 3.3 per cent to 4.0 per

---

1. Between 1911–13 capital outflow from Britain amounted to about 10 per cent of GDP (see Peter Mathias, *The First Industrial Nation – An Economic History of Britain*, 1974). Over the 1990s, outward flows of direct and portfolio investment have also equalled 10 per cent of GDP (ONS Pink Book 1999). What is different, however, is that the flow is now both ways, with the annual outflow of 10 per cent of GDP being offset by a 7 per cent inflow. Between the developed economies it is the two-way flow of all types of capital (rather than a stable pattern of capital exporters and capital importers) which is the distinctive feature of the present phase of globalization.

cent and the equity rather than debt element up from 0.4 per cent to 2.2 per cent. Capital flows to developing countries in 1975 largely meant bank loans to state and parastatal organizations. A large share now is direct investment by multinationals and that has quite different consequences for integration in the global economy.

Greater openness to trade and capital flows, moreover, has typically been accompanied by domestic liberalization. The dismantling of the Indian regime of industrial licensing, privatization in many countries of both industrial companies and utilities, deregulation of telecoms markets, the liberalization of private commercial activity in China, all these have shifted many developing economies in a market-oriented direction. These changes are not strictly speaking globalization (in theory India could have liberalized internally while remaining largely closed to the world) but they are part of the package we usually mean by that term, and the package is perceived by governments as an integrated whole. Above all indeed it is the approach to economic policy, the philosophy of free markets, which has been globalized.

That globalization process has delivered major economic benefits to many developing countries. The key evidence for that has already been set out in Chapters 1 and 5 – the acceleration of rates of economic catch-up achieved over time. Korea, Thailand, China and India are catching up in GDP per capita far faster than say Sweden versus America in the early years of the twentieth century and faster even than Germany, Italy or France in the 1950s. Catch-up is possible wherever existing productivity levels are below world best practice. Catch-up is facilitated if there are powerful incentives to pursue productivity improvement (intense internal competition, access to foreign markets, potential import competition) and if there are mechanisms for transferring capital and ideas across the world. Globalization provides both those incentives and those mechanisms.

That conventional wisdom is of course disputed, and some of the criticisms of it are valid. We should not overstate the benefits or rewrite economic history to make totally free markets the universal answer, the only route to growth. Economists such as Jagdish Bhagwati at Columbia University and Dani Rodrick at Harvard have pointed out that the benefits of free movement of capital are by no means clear cut.[2] China

2. See Jagdish Bhagwati, 'The Capital Myth', *Foreign Affairs*, May–June 1998;

and Japan both achieved high growth rates before easing of capital movement, as did Western Europe after the Second World War. All really high catch-up rates have depended vitally on high levels of domestic savings, and early capital market liberalization might actually have reduced that saving.[3] Free movement of short-term capital can bring with it severe macroeconomic problems. And the use Japan and Korea made of infant industry protection tariffs in the early stages of industrial growth should not be airbrushed from history simply because it doesn't fit the latest intellectual fashion.

All that said, however, the evidence of the very high catch-up rates achieved by those countries which have 'globalized' in the 1980s and 1990s is compelling. India's performance is particularly notable – a country which for many years turned its back on market economic doctrines but which has achieved a step change in its rate of growth per capita since it commenced external and internal liberalization in the late 1980s. And at the other end of the scale, the countries which score lowest for economic freedom and integration in the world economy – for instance the Congo, Zimbabwe or Myanmar – are also among the poorest. The whole package is beneficial even if we can cast theoretical and empirical doubt on whether all elements of the package are essential.

Another attack on globalization bemoans its impact on inequality. Globalization, it is claimed, 'has dramatically increased inequality between and within nations'.[4] Whether that is true is fiercely disputed.

Dani Rodrick, 'Who Needs Capital Account Convertibility?', *International Finance*, No. 207, Princeton University, 1998.

3. The fact that financial market liberalization can reduce the savings rate follows from the discussion of savings-rate elasticity in Chapter 8. While it is often simply assumed that people save more the higher the return they achieve this is not necessarily so. Lower returns can sometimes generate higher saving if people are motivated by target levels of wealth and income for retirement. Japan's very high rates of savings via low-return savings accounts in the 1950s and 1960s might therefore have been lower if domestic market liberalization and freedom from capital controls had enabled the Japanese investors to achieve higher returns. Indeed it may be the case that very high rates of growth always depend on somewhat artificial mechanisms to stimulate savings above a natural free-market level.

4. Jay Mazur, 'Labour's New Internationalism', *Foreign Affairs*, January–February 2000.

The best judgement is that the first half of the claim ('between . . . nations') is wrong but that the latter ('within nations') is at least partially true.

The claim that globalization has increased inequality between nations clearly cannot be true in respect of the emerging economies set out in Table 1.2. If China and Korea (together with many other Asian countries) are growing faster than the US or Europe then inequality between them and the already rich is obviously falling. Arguments that inequality between nations has increased therefore depend upon the observation that many very poor countries – concentrated particularly in Africa – have actually got poorer in the last twenty years while both the Asian tigers and the developed world have got richer. But to claim that this is due to globalization is surely wrong. The reasons why the Congo, Rwanda or Zambia have remained poor or got poorer while Korea has gone from a similar standard of living in 1950 to approaching Western levels in 2000 are complex, difficult to discern, and vitally important for us to understand. But claiming that it is because they have been exposed to globalization is as trite as suggesting that a dose of globalization and liberalization would magically cure all their ills. We don't actually understand some of the more subtle drivers of economic success. But the evidence suggests that openness to the world economy, to its capital flows, trade flows and ideas, while not a sufficient condition to ensure success is close to a necessary one. As a result globalization is a force for reducing inequality between countries.[5]

Within countries inequality does seem, however, to have increased both in the developed and in the developing world, and in the latter (far more than in the former) it may well be a product of greater

---

5. The debate can be expressed numerically in terms of gini coefficients – one of the best standard measures of inequality. Boltho and Toniolo's work (*Oxford Review of Economic Policy*, 15: 4, 1999) shows the inter-national gini coefficient falling in the 1980s and 1990s for the first time since the Industrial Revolution. Their sample of countries (forty-nine in number) excludes, however, some of the poorest ones which play close to no part in the world economy. Studies by Firebaugh, Milanovic and Schultz, which do include those latter countries, show the inter-national gini coefficient both higher and rising (*American Journal of Sociology*, 1999; World Bank, 1999; *Journal of Population Economics*, 1999). But Boltho and Toniolo's is still a better measure of globalization's impact given that it covers the countries which have actually opened themselves to globalization.

openness combined with greater domestic liberalization. Privatization has opened the way to managerial salary increases unacceptable in the public sector. New opportunities for business mean big new rewards for the entrepreneurial. More importantly (since this affects the bottom end of the income distribution), the removal of subsidies, dismantling of tariff protection and liberalization of prices have often reduced real wages for low-paid workers. We need to recognize that fact and the fears and resistance it engenders. Supporters of globalization should have enough confidence in the overall case for the market not to feel the need to deny any problems.

Globalization is beneficial but it is not a win-win process for all and not all aspects of it are necessarily beneficial. Two implications follow. The first is that openness to the global economy is not enough, that governments of developing countries, as of developed, still have enormously important roles to play in making capitalism workable socially and indeed in underpinning its long-term economic success. Professor Amartya Sen's criticism of India is pertinent. The liberalization process, he noted, could lead to a more appropriate focus in the role of the state. Prior to liberalization, 'The state was doing things it wasn't very good at, namely running industries by issuing licences, and not doing things it would be expected to do, namely providing good schools, healthcare and land reform.' The danger in its current policy, he believes, is not that it has withdrawn from the former activity but that it has still not taken adequate and effective responsibility for the latter.[6]

The second is that we should look carefully at the overall package of globalization and identify which elements are clearly beneficial and where a more nuanced approach to liberalization is required. Above all it is needed in respect to liquid financial markets. For the case for immediate liberalization of all financial markets is much less compelling than for most product markets. The reasons why that is so are rooted in some economic theory relevant to our overall approach to free markets and to the capitalist system.[7]

---

6. Comments to World Bank Development Conference in Paris, June 2000.

7. The separate issue of whether globalization has adverse consequences for the environment is covered in Chapter 11. The brief answer is that globalization creates environmental challenges because it makes people richer, but that if there was a non-globalized autarkic route to prosperity it would almost certainly cause

All markets are different

Market economists use models of perfectly competitive markets as an analytical tool. Perfectly competitive markets are ones where perfect information is available immediately to all participants and where individuals react rationally in response to the information before them. Market fundamentalists believe, or at least care to assume, that such markets actually exist in large numbers; serious market economists do not. The purpose of the models indeed is not to describe reality but to serve as tools of understanding: it is easier to understand how real world imperfect markets work by starting with an unreal perfect model and then folding in real world complexities bit by bit than by diving immediately into a description of imperfect markets.

'All perfect markets are perfect in the same way: all imperfect markets are imperfect in their own different way.' Not, sadly, my own neat adaptation of Tolstoy but Paul Krugman's. It captures a vital insight. Different markets differ from the model of perfect competition in importantly different ways. Markets are both imperfect and highly diverse. Indeed if you ever hear someone asserting that such and such a market is 'a market like any other' or that a specific price is 'a price like any other' it is usually a sure sign that they really don't understand market economics.

Some markets are more like the theoretical model than others. Many physical product markets are sufficiently close in behaviour to the theoretical model that we can largely base economic policy on the assumption that they are perfect, especially if we take regulatory measures to offset market imperfections such as monopoly and abusive competitive behaviour. Two of the most important markets in capitalist economies, labour and financial markets, tend, however, for quite fundamental reasons to be significantly imperfect but in diametrically different ways.

Labour markets are imperfect because both individuals and society are unwilling to treat labour as a 'commodity like any other' and because workplace relations are social as well as economic. Even in a

more damage, and that globalization provides us with some of the tools with which we can address the inevitable implications of greater prosperity.

legally completely free labour market – no trade unions, no rules on dismissal, no minimum wages – there are important sociological and economic barriers to flexible wage-setting. If a manager observes that the average secretarial wage in the local labour market has dropped 2 per cent in the last three months, he or she does not (on the whole) call in his or her secretary and cut his or her wages.[8] Labour markets are therefore naturally 'sticky' – relative prices in labour markets do not move as rapidly and smoothly as perfect market theory suggests to the 'market clearing' level which ensures that all labour is employed. And they are made stickier by the rules which society has introduced to give expression to our social concern for labour as a very special form of economic input. We accept or encourage trade-union collective bargaining while we would normally ban cartels: we introduce minimum wages and rules on dismissal and on consultation. The optimal approach to such rules and thus to labour-market flexibility has been discussed in Chapter 6. But however one resolves that debate labour markets will be to some degree special and that has implications for many aspects of economic policy. The argument for positive and symmetrical inflation targets (rather than zero or less) rests in part, for instance, on the inherent inflexibility of labour markets.[9]

Liquid financial markets are special in precisely the opposite sense – they have an inherent tendency to be more volatile than perfect market theory suggests and can display price movements which 'over- shoot' equilibrium levels, which are inherently irrational and which

---

8. In many ways, of course, this behaviour is economically rational once account is taken of the economic benefits of employee loyalty, accumulated knowledge and training, etc. There is indeed a fine philosophical point to be argued as to whether some apparently irrational markets are rational if you get down to more detailed definitions of rationality or if we consider 'near rational' behaviour in conditions of uncertainty and with decision-making costs taken into account. The implication that simple perfect market models are unrealistic is, however, unchanged. See Akerlof and Yellen, 'A Near Rational Model of the Business Cycle', *Quarterly Journal of Economics*, 100 (1985), for discussion of the implications of 'near rational' behaviour.

9. Low but positive inflation makes it easier to achieve small adjustments in relative real wages – freezing specific nominal wages when inflation is 2 per cent is much more socially acceptable than cutting those nominal wages by 2 per cent when inflation is zero, and less likely to produce cycles of declining consumer confidence and demand.

have harmful economic effects. Exchange-rate movements overshoot rational equilibrium values by as much as 15 or 20 per cent and for years not just months: stock markets can be irrationally high or irrationally low by at least similar margins. Three factors create this potential for volatility and irrationality. The first is the inherent difficulty of estimating fair value. Financial instruments are not real products or even usually claims on specific real products, but claims on bundles of real products and often on extremely complex bundles. The 'correct' price of a share depends on an enormously complicated set of assumptions about future company performance, future macro-developments, and future relative prices for different products and wages. A very wide range of estimates of value can therefore be logically supported. The second factor is that transaction costs are low, much lower than for most products: minute movements in share price or exchange rate can therefore deliver profits which cover trading costs. The third is that many individuals involved in trading face asymmetric risk return trade-offs: they will make lots of money if they speculate well but are not personally liable if they lose; and they may be criticized for failing to make profits when other market participants make them, but not usually for making losses as long as others do as well.

Those three factors can generate price-setting behaviour focused not on the estimation of inherent value – not therefore on what perfect market theory would suggest – but on an essentially self-referential process of guessing before the rest of the market the guesses which the market will make tomorrow. Or, as Keynes famously put it, investing in financial instruments can at times come to be like

> those newspaper competitions in which the competitors have to pick out the six prettiest faces from a hundred photographs, the prize being awarded to the competitor whose choice most nearly corresponds to the average preferences of the competitors as a whole; so that each competitor has to pick, not those faces which he himself finds prettiest, but those which he thinks likeliest to catch the fancy of the other competitors, all of whom are looking at the problem from the same point of view. It is not a case of choosing those which to the best of one's judgment are really the prettiest, nor even those which average opinion genuinely thinks the prettiest. We have reached the third degree where we devote our intelligence to anticipating what average opinion expects the

average opinion to be. And there are some, I believe, who practise the fourth, fifth and higher degrees.[10]

Periodic bouts of volatility and overshooting are as a result inherent to all liquid financial markets. That fact has been described in numerous precise ways and is supported by a wealth of theory and empirical analysis. Robert Shiller's *Irrational Exuberance* provides compelling evidence that the overall level of stock-market valuation is subject to occasional irrational booms and busts, and describes the key amplification mechanism as a 'naturally occurring Ponzi process', i.e. a pyramid scheme in which you make the most money by getting out before everybody else realizes the game is up.[11] George Soros, who ought to know a little bit about this subject, refers to 'reflexivity', a process of feedback loops in which market movements generate market movements. Barry Eichengreen describes how 'self-fulfilling speculative attacks' can undermine exchange-rate policies which ought, in fundamental terms, to be sustainable. But however you describe it the phenomenon is clear. Financial-market prices must eventually oscillate around sensible fair values – they cannot limitlessly diverge from economic reality – but over significant periods of time they diverge significantly on the basis of self-fulfilling waves of sentiment. Nasdaq's valuation of Internet companies in March 2000 was not rational: the fact that it fell by a third between then and mid-April was not because of new information, but because of a change in sentiment, a highly judgemental response to largely unchanged information. And the oscillations of the yen against the dollar throughout the 1990s (see Figure 10.1) cannot be explained by any flow of new information – instead they were heavily driven by waves of sentiment heading first in one direction then in another.

Most market economists accept that liquid financial markets overshoot, though they may disagree about the extent and the implications. Almost everybody who actually trades in financial markets accepts it as

10. John M. Keynes, *The General Theory of Employment, Interest and Money* (Macmillan, 1973), Chapter 12.

11. Robert J. Shiller, *International Exuberance* (Princeton University, 2000). Charles Ponzi was the creator of one of the first and largest pyramid selling schemes, which gripped the US in 1920. See also Barry Eichengreen's analysis of the possibility of 'Self-fulfilling speculative attacks' in *European Monetary Unification: Theory, Practice and Analysis* (MIT, 1997).

Figure 10.1 Yen:$ exchange rate

1992–2000

February 1998–December 1998

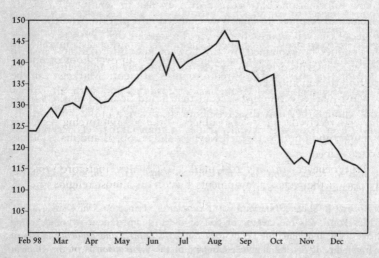

Source: Datastream.

obvious, a fact of life reflected in the language of trading rooms, the 'waves of selling', 'waves of buying', 'panic selling', 'rising confidence', 'trading support levels' and 'psychological barriers', with which movements in price are explained. It is nevertheless denied. The arguments used for denial are, however, a mixture of the technical but irrelevant and the quasi-metaphysical.

The technical argument relates to 'efficient market theory'. This theory is well founded, analytically valuable and carries some useful implications for public policy. It just happens to be irrelevant to the issue of overshoots. Indeed it was never intended to deny the possibility of overshoots, even though it is often wrongly assumed to do so. It asserts that prices in well-run liquid stock markets (as against some illiquid badly regulated Third World markets) are efficient in the specific sense that all information is rapidly disseminated and, as best we can judge, is factored rapidly into price estimates by all participants. It also argues that there are no observable patterns in stock-market movements (which instead follow 'random walks'), and that it is therefore impossible to make money in stock markets on the basis of knowledge of past patterns of price movement. Some 'strong forms' of the hypothesis go further indeed and argue that even those with privileged information can only rarely use it to make superior returns.[12] These findings are interesting. Their most important implication is that the *relative* price of different shares (at least within broad industry sectors) may have a strong tendency to be rationally estimated by market prices – a finding which supports the role of stock markets as mechanisms for allocating capital between firms. But none of the efficient market tests in any way disprove the assertion that the overall market can overshoot or under-shoot on the basis of self-reinforcing sentiment. Markets can be efficient, reasonably free from insider trading, and with all parties trying their best to assess the meaning of new information simultaneously received, but still be subject to the self-reinforcing waves of pessimism and optimism which Keynes, Shiller, Soros and many others have described.

True believers in universal market rationality therefore typically rely not on the technical arguments but on an almost religious belief,

---

12. See Lorie and Hamilton, *The Stock Market, Theories and Evidence* (Richard D. Irwin Inc, 1973) for a good summary of the various forms of the efficient market theory.

and on those grounds of course they become unanswerable. For it is always possible to look at the oscillations of Figure 10.1, or of any other market price, and to assert that they *must* have been rational even if we cannot immediately see why. If we cannot identify the new information which justified the rise or fall, that must be because we were not close enough to the market. If to us it seems that the available new information did not support the rise or fall we observe, that must be because we are drawing wrong inferences, different from those which the all-seeing market rightly drew. Since we know that markets are rational, there must have been information and rational inference which justified the price movement, even if for now that truth is hidden from our eyes. Arguing with such people is like arguing with anti-Darwinists who believe that God put the fossils in the rocks to test our faith in the biblical creation myth. The common sense conclusion is that the fossils prove that the world was not created in seven days, and the common sense reaction to the observed behaviour of liquid financial markets is that they are susceptible to significant irrational volatility and overshoots.

The inherently special characteristics of financial markets are most obvious in liquid trading markets. But the same factors also make bank-lending markets special too. For a tendency to herd behaviour – the need to get out of loss-making positions before everybody else does – is what creates systemic risk in the banking system. Banks which have made losses, or which are rumoured to have made losses, can be subject to 'liquidity runs' which make the problems worse. Queues of depositors seeking to get their money out make more people join the queue. Attempts in the wholesale market to offload exposure to suspect banks provoke others to do the same. Falling confidence can lead to collapses in market liquidity out of all proportion to the initial problem, and can drive basically sound banks out of business simply because they have to liquidate assets fast – fire sale values are always low. Unregulated banking markets are therefore prone to periodic extreme instability and for that reason banking markets are never, in fact, left unregulated. But regulation and implicit government support can itself create new problems and a new imperfection. Guarantees to depositors, implicit or explicit, created a 'moral hazard' – both for depositors and for bank managers. Why care whether your bank's lending policies are sound if the government guarantees your deposit? Why not manage your bank's lending for higher risk and higher return if the cost of one's deposits will not increase since risk to depositors is removed by government guarantee? Banking markets, like liquid financial markets, are inherently different from others.

Because both banking markets and liquid financial markets are different they can never be left unregulated. And because there are different, the case for their liberalization is more complex and more debatable than the case for free markets in other areas of the economy.

Pragmatism and religion in financial markets

Financial-market liberalization has many potential benefits. Stocks markets, as Chapter 6 argued, can be more effective mechanisms for the rapid allocation of capital to new ventures than bank finance, and the case for Europe to develop further an equity culture characterized by transparent corporate governance, explicit management targets, an extensive venture-capital industry, and an active market for corporate control is therefore a strong one. Bank ownership is undoubtedly best in private hands. Whatever the inherent difficulties of bank regulation, the problems created by corruption and bad lending policies in state-owned banks throughout the world have been worse. Long-term capital-investment flows are undoubtedly beneficial and those will only occur where exchange-control rules support repatriation of profits. Well-developed derivatives markets have a role to play in risk management in mature economies. The issue is not therefore the general case for a movement towards liberalized financial markets; it is the need for a pragmatic rather than religious approach to the question of which markets, how and when.

Bad liberalization has had its costs even in developed economies where the special-case character of financial markets has been clearly apparent. The benefits of the deregulation and privatization of the last two decades in telecoms, airlines and electricity are clear and close to undisputed. But in both the US and the UK the impact of deregulation in retail financial services remains debatable. America's botched deregulation of its savings and loans institutions, with inadequate attention to the dangers of moral hazard and interest-rate mismatch, ended up costing the American taxpayer over $150 billion. Sleepy old mortgage banks which had served their communities adequately for decades were freed to invest in speculative real-estate ventures, lost spectacularly and the taxpayer picked up the bill. The UK's equivalent deregulation had less disastrous effects, but the unanticipated macroeconomic consequences of mortgage-market competition played a role in generating the boom of 1987-9 and thus the subsequent bust. It is a moot point whether the micro-efficiency benefits of increased competition have yet paid for the macroeconomic disadvantages. The story is now in the past, water under the bridge, but the general point that some liberalization is best done slowly and carefully remains valid.

It is in the wholesale arena and in respect to developing economies, however, that the need for a non-religious approach is greatest. For the best explanation of the financial-market turmoil of 1997-8 is that the inherent potential irrationality of liquid financial markets played at least as important a role as fundamental economic and political factors.

Fundamental internal factors were of course present. In Thailand, the initial trigger of the crash, bad bank-lending practices were key. Unhedged and irresponsible lending by the banking sector (borrowing in dollars to lend in baht to real-estate companies building in an oversupplied market) created a major potential for disaster. This was a financial-market problem but it was in a sense 'structural'. In Russia, the trigger for the second wave crisis of autumn 1998, it was fundamental internal defects which brought collapse and default, not global financial-market overreaction. The Russian state was bankrupt because it didn't have the effective power and administrative efficiency to raise taxes.

But once the crisis started, and then restarted, overshoot and contagion and liquidity run effects played an enormously important role. Foreign-exchange markets overshot – exchange rates shooting down in the initial crash periods to absurdly low levels from which they rebounded later when sentiment rather than objective facts changed. The Thai baht was overvalued at twenty-five to the dollar in June 1997, but its collapse to a low of fifty-three, followed by a return to thirty-nine, all within nine months made little rational sense. The Indonesian rupiah's gyrations were even more extreme. Between 1997 and the summer of 1998 it lost more than 80 per cent of its value, only to double in value by November 1998. Portfolio-investment flows were also irrationally volatile, the same managers who had invested without adequate attention to fundamentals in 1995 and 1996 pulling out in a panic reaction in 1997 and 1998. Contagion effects played a key role – falling prices in one market producing collapsing confidence in others deemed to be in the same category irrespective of the market's prior attitude to the latters' prospects. Because the baht collapsed in July 1997, therefore the Malaysian ringit followed, and after a delay the

Indonesian rupiah. The common factor was simply that they were all East Asian countries whose prospects the markets had previously lauded to the skies. In August and September 1998 Brazil was hit by huge capital outflows. Partly they were justified by too high an exchange rate: but they were amplified by the market perception that Brazil was the 'next Russia', a comparison simply incredible to anyone who had given a moment's thought to the gulf in economic performance and sophistication separating the two countries.

And in the final stages of the crisis, it was liquidity and confidence effects which appeared to threaten global rather than developing country-specific disaster. September 1998's Wall Street crash reflected only to the most minor extent changes in the earnings prospects of American companies and to a huge extent a self-fulfilling crisis of confidence. The danger of a further crash in Wall Street was in turn the greatest potential threat to American and European growth. If American consumers, shocked by the disappearance of some of their perceived wealth, had increased their savings rates by just 4 per cent, that would have had as big an impact on world demand as the absolute and total disappearance of the whole of the Russian economy. And the crash of Long-Term Capital Management in late September, a huge enough event in itself, threatened to be more worrying still if it generated a global 'credit crunch', banks unwilling to lend even to good-quality risks at reasonable rates for fear that others in the system were also pulling in their horns. Just because complete disaster was averted, it would be unwise for us to forget that it seemed possible. And it was possible above all because of the inherent features of liquid financial markets.

That conclusion, however, horrifies ultra-liberals because it casts doubt on the proposition that market liberalization is always and in all respects right. Their analysis of the crisis is therefore different – the causes almost entirely structural, the role of market contagion nil or very slight, exchange-rate and stock-market movements rational reactions to available information. If the Thai baht lost half of its value in five months that must have been a rational reaction to bad structural factors. And those bad structural factors are obvious for all to see – corruption, crony capitalism, non-transparent governance, bad accounting – fundamental faults requiring structural reform, the financial-market reaction a symptom not a cause.

The trouble with this explanation, however, is that it ignores two glaringly obvious facts. The first is that East Asian economies in the late 1990s were no more characterized by crony capitalism, opaque governance or corruption than they were in the 1980s or early 1990s. If those are indeed features of these economies they were as much features in 1994 and 1995 when we were all worshipping them as the wave of the future. Crony capitalism and non-transparent governance indeed seem to have more than a passing similarity to the 'trust-based implicit relationships' which only a few years before were perceived as a clue to superior Asian performance. The second fact is that the relationship between those who suffered most and those with the worst structural problems is just not there. In an Asian competition for the country most riddled with cronyism, opaque governance, bankrupt banks and bad accounting, China would be a clear winner. But China's GDP did not fall between 1997–8, it simply grew less fast, i.e. 'only' 8 per cent. China's relative stability, moreover, was crucial not only for itself but for its neighbours. A dramatic fall in China's GDP or a sudden devaluation of its exchange rate would have exacerbated the regional crisis severely. And the reason for its relative stability seems clear – China was not subject to financial-market overshoots because its currency is not convertible and portfolio capital flows are still controlled. Incomplete liberalization saved China and the region from worse problems still.[13]

Despite the protests of the ultra-liberals, therefore, the best explanation of the 1997–8 turmoil cannot fail to ascribe pride of place to financial-market overreaction. Such financial-market overreaction in turn is the real way in which globalization can conceivably hurt the economic prospects of the rich developed world. A 3 per cent rise in American and European savings rates, in response to stock-market collapses and falling confidence, has as much impact on demand in our economies as a 50 per cent collapse in our exports to developing countries. But that is the least important implication of this story, for developed rich countries have available policy responses which can largely offset such demand effects. More important is that financial-market overreaction can impose large economic costs on developing

13. During the mid-1990s China had in fact been discussing making its currency convertible, encouraged by many Western experts. And in April 1997 an IMF committee had recommended that liberalized capital accounts (i.e. full convertibility) should be a formal aim in the Fund's articles, an express and general objective of policy. See Krugman, *The Return of Depression Economics*.

nations, costs quite out of proportion to any initial structural policy mistakes. Countries faced with irrationally collapsing exchange rates and capital outflow are forced either to accept inflation or to jack up interest rates in a way which can cut activity and make a banking crisis worse. Countries seeking to regain the confidence of the markets are sometimes required to take actions with no apparent relation to the initial problem. The Asian crash of 1997 was one crisis whose roots did not lie in profligate government spending and deficits, but cutting government spending was still part of the package many in the market wanted to prescribe. Financial-market overreaction can as a result impose real economic harm on societies and on the most vulnerable individuals within them, and by doing so undermine support for the overall benefits of openness to the world economy.

Faced with this reality, what are the implications for policy? It would be wrong to imply there are easy solutions. Opening to the global economy involves both advantages and disadvantages and some of the former may be unattainable without the latter. And overall the package works: almost all of the countries of East Asia have now comfortably overtaken their pre-crash prosperity; all are far more prosperous than ten years ago. But we should at least face the reality of the disadvantages as well as advantages and seek to minimize the former, not deny their existence. Four implications follow.

The first is that those dry technicians of the world financial architecture still have an important job to do. Offshore financial institutions which escape regulatory oversight can introduce dangerous systemic risk: financial markets must always be regulated, but since we have no world government some can escape the net; that remains a vitally important issue. International bank supervision, especially of currency exposures, is vitally important and needs continuous improvement. The debate on what is called 'private-sector involvement' is a crucial one: too often the private sector can emerge scot-free from financial crises – effectively underwritten by the IMF and other inter-governmental support mechanisms; the moral hazard thus created is an open invitation to irrational exuberance when markets, lending volumes, and currencies are on the up. Presidents and prime ministers may have forgotten the issues on which they opined so urgently in autumn 1998, but they need to preserve some of their attention and political will to ensure that the technicians can deliver the improvements required.

The second is that we need an open mind on capital-market liberalization. The benefits and costs of free capital movement are debated, but one conclusion seems clear – there is a big difference in the balance of pros and cons between direct investment and portfolio investment. Foreign direct investment, whether it be organic development or acquisitions of existing companies or of assets being privatized, is beneficial in almost every respect. It brings with it new technology, new management techniques and often indeed higher environmental standards and better workplace safety. It is also more stable. Foreign direct investment in Asian emerging countries fell only 10 per cent between 1996–8, from $55 billion to $50 billion, but portfolio investment and bank-lending went, on IMF estimates, from an inflow of $49 billion in 1996 to an outflow of $104 billion in 1998. While the case for free movement of long-term capital is therefore overwhelming, the case for total and immediate liberalization of short-term flows is far less clear. Chile's restraints on short-term inflows were always attacked by free-market true believers as a heretical divergence from the creed, but the Chilean authorities argue persuasively that they played a key role in reducing Chile's exposure to the financial contagion which swept Latin America in the 'tequila crisis' of 1994–5. Malaysia's post facto imposition of controls on capital outflows in summer 1998 is open to far greater criticism in principle – allowing free inflows but then restricting outflows is a breach of trust. But it has not been one which, despite dire warnings, has prevented the Malaysian economy from bouncing back at almost exactly the same pace as the IMF's favourite pupil, Korea. The free-market creed says liberalize all capital flows; and the case for eventual liberalization is strong – mature developed economies gain benefits from liquid equity markets and are robust enough to deal with the volatility. But we should be more pragmatic and less religious about the pace of liberalization.[14]

---

14. We should also be less arrogant in our dismissal of local financial leaders making judgements in difficult circumstances. In August to September 1998 Donald Tsang, Financial Secretary of Hong Kong, used the reserves of the Hong Kong Monetary Authority to intervene massively in the Hong Kong stock market which he believed was being deliberately sold short in a complex attempt by hedge funds (in some cases the most misnamed funds in financial history) to force a devaluation of the Hong Kong dollar. He was roundly attacked by free marketeers for this infringement of the canon: Milton Friedman called the policy 'insane'. Two years later the avoidance of a crisis devaluation of the Hong Kong dollar looks to have been one of the factors which helped to contain the contagion, and the Hong Kong Monetary Authority has made a huge capital gain.

The third implication conversely is that in one key respect some countries should liberalize more, removing restrictions on foreign competition in domestic banking markets. Such participation – whether via organic growth of newly licensed operations or the acquisition of existing banks – is a specific form of foreign direct (rather than portfolio) investment, and a particularly valuable one for two reasons. First, because foreign banks bring with them skills in risk management and credit analysis often undeveloped in local institutions. Second, because their participation helps cut systemic risk, reducing the danger that a local credit crisis (e.g. Thailand's property crash or the Russian government's debt default) in turn cripples a large proportion of local banking capacity. Well-capitalized international banks can keep lending to good credits even in a generally collapsing economy; local banks, with less diversified portfolios, are often unable to do so since they are themselves bankrupt or close to it. Limits on foreign competition in the Russian banking market, for instance, have made the Russian economy more vulnerable to shocks than Poland's, where foreign stakes in local banks were deliberately encouraged. Economic nationalism – the still lingering notion that there are economic 'commanding heights' which must be nationally controlled – can be as much a threat to sensible policy as a slavish commitment to liberalization in all markets immediately.

The fourth implication is that we need a pragmatic rather than religious attitude to currency regime. Fully convertible and floating exchange rates are not always best. And there may well be a case for preferring fewer currencies or currency blocs across the world. The reason why is rooted in this chapter's earlier discussion of market imperfections.

Fewer currencies better?

The economic case for multiple floating-rate occurrences is that they act to offset imperfections in other markets. If all other markets acted in the perfectly rational and self-correcting fashion described by perfect market theory, we wouldn't need multiple currencies and we would dispense with them simply to get rid of the hassle.[15] In particular,

---

15. One very bad argument made by opponents of currency unions and fixed-rate

floating-rate currencies compensate for imperfections in labour markets. If competitive conditions in specific sectors change (through new technology, changing consumer demand, new supplies of raw material or whatever) that can require that real wages in a country exposed to those sectors need to fall. But nominal wage rates are sticky – they do not easily fall to market clearing levels. So necessary downward adjustments in real wages can sometimes be more easily achieved via currency devaluations than by actual wage cuts.

The case is theoretically strong, but it depends on one crucial assumption – that foreign-exchange markets are rational, that they actually move in the direction and to the extent required to bring real wages into a new equilibrium. If instead they oscillate irrationally, overshooting equilibrium values by significant amounts and for significant periods of time, then far from helping to offset imperfections in other markets they can make the situation worse. If the real circumstances require devaluation but the exchange rate actually revalues, that increases rather than decreases the burden of adjustment on inflexible labour markets. Almost every serious economist accepts that foreign-exchange markets are to a degree imperfect and irrational for the reasons inherent to any liquid financial market – the disagreement is simply about to what degree.

The choice between fixed and floating exchange-rate regimes therefore essentially comes down to a judgement on which markets are more imperfect. It can be illustrated by a simple matrix (Figure 10.2). The vertical axis represents our judgement on labour-market imperfection – from totally flexible to highly inflexible; the horizontal our judgement on the foreign-exchange market, from rational and smoothly adjusting to irrational and subject to significant overshoots. If your beliefs put

---

regimes is to say that interfering with the exchange-rate price is to deny the market, that it is 'exactly like fixing a price for any other product' since an exchange rate is 'a price like any other'. In fact more than any other price, exchange rates are not 'prices like any other' since they do not need to exist and we choose how many exist. Market theory tells us that efficient markets require the existence of prices for all products we actually consume and for all inputs needed in production processes. Currencies fall into neither of these categories. Instead currencies are essentially 'numeraires' or measuring rods required to express other prices and to act as stores of value which can be exchanged for real goods and services. Multiple currencies – i.e. multiple measuring rods – are not inherently essential or desirable but can be appropriate because other markets are imperfect.

Figure 10.2 Fixed versus floating exchange rates – a balance of market imperfections

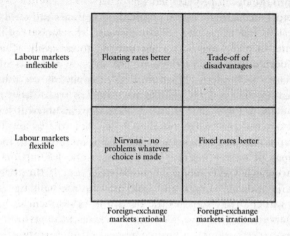

you in the bottom left-hand corner your policy choice makes no difference – you are in a beautifully perfect world in which all markets are perfect: you might as well have one currency to get rid of bureau de change hassle but the decision is really no big thing. Those in the top left corner will prefer floating rates; those in the bottom right fixed rates and currency unions. If you are in the top right, you have a difficult choice and you need to decide precisely where in that quadrant reality lies. Most sensible people are in the top right box – aware that choice of currency regime involves a difficult trade-off between two imperfections, two sources of potential economic harm.[16]

The trade-off is extensively debated and its optimal resolution depends on specific circumstances. This book can only touch the surface of that debate. But it seems likely that whatever the optimal balance, changes in the world economy have shifted it in the direction of fixed exchange-rate regimes. This does not imply one world currency but

---

16. In fact the definition of the vertical axis involves a simplification. Ideally it should reflect the flexibility and efficiency of all relevant markets, not just labour markets. But labour markets are usually the most important to the trade-off.

perhaps a smaller number of currencies and currency blocs than exist today.[17] One factor certainly pushes us in that direction and is general to the world financial system; another may do so but is specific (at least for now) to the developed rich world.

The general factor is increasing trading volumes in liquid financial markets. This rise in trading activity increases the dangers of irrational overshoots – on the matrix we are moving to the right. Transaction costs in foreign exchange markets are not only low but also falling as a result of new technology. Liberalization of capital flows is increasing the percentage of total FX trading unrelated to trade flows and thus increasing the danger that exchange-rate movements will be disconnected from the real wage misalignments they are meant to offset. Market volatility and contagion effects seem, moreover, to increase as the number of interconnecting markets multiply. Interaction between foreign exchange and equity markets, between principal and derivatives markets, confidence surges and collapses in one spilling over into another, was the truly striking feature of the 1997–8 crisis. The world financial system may be unstable simply because the number of different interconnections is now too large: financial instability appears to be a cumulative (and perhaps more than linear) function of the number of liquid markets involved. Removing one source of potential instability may therefore be essential, and currency instability is by far the best

---

17. Some opponents of currency unions claim that anyone who favours European currency union (or any other specific fixed-rate regime) must be in favour of one world currency. This is as fatuous as accusing an opponent of monetary union of wanting to break up all existing currency unions (such as the UK's) into as many currencies as possible – a currency for every county or street or person. The optimal size of currency union depends on a balance of two forces. One argues for larger blocs but becomes steadily less important the bigger the bloc already in place; the other argues for smaller blocs and becomes more important the bigger the size already achieved. Thus, the bigger the existing currency union the lower the marginal benefit from exchange-rate fixity available from further expansion: EMU has already reduced the external trade sector of Eurozone economies by 60 per cent (from 30 to 11.5 per cent of Eurozone GDPs) and it has thus already eliminated 60 per cent of the volatility disadvantage – making it wider still can give only marginal additional benefit to existing members. But the wider we make it the more severe the economic management problems created by a one-size-does-not-fit-all interest rate. A move from European national currencies to the euro can thus be beneficial even if a further move to a world currency is not.

candidate for removal. Freely moving stock-exchange prices and freedom of most capital flows are inherent to the market economy in a way that multiple currencies are not.

The second factor is far less certain, a hypothesis for consideration rather than a clearly established fact. It follows from Chapter 2's analysis of the structure of the economy, from the tendency in richer economies for inherently local activities (such as face-to-face services) to account for an increasing share of the total economy. The more that economic activity in any region is both inherently local and inherently similar to that in other regions (the same increasing role of education and health and leisure services, etc.) the less likely that exchange-rate movement is required to offset competitive trends and shocks which depress that region's economy. Some opponents of a European currency union argue the historical case that the southern states of the US would have been better able to cope with the long decline in cotton prices if they had had their own specific currency in the post-civil war period. But no region of Europe has a dependence on any one industry remotely comparable to that of the southern states on cotton in the late nineteenth and early twentieth centuries. Nor indeed does Britain or any other European country now have concentrations of sectoral-specific employment comparable to those which existed when coal mining, steel, shipbuilding and agriculture still employed huge numbers of people in 1950 or even 1970. In the increasingly service-intensive economy, regional unemployment is increasingly specific to small sub-regions – specific housing estates and towns – and increasingly explicable by cycles of social deprivation, attitude and skill levels, not by sectoral factors. And the latest technology shock we face – accelerated productivity growth in interactive activities through the application of ICT – will have a roughly proportionate effect across all sectors and regions, unlike, say, productivity improvements in coal mining and the emergence of alternative fuels which had regionally concentrated effects. In the rich developed world exchange-rate adjustment to offset changes in sectoral competitiveness and relative price may be becoming less necessary as well as less dependable. Certainly many of the historical examples cited in favour of floating currencies are irrelevant to economies in which the nature of regional specialization is changing.[18]

---

18. The other argument against wide currency areas – the problems created by a one-size-does-not-fit-all interest rate – however, are not necessarily reduced by this

The first factor certainly suggests a general case for fewer currencies. In Europe it provides the macro-case for monetary union, reinforcing the micro-supply-side case set out in Chapter 6. In developing countries the specific implications are less easy to decide and intensely debated. Increased capital flows and potential instability can indeed be used to argue for more floating rather than less, since they almost certainly make intermediate solutions such as managed floats increasingly untenable. The emerging consensus in favour of 'corner' solutions – either fully floating regimes or rigidly fixed (currency boards, dollarization or monetary union) – seems to be well founded. But if the precise solutions are uncertain the need for a pragmatic approach is clear. Full convertibility of the Chinese renvimbi is by no means an obvious short or medium-term priority. Hong Kong's successful defence of its dollar parity is not an offence against free-market theory. And discussions of dollarization (such as in Argentina) or of the potential for regional monetary unions, however difficult to achieve in practice, should not be seen as rejections of free-market economics, but as potential means to produce a more efficient market result.[19] [20]

Pragmatism not dogma is therefore required if we are to manage global capitalism to best effect. Pragmatism in management of the

---

changing shape of the economy. Regionally specific property booms are still possible even if regions have become more similar in sectoral terms. Potential problems arising from one interest rate across Europe are in fact a much better argument against the euro than the assertion that floating exchange rates are needed to offset changes in sectoral demand.

19. Senior figures in the administration of the new President of Mexico – Vincente Fox – have, for instance, raised the issue of whether Mexico should pursue a 'dollarization' strategy as a logical next step after NAFTA, or even (though this of course requires US co-operation) a full monetary union with the US.

20. Given the problems created by overvolatile and overshooting exchange rates there are also at least theoretical attractions in James Tobin's proposal of a tax – levied at a very low rate – on foreign-exchange transactions. While it is unlikely that this would make more than a trivial difference to the likelihood of overshoots (since potential speculative gains would be massively larger than any sensible tax rate), it would probably prove a less distortive tax than most alternatives (e.g. labour and profit taxes). The key arguments against it are therefore not theoretical but simply the impracticality of enforcing it and deciding on division of revenues in a world of multiple nations and governments.

global financial system, and both pragmatism and realism also in domestic liberalization. The Russian example illustrates this point.

Russia – market fundamentalism rampant?

The market economy is the best mechanism we know to deliver economic prosperity. It is also, over the long term, a stimulus to the emergence of governments founded on democratic and liberal values – its rule-driven nature ultimately incompatible with arbitrary rule. Following communism's catastrophic failure – economic, social, political and environmental – Russia's aspiration to become a market economy was inevitable and wise.

Russia's transition to the market became therefore in the 1990s the central project of the country's elites. But also a central project for global capitalism, for the institutions of the world financial order, the IMF and World Bank, and for the army of consultants and bankers who flew in and out of Moscow to provide advice and finance – myself among them between 1992 and 1995. The project was pursued with vigour if not always with consistency. The currency was made convertible, prices were liberalized, stock markets were created, and, above all, a massive privatization programme put in place. Large IMF and World Bank loans supported the programme, the former on conditions outside normal IMF rules, any doubters swept aside by the West's clear geopolitical interest in preventing a nuclear power falling into either anarchy or belligerent nationalism.

But at the end of August 1998, the project appeared to be in tatters. The Russian government could not pay its debts, income per capita was well below 1989 levels, and the privatization programme was perceived to have created a corrupt oligarchy rather than modern business owners and managers. Living standards for the poor had declined sharply, but for a few rich had shot skywards, the death rate was up, the birth rate sharply down, the population falling by three-quarters of a million per year. For those convinced that capitalism provides easy answers it was a sobering sight.

What went wrong is and will be extensively debated. To John Gray, Russia's collapse into 'anarcho-capitalism' was the inevitable consequence of market fundamentalism and of the simplistic notion that the free market is a universal model which can be applied irrespective of historical traditions and cultural context. To true believers in the universal model the fault lay instead in insufficient radicalism, the absence indeed of the 'shock therapy' applied so successfully in Poland under Balcerowicz's tenure at the finance ministry. Whether a better way was actually possible can be debated too. Russia entered the transition process without several of the advantages other countries, such as Poland, enjoyed – no folk memory of a pre-war market system, no extensive private agriculture to provide at least some experience of the market, no large and entrepreneurial diaspora of émigrés keen to do business in the old country, but continued unaffordable aspirations to great power status and a huge military-industrial complex needing to be downsized. But at the very least, and despite these disadvantages, the Russian experience should give believers in free markets pause for thought. For in several ways Russia's path to the market may have been made more painful and less successful by market principles too simplistically applied, by an overconfident free-market ideology. And what was lacking above all in Russia was not a commitment to free-market principles but a state strong and efficient enough to make the market economy work.

Between 1992 and 1996 Russia executed the most rapid privatization programme ever seen, first via the granting of 'vouchers' to managers, employees and the general public, then via the 'loans for shares' scheme of spring 1996, state assets sold at low prices to commercial banks in return for loans to cover the budget deficit. The philosophy was that faster was more important than better, that it was more important to get assets in private hands quickly than to ensure that those private hands were clean and competent. Private ownership, the theory was advanced, would automatically in time create good governance and management competence. But speed had inevitable consequences. It increased the relative power of the well-financed and well-connected, who could buy assets cheap and establish monopolistic positions. And it generated a culture of capitalism focused on asset trading and asset stripping rather than on restructuring and building businesses: it taught Russian people, both the winners and losers, that 'get rich quick' through corrupt connections is what capitalism is all about. No privatization process in transition countries can be perfect but other economies managed it better and slower. In Poland privatization of the existing big industrial assets was not an early priority, in China it still is not. Instead, capitalism (or whatever the latest euphemism the Chinese authorities prefer) has been built bottom up, privatization of small and medium companies and organic growth of entirely new businesses providing economic dynamism and the experience of business creation before opportunities for asset plays become available on a large scale. In Poland and Hungary, moreover, a deliberate policy of encouraging foreign strategic investors was pursued, particularly in the banking sector, as a means to ensure the transfer of foreign technique and management skill. Private ownership is not sufficient: managerial competence matters a lot too and governments need to think through how they are going to foster or import it.

In the financial system too the early stages of reform were years of simplistic beliefs and misplaced focus. Rapid moves to foreign-exchange convertibility and initially to a floating exchange rate won plaudits from the world financial community, and arguably were inevitable: Russia simply lacked the social control levers to pursue a non-convertible policy of the type that works in China. But convertibility made massive capital flight easier and exposure to financial-market speculation has clear disadvantages for fragile emerging economies – short-term shocks are much more difficult to manage if some basic dynamism of real activity has not yet been established. More obviously wrong because more avoidable was the sequence and priority of financial-institution reform. Moscow in the mid-1990s was buzzing with consultants, many paid for by Western taxpayers, advising on how to establish stock exchanges and commodity exchanges, how to do futures trading, and how the new Russian banks could make profits from wholesale trading. It should have been buzzing with consultants trying to reform Sberbank, the giant savings bank with branches throughout the country, and helping to build small business lending institutions able to lend secured against well-defined property rights. A liquid capital market capable of attracting foreign portfolio investors was seen as a priority; the enforceable property rights and coherent tax rules required to attract long-term strategic investors were in reality much more important. Liquid stock markets and futures trading have their roles in a developed market economy but in the development of capitalism Credit Agricole and the Midland Bank come sequentially and logically before MATIF and LIFFE. Reverse the sequence and you have a sophisticated economic superstructure based on foundations of sand.

The Russian story can thus be seen as one of market economics too simplistically applied. The counter-argument, well set out in Andrei

Shleifer and Daniel Treisman's book *Without a Map*[21] is that the political context and constraints need to be understood and that if Russia performed worse in transition than Poland or Hungary that was simply because the problems were inherently more difficult. The initial voucher privatization programme was imperfect but to Shleifer and Treisman it was the only way rapidly to create a constituency of support for private enterprise and to deal with the reality that enterprise managers and workers were in a position of de facto power. Huge concentrations of economic and political power, which had to be bought off through compromises in each step of the reform process, were the inevitable consequence of an economy so dependent on natural resources concentrated in specific regions. The financial superstructure of commercial banks was parasitic and disconnected from lending to the domestic economy but the key fault lay not in a simplistic commitment to market principles but in the political reality of nationalism and vested interests – the reformers never had the political power to allow the foreign entry into the banking system (whether as licensed competitors or as acquirers) which in Hungary and Poland played a crucial role in the development of a competent and relevant banking industry. And those who believe there was a better alternative – a gradualist path to capitalism from the starting point not of Poland or China but of the former Soviet Union – need to face the fact that the countries which shared that background and which pursued the gradualist route – the Ukraine and Belarus – did worse still.

Above all, however, Shleifer and Treisman's analysis identifies the vital failing of the Russian reform process as the inability of the central state to raise adequate taxes. The essential cause of the 1998 collapse indeed was that capitalism's beneficiaries were unwilling to pay the tax required to support even a greatly reduced state and that the state lacked the technical competence, but even more importantly the political power, to design a simple and enforceable tax code and to structure a workable fiscal relationship with the regions. The result was that necessary functions of social amelioration had to be pursued via distortive special deals and implicit subsidy flows (e.g. through permitted payment delays to keep bankrupt companies afloat) rather than through the state provision of a minimum social welfare net; and that even after

---

21. Shleifer and Treisman, *Without a Map – Political Tactics and Economic Reform in Russia* (MIT, 2000).

massive cuts in government expenditure, the central government could not pay its debts.

The irony for those who believe that free markets flourish with minimal states indeed is that Russia's path to capitalism was above all undermined by the inadequacy of the state. Poland was the star transition economy with government revenues reasonably stable at around 44–47 per cent of GDP, Russia the disaster with the size of the state shrinking from 44 per cent in 1992 to 34 per cent in 1997.[22] Recovery since 1999 has been heavily reliant on action to at last create a more effective tax-raising system.

There were no simple answers in Russia but there are important lessons. Flourishing market economies cannot be created overnight by privatization alone, irrespective of political and economic traditions, of management competence or of whether commercial relationships are law-based and enforced. Nor can they be created without an effective state power. Probably in Russia's case, the conditions for a smoother transition were simply never present, however carefully designed the process. But we should at least have known that in advance. That on the whole we did not reflects a dangerous tendency among many of capitalism's proponents to see free markets as a universal and an easy answer, rather than an answer which is generally but not always right and certainly not easy.

* * *

To John Gray, writing in his book *False Dawn*, the crisis of 1997 to 1998 proved that the whole edifice of global capitalism was unstable, destructive of countries' rights to independent economic and social choice, and bound to end up 'swallowed into the memory hole of history'. To demonstrators in Seattle and Prague the inherent evils of global capitalism are equally apparent. Some of the specific points which Gray and those demonstrators make are worthy of a hearing and a considered response. The global capitalist system is not a faultless

---

22. Ibid, Table 5.2. Figures are for total revenues in consolidated budgets federal and regional, including ex-budgetary funds, such as pensions. The decline of Russian federal tax revenue was even more dramatic, falling from 18 per cent in 1992 to 10 per cent in 1997.

route to a win-win nirvana: not all markets are or ever will be equally rational, efficient and therefore beneficial, and government's role in making modern capitalism socially workable and stable remains as essential as ever. Markets are means by which we achieve desirable ends, not ends per se, and if many people around the world fear global capitalism, the intellectual arrogance of market fundamentalism – the assertion that markets are the answers to everything – has played a role in provoking a response. Where the left-wing pessimists go wrong, however, is in their pessimism. The global capitalist system is not perfect but it is a better route to increased living standards than any other we know. And its undoubted imperfections can be reduced if we recognize them and develop specific responses to them rather than wring our hands in despair.

11. Free Trade, Mercantilism and Morality

Global free trade incites strong passions. To anti-capitalist protesters on the streets of Seattle and Prague it is a threat to jobs and the environment, and the World Trade Organization (WTO) a threat to the rights of individual countries to make their own social and cultural choices. To market fundamentalists it is a creed to which no exceptions must be allowed, and attempts to burden the WTO with irrelevant social issues threaten to unleash waves of protectionism which will make us all poorer. To business lobbyists exports are the lifeblood of our economy and in a harsh competitive world governments must support their fight for market share undeterred by sentimental qualms about the arms trade, the environment, or human rights.

But though the conclusions are different, the three groups often share a common starting assumption – that the economic prosperity of the developed world depends crucially on its trade with emerging economies, and that further trade liberalization serves the vital economic interests of the already rich and developed economies. In fact, however, that is largely untrue – rich developed economies are far less reliant on global trade with emerging economies than conventional wisdom assumes and have only little to gain from further trade liberalization.

That does not mean that free trade is undesirable, for freer trade has the potential to make *developing* countries both richer and, indirectly, more democratic; and free markets are less likely to cause environmental harm than any alternative development path we know. But it does carry implications for *how* we pursue trade liberalization and for how we balance commercial interests versus ethical and political concerns. It implies that our approach to trade liberalization should be pragmatic not religious, recognizing trade-offs and exceptions required to make capitalism serve wider social objectives. And it implies that moral principles which ought in any case to guide our conduct involve less economic sacrifice than some business lobbyists often suggest.

From wrong assumptions indeed, some opponents of global capitalism derive specific policy conclusions with merit. But the required policies should be seen for what they are, not rejections of globalization but actions designed to gain its full potential benefits.

Free trade and the already rich

The idea that rich countries depend crucially on trade with poorer ones unites left-wing anti-capitalists and business lobbyists. For both indeed it serves a useful polemic purpose. To one side capitalism is unjust because it is based on the exploitation of poorer nations; to the other, access to emerging markets (of undoubted value to individual companies) is also so vital to national economic interest that governments must sacrifice all other concerns in its pursuit.

But the figures set out in Chapter 1 tell us clearly that this is not true. The vast majority of the economic activity of developed economies is either not traded at all or traded with other economies of roughly equivalent income. Only 6 per cent of the GDP of the rich developed economies (Japan, the US, the EU and Australia/New Zealand combined) is traded with the rest of the world outside those countries, and that percentage has fallen not risen in the last twenty years despite further trade liberalization. The implication drawn in Chapter 1 was that the threat of imports from low-income countries is not the key driver of change within developed rich societies, and that most of the changes we see in mature economies would be occurring even if globalization was not occurring, even indeed if the rest of the world did not exist. The corollary must also, however, be true: the role of exports to the developing world is less crucial to rich economies than often asserted, and the role of exploitative terms of trade between rich countries and poor raw material producers can make only a very small difference to rich country incomes. What matters to the prosperity of the already rich world is that they achieve rapid productivity growth in all sectors of their economy, traded and non-traded alike. Growing trade flows with the rest of the world are of secondary importance.[1]

---

1. We should note one exception to this story of the relative unimportance of trade flows outside the developed world: this relates to the input of oil and other raw materials used not as final consumption products but as inputs to industrial processes. Raw material imports from the developing world in total account for only about 2–4 per cent of developed world GDP, and as a result even very large

The economic interest of the already rich economies in further trade liberalization is as a result fairly slight. For the trade which matters most to them – trade amongst themselves – is already largely free of tariffs. And the key drivers of further prosperity growth relate to the structure of their internal markets and the quality of their infrastructure and skills. More intense product and capital market competition within the European single market has more potential to drive European productivity growth than the small remaining opportunities which further trade liberalization would create for comparative advantage-based specialization between Europe and the emerging economies. The decisions which the US takes on education, public R&D funding and long-term social-security reform will have more influence on America's economic prospects than any amount of trade liberalization. NAFTA has been easily the biggest driver of the growth in America's trade intensity during the 1990s, but most economic studies suggest that its total impact on US GDP per capita, though undoubtedly positive, has not exceeded 0.1 per cent.[2]

The figures and logic are close to undeniable and on the whole indeed are not denied. But despite that, trade liberalization is a major policy priority for several developed countries and sold to electorates as a key potential driver of increased national prosperity. Washington DC employs so many trade specialists in the government, in think tanks, and in lobbying firms (both for and against) that trade liberalization could be considered a business activity in its own right. No US administration or EU Commission would ever say that trade liberalization was not high on its agenda. Anti-capitalists can be forgiven for assuming that it is in the vital economic interests of rich countries to force trade liberalization on the rest of the world since it is in terms of

---

changes in terms of trade can have only a small impact on developed world GDP, e.g. a doubling of raw material prices reduces GDP by 1.5 per cent (less than a year's growth). But sudden changes of price of raw materials used as a key production input – above all oil – can have more significant shock effects on developed economies. This does not, however, challenge the separate assertion that improved market access to emerging economies for developed country exports and investments is now of slight importance to developed country growth.

2. Krugman, *Pop Internationalism*, Chapter 10: 'The uncomfortable truth about NAFTA'.

a national economic interest in further liberalization that politicians usually speak. Three factors explain this disconnection between relatively small economic interest on the one hand and major activity and rhetoric on the other. The first is business lobbying: improved trade or investment access into emerging countries can matter a lot to individual companies even if its potential benefit to the overall national economy is small, and Western governments respond to vested-interest business lobbying, particularly in America. Second, administrative inertia: liberalizing trade between developed countries *was* very important and the administrative machines which achieved that liberalization are in place, and staffed with trade experts anxious to employ their skills. And they might as well – trade liberalization is far from the highest priority for developed rich economies, but 0.1 per cent of US GDP is still a very big number in absolute terms. The third is a mixture of fear, altruism, geopolitics and ideological faith: fear that if liberalization does not roll forward it could be rolled back; altruistic belief that trade liberalization is good for developing countries; geopolitical concerns that key allies must be strengthened (the real justification for NAFTA); and simple ideological attachment to free trade as an end per se, an article of faith which keeps trade specialists motivated amid the mind-numbing detail which trade negotiations entail.

All or some of which might be good reasons for still pursuing trade liberalization. But the fact that those are the motivations has implications for *how* developed nations should pursue the trade-liberalization agenda. From the developed country point of view we are not liberalizing because we have to – there is no economic imperative which must overwhelm all other considerations.

The case for global free trade

Contrary to the assertions of both anti-capitalists and business lobbyists the economic case for further trade liberalization is based on its benefits not for the already rich world but for developing economies. For the overall case for trade liberalization remains strong and the arguments advanced against it overstated or simply wrong.

Trade liberalization can still play a major role in developing country growth for two reasons. First, because some developing economies, unlike developed, still have economic structures severely distorted by their import trade barriers; second, because they face sectoral-specific restrictions on exports to the developed world which are significant barriers to their growth, even though relatively unimportant in their effects on developed-economy structures. Estimates suggest that the economic benefits to the US from NAFTA may be only 0.1 per cent GDP, but the same estimates calculate the benefits to Mexico at 4 per cent of GDP.

The first factor means that reduced trade barriers between developing countries can be of major economic benefit, and indeed that easier trade access into developing countries from developed can have benefits to the importer. The creation of the Mercosur trading bloc in Latin America in 1991 (linking Brazil, Argentina, Uruguay and Paraguay with Chile as an associate member) has had an effect in stimulating trade growth and industrial restructuring analogous to that unleashed by the European Economic Community in the 1950s. Brazilian trade (exports and imports combined) grew over two and a half times between 1991 and 1998. Further intensification of that bloc towards not just a free-trade area but a single market could deliver more benefits. Those benefits come in two forms. First, there are the classic trade theory benefits of comparative advantage-based specialization and economies of scale. Prior to the 1990s the countries of Mercosur were each duplicating capability in every industrial sector rather than developing strong capability and clusters in areas of specific strength. Second, and in the long run perhaps more important still, there are the benefits of market contestability: companies enjoying tariff protection, especially in relatively small national economies with few domestic players, tend to enjoy monopolistic positions which remove incentives to efficiency. Trade liberalization, along with the domestic-liberalization measures which usually accompany it within the package of 'globalization', is one of the factors which has helped unleash the accelerated rates of economic catch-up enjoyed by emerging economies in the last twenty years.

Trade liberalization could deliver further economic benefits if the developed economies were willing to liberalize access to economic sectors which are still significantly protected and/or subsidized – heavy industries such as steel and shipbuilding, textiles and, above all, agriculture. Most industrial products from emerging countries now enter developed countries at tariff rates sufficiently low to make little difference to competitive conditions, and in most industrial sectors in developed economies subsidy levels are minimal. But through a mixture of direct subsidies, price support, tariff protection and export subsidy all three major developed economies – Europe, the US and Japan – massively distort the world market in agricultural produce. Total European subsidies amount to $126 billion per annum, total American to $97 billion.[3] Removing those subsidies and allowing more open trade would deliver a small but useful benefit to rich-country GDP – small simply because agricultural sectors in total only amount to 2–3 per cent of developed economies, and lower prices for agricultural products can therefore only deliver a benefit equal to a percentage of this percentage. But they would considerably ease the economic transition and growth prospects of countries with large potential agricultural exports, such as Mexico, Argentina, Egypt or the countries of Eastern Europe. On the streets of Seattle in autumn 1999 Jose Bové, the leader of French agricultural protectionism known for his attacks on McDonald's restaurants, was present alongside demonstrators convinced that rich-country capitalism is denying the developing world its economic birthright. They are strange allies in opposition to liberalization. Anyone with an altruistic concern for global economic equity should favour more trade liberalization in agriculture not less.

The case for developing a rule-driven approach to international trade – the hallmark of the WTO – is also strong. Opponents of both right- and left-wing persuasion, protectionist and green, view the WTO with intense suspicion. To some it is the enemy of Third World development, preventing the EU from allowing preferential trade access to bananas from poor African and Caribbean countries. To John Gray in *False Dawn* it is an instrument of ideological warfare – 'the role of the WTO is to project free markets into the economic life of every society'. To some American senators of isolationist persuasion it is an intolerable infringement of US sovereignty, an international body granted the right to find the US guilty of bad practice and to instruct it to desist. But in fact its existence and rule-driven approach have profound international and domestic political advantages. Internationally it creates a robust set of arrangements for avoiding the tit-for-tat escalation of trade disputes. The danger of 1930s-style tariff wars – which played a major role in exacerbating the Great Depression – is very slight, but it is good to have rules that diminish it further. And criticism of the WTO for the undoubted injustices that can occur in international trade is like shooting the messenger and the referee; it also

---

3. OECD quoted in *The Economist*, 24 June 2000.

fails to ask what the alternative is. The 1999–2000 banana dispute excites justifiable concern: a large US company has been able, because of its political influence in Washington, to persuade the American government to pursue a case in which the American national economy has minimal interest and which is to the detriment of some very poor banana-producing countries, and the WTO, because rules are rules, has permitted the US to impose sanctions (for instance against cashmere sweater imports) in pursuit of its legal rights. A sorry story. But the alternative is not no US sanctions, but that the US would have simply imposed whatever sanctions it wanted, possibly more severe, with no referee to limit its actions to proportionate response. You don't have to like every decision a referee makes, or every word of the rulebook, to realize that a world governed by agreed rules and procedures is likely to be more pleasant than one governed simply by economic power.

The long-term domestic implications of the WTO rule-driven approach may, however, be even more profound and beneficial. For there is a complex yet powerful symbiosis between the rules essential for the effective workings of market economies and the rules which constrain arbitrary state power. Chapter 10 made the point that one of the delusions of Russia's transition to capitalism was to imagine that a market economy can simply be created overnight irrespective of the inherited political and legal context, of the degree of respect for property rights, of the existence of courts capable of enforcing contracts, of the ability of the state to raise taxes in an efficient and non-arbitrary fashion. The converse also applies. The rules and procedures of capitalism have a spin-off benefit in their political effect. Once you are required by WTO obligations to respect commercial intellectual property rights, it becomes subtly more difficult to treat intellectual rights of expression in a completely arbitrary fashion. Once the commercial property rights of foreigners need to be respected, laws and court systems develop which make it more difficult to treat domestic property rights arbitrarily. Martin Lee, the leading campaigner for greater democracy in Hong Kong, has noted: 'participation of China in the WTO would not only have economic and political benefits, but also serve to bolster those in China who understand that the country must embrace the rule of law'.

A final charge made against free trade and globalization more generally is that it causes huge environmental destruction: trade negotiations should therefore include an environmental dimension. The latter proposal, as we shall see later, has merit, but the charge is confused nonsense: a prime example of right conclusions from wrong assumptions.

Severe environmental damage is occurring throughout the developing world but the reason is simple – people are getting more numerous and they are getting richer. As they get richer they want the cars and larger houses and electricity supplies and opportunities for travel that we in the West already enjoy, and that produces pollution and countryside destruction. The early stages of economic growth always have environmental consequences. England is not as green and pleasant a land as when it had a population of 8 million people living a primarily agricultural life. Unless the proposition, therefore, is that low-income countries should remain in a state of aesthetically pleasing poverty, we face environmental problems with which we have to deal. But all the evidence is that globalization, while not providing magic and sufficient answers, helps rather than hinders us in that challenge. The environmental record of Soviet-era planned economies pursuing autarkic rather than open-economy approaches to growth was catastrophically worse than that of the capitalist economies. Multinationals investing in emerging countries almost always introduce higher environmental standards than domestic industry because they have technologies available for transfer and because they increasingly respond to the pressure of home country public opinion. And rapid growth in prosperity and in the global flow of ideas will be a key driver of the most important development of all for the environment – a stabilization of world population. In every single society where three conditions are achieved – prosperity, a high level of women's education and a supply of contraceptives which are cheap, effective, safe and free of moral stigma – birth rates fall towards replacement rather than rapid growth levels. The faster globalization spreads prosperity, demand for skilled labour and ideas, the faster world population will stabilize.

Trade liberalization as tool not dogma

The overall case for trade liberalization (as for the wider process of 'globalization') is therefore strong, but it is strong today because of its economic benefits for emerging economies, not because the developed world has a pressing economic self-interest in further steps to wholly free trade. The case, moreover, should be based upon the pragmatic observation that trade liberalization *in general* has beneficial effects,

not on a philosophical certainty that it is always and in all circumstances the only true path. Japan used tariff protection to no economic
disadvantage and arguably to some advantage during its economic
take-off in the 1950s and 1960s, Korea the same in the 1960s and
1970s. Nor should trade liberalization and globalization more generally
be seen as a panacea. It is not a win-win process, there are losers as
well as winners, and there are major global problems, such as environmental ones, which while not created by globalization are not magically
cured by it.

Three implications follow for how we should pursue trade liberalization. First, that some exceptions to liberalization should be accepted,
not condemned as heresy. Second, that we should recognize trade
liberalization as an inherently political rather than simply economic
issue. Third, and as a result, that we need to accept that other global
issues – environmental in particular – will have to be increasingly
integrated with discussions of trade.

We do not need to liberalize all markets and perhaps there are some
we should not. The French government has always insisted that some
cultural services – films and television programmes in particular –
should be exempted from the principles which increasingly govern trade
in other sectors – zero tariffs and no quotas, no subsidies, no restrictions
on foreign ownership and no requirements for national content. Its
argument is that it needs the freedom to interfere in these markets to
defend cultural identity, that these are not 'goods like any others but
instead essential determinants of people's cultural identity'.[4] The pros
and cons of this French attitude in terms of its influence on culture can
be debated. But what cannot is the fact that if the French want to take
this attitude the economic disadvantage to others is so minuscule as to
be simply not worth the argument. The impact on American GDP of
American film companies gaining totally free access to the French
market would be as near nil as makes no difference. And yet French
cultural exception is treated as a perpetual bone of contention in trade
negotiations, a sort of totem pole deeply indicative of one's ideological
commitment to the pure and beautiful principles of free trade. The issue
should simply be dropped. Arguing over it only provokes a suspicion in
French public opinion of the wider benefits of globalization and diverts

---

4. Pierre Moscovici, French Minister of European Affairs, interview in *Le Figaro*,
autumn 1999.

attention from really significant issues, such as agricultural protection. And maybe, after all, the French cultural nationalists have a point.

The second point concerns more the need to admit reality than actually to change policy. The primary interest of the major developed economies in further liberalization of world trade is political not economic. The West's greatest strategic interest in China's accession to the WTO lies not in the economic benefits to the US and European economies of a more open Chinese market but in the closer engagement of China in a rule-driven approach to global governance. NAFTA was sold politically to the American people on the basis of the economic benefit to the US, but its fundamental rationale lay in America's geopolitical interest in the economic prosperity of Mexico and in the success of Mexican governments friendly to capitalism and the US. The brutal truth is that the economic prosperity of Africa has only limited potential to make Europe richer through increased trade, but that Europe has a major long-term interest in doing whatever it can to foster African prosperity, because otherwise it faces to its south a major potential source of instability and uncontrolled migration.

In practice this reality of limited economic self-interest already affects Western policy. The fundamental reason why the Seattle WTO conference in autumn 1999 'failed' (i.e. failed to result in the launch of a new tariff-reduction round) was not the demonstrations in the streets but that Western nations do not have a pressing economic self-interest in further trade liberalization, and that the developing world is unwilling to accept some aspects of the West's increasingly political agenda. That reality, however, will increasingly have to be accepted. Western policy towards trade liberalization is going to stop being a rather technical thing driven by trade-policy experts negotiating on behalf of their business sectors, confident that trade access for their companies has a major economic benefit, that 'what is good for General Motors is good for America'. And given that our interest is primarily political rather than economic we cannot, even on the grounds of self-interest let alone altruism, exclude political issues – human rights, the environment, labour standards and the economic development of the poorest nations – as illegitimate considerations in trade-policy debates.

The case for some integration between environmental issues and trade issues in particular is strong and will get stronger for two reasons. The first follows from Chapter 9's discussion of the competitiveness effects of environmental regulation. The point was made there that competitiveness concerns are more valid in respect to environmental regulation than in respect to labour regulation or general taxation because of the sectorally specific nature of environmental constraints. If Sweden cares to have higher taxes and government expenditure levels than Korea, or more generous maternity-leave rules than Portugal, that has no consequence for any meaningful concept of competitiveness. But a specific industrial sector might suffer a competitive disadvantage from environmental rules applied in Sweden but not elsewhere, and this could produce both a small prosperity effect (through changes in the terms of trade) and a harmful environmental effect (polluting industries moving to countries with low standards). As a result there is an overwhelmingly strong rationale for pursuing environmental regulation at European Union rather than national level and an inherent incompatibility indeed between a truly complete single market and competing environmental standards. The same logic must to a degree apply also at global level: free trade without any environmental rules creates the danger that polluting industries will migrate to countries with the lowest standards, that there will indeed be some sort of race for the bottom.

That rationale, moreover, is reinforced by the interconnected nature of the global environment. Fishing stocks, acid rain and global warming are all inherently international issues: polluting and stock-depleting activities by one country affect the self-interest of all others. And such issues are inherently plagued by the problem of free riders: for any individual country the best purely selfish policy is to let others make the economic sacrifices to achieve the environmental benefits all will enjoy. Our ability to deal with such issues will be limited if we reject in principle the possibility that at some stage trade sanctions would be applied against countries refusing to join internationally agreed approaches. The complexities of how we integrate these agendas are immense, but unless we at least start down that road, we should not be surprised if people who care for the environment perceive free trade as a threat not an opportunity.

On labour standards the case for linkage is less clear, both because low labour standards in one country have less implications for others than lower environmental standards, and because the dangers of a labour agenda being a Trojan horse for simple protectionism are greater. High labour standards (minimum wages, trade-union rights, etc.) applied across the board do not create a competitiveness problem (though they may create a separate and wholly internal problem of inflexibility). Global trade, moreover, is probably not the most important driver of rising inequality or job insecurity in the developed world – internal technological developments look far more likely to be the culprit. And low pay cannot be seen as unfair competition: if developing countries cannot compete in international trade on the basis of initially low pay, earning profits and generating savings which are then reinvested to increase productivity, we are denying them a key route through which they will eventually become high-income countries. But equally the concerns of public opinion about the more extreme issues of basic labour standards – prison labour, child labour, debt-indenture-based dependency, lack of association rights – cannot be simply swept aside. For if the West's fundamental interest in further trade liberalization is now political rather than economic, we cannot ignore the political issues which public opinion defines. Trade negotiators cannot talk the tough language of representing their national interest in trade-offs with other countries and exclude the possibility that national consumer preference might wish to see that trade-off take the form of increased access to Western markets negotiated against action on basic human rights. As Leon Brittan, the former EU commissioner for external trade and in general a rigorous free-trader, put it: 'labour standards and other apparently domestic political issues are now the legitimate concern of the WTO because they are the concern of our constituents'.

Environmental, labour and other political issues are bound therefore to be increasingly entwined with trade debates. How we do that in institutional terms is by no means clear. Simply landing these issues on the WTO may well not be the answer: it could simply undermine the WTO's ability to deal competently with its existing important functions, without creating any real potential for progress. Separate institutions, on the environmental front in particular, may be required. And the political sensitivities will need to be handled with extreme care. The biggest opposition to linking trade and the environment and trade and labour comes from developing countries who believe these links will be used as an excuse for protectionism: the most virulent antipathy to the demonstrators of Seattle and Prague came from emerging-country leaders who believe that privileged people in the developed world want to deny poor countries their chance to enjoy the economic opportunities the rich already enjoy. But increasingly the world will need to find mechanisms to discuss common environmental, labour and human-rights concerns. And increasingly over time trade rules may have to entail some environmental conditionality.

That conclusion horrifies the ideologues of free trade and the mercantilists of business lobby groups. The former treat the introduction of other contaminating issues as a heresy against the free-market creed. The latter still dream that specific company interests in improved market access will continue to be the primary and preferably sole driver of developed-country trade policy. But in both camps also there are those who accept the logic of the linkage but oppose it out of fear – fear that the whole framework of global free trade will 'unravel' if new complications are introduced, fear that trade liberalization will go backwards if forward 'momentum' is not maintained.[5] That is surely, however, the wrong concern. The benefits of free trade between developed countries are sufficiently clear, undisputed and embedded in myriad business relationships that any likelihood of a serious step backwards towards protectionism is very, very small. And the benefits of globalization are sufficiently apparent in the rising prosperity of emerging nations for rejection by them to be extremely unlikely also. We should have enough confidence in the overall case for globalization and market economics not to scare ourselves with a bogey that it is all about to unravel. The danger instead is the opposite: if the institutions of global governance do not evolve to deal with people's concerns on issues other than the narrowly economic, that will undermine support for globalization and will prevent us indeed from gaining its full benefits. Free-market capitalism at national level required the development of the active state in the late nineteenth century to manage its rough edges and to reap its maximum benefits; global free markets will increasingly need to be balanced by other forms of global dialogue and agreement if it is to deliver the benefits of which it is capable.

For that is what the evolving agendas of trade and environment and trade and labour are really about – not a rejection of globalization but its logical development. The anti-capitalists are wrong. We do not need an environmental dimension because globalization is destroying the

---

5. The doctrine of 'momentum' is fundamental in trade-policy circles. Throughout Bill Clinton's presidency a common refrain was that Clinton had been a failure on trade issues because he had been unable to persuade Congress to grant him 'fast-track authority' (a legal ability to make trade deals which cannot get bogged down by subsequent Congressional amendment). If you asked the trade experts what economic benefits would be achieved with fast-track authority, however, the answer given was almost always couched in terms of its symbolic importance and of 'momentum', rather than in terms of any specific trade deals or of income or employment effects.

environment – the global free market is already better than the only available alternatives. But globalization provides us with an opportunity to pursue the aim of global environmental responsibility as well as economic prosperity and we should not be afraid of pursuing that opportunity. We need to widen the scope of globalization to do better still, not reject globalization because we are heading for disaster.

Mercantilism and morality: why we don't need to sell arms to brutal regimes

Free trade is in general a good thing. It is beneficial because it allows countries to concentrate on economic activities where they have a comparative advantage, because it allows them to achieve economies of scale whether in industrial plants, companies, or in terms of clusters of related activity and, perhaps most importantly, because it increases the contestability of markets – increasing the intensity of actual or potential competition, and thus stimulating productivity improvement and product innovation. Britain and Europe are both better off because we have largely free-trade policies both internally and externally.

Because we have free trade we export. Exports are therefore in turn a good thing – they enable us to buy imported goods and services more cheaply (i.e. with a smaller commitment of resources) than if we produced them internally. But to many people exports seem more than simply the inevitable implication of free trade and the necessary price for desirable imports – they seem to be the lifeblood of the economy, the essential source of wealth on which all other sectors rely. And because they are so vital, especially in the harsh competitive world of global competition, it follows that governments must subsidize and promote them, and that our vital economic interest in exporting must overwhelm any political, ethical or environmental concerns. British trade ministers should be the 'head of sales of UK plc', US commerce secretaries should spearhead America's overseas sales drive; export credit guarantees must be competitive with those of other nations; and arms sales restrictions must not be allowed to threaten British jobs, or demonstrators in favour of Tibetan rights be allowed near visiting Chinese dignitaries for fear that British economic interests in China will be harmed. Competitiveness constrains us to reject squeamish consideration of ethical concerns.

The premise of these conclusions is, however, both wrong in theory and wrong in its empirical description of the world. For as Chapter 1 outlined, the very concept of competitiveness is close to meaningless at the level of a large national or continental economy, and the reliance of the developed economies on their trade with the less developed world is far less than usually supposed, and not rising. The key to the prosperity of developed economies lies in productivity growth in all sectors of the economy, traded and untraded, and in the intensity of trade, capital and idea flows between them and other economies of roughly equal wealth and, fortunately, similar values and geopolitical interest. The ultimate case for ethical conduct is that it is right to act morally, but the good news is that the cost of ethical conduct in the trade affairs of developed countries is massively less than often supposed. We are not condemned by some economic necessity in a harsh competitive world to sell arms and instruments of torture to dictatorial regimes, or to stay silent about human-rights violations, and our attainable rate of employment will not be reduced if we cease doing so.

The impact of tighter restrictions on arms sales is exactly analogous to the impact of a sectorally specific environmental regulation or tax considered in Chapter 9. Just as an energy tax applied in the UK but not elsewhere would lead to a shift in Britain's sectoral mix towards less energy-intensive sectors, so tight restrictions on arms exports to brutal regimes would (unless compensated by increased domestic defence expenditure) lead to a sectoral shift from arms production to other sectors of the economy. That would have (as with the energy tax) no implications for the long-term level of employment, but it would have two effects – a prosperity effect through changed terms of trade, and a transitional employment effect as labour shifted from one sector to the other. In the case of the energy tax those effects are potentially sufficiently large to provide a strong argument either for the special treatment of energy-intensive traded sectors or, preferably, for a pan-European approach. In the case of arms sales, fortunately, the total scale of the effects would be very small. That small scale has been spelt out by Sir Samuel Brittan in a number of articles in the *Financial Times*.[6] Total British arms sales were in the region £3.5 billion in 1998. Of these something like 25 per cent go to other NATO countries. The

---

6. See Samuel Brittan, 'There Is No Need to Sell Arms to Odious Regimes', *Financial Times*, 9 December 1999, and 'The Hidden Cost of Promoting Arms Sales', 6 January 2000.

remainder represents about 0.4 per cent of GDP, some to dictatorial and unstable regimes, but some to stable democracies and natural allies such as Australia. Even, however, if all the non-NATO sales were stopped, and even if the alternative export industries which would emerge over time to pay for desirable imports enjoyed terms of trade only half as favourable, the total diminution in GDP would be just 0.2 per cent, about six weeks' GDP growth, national income in, say, mid-February 2001 reaching what it would otherwise have reached at the end of December 2000. And against that effect has to be weighed the large direct and indirect subsidies which the arms trade enjoys, estimated at £228 million in a recent study.[7] In terms of the prosperity effect this is a moral decision we can afford to make.

In terms of transitional employment effects it is more difficult but still not insuperable if handled gradually. Arms exports employ about 130,000 workers: the majority of these, in almost any scenario, would keep their jobs to support arms sales to allied and acceptable regimes. And well over 3 million people leave and join the unemployment register every year, a natural feature of a dynamic market economy in which changes in jobs and skills are key to productivity growth and essential responses to changing consumer demands. If we choose to make this transition, it would be a far easier one than many others our economy has experienced in the past or is now experiencing – the decline in mining, shipbuilding and dock labour, the perpetual restructuring of our automobile industry, the shake-out of jobs in retail financial services.

The best arguments against tight controls indeed have nothing to do with economics but instead are military – the need for an adequate supplier base to support our military capability in a still very dangerous world. But if that is the argument we should face it head on, with greater integration of the European defence and aerospace industries to achieve economies of scale and with increased defence expenditure in Britain and across Europe. The policy of defending our essential long-term military capability by selling arms to Iraq, which then used those arms in military action against us, was strategic lunacy as well as economically unnecessary. It was also, of course, immoral.

7. Stephen Martin, 'The Subsidy Saving from Reducing UK Arms Exports', *Journal of Economic Studies*, 26: 1 (1999).

Managing global capitalism

Global free trade cannot be pursued outside the context of other global issues, and Britain's (or preferably all of Europe's) export policies should not be pursued without a moral concern for human rights and for the uses to which our exports will be put. To some free marketeers and to some business interests these assertions will be anathema, an attack on market economics. But they are not. For market economics should never be dogma, but a set of propositions about how we best achieve desirable ends. And free markets should never be thought sufficient in themselves to meet the full range of human aspirations: they have to be managed and moderated, domestically and inter-nationally, to offset imperfections, to achieve inherently collective rather than individual objectives, and to deal with distributional issues.

Criticisms of the simplistic creed of global free markets are therefore well founded. But the case is badly made when expressed as a general-ized attack on globalization and capitalism, and when based on a confused belief that the West's prosperity rests on the exploitation of poorer nations. The assertion that our prosperity depends crucially on unfair trade, indeed, plays into the hands of mercantilists telling us that any constraint on their freedom to export will seriously damage our prosperity. And the case is badly made too, when the undoubted benefits of globalization are denied, and when the whole process of globalization is presented as a sort of conspiracy by which Western interests pursue ideological aims. Globalization has occurred because the collapsing costs of transport and communications increase the intensity of the links bound to exist between different people, and because governments throughout the world have observed that open-market economies produce in general better effects than autarkic and planned ones, in both economic and political terms. But global free markets are not a magic panacea: they are neither perfect in their own direct effects nor do they provide automatic solutions to the other naturally arising and global consequences of prosperity, such as environmental damage. Global free markets are therefore not enough. We need to supplement global free markets with mechanisms to cope with other global problems. We need to manage capitalism at the global level as well as at home.

12. The Third Way or Liberalism Reborn?

'We are all socialists now,' said Sir William Harcourt, one of Gladstone's chancellors of the Exchequer reflecting, in his case with very considerable exaggeration, the growth of collectivist ideas in the late nineteenth century. 'We are all capitalists now' would be, with considerably less exaggeration, the equivalent today. Communism has collapsed, socialism has ceased to believe in itself: even the Chinese government is building a capitalist economy under the cloak of a successive series of euphemisms. The market economy is triumphant more completely and across more of the world than ever before.

Overall that is a good thing because capitalism is the least bad system we know for organizing economic activity and for underpinning personal liberty. The market economy provides a more efficient mechanism than planning ever could for co-ordinating the independent activities of numerous individuals and firms: it works better than the alternatives because its acceptance of individualist motivation reflects an important dimension (but not the only dimension) of human nature. And because capitalism as an economic system relies vitally on respect for the law and for property rights, and on a limitation of arbitrary state power, it tends also to foster a law-based society which respects individual political freedoms. Emerging economies which embrace global capitalism are now achieving faster rates of economic catch-up than ever seen before. More people are getting richer faster than ever before in human history: and their material wealth is not just the worthless 'consumerism' attacked by anti-capitalists; it is better health-care and sanitation, better food and longer lives, the freedom of personal mobility to travel to new places – the things people in the West already enjoy. The anti-capitalist protesters of Seattle and Prague are, in their blanket attacks on global capitalism, simply wrong.

But capitalism pure and simple is not a sufficient answer to all problems. Proponents of a market economy should neither believe that it is perfect nor capable of being made perfect. The case for the market economy rests instead on the empirical observation that it is a better system for the organization of society than any available alternative and that its undoubted deficiencies are to a degree capable of amelioration provided we design our actions on the basis, not of a belief in a perfect world, but of an empirical understanding of the imperfections which necessarily exist.

Capitalism pure and simple, unmoderated by the intervention of the state, suffers from four key deficiencies.

First, it does not ensure an acceptable distribution of economic opportunities or results. Theory tells us that a market economy will tend to maximize the size of the economic cake and real world evidence confirms that it does that more effectively than any other system. But market theory tells us nothing about the distribution of property rights with which different people will or should participate in a competitive market, or whether the outcome in terms of relative income will be acceptable. Conservatives and market fundamentalists – believers in the status quo either as an end per se or as a principle of ultra-free-market theory – seek to avoid the distributional issue in two ways. One is to assert the philosophy of property rights proposed in the seventeenth century by John Locke. To Locke property, above all land, becomes rightfully owned because it is 'mixed with labour': the homestead of the American frontier, as it were, becoming rightfully private because of the labour which went into its creation.[1] But as a justification for property rights in the modern world this is woefully inadequate. It ignores the fact that key forms of property are in limited supply, that they are positional, and that as a result John Locke's own qualification of his theory of property – that there should be, after private appropriation, 'good and enough left over' for others to appropriate – simply does not apply. It fails to provide a coherent resolution of debates over inheritance – whether I should enjoy property rights because my ancestors mixed *their* labour with real assets. And it fails to recognize that the actual pattern of inherited wealth reflects not just labour mixed with assets in previous generations, but also a sizeable dose of political power, criminality and unscrupulousness mixed in as well.

Recognizing these realities, conservatives tend also to present a second defence, the assertion that the market is so powerful an economic device that it will generate prosperity for all, that we do not need

---

1. Even in this example, of course, native Americans quite reasonably question the purity of the process.

to worry about equality because we will all be rich, and that unfettered inheritance and the lowest possible income taxes will themselves increase the size of the cake. But these arguments also do not hold in the face of reality. For there is no necessary reason to believe that the distribution of income arising from the free flow of market forces will result in acceptable absolute incomes for all, nor that the common panaceas – such as investing in skills – can be relied upon to release us from that reality. However much we increase individual skills, people with the lowest relative skill will have the lowest-paying jobs, and market theory tells us nothing about whether the incomes they derive from those jobs will be adequate or acceptable. Poverty, moreover, for the reasons discussed in Chapter 8, must be defined in a part relative as well as part absolute sense. Relative income affects absolute standard of living.[2] And while taxes above a certain level will reduce incentives, there is no good case for believing that zero inheritance taxes on larger fortunes deliver economic advantages or that a 30 per cent top rate of income tax rather than a 40 per cent rate will increase prosperity. In the face of the facts of poverty and disadvantage, whether within rich societies or globally, we cannot simply avoid the issue of distribution. In terms of philosophy, there is no escaping the need to consider – as in John Rawls's theory – what our attitude to inequality would be if we did not know in advance our allocated set of genetic, environmental and financial inheritances.[3] And in terms of practice, the state should be to a degree redistributive. The philosophy this book proposes is one of redistributive market liberalism – not market liberalism pure and simple.

The second deficiency is that totally laissez-faire markets will either not provide at all, or will underprovide, inherently collective goods. Consumer preference includes the desire for high-quality public space, for clean air and rivers, for the beauty of countryside, for cities free of pollution and excessive traffic congestion as much as for new washing machines and more restaurant meals. And if these collective goods are underprovided, true prosperity will be less than measured GDP suggests. To provide these goods and services, we need a state taxing and spending and regulating. To decide on the level of those collective

---

2. See Brittan, *The Poor Need Not Always Be With Us*.

3. John Rawls, *Theory of Justice* (Oxford, 1972).

goods we need to express our preferences through political processes as well as through our private purchase decisions.[4] To make sensible decisions about long-term issues like global warming, where present market prices fail to reflect not only unmeasured environmental benefits but even narrowly economic but far distant costs, we need determined government action at national level, at European level, and increasingly through development of the institutions and mechanisms of global governance.[5]

Third, some markets act, for inherent reasons, in imperfect ways – ways so different from the perfect models of market theory that they cannot be relied upon even to maximize the size of the cake. Labour markets are inherently 'sticky' because of the social nature of employment relations. Housing markets do not clear in the fashion described by pure market theory, but display both irrational upward volatility in booms and irrational downward stickiness in depressions.[6] And more

---

4. What we must not assume, of course, is that political processes are themselves perfect: indeed they are inherently subject to imperfections and failures closely analogous to those which affect markets. Voting processes reflect consumer preferences imperfectly, and can deliver both harmful 'winner takes all' results and simple incoherence (sequential majorities for endless changes of direction). Lobby groups which support specific expenditures more passionately than the majority of people oppose them, can produce 'ratchet' effects which increase the size of the state above a reasonable reflection of popular preference. Governments have imperfect information as well as markets. All these factors are among the reasons for massively preferring capitalism to socialism in general: all provide a rationale too for clearly stated limits on the size of the state (e.g. 'government expenditure not to exceed X per cent of GDP') of the sort discussed in Chapter 8. (See Samuel Brittan, *Participation Without Politics – An Analysis of the Nature and the Role of Markets*, Institute of Economic Affairs, 1979.)

5. Market failures, of course, can often be attributed to an insufficient definition of property rights, e.g. the lack of a right to clean air. Analytically this is a useful insight; and in a few specific instances practical policy implications can follow (cf. the discussion in Chapter 9 of emissions trading and of full compensation for house price effects). In many more cases, however, the only practical offset to market imperfection is through politically determined and general decisions (e.g. to have high fuel taxes to reflect environmental damage), not through the actual definition of property rights.

6. See Krugman, *Peddling Prosperity*, Chapter 8, 'In the long run, Keynes is still alive'.

generally, for the reasons which Keynes explained in the General Theory, economies have no natural or automatic adjustment mechanisms to ensure rapid recovery from general demand deflation. Keynesianism was abused and misused in the pursuit of inappropriate objectives in the 1960s and 1970s, but Keynes's central propositions remain as important as ever. Correctly applied, as in Britain's current fiscal and monetary-policy arrangements, they produce a good result; ignored, as in Japan in the 1990s, they produce unnecessary depression.

Liquid financial markets meanwhile are imperfect in a different fashion – inherently subject, as Chapter 10 described, to volatility and irrational overshoots, and liable when they do overshoot to cause macroeconomic damage such as the Asian crashes.[7] Faced with that reality, liberalization of short-term liquid financial markets should not be either a priority of reform processes or a universal principle: taxes on liquid transactions – such as James Tobin's proposal for a tax on foreign-exchange transactions – should not be dismissed out of hand. And the debate about floating or fixed exchange rates should be approached dispassionately rather than with ideological fervour.

Fourth, self-interested economic motivations are not the only motivations which govern human behaviour and that has vital implications for the application of market principles to areas such as health and education. Healthcare markets indeed would be subject to inherent imperfections of the sort described above, even if motivations were entirely self-interested. The asymmetry of information and knowledge between doctor and patient destroys the conditions for efficient market operation in the way described by Kenneth Arrow in a classic article.[8] Doctors and patients interacting in a purely self-interested fashion may well tend to overprovide services – doctors expanding their own business and covering themselves against liability claims, patients claiming to the maximum against insurance policies whose premiums they have already paid. America's healthcare industry – absorbing 14 per cent of GDP in total, compared with 10 per cent in France or Germany but without commensurately superior results – is not an efficient solution,

---

7. Liquid financial markets may also have a tendency to attract more skilled human resources than is socially optimal, for reasons explained in Joseph E. Stiglitz, *Whither Socialism?* (MIT Press, 1994) and in W.J. Baumol, *Entrepreneurship, Management and the Structure of Payoffs*.

8. Arrow, 'Uncertainty and the Welfare Economics of Medical Care'.

even on narrowly economic terms. But the complexities of human motivation suggest further reasons to treat healthcare and education as special cases. For the natural reaction of patients and doctors to the existence of their asymmetric knowledge has been to treat medical service not as a consumer good like any other, but as a 'profession' – to construct the relationship between patient and doctor on the basis of trust rather than contract, and to respect among healthcare providers motivations other than the purely commercial. Those non-commercial motivations – what the Swiss economist Bruno Frey has called 'intrinsic' rather than 'commercial' motivations – may be vital to the attainment of an optimal result.[9] And there is a danger that the introduction of overt commercial relationships cannot be achieved without eroding those intrinsic motivations. The challenge in healthcare may thus be to introduce the allocative efficiency benefits of market organization while not undermining the 'ethos' of public and professional services which is in this special case important to an optimal overall result. It is wrong and, as Sir Samuel Brittan has said, 'merely childish' to reject without examination the possibility that internal market structures may be needed to drive value for money in health-service administration:[10] But it is wrong also to imagine that healthcare can be simply a market like any other, and that the complete marketization of patient/provider relationships would be desirable. The market economy is a tremendously powerful tool to achieve ends, but it should not pretend to reflect the full range of human motivation and aspirations.

Capitalism is therefore not enough. Capitalism needs to be moderated by the state, by the political process. Laissez-faire capitalism needs to be made human and efficient through redistribution, through the adequate provision of collective goods, through correctly focused Keynesian demand management, through the recognition that not all markets can be perfect, and through respect for motivations other than those of commercial self-interest. European capitalism should continue its evolution towards freer product, capital and even labour markets – but should not reject as either undesirable, unnecessary or unattainable

9. Bruno S. Frey, *Not Just for the Money: An Economic Theory of Human Motivation* (Edward Elgar, 1997).

10. See Samuel Brittan's essays on 'Liberal Individualism' in *Essays, Moral, Political and Economic* (1998) on this and many other arguments relevant to this chapter.

the objectives of social inclusion which have been the distinctive ends of the European social model. And in the design of the interventions and offsets by which those ends are achieved, the guiding philosophy should be rooted in empirical observation of what works, not in a belief in 'the market' as a creed or ideology.

Belief in the market as a creed is, however, an important strain in current political and economic life, and one strongly allied in Britain with virulent Euro-scepticism. Many ultra-liberals and conservatives will therefore disagree strongly with the conclusions and indeed the philosophy of this book. For to the true believer in the market, this talk of exceptions and special cases, of market imperfections and market failures, and of the need for a strong state, is just dangerous backsliding towards a socialist past. And, as with any creed, there is no empirical evidence that will lead the true believers to doubt their beliefs. If the economic and social consequences of New Zealand's experiment in radical market reforms appear to the empiricist to cast doubt on any simplistic belief in unmoderated markets, to the true believer it simply proves that New Zealand did not liberalize enough. If Britain's relative economic performance has been adequate rather than stellar, more deregulation must be required. If the Asian crashes look like the consequences of financial market overreaction, that must be because we haven't looked hard enough for the structural causes which are bound to lie in inadequately liberalized markets. If the theory and correlations presented in Chapter 8 cast doubt on the proposition that lower taxes are always limitlessly better, there must be some other correlations which will confirm the true believers in their certain belief. Market fundamentalism appeals because it gives to its true believers that absolute certainty which so many intellectuals who should have known better derived from Marxism between the 1920s and 1970s. A notable feature of meetings at Britain's more right-wing think tanks, or of debates on European issues with representatives of the ultra-liberal right, is the presence of young men in particular who seem to glow with that inner warmth of absolute conviction which one saw on the faces of Marxist students in the 1960s and 70s.

Even indeed in the writing of one of the most powerful and respected exponents of market liberalism, that tendency to seek absolute certainty was always present. F.A. Hayek's The Road to Serfdom is rightly recognized as a brilliant criticism of the intellectual fallacies and delusions which helped foster totalitarianism. But as Ralf Dahrendorf has written, Hayek's contribution to liberal thought is undermined by his 'fatal tendency to hold another system against socialism . . . one complete in itself and intolerant of untidy realities'.[11] Hayek's condemnation of the 'fatal conceit that man is able to shape the world around him according to his wishes' is, in its rejection of any collective ability to improve the world, a statement of dogma. Karl Popper's insistence in *The Open Society and Its Enemies* that we should both reject the idea of a utopian reordering of the world but pursue the possibility of piecemeal improvement based on empirical observation of causes and effects, is a far better and more humane guide to action.[12] [13]

---

11. Ralf Dahrendorf, *Reflections on the Revolution in Europe* (Chatto & Windus, 1990). F.A. Hayek, *The Road to Serfdom* (first published in 1944), *The Fatal Conceit* (Routledge, 1988).

12. Hayek himself quotes with approval Popper's commendation of 'piecemeal improvement' but makes it apparent how very limited he perceives the potential for such action. His comments on the need to evolve the approach to property rights, for instance, are focused entirely on the technical issue of whether intellectual property (such as copyright and patents) should be owned as exclusively as real property, rather than on the more fundamental issue of our attitude to the distribution and inheritance of property rights. While Hayek actually wrote an essay on 'Why I am not a Conservative', his rejection of even the most limited ability to guide the 'spontaneous order' of capitalism via political interventions makes him essentially conservative. (See *The Fatal Conceit*, Chapters 4 and 5).

13. John Gray notes in *False Dawn* another striking similarity of Marxism and extreme free-market belief, the delusion that it is possible to create an economic system so productive that all issues of scarcity and distributional conflict are resolved. 'Free marketeers tell us that the unprecedented productivity of a rational economic system will remove the sources of social conflict. Marxists used to assure us that socialist planning would make scarcity a thing of the past.' Perversely, however, Gray uses this to condemn both Marxism and market fundamentalism as utopian expressions of an enlightenment tradition of rational utilitarian thought, contrasting them with the more organic particularities of culture and nation. But as Karl Popper described in *The Open Society and Its Enemies*, utopianism of any sort – the belief that there is any perfect world – is not an expression but a perversion of the Enlightenment tradition, and Marxism, while superficially rationalist in its approach, was actually in its eventual development part of the 'revolt against reason' through which people tried to replace the lost certainties of religious faith with a secular ideology. Market fundamentalism serves the same psychological need for absolute certainty, the desire for a model absolutely and universally applicable. Both Marxism and market fundamentalism reflect an unwillingness to accept models as simply tools to understanding and as means to achieve ends, and

Simplistic market fundamentalism can be as dangerous to sensible market liberalism as was Marxism. Capitalism can have a human face, but governments and political processes need to ensure that it does. Those who oppose that necessary role in the name of a pure and beautiful theory, or out of the simple vested interest of the already rich, will undermine both capitalism's long-term success and its popular support.

The issue remains, however, of *how* we should pursue those interventions and offsets which make capitalism serve the full range of social objectives. Two different approaches can be pursued – the classical liberal model in which wider objectives are achieved through the constraints of tax and regulation within which individuals pursue their own self-interest, or the 'communitarian' or 'stakeholderist' model which seeks to humanize capitalism by asking of individuals and corporations that they take upon themselves a wider set of responsibilities. The latter is currently fashionable. The former is a sounder base on which to pursue desirable, economic and social objectives and on which to build a robust respect for individual liberty.

The classical liberal model accepts Adam Smith's essential insight, that it is possible and indeed necessary to construct a model through which individuals are, in their economic activities, 'led by an invisible hand' to promote the good of society. This model involves accepting that individuals in their career and in their business life, and companies in their business operations, will normally act in a self-interested fashion, pursuing their own profit, rather than trying themselves to ensure that their own specific actions serve desirable social goals. It does not deny the possibility and desirability of altruism; it simply seeks its expression through different means. For in this model wider social objectives are achieved not by the actions of firms or by individuals in their economic activity, but through the laws and taxes to which they are subject. Redistribution is achieved through the income and inheritance taxes which people pay and through benefits paid, not through firms deciding to pay 'just' wages. Collective-services provision is achieved through the tax-financed expenditures of the state and through its regulations; environmental objectives through regulation and appropriate taxes; market failures are compensated by specific

---

a refusal to accept the disciplines of empirical observation, trial and error, and piecemeal rather than utopian change, which Popper rightly commended.

interventions. Nor does the model preclude the possibility that many companies may in pursuit of long-term self-interest take many actions – to train workers, to build brands, to create trust among consumers – which are at the expense of short-term profit and which look (and indeed are described in annual reports) as if serving a wider set of societal or stakeholder objectives. And the model certainly does not preclude the possibility that the individual who competes successfully and self-interestedly in the marketplace, and who enjoys the fruits of success, may in his or her political life give expression to wider social concerns, choosing, for instance, to vote for political parties which support higher rather than lower levels of redistributive taxation. But the philosophical approach of the model is clear; and it is that of the classical liberal philosophers. It takes the essential insights of Adam Smith, Jeremy Bentham and John Stuart Mill, but applies them to achieve a wider set of objectives than Smith and the other founders of classical liberalism originally believed legitimate.[14]

It is for that liberal philosophy that this book argues. For that

---

14. The founders of classical liberalism should not be castigated post facto for failing to envisage or support the range of objectives to which their model could be put, or indeed for having failed to develop ethical approaches – for instance to poverty – outside the range of predominant contemporary belief. It is, however, worth noting that from the very earliest stages of the development of liberal thought, the foremost thinkers were aware that their model could and should accommodate a wider set of constraints than those laws and regulations required for the efficient conduct of commerce. Adam Smith recognized a state role in 'erecting and maintaining certain public works and certain public institutions which it can never be for the interest of any individual or small number of individuals to erect and maintain' (i.e. collective goods). Bentham set out numerous exceptions to a generally laissez-faire rule. And John Stuart Mill, above all, in his *Principles of Political Economy* and in his four chapters on socialism (originally intended as part of a larger work), recognized clearly that the classical liberal model of laissez-faire had to evolve to deal with the issues of externalities, collective-goods provision and distributional equity. 'In attempting to enumerate the necessary functions of government, we find them to be considerably more multifarious than most people are first aware of, and not capable of being circumscribed by those very definite lines of demarcation which it is attempted to draw round them.' A philosophy of redistributive and humane market liberalization is not therefore a rejection of the insights of the early liberal philosophers – it is its logical development in the face of the complexity of the real world. See John Stuart Mill, *Principles of Political Economy*, first published in 1848.

reason many on the left, as well as market fundamentalists, will find its philosophy – far more than its specific policy conclusions – difficult to accept. For while socialism has lost the great ideological battle of the twentieth century, and most former socialists, whatever they now call themselves, accept the power of the market, that acceptance has not come easily, at least at a philosophical rather than practical level. For socialism was a creed which sought to praise and promote the intrinsic noble purposes not just of individuals but of societies as a whole: its roots were both Marxist and, in Britain, Methodist, its natural tone messianic. Socialists therefore respond uncomfortably to the prosaic rationality and empiricism of liberalism. More fundamentally still, they respond uncomfortably to the idea that we should accept the significant role of individual self-interest, even if we can demonstrate that the constraints imposed can make that self-interest serve wider social goals. The liberalism of this book is therefore likely to be opposed from two left-wing directions.

It will be opposed by those who still hanker for the role of the state as an active agent in the economy, and as an expression of some innate national or social identity. That means, unfortunately, that some potential readers in France who could agree with my specific conclusions, will reject the liberal philosophy, probably indeed dismissing unread a book with the word 'liberal' in the title. But what is striking is how rhetorical rather than substantive such opposition now is. French socialists, more than any others in Europe, may still feel the need to pay homage to the Colbertian tradition of the economically activist state: French autoroutes may still display signposts reminding French citizens of an active state role – '*ici l'état investit pour votre avenir*'. But the French state, under a socialist government, is close to completing an almost total withdrawal from the ownership of economic assets, and the de facto model to which it is moving is one in which social objectives are achieved not through the activism of state technocrats but via the laws and taxes which constrain private economic behaviour and through the public expenditures on benefits and collective goods which those taxes support.

The liberal model proposed in this chapter may be attacked more generally, however, from a communitarian or stakeholderist direction. For even many on the left who have moved far from love of the state (or indeed never shared it) feel uncomfortable with the idea of 'self-interest', however effectively constrained. They therefore hope to pursue the good society not merely through constraints, laws, taxes and the provision of collective services, but through persuading and encouraging companies or individuals to take into account in their economic decisions a wider set of objectives than those of profit maximization and self-interest. 'The balance sheet of gains and losses [to society],' writes Will Hutton, 'is much wider than the simple calculus of one firm's profitability.'[15] Companies therefore should serve the interests of a wider set of stakeholders, not shareholders alone. Companies should be encouraged to become more 'rooted' in their communities. And more widely too the good society will be achieved if people are highly conscious – in all their activities – of their membership of communities, their inherently social nature. The good society will be achieved because people in their economic as well as political lives act in a good way, not because laws, taxes and public expenditure produce a good result from largely self-interested actions.

It all sounds rather attractive. But as a guide to practical policy it is at best a cul-de-sac, at worst dangerous. It sounds attractive to ask corporations to think through the wider social 'balance sheet of gains and losses' but in practice it is an almost totally inoperable principle. Corporations can just about imperfectly identify the complex set of actions which will maximize their own profit within given constraints, but they are ill-equipped to calibrate the second and third and nth order social consequence of their actions and lack the legitimacy to make the trade-offs involved. Is it better socially to downsize rapidly to preserve the remaining business and to free up resources for work elsewhere, or to keep workers in existing jobs at the expense of the firm's long-term prospects and the productivity growth of the whole economy? That is a social decision which should be reflected in the rules which govern hire and fire, not one which directors of companies are competent to make or justified in making. The complexity of economic interactions and effects makes it impossible for companies and individuals to be the effective agents of wide-ranging social objectives, and it is for that reason that the only practical way to proceed is through the classical liberal model.[16] Adam Smith's great insight, indeed, was to identify that the complexity of economic interfaces is so great and their number so

15. Will Hutton, *The State to Come* (Vintage, 1997).

16. For a more detailed discussion of this issue see the author's Napier Enterprise Lecture: 'Shareholders, Stakeholders and the Enterprise Economy', Napier University, 8 May 1997.

numerous and each of us so dependent on the behaviour of others, with only a few of whom we could ever hope to have bonds of friendship rather than contract, that we have to construct a system which makes self-interest compatible with civilized behaviour, rather than relying on a generalized disposition to benevolence.

The stakeholder model thus collapses in impracticability. Indeed what is striking in stakeholderist writing is how limited are the actual policy prescriptions from so grand a theme – rhetoric collapsing to minimal 'voluntarist' initiatives, or to tinkering with company law, when faced with the specific question of what changes could make a difference, what actions could make individuals more benevolent in their economic behaviour. That in turn illustrates the dangers of stakeholderist and communitarian approaches. For the more that we hope to civilize capitalism by vague admonitions to corporate responsibility and communitarian ethics, the more we may be diverted from identifying and implementing those specific interventions – redistribution, collective-goods provision, or regulation – which will make capitalism more humane. And the more that governments draw business into a 'joint endeavour' to pursue noble purposes in voluntary ways, the less they may be willing to play their role as the robust definers and enforcers of the constraints under which those businesses ought to operate. The good society is delivered by a robust tension between politically defined constraints and the self-interest and animal spirits of business and entrepreneurs, and it is not always wise to muddy that division of roles.

The greatest social duty incumbent on business is to obey the laws and pay the taxes which the government imposes. Russian capitalism did not collapse in 1998 because the oligarchs failed to act in nice communitarian ways towards their workforces and local communities; it collapsed because they didn't pay the taxes due. And the self-denying ordinance which we might reasonably expect business leaders to accept as an expression of their social nature, is not that they take on themselves the burden of thinking through all the indirect consequences of their economic activities, but that they desist from using the influence which money and power can buy to oppose unreasonably the constraints which society legitimately seeks to impose. The biggest threat to America's ability to create a more humane form of capitalism lies not in the actions of individual businesses downsizing their workforces, but in a political system which gives too much influence to specific businesses opposing valid environmental and social objectives.

Capitalism flourishes within a clearly understood role for the state, as the definer and implementer of wider social objectives. It should be a limited role, eschewing in almost all cases the ownership and management of commercial assets, or strategic interventions in competitive markets based on judgements which governments are ill-equipped to make. It should be a role limited by an understanding that some level of taxes will blunt incentives, distort markets and destroy popular consent, and that too large a state generates ratchet effects which make it larger still, the state growing not to meet the desirable objectives of society but the self-interest of producer groups. But, though limited, it is a vital role, and a far more sustainable one than much current rhetoric about competitiveness, incentives and tax base erosion suggests. European welfare states are affordable if people want them. Price-based incentives to pursue environmental responsibility can and should be introduced without significantly reducing growth. Europeans can stop selling arms to brutal regimes and ignoring human-rights abuses at only minimal cost to their economies. Developed rich societies are largely free to choose their own destiny.

A partial exception to that optimistic picture should, however, be admitted. In some emerging countries, and in relation to some global problems, social choice is less easily empowered and the classical liberal model less purely applicable. Corporations in emerging countries are less constrained if the state is less effective. Global corporate responsibility is therefore a more important issue than corporate responsibility at home, and attempts to encourage it, through codes and consumer pressure, are valid attempts to compensate for inadequate state power. Free riders on the global environment, moreover, are left unconstrained by the absence of anything resembling a global government. The steady development of the institutions and rules of global governance (rather than government) should not therefore be seen as a denial of the global free market but as its necessary corollary. World trade rules and world environmental agreements cannot forever continue along totally unlinked paths.

Both domestically and internationally therefore capitalism needs to be moderated and constrained to serve wider social objectives. What is striking is how many on the left of politics lack the confidence that that is possible, how much indeed they accept the assumptions of the right that competitiveness imposes severe external constraints. In the global arena, their lack of confidence is partially, but only partially, justified; in the domestic arena in rich developed countries hardly at all. It is therefore worth pondering why many former socialists are not more confident in their assertion of a limited but still important state role, why they prefer the fuzzy rhetoric of stakeholders and communities to the more concrete robustness of a market liberalism which is also redistributive and humane.

Three reasons seem to explain this. The first is that competitiveness is a compelling delusion, the idea of external economic constraints truly believed by those who have not analysed the economics with sufficient care. The other two reasons are rooted in the practical politics and emotional difficulties of socialism's retreat. Parties of the left are keen to prove their market- and business-friendly credentials – to demonstrate clearly that their high tax days are behind them. From that follows a reticence in speaking clearly about even the more limited set of redistributive and collective objectives which non-socialist states should pursue. But parties of the left are also unwilling to let go of their sense of noble purpose, their mission to make people more caring, more individually humane. From that combination we get the strange paradox of the 'third way' – an unwillingness to say bluntly that one purpose of taxes is to support redistribution, matched by fuzzy talk of communities, stakeholders and social responsibility.

Amid the intellectual retreat of socialism, therefore, the search for the Holy Grail of the third way has been launched and continues. Seminars and conferences across the world pursue its elusive trail. Tony Blair and Bill Clinton have discussed it. Gerhard Schroeder was happy to couple it with his *Neue Mitte* (new middle). President Cardosa of Brazil is keen on it, Prime Minister D'Alema of Italy pursued its Italian translation.[17] It is a search for a position not merely equidistant between capitalism and socialism, but tangential to that well understood distinction, a new beginning, a new insight.

This book agrees with many of the policy implications which that search for a third way has inspired. The present British government was right to introduce significant redistribution through the working-family tax credit given the strong trend towards inequality Britain has faced for many years. It is right to increase public spending on Britain's

---

17. Even President Menem of Argentina once explained to me his insight that Peronism was the true and only third way, a way enjoying the great advantage that Peronism is whatever the Peronist party does – corporatist under Peron himself, close to ultra-liberal under Menem. He said it, however, with a broad smile.

National Health Service and investment in our public transport system. From Britain's position in 1997, it was desirable to shift the balance a bit towards the collective and redistributive direction. But I can see no good reason and some danger in labelling as the third way an approach which is not new but has a deep historical roots, and which is not a third way either between or tangential to socialism and capitalism, but is instead capitalism with a human face.

The fundamental issue is how to reconcile a dynamic economy and the liberating effects of individual economic freedom with the objective of an inclusive society, recognizing that totally free markets will not achieve that end. This is not a new issue and we are not the first generation to consider it. It intrigued John Stuart Mill and John Maynard Keynes. Its philosophical and political implications were explored by Karl Popper, its economics explored in depth by James Meade. It is a theme frequently present in the writings of Paul Krugman, Samuel Brittan and Ralf Dahrendorf. And in the world of practical politics it found its first expression across Europe in the social-insurance schemes and urban improvements of the late nineteenth and early twentieth centuries, and in Britain in the liberal welfare reforms of 1906–14 and in Lloyd George's budget of 1909. From the rigorous but limited principles of Gladstonianism a liberal tradition has been in a continual process of evolution, even if not always overtly called by its true name, and even if political liberals, throughout the twentieth century, were often forced by the existence of socialism into an alliance with purely conservative forces.[18] The precise policies pursued need continual fine-tuning to meet changing economic reality. But the core philosophy does not need a new name because it exists already. It is called liberalism.

18. Indeed many people happy to call themselves Conservatives with a big 'C' have been in their essential beliefs redistributive market liberals. In 1994 Kenneth Clarke, then the British Chancellor of the Exchequer in a Conservative government, began a lecture with the words: 'I intend to extol the virtues of both flexible labour markets and a strong welfare state.' (Mais lecture, City University Business School, 1994.) That is very close to the philosophy of this book.

Afterword: January 2002

Just Capital was written during 2000, the year which marked the apogee of free market triumphalism and belief in benign globalization. Three economic certainties marked the conventional wisdom of business and political elites. Information and communications technology was creating a 'new economy' with new rules of competition, new rules of valuation, and profound social effects. Globalization and the need to compete in the global market were the unavoidable, but in general benign, facts of economic life. And a rigorously free-market version of capitalism – the American version – was clearly the best, liberalization and structural reform the means to attain it.

Those economic beliefs, moreover, underpinned a more wide-ranging world view. For the optimists of global capitalism saw free markets, prosperity, and democracy linked together in a package which would overcome historical divisions, uniting the world in a consumerist paradise, as heralded ten years previously in Francis Fukuyama's 'The End of History' as the likely and natural consequence of the fall of communism.[1,2]

Just Capital questions and finds wanting the economic premises of that free market triumphalism. But the year 2001 shocked the certainties on which it seemed based more suddenly than I anticipated. The inflated equity prices of the new economy collapsed with Nasdaq down over 60 per cent. Most dotcoms and e-retailers have ended not in business and social transformation but in bankruptcy. The sharp downturn in the US has taken the gloss off the miracle American economy. Argentina's ecnomic collapse has reminded us that market liberalization is no panacea. But above all the terrible events of September 11th came

---

1. Francis Fukuyama, 'The End of History' (*The National Interest* – Summer 1989)

2. For a fuller exposition of the themes of this Afterword, see the author's lecture 'Capitalism and the End of History' to the Royal Society of Arts, London, 26 November 2001.

as a brutal reminder that history has not ended, that religious and historical enmities, cultural dislocations and perceived injustice, have the capacity to generate terrorism and wars. In autumn 2001, Samuel Huntingdon's 'The Clash of Civilisations', the classic rejection of Fukuyama's optimism, seemed more prescient than *The End of History*.[3] And in the weeks after September 11th newspapers and journals were full of articles certain that all had changed utterly.

What did change, what not? We should be wary of the assumption that all has changed. For as the introduction to *Just Capital* describes, there is a tendency in political and economic discussion to assert that everything has changed every two to three years.

Only twelve years ago Japanese economic domination was inevitable: only six years ago the Asian tigers were unbeatable. And the hyper-optimism of 2000 followed only two years after the global uncertainty of 1998, the Crisis of Global Capitalism (in George Soros' words) which would usher in the Return of Depression Economics (in Paul Krugman's). Now again in 2002 we face a new era with all previous certainties gone.

In the economic and social sphere at least, much of this new new-era talk will prove as misleading as the old. September 11th has played only a minor role in accelerating the global economic slowdown which began in late 2000, and will not prevent a strong American bounce back as monetary relaxation produces its effects. It did not kill off the new economic paradigm, since there never was one, but nor will it prevent information technology continuing to be an important driver of growing prosperity. It has had minimal impact on the course of Japanese economic performance, which continues to be depressed by the self-inflicted wound of bad macro-economic policy. It has few implications for debates on tax and public expenditure, health services and transport plans, or the case for and against the Euro, the issues which were central to political discourse before September and will be so again in 2002. Even indeed in the sphere of individual human behaviour its impact may be less profound and certainly less sustained than many suggest. People will fly again, indeed already are in large numbers, and within a short time the bigger problem will probably not be persuading people that air travel is reasonably safe, but maintaining security vigilance in the face of

---

3. Samuel Huntingdon, 'The Clash of Civilisations' (*Foreign Affairs*, Summer 1993)

people's regained (and rational) assumption that the risks to them personally are very small.

September 11th will not in the economic and social spheres augur a definable new era. But it should change our assessment of the importance of economic and business issues relative to political. And it reinforces a major theme of *Just Capital*, that free markets alone will not solve all problems, that the role of governments and of political choice is vital.

One key message that we should take from September 11th is the primacy of politics. The conventional wisdom of 2000 tended to deny that, asserting that politicians were powerless in a world of global competition, and that economic prosperity itself (driven by free markets) would solve all problems: that Bill Gates was more important than Bill Clinton. We now know that is not true. Our ability to find a lasting solution to the Middle East conflict is more important to the future of humanity than the last percentage point of GDP growth. The judgements that President Bush makes on military action, on coalition building, on America's involvement or disengagement in post-war Afghanistan, or on America's relationship with Israel and the Palestinians, have far greater potential to affect the world for good or ill than the details of Microsoft's latest Windows release.

Likewise any mechanistic assumption that global free-markets drive prosperity, and that prosperity drives democracy and a convergence of values, seems contradicted by the continued economic failure of many countries, particularly in Africa and the Islamic world, by huge inequalities in others, and by Islamic fundamentalism's often violent rejection of Western values.

Faced with those realities, much that was written and assumed in the late 1990s and 2000 now seems over optimistic; too easily certain of the benefits of market capitalism; too mechanistic in its assumed linkage of economic and political developments. But the danger today is that we swing to the other extreme. For there is nothing in the events of last year which undermines the fundamental case for the market economy nor which should change our attitude to globalization. It is still true that the spread of market economies at the expense of state-run systems, and of open economies at the expense of closed, has freed more people from poverty faster over the last thirty years than ever before in history. And in many countries that rising prosperity has been accompanied by increasing political liberalism, by greater respect for individual rights of expression, by improved rights for women and by increasing democracy. A larger proportion of the world population now lives under democratic rules, however imperfect, than ever before in history. The case for the market economy as the least bad system we know for generating economic prosperity and for supporting political liberty remains a robust one.

The implication of 2001 is neither that optimism is impossible, nor that the links between economic development, political liberalism and peace are non-existent. Rather it is that optimistic outcomes are not inevitable, and that the links between economic and political developments are not mechanistic. Liberal capitalism can be a force for prosperity, political liberalism and improved prospects for peace, but only if accompanied by political actions and policies which electorates and politicians are free to choose or to reject. And the policies chosen need to include those designed to offset the insecurities and inequalities which capitalism itself undoubtedly creates.

A successful transition to prosperity, democracy and political liberalism is not inevitable in the developing world today. It was not inevitable in Western Europe. Looking back over the last 500 years, we can see clear linkages between the development of market capitalism, political liberalism and attitudes of secular modernity.[4] We can recognize a self-reinforcing pattern even while rejecting the Marxist idea that one dimension of change, the economic, was primary and drove all the others. One cannot imagine the Western Europe of today as prosperous as it is without political liberalism, or as liberal and peaceable as it is without prosperity. But there was nothing *inevitable* which took us from the poor, feudal, agricultural, warring and superstitious Europe of 1500, to the rich, capitalist, peaceable and largely secular Europe of today. Indeed the very processes of economic change which played a key role in that transformation, produced along the way such huge dislocations – movements of people, increasing inequalities, uprooting

---

4. David Landes *The Wealth and Poverty of Nations* sets out a compelling account of the links between economic and cultural development. Among the features he identifies as crucial to European economic take-off was the development of a rational, and to a degree, secular world view. This does not deny the possibility of extensive private religious belief, but it does imply that economic success and political liberalism are best fostered when societies have found ways of reconciling private religious belief with an open spirit of intellectual enquiry, with what Landes labels 'intellectual autonomy'.

of traditional communities and beliefs – that they fostered the development of fundamentalist political reactions – communism and fascism – which almost blew that progress quite apart. History can reveal a pattern without that pattern being inevitable.

Market capitalism was not a faultless route to a win-win nirvana in Western Europe, any more than in the developing world today. Even while free markets can create the prosperity that helps resolve social and environmental problems, they can create the social dislocations and environmental problems that need to be resolved. In Europe their resolution has depended on the emergence of governments powerful and competent enough to balance the dynamism of free markets with the regulation, collective goods provision, and income redistribution needed to make capitalism just and socially viable. Capitalism was saved from its own exesses by the countervailing power of the regulatory and welfare state.

That evolution of European capitalism provides the background to one of *Just Capital*'s key themes, the need for countries to choose between different models of capitalism, and the wide degrees of freedom which developed nations enjoy in doing so – the absence of one inevitable model of capitalism to which all countries must converge. That message is neither significantly challenged nor reinforced by the events of 2001: it is equally relevant today as it was a year ago.[5] But the history of European capitalism also carries implications for developing countries today, and for the global capitalist system, implications which were thrown into starker relief by the pessimism of autumn 2001.

Europe's historic path of capitalist development was neither smooth nor inevitable, either in economic or social terms. Developing economies today enjoy both advantages and disadvantages relative to Europe

---

5. At the beginning of 2001 some commentators anticipated that superior European economic performance during 2001, and America's relative decline would shift the balance of debate in favour of the European model. In fact, while America's performance declined, Europe's also disappointed. There are good arguments for believing that some of that disappointment was the unnecessary product of the ECB's too restrictive monetary policy. Overall, however, the conclusion on comparative economic performance remains as it was a year ago: on a long-term basis the performance of different models of mature capitalism is greatly more similar than different and the scope for societies to make their own distinctive social policy trade-offs is, as a result, far greater than much rhetoric suggests.

as they attempt to pursue similar paths. The advantage is that globalization and freer markets can, in some circumstances, dramatically increase the attainable pace of economic catch-up. Global transfers of technology, know-how and capital have enabled countries like South Korea to rise from the income level of the Congo in 1950 to approaching European levels of prosperity today, a pace of progress far more rapid than any found in the history of Western Europe. And where that growth is achieved, the pace of political and social development can be rapid also, Fukuyama's optimistic model of political and cultural convergence is a possible and rapid result. But openness to the global economy also implies, when compared with Europe's historic development, more rapid social change, more rapid dislocation of existing patterns of employment and social structure, more sudden challenges to traditional cultures and religious assumptions, more rapid inflation of expectations, greater rewards to corruption, and easier and earlier access to the destructive potential of modern weaponry. The uneven transfer of modernity, moreover, creates for some countries the challenge of super rapid population growth. For it is far easier to transfer the vaccines and basic health care which dramatically cut infant and child mortality, than to develop the prosperity, female literacy, and attitudes that cut birth rates. Several developing nations, in Africa and the Islamic world in particular, are as a result attempting a transition to prosperity while facing population growth rates far higher than any observed in European and American economic history.

Taken together, these advantages and disadvantages have made it almost inevitable that the recent pattern of economic development provides ammunition for optimists and pessimists alike – stunningly rapid improvement in some countries, other societies failing completely to participate in rising world prosperity, and sometimes rejecting violently the political and social attitudes with which mature capitalism is typically associated.

There are no magic wands with which to overcome the reality of highly divergent economic performance and of hugely varied social progress. Neither more free markets (as ultra-liberals urge) nor any known set of global and national interventions (as anti-globalization protestors desire but rarely specify) will magically smooth out the uneven pattern of development. To a degree the lesson of 2001 is that the world is imperfect and will remain so. But the fact that we are neither omniscient nor omnipotent does not mean that we know nothing, nor that policy choices, at national and global level, make no difference. And the policy choices likely to produce more favourable results imply an agenda of global engagement more nuanced and in some senses more overtly political than the free-market triumphalism of the late 1990s.

Late 1990s market triumphalism tended to deny the importance of government, to imply that smaller states, lower taxes and less fettered markets were always and without limit better for prosperity. But the experience of the last several years has reminded us that market economies can only flourish, socially or even economically, within frameworks set by effective states. Without great fanfare, the remarkable economic success of 2001 was Russia, growing at close to 5 per cent amid the slowing world economy, continuing a strong recovery which began in 1999. Partly that success has been driven by higher oil prices. But partly too it reflects the fact that since 1998's economic and political debacle, Russia has managed to create a more effective and slightly less corrupt state, capable of designing and enforcing a workable tax system, of paying its debts, and of performing some of the basic functions of the supportive state. However imperfect Russia's democratic and liberal credentials today, it is easier to see a transition to prosperity and full democracy from its present condition, than from the anarchic variant of capitalism unleashed by the 1990's experiment in crash market liberalization.

The implication is that market liberalization is not enough, that the politics and statecraft of economic and social transitions matter greatly. A further implication of that, and of the events of 2001, is that the rich developed world has a far greater self-interest in fostering steady development, political as well as economic, than it has in the direct economic benefits accruing to its own companies and consumers from market liberalization alone. The West's primary self-interest in global trade negotiations, for instance, lies not in the commercial benefits we can gain from access to developing markets, but in the potential for trade access to our markets to enhance the growth prospects of developing economies, and in the long-term political consequences of that growth. Our objectives in world-trade negotiations should be focused on benefits to others, not benefit to ourselves. There is, meanwhile, no selfish commercial benefit Western nations can gain from arms sales to poor, unstable, or dictatorial regimes, which can outweigh their likely negative impact on political and economic development. And if we have any ability, through our aid programmes and political engagement – admittedly a big if – to help foster the emergence of stable and uncorrupt states where presently these are non-existent, we should aim to do so and increase our aid programmes substantially.[6] Just as the development of capitalism in the West had to be supplemented by the overt political interventions of a socially supportive, liberal state, so global capitalism's ability to produce beneficial results needs to be nourished by an overtly political approach to issues of economic development, and by some aspects of global governance.

Just Capital deals primarily with the already developed world, turning to global issues only in Chapters 10 and 11. Its focus is mainly on economic and social issues, rather than culture, politics or international relations. The events of autumn 2001 have forcibly reminded us that political conflicts and the potential for international terrorism are more important issues than economics. Those events have also dented the late 1990s optimism that free markets, prosperity and a peaceable 'end of history' were inevitably linked. But the links between market economics, prosperity, political liberalism and social peace, though neither inevitable nor mechanistic, are powerful. And the best hope for improving an inevitably imperfect world lies in combining the dynamism of market capitalism, with the interventions at global and national level needed to make capitalism humane and to spread its benefits widely. The events of 2001 reinforce rather than undermine that belief.

---

6. In fact, one of the most obvious things we could do to help foster stable societies and less corrupt states would be to cease our totally ineffective 'war on drugs', dealing with drug abuse in our own societies through education and rehabilitation, rather than through attempted prohibitions which fail utterly to stop drug use but which have helped destroy the social and political cohesion of countries like Colombia and Afghanistan, and which funnel huge funds to international criminal and terrorist networks. One interesting instance where more market liberalization undoubtedly would be beneficial, though one which many otherwise ultra-liberal right-wingers are unwilling to accept. A theme, however, which I will leave to another book.

Bibliography

Books and articles

Akerlof, George and Janet Yellen, 'A Near-Rational Model of the Business Cycle', *Quarterly Journal of Economics*, 100, Issue Suplement (1985).

Albert, Michel, *Capitalism Against Capitalism* (London, Whurr Publishers, 1993). [First published as *Capitalism Contre Capitalisme* in 1991 by Seuil, Paris.]

Arrow, Kenneth, 'Uncertainty and the Welfare Economics of Medical Care', *Collected Papers of Kenneth Arrow* (1985), vol. 6: *Applied Economics*.

Atkinson, A. and Gunnar Mogensen (eds.), *Welfare and Work Incentives: A North European Perspective* (Oxford University Press, 1993).

Ball, James, *The British Economy at the Crossroads* (London, Financial Times Pitman Publishing, 1998).

Barker, Terry, Paul Ekins and Nick Johnstone, *Global Warming and Energy Demand* (London, Routledge, 1995).

Barnett, Correlli, *The Audit of War – The Illusion and Reality of Britain as a Great Nation* (London, Macmillan, 1986).

Baumol, W.J., 'Macroeconomics of Unbalanced Growth', *American Economic Review*, 57: 3 (1967).

   Entrepreneurship, Management and the Structure of Payoffs (Cambridge, Massachusetts/London, The MIT Press, 1993).

Bhagwati, Jagdish, 'The Capital Myth', *Foreign Affairs*, May–June 1998.

Boltho, Andrea and Gianni Toniolo, 'The Assessment: The Twentieth Century – Achievements, Failures, Lessons', *Oxford Review of Economic Policy*, 15: 4 (1999).

British Cabinet Office, *Performance and Unit Report on Business and Consumer Internet Use* (September 1999).

Brittan, Samuel, *Participation Without Politics – An Analysis of the Nature and the Role of Markets*, Hobart Special Paper 62, 2nd edition (Institute of Economic Affairs, 1979).

Capitalism with a Human Face (England, Edward Elgar, 1995).

Essays, Moral, Political and Economic. Human Papers on Public Policy, 6: 4 (1998).

The Poor Need Not Always be With Us (Joseph Rowntree Foundation, spring 2000).

Brookes, Martin and Zaki Wahhaj, *The Shocking Economic Effect of B2B*, Goldman Sachs Global Economics Paper no. 37 (3 February 2000).

Brown, C.V., *Taxation and the Incentive to Work* (Oxford University Press, 1983).

'Will the 1988 Income Tax Cuts Either Increase Work Incentives or Raise More Revenue?', *Fiscal Studies*, 9: 4 (1988).

CBI, *Filling the Gaps – Skills for Tourism* (July 1995).

World Hosts – International Benchmarking in the Hospitality Industry (November 1995).

Missing Links, Transport Strategy Report (1995).

Moving Forward, Transport Strategy Report (1995).

Fit for the Future, National Manufacturing Council Report (1998).

Creating a Europe That Works: A Study of Labour Market Flexibility (1999).

Clarke, Kenneth, Mais Lecture given to the City University Business School, 1994.

Dahrendorf, Ralf, *Reflections on the Revolution in Europe* (London, Chatto & Windus, 1990).

Daveri, Francesco and Guido Tabellini, 'Unemployment, Growth and Taxation in Industrial Countries', discussion paper no. 1681 (Centre for Economic Policy Research, 1997).

David, Paul, 'General-Purpose Engines, Investment and Productivity Growth: From the Dynamo Revolution to the Computer Revolution' in E. Deiaco, E. Hornell, G. Vickery (eds.), *Technology and Investment: Crucial Issues for the 1990s* (Columbia University Press, 1990).

Department for Education and Employment, *Skills for All: Proposals for a National Skills Agenda, Final Report of the National Skills Task Force* (2000).

Department of the Environment, *House Prices: Changes Through Time at National and Sub-National Level*, Government Economic Service, Working Paper 110 (1990).

Department of the Environment, Transport and the Regions (DETR), *Transport 2010, The 10 Year Plan* (July 2000).

Panel Report on South East Regional Planning Guidance (May–June 1999).

Eichengreen, Barry, European Monetary Unification: Theory, Practice and Analysis (Cambridge, Massachusetts/London, The MIT Press, 1997.)

EU, Growth, Competitiveness and Employment White Paper (European Commission, 1994).

Firebaugh, Glenn, 'Empirics of World Income Inequality', American Journal of Sociology, 4 (1999).

Forum for the Future, The 20% Solution (Insights Publication Series, November 1999)
    Solar Millenium: A Renewables and Energy Efficiency Development Initiative for the UK (Cambridge Econometrics, 1999).

Frey, Bruno S., Not Just for the Money: An Economic Theory of Personal Motivation (England, Edward Elgar, 1997).

Goldsmith, James, The Trap (London, Macmillan, 1994).

Gordon, Robert, 'Has the "New Economy" Rendered the Productivity Slowdown Obsolete?', Mimeo, Northwestern University, 14 June 1999.

Gray, John, False Dawn – The Delusions of Global Capitalism (London, Granta Books, 1999).

Greenwood, Jeremy, The Third Industrial Revolution – Technology, Productivity and Income Inequality (American Enterprise Institute, 1997).

Gregg, Paul and Jonathan Wadsworth, 'A Short History of Labour Turnover, Job Tenure and Job Security 1975–93', Oxford Review of Economic Policy, 11:1 (1995).

Gust, Christopher and Jamie Marquez, Federal Reserve Bulletin, October 2000.

Hale, David, Why the Equity Market is an Experiment in Corporate Resource Allocation (Zurich Financial Services, January 2000).

Hansson, Ingemar and Charles Stuart, 'Sweden: Tax Reform in a High-Tax Environment' in Michael Boskin and Charles McLure Jr (eds.), World Tax Reform: Case Studies of Developed and Developing Countries (San Francisco, ICS Press, 1998).

Hausman, Jerry, 'Taxes and Labor Supply' in Alan J. Auerbach and Martin Feldstein (eds.), Handbook of Public Economics (New York, North-Holland, 1985).

Hayek, F.A., The Road to Serfdom (1944; London, Routledge and Kegan Paul, 1976).

The Fatal Conceit – The Errors of Socialism, ed. W.W. Bartley III (London, Routledge, 1988).

Hutton, Will, *The State We're In* (London, Jonathan Cape, 1995).

The State to Come (London, Vintage, 1997).

Institute for Fiscal Studies, *Taxing Profits in a Changing World*, 1997.

The Petrol Tax Debate, Briefing Note No. 8 (July 2000).

Kelsey, Jane, *Economic Fundamentalism* (London, Pluto Press, 1995).

Keynes, John M., *The General Theory of Employment, Interest and Money* (1936; London, Macmillan, 1973).

Kissinger, Henry, 'Global Capitalism is Stoking Flames of Financial Disaster', *Daily Telegraph*, 7 October 1998.

Krugman, Paul, *Peddling Prosperity – Economic Sense and Nonsense in the Age of Diminished Expectations* (New York, W.W. Norton & Company Inc, 1995).

Pop Internationalism (Cambridge, Massachusetts/London, The MIT Press, 1997).

The Accidental Theorist and Other Dispatches from the Dismal Science (New York, W.W. Norton & Company Inc, 1998).

The Return of Depression Economics (London, Allen Lane, The Penguin Press, 1999).

Landes, David, *The Wealth and Poverty of Nations – Why Some are so Rich and Some are so Poor* (London, Little, Brown & Co, 1998).

Layard, Richard, 'Human Satisfactions and Public Policy', *Economic Journal*, 90 (December 1980).

Tackling Unemployment (Hampshire, Macmillan Press; New York, St Martin's Press, 1999).

Layard *et al.*, *The Case for the Euro* (Britain in Europe, June 2000).

Leadbeater, Charles, *Living on Thin Air – The New Economy* (London, Viking, 1999).

Lorie, James T. and Mary T. Hamilton, *The Stock Market: Theories and Evidence* (Illinois, Richard D. Irwin Inc, 1973).

Low Pay Commission, *The National Minimum Wage: The Story So Far*, 2nd Report (February 2000).

Luttwak, Edward, *The Endangered American Dream – How to Stop the United States from Becoming a Third World Country and How to Win the Geo-economic Struggle for Industrial Supremacy* (New York, Simon and Schuster, 1993).

Magaziner, Ira and Robert Reich, *Minding America's Business – The Decline and Rise of the American Economy* (US, Harcourt Brace Jovanovich, 1982).

Martin, Stephen, 'The Subsidy Saving from Reducing UK Arms Exports', *Journal of Economic Studies*, 26: 1 (1999).

Mason, Geoff and Mary O'Mahony, 'Capital Accumulation and Manufacturing Productivity Performance: US-European Comparisons', Discussion Paper No. 124 (National Institute of Economic and Social Research, December 1997).

Mathias, Peter, *The First Industrial Nation – An Economic History of Britain* (London, Methuen & Co, 1969).

Mazur, Jay, 'Labour's New Internationalism', *Foreign Affairs*, January–February 2000.

McKinsey & Co, 'A Revolution in Interaction', *McKinsey Quarterly*, No.1, 1997.

'Driving Productivity Growth in the UK Econmy', McKinsey report to the UK government (1998).

Meade, J.E., *The Intelligent Radical's Guide to Economic Policy: The Mixed Economy* (London, Allen and Unwin, 1975).

Liberty, Equality and Efficiency (London, Macmillan, 1993).

Milanovic, Branco, 'True World Income Distribution, 1988 and 1993: First Calculation Based on Household Surveys Alone' (World Bank, 1999).

Mill, John Stuart, *Principles of Political Economy* and *Chapters on Socialism* (1848; 1879; published in one volume by Oxford University Press, 1994).

Minford, Patrick and Andrew Holdenby, *The Price of Fairness* (Centre for Policy Studies, June 1999).

Nickell, Stephen, 'Unemployment and Labour Market Rigidities: Europe Versus North America', *Journal of Economic Perspectives*, 11: 3 (1997).

OECD, *Literacy Skills for the Knowledge Society* (1997).

O'Mahony, Mary, *Britain's Productivity Performance 1950–1996: An International Perspective* (London, National Institute of Economic and Social Research, 1999).

Owen, Geoffrey, *From Empire to Europe – The Decline and Revival of British Industry Since the Second World War* (London, Harper-Collins, 1999).

Popper, K.R., *The Open Society and Its Enemies* (1945; London, Routledge & Kegan Paul, 1974).

Prestowitz, Clyde, *Trading Places: How We Allowed Japan to Take the Lead* (New York, Basic Books, 1988).

Rawls, John, *Theory of Justice* (Oxford University Press, 1972).

Richardson, Ray and Marcus Rubin, 'The Shorter Working Week in

Engineering: Surrender Without Sacrifice' in Metcalf and Milner (eds.), *New Perspectives in Industrial Disputes* (1993).

Rodrick, Dani, 'Who Needs Capital Account Convertibility?' in Stanley Fischer *et al.* (eds.), *Should the IMF Pursue Capital-Account Convertibility, Essays in International Finance*, no. 207 (Princeton University, Department of Economics, International Finance Section, 1998).

Rose, Andrew, *EMU's Potential Effect on British Trade* (Britain in Europe, July 2000).

Rosen, Sherwin, 'The Economics of Superstars', *American Economic Review*, 71: 5 (1981).

Schultz, Paul, 'Inequality in the Distribution of Personal Income in the World: How it is Changing and Why', *Journal of Population Economics* (1999).

Shiller, Robert J., *Irrational Exuberance* (Princeton University Press, 2000).

Shleifer, Andrei and Daniel Treisman, *Without a Map – Political Tactics and Economic Reform in Russia* (Cambridge, Massachusetts/London, The MIT Press, 2000).

Skidelsky, Robert, *Beyond the Welfare State* (London, Social Market Foundation, 1997).

Smith, Adam, *The Wealth of Nations* (1776; London, Penguin, 1999).

Smith, David, *Will Europe Work?* (London, Social Market Foundation, 1999).

Soros, George, *The Crisis of Global Capitalism – Open Society Endangered* (London, Little, Brown & Co, 1998).

Stiglitz, Joseph E., *Whither Socialism?* (Cambridge, Massachusetts/London, The MIT Press, 1994).

Tanzi, Vito and Ludger Schuknecht, *Public Spending in the 20th Century* (Cambridge University Press, 2000).

Taylor, Arthur, J., *Laissez-Faire and State Intervention in Nineteenth-Century Britain* (London, Macmillan, 1972).

Thurow, Lester, *Head to Head – The Coming Economic Battle Among Japan, Europe and America* (London, Nicholas Brealey, 1992).

Triest, Robert, 'Fundamental Tax Reform and Labour Supply' in H.J. Aaron and W.G. Cale (eds.), *Economic Effects of Fundamental Tax Reform* (Brookings Institute Press, 1996).

Turner, Adair, 'Shareholders, Stakeholders and the Enterprise Economy', Napier Enterprise Lecture, 8 May 1997.

'Growth, Productivity and Employment', lecture given at the London School of Economics and Political Science, 18 October 1999.

'Globalisation, Technology and the Service Economy – Implications for Job Creation', lecture given at the London School of Economics and Political Science, 7 March 2000.

'Choosing The State We Want', lecture given at the London School of Economics and Political Science, 31 October 2000.

UK Government, *Draft Climate Change Programme* (2000).

UK Royal Commission on Environmental Pollution, 22nd Report, *Energy – The Changing Climate* (2000).

UN, International Panel on Climate Change, *Second Assessment* (1995).

UNICE, *Benchmarking Europe's Competitiveness: From Analysis to Action* (1998).

Ussher, Kitty, *The Spectre of Tax Harmonisation* (Centre for European Reform, 2000).

Utton, M.A., *Industrial Concentration* (London, Penguin, 1970).

Wiener, Martin, *English Culture and the Decline of the Industrial Spirit, 1850–1980* (Harmondsworth, Penguin, 1985).

Wolf, Alison, 'Education and Economic Growth', *IPPR New Economy*, March 1999.

Data sources

US

Bureau of Economic Analysis – *Survey of Current Business*.

Bureau of Labour Statistics – *Monthly Labour Review*.

Council of Economic Advisers – *Economic Indicators*.

Economic Report of the President and Annual Report of the Council of Economic Advisers.

US Census Bureau – *Statistical Abstract of the U.S.*

UK

Department of the Environment, Transport and the Regions (DETR), *Housing and Construction Statistics*.

HM Treasury, *Budget*.

Joseph Rowntree Foundation, *Poverty and Social Exclusion in Britain* (York, 2000).

Office for National Statistics (ONS), *Consumer Trends*.

Digest of UK Energy Statistics.

Economic Trends.

Family Spending.
Financial Statistics.
Labour Market Trends.
Monthly Digest of Statistics.
Public Finance Trends.
Social Inequalities.
Social Trends.
UK Economic Accounts.
UK National Accounts – The Blue Book.

Europe

DG5 Employment and Social Affairs, *European Employment Strategy 1997–2002* (1999).

European Commission, *Employment in Europe, 1999.*

European Foundation for Improvement of Living and Working Conditions, *Survey* (1993).

International

International Monetary Fund (IMF), *World Economic Outlook.*
  International Financial Statistics.
  Government Finance Statistics.
Organisation for Economic Co-operation and Development (OECD), *Economic Outlook.*
  Employment Outlook.
  Historical Statistics.
  Jobs Study 1994.
  Main Economic Indicators.
  Monthly Statistics of Foreign Trade.
  National Accounts, Volumes 1 and 2.
  Quarterly Labour Force Statistics.
  Quarterly National Accounts.
United Nations Conference on Trade and Development (UNCTAD), *Handbook of International Trade and Development Statistics 1996–97.*
  Trade and Development Report 1999.
World Bank (WB), *World Development Indicators.*
  World Development Report 2000–01.
  Global Development Finance CD Rom.

Index